Muslim Women and Sport

Examining the global experiences, challenges and achievements of Muslim women participating in physical activities and sport, this important new study makes a profound contribution to our understanding of both contemporary Islam and the complexity and diversity of women's lives in the modern world.

The book presents an overview of current research into constructs of gender, the role of religion and the importance of situation. It addresses what Islam has to say about women's participation in sport and what Muslim women have to say about their involvement in sport. It highlights the challenges and explores the opportunities for women in sport in both Muslim and non-Muslim countries, utilising a series of extensive case studies in various countries which invite the readers to conduct cross-cultural comparisons. Material on Iraq, Palestine and Bosnia and Herzegovina provides rare insights into the impact of war on sporting activities for women. The book also seeks to make important recommendations for improving access to sport for girls and women from Muslim communities.

Muslim Women and Sport confronts many deeply held stereotypes and crosses those commonly quoted boundaries between 'Islam and the West' and between 'East and West'. It makes fascinating reading for anyone with an interest in the interrelationships between sport, religion, gender, culture and policy.

Tansin Benn is an Associate Professor in the School of Education, University of Birmingham, UK. **Gertrud Pfister** is Professor in the Department of Exercise and Sport Sciences, University of Copenhagen, Denmark. **Haifaa Jawad** is Senior Lecturer in Islamic and Middle Eastern Studies, Department of Theology and Religion, University of Birmingham, UK.

International studies in physical education and youth sport

Series Editor: Richard Bailey
University of Birmingham, UK

Routledge's *International Studies in Physical Education and Youth Sport* series aims to stimulate discussion on the theory and practice of school physical education, youth sport, childhood physical activity and well-being. By drawing on international perspectives, both in terms of the background of the contributors and the selection of the subject matter, the series seeks to make a distinctive contribution to our understanding of issues that continue to attract attention from policy-makers, academics and practitioners.

Also available in this series:

Muslim Women and Sport

**Edited by Tansin Benn,
Gertrud Pfister and Haifaa Jawad**

Routledge
Taylor & Francis Group

LONDON AND NEW YORK

First published 2011
by Routledge
2 Park Square, Milton Park, Abingdon, Oxon OX14 4RN

Simultaneously published in the USA and Canada
by Routledge
270 Madison Avenue, New York, NY 10016

Routledge is an imprint of the Taylor & Francis Group, an informa business

Typeset in Times by Wearset Ltd, Boldon, Tyne and Wear
Printed and bound in Great Britain by CPI Anthony Rowe, Chippenham,
Wiltshire

British Library Cataloguing in Publication Data
A catalogue record for this book is available from the British Library

Library of Congress Cataloguing in Publication Data
Muslim women and sport / edited by Tansin Benn, Gertrud Pfister and
Haifaa Jawad.
p. cm.
Includes bibliographical references and index.
1. Sports for women–Islamic countries. 2. Muslim athletes–Southeast
Asia. 3. Women athletes–Islamic countries. 4. Women–Islamic countries.
I. Benn, Tansin. II. Pfister, Gertrud, 1945– III. Jawad, H. A.
GV709.18.I74M87 2010
796.088′297–dc22

2010002182

ISBN: 978-0-415-49076-4 (hbk)
ISBN: 978-0-203-88063-0 (ebk)

This book is dedicated to all who take positive action to build bridges between people; also, to those whose love and inspiration has enabled all authors and participants to fulfil their ambition to contribute to this volume, including loved ones who sadly died before seeing its fruition.

Contents

PART II
National perspectives 77

Illustrations

Figures

Tables

Contributors

Mona Al-Ansari is an Associate Professor in the College of Education, University of Bahrain, where, since 2005, she has been Chair of the Physical Education Department. She was educated in Bahrain, the UK (Scotland and Leeds) and the USA, and has been highly influential throughout her career in developing opportunities for girls and women in physical education and sport in Bahrain. She has worked in the Ministry of Education, as Women's Programmes specialist, and as Head of Sports Programmes in the General Organisation for Youth and Sports at the Bahrain Sports Institute.

Yousra Al-Sinani is a Lecturer in Physical Education in the Education Faculty of Sultan Qaboos University, Muscat, Oman. She was the first Omani woman to gain a PhD in the subject through her studies in England. In July 2009, Yousra was awarded the Kluka Love Award for her presentation at the IAPESGW World Congress in South Africa. She made an outstanding contribution to the management of the IAPESGW 2008 International Study Week, hosted by her university, which led to the idea for this publication.

Nadhim Shakir Yousif Al-Wattar is a Professor at Mosul University, Iraq. His particular interest is in sports psychology and he is an advocate for women's participation and rights in the sporting field.

Tansin Benn is Associate Professor in the School of Education, College of Social Sciences, University of Birmingham, England, and President of IAPESGW 2009–2013. Her specialist research and publication field is the interface of gender, ethnicity, religion and physical education/sport. Her research into the life experiences of British Muslim women in teacher training started in the 1990s and has involved work linking policy, theory and practice at national and international levels. The award of a Leverhulme Research Fellowship to conduct a study in Oman in 2008 resulted in establishing the networks evident in this publication.

Symeon Dagkas is Lecturer in the School of Education, College of Social Sciences, University of Birmingham, England. His international studies have included comparative investigations, for example of Muslim girls' experiences in Greece and England. He is currently interested in intersectional research, examining overlays of disadvantage such as socio-economic factors, ethnicity, gender and religion, and in the health benefits of physical activity.

Fatima El Faquir is Professor of Higher Education at the Moroccan National Institute of Sport. She graduated from the University of Montreal, Canada, and the University of Bucarest, Romania. She has directed the training of the women's and men's national athletics team in Morocco after a high-level career as an athlete. Fatima was the first African Champion in 400 m hurdles and she participated in the Olympic Games of 1972. She holds Presidential positions on the Confederation of African Athletics, North Africa, and the National Association of Women's Physical Activities and Sport. Fatima has been awarded many honours for her lifetime contribution to the development of athletics in North Africa.

Nour El-Houda Karfoul is Secretary General of the Syrian Olympic Committee and President of the Sport Association for Arab Women (SAAW). Originally she was a physical-education teacher, then Director of the Sport Education Institutes in Aleppo and Damascus respectively. Nour gained a Master's degree in Sport Education from the Central Institute of Physical Education and Sport in Moscow in 1970. She is a Vice President of the Sport Movement History Commission in Syria. As an author, she contributed in issuing the first and second volumes of the book, *History of Sport Movement in Syria*. In her lifetime of commitment to sport, Nour has presided at a number of the Syrian sport delegations in Arab, Mediterranean and Asian events. She has delivered presentations in many international conferences on Women and Sport (IOC, OCA, AWG, IWG, IAPESGW), and is a holder of the 2000 International Olympic Committee Order of Merit.

Ilhaam Essa is a Lecturer in the Division of Nursing, Faculty of Health Sciences at Stellenbosch University in South Africa. She is currently completing her Master's degree in Higher Education. Her research focuses on student completion and retention rates in higher education.

Eman Gaad taught children with special needs in the UK and Egypt before moving into higher education at the University of East Anglia (UK) and then to UAE University as a lecturer on issues of people with special needs. Dr Gaad has been a Senior Lecturer at the British University in Dubai since 2004, where her special research interests centre on the inclusion of children with special educational needs in mainstream education, especially in Arab/Islamic countries. She is currently seconded to the Government of Dubai as a Director of Disability Services in the Community Development Authority.

Petra Gieß-Stüber is Professor and Head of the Department of Sport Pedagogy at the Institute of Sport and Sport Sciences of the Albert-Ludwigs University, Freiburg. Her main fields of research and teaching are gender-related sport pedagogy as well as sport and interculturality in physical education.

İlknur Hacısoftaoğlu is a Research Assistant, currently studying for a PhD at Hacettepe University, Ankara, Turkey. Her particular research interests are the sociology of the body as well as gender and nationalism in sport and physical activity.

Alla Abdullah Hussein is Assistant Professor in the College of Physical Education, University of Mosul, Iraq. In addition to participation in many sports, including athletics, volleyball, taekwondo and basketball – and contributing to women's sport in coaching and officiating capacities – she gained her Doctorate in 2003. Her research interests include sports psychology, gender studies, philosophical enquiry and comparative studies in school, rural and city (including Alfatat sports club) contexts.

Fatima Hussein, a former athlete, was headmistress of two secondary schools, Aisha school for girls and Al-Fafdeal school for girls, in the Ninevah Educational Directorate. She gained her Master's degree in 2005 and is currently a PhD student at Mosul University, Iraq.

Fadila Ibrahimbegovic-Gafic is a Professor at the University of Sarajevo and Member of its Governing Board. Until 2005, she was Head of the Physical Education Department in the Medical Faculty, and Professor for Rhythmic Gymnastics in the Faculty of Sport and Physical Education. She was the first Muslim woman in Bosnia and Herzegovina to gain a PhD in the subject of Physical Education and Sport, and she has researched the ways in which physical activity and recreational sport can be used to improve the quality of life and emotional well-being in the rehabilitation of war-traumatized women in Bosnia and Herzegovina.

Haifaa Jawad is Senior Lecturer in Islamic and Middle Eastern Studies, School of Philosophy, Theology and Religion, University of Birmingham, UK. She is Associate Editor of *The American Journal of Islamic Social Sciences* and the *Journal of the Study of Islam and Christian–Muslim Relations*. In 2004, she was a visiting Professor in Contemporary Islam at the University of Alabama, USA. From 2006 to 2008, she was a visiting lecturer at the Irish School of Ecumenics, Trinity College, Dublin. She has specialised in the socio-political study of Islam, Islamic thought, women in Islam, and British Islam, especially new Muslims. She has interests in Islamic spirituality and ethics. Among her recent publications are: 'Islamic Spirituality and the Feminine Dimension', in Howie and Jobling (eds), *Women and the Divine*, Palgrave, Macmillan, 2009; 'Islamic Feminism: Leadership Roles and Public Representation', *HAWWA: Journal of Women of the Middle East and the Islamic World*, Brill, 7, 1, 2009. Haifaa is currently working on *The Contribution of European Converts to Islam: Britain as a Case Study*, for Continuum International.

Christa Kleindienst-Cachay is Professor of Sport Pedagogy at the University of Bielefeld, Germany. She has researched and written extensively on gender, physical education and sport, with a particular interest in the participation of Muslim girls and women in sport and physical activity.

Canan Koca gained her Doctorate at Hacettepe University, Ankara, Turkey. She worked as a researcher at Edinburgh University, Scotland, before returning to Hacettepe University. Her research interests centre on physical education, gender and sport.

Maryam Koushkie Jahromi was appointed as an Assistant Professor of Shiraz University in 2003 and Head of the Physical Education Department 2004–2009. Her specialisation is in exercise physiology and women's health, with a particular interest in Muslim women and sport. Maryam has presented papers at international conferences in Canada, China, Oman, Saudi Arabia and South Africa, and has published books and articles in national and international journals.

Sarah Kremers is a graduate of the Albert-Ludwigs University who carried out the research for the chapter about the Palestinian women's national football team under the direction of Professor Gieß-Stüber. She is now a teacher.

Steffen Luft is a graduate of the Albert-Ludwigs University who carried out the research for the chapter about the Palestinian women's national football team under the direction of Professor Gieß-Stüber. He is now a teacher.

Gertrud Pfister is Professor at the Institute of Sport Sciences at the University of Copenhagen. She conducted major international research projects on women and sport, serves on the editorial boards of several academic journals and holds a number of international offices including Vice-President of the International Sociology of Sport Association. Gertrud has authored several books, published numerous articles and is co-editor of the *International Encyclopedia of Women and Sport*.

Jonathan Schaller is a student at the Albert-Ludwigs University who carried out the research for the chapter about the Palestinian women's national football team under the direction of Professor Gieß-Stüber. One of his roles was to coach the team in the investigation.

Margaret Talbot OBE was Professor and Head of Sport at Leeds Metropolitan University, England, before becoming the Chief Executive, successively of the Central Council of Physical Recreation, then the Association for Physical Education (UK). Margaret was President of the International Association of Physical Education and Sport for Girls and Women from 1997–2005, and is currently President of the International Council of Sports Science and Physical Education. She has contributed at the highest levels to research, policy and delivery of sport and physical education at national and international levels.

Foreword

Professor Darlene A. Kluka

The issue of women, sport and empowerment continuously remains on the agenda of global social change. The concepts of women's empowerment, gender mainstreaming, gender equality and gender equity have been identified as key drivers for promoting women's quality of life. The increased emphasis on the position of women and sport during the last half-century has now been embedded in the broader context of globalization. A record of this can be found in sequential United Nations policy documents, as well as proceedings from the 16 quadrennial IAPESGW World Congresses. These documents track increased global attention to women's rights and have served to facilitate a greater interest and participation in women's sport. IAPESGW has, historically, supported the involvement of girls and women in physical education and sport since its inception in 1949. A half-century later, in 1999, IAPESGW, through its members and leaders, responded to members' requests to work more closely with and for Muslim women in physical education and sport. The strategic initiative involved acknowledging and combating negative stereotypes of Muslim women (predominantly held in the West, but also held in other parts of the world) as oppressed and virtually invisible in the sports arena; and bringing forth understanding, through knowledge exchange, about the diverse experiences of Muslim girls and women in and through physical education and sport internationally. One forum created was in locating the IAPESGW World Congress in Alexandria, Egypt, in 2001. This provided a world platform from which to facilitate an international agenda for the discussion of challenges and opportunities for Muslim girls and women in sport.

During the following 2005 IAPESGW World Congress in Edmonton, Canada, two important events coincided, the opening keynote by the then President, Professor Margaret Talbot, and a seminar on Muslim women in sport. The former raised concerns about the exclusion of Muslim girls and women from physical education and sport, while the latter identified contested views concerning the participation of Muslim women in the Olympic Games. As a result of subsequent discussion between a group of scholars with mutual interest in facilitating the participation of Muslim women in sport, a commitment to pursue an opportunity for extended dialogue at an international level was agreed. Dr Tansin Benn, then an Executive Board member of IAPESGW, and the current President, was invited by the group to coordinate a study group initiative. Eventually, under the aegis of IAPESGW and with the generous support of Sultan Qaboos University, Oman, a study week on 'Improving opportunities for Muslim girls and women in physical education and sport' took place in February 2008. The result of intense debate and discussion resulted in the 'Accept and Respect' Declaration, as well as this significant book.

This publication is edited by Tansin Benn, Gertrud Pfister and Haifaa Jawad, who are established researchers in socio-cultural, gender and Islamic studies. It presents examples of the diversity in international experiences of young Muslim women through sport and physical education; identifies challenges and achievements; links theory, practice and reflection; contributes to the knowledge-base of multiple realities that defy stereotypes; and opens understanding of different worldviews. This is the first book of its kind that brings Muslim and non-Muslim authors together on this scale of collective authorship, with the mutual interest of increasing knowledge and understanding for and about the sport-related experiences of Muslim women. It will be of value to those genuinely interested in shared knowledge and provision of greater inclusion in all fields of physical activity: policy-makers, leaders, sports governing bodies, organisers, coaches, educators and participants.

This seminal work is testament to the agency of women and the power of collaboration in pursuit of broadening knowledge. IAPESGW, recently celebrating its Sixtieth Anniversary at its 2009 world congress in Stellenbosch, South Africa, is proud to be associated with this groundbreaking book that provides new insights into religious, cultural and social influences on the lives of women through the life experiences of Muslim women in sport.

Acknowledgements

Thanks must go to the Leverhulme Trust, the Westhill Trust, the College of Education at Sultan Qaboos University, Oman, and the International Association of Physical Education and Sport for Girls and Women, who made the idea for the book possible.

Deepest appreciation goes to all contributors and participants, translators and readers, especially Barry Benn and Gerald Nixon, for their endeavours, skills, patience, perseverance, generosity and kindness in making this dream into a reality.

Introduction

Muslim women and sport

Tansin Benn, Gertrud Pfister and Haifaa Jawad

> Today we are trying to live ever closer to the lives about which we write ... we
> are trying to show not that we can live those lives but that we have lived close
> enough to them to begin to understand how the people who live those lives have
> constructed their worlds.
>
> (Denzin and Lincoln 2000: 1058)

Muslim Women and Sport is a collection of accounts of ways in which people
construct and live their lives in different situations. The term 'sport' is used in its
widest sense to cover all aspects of physical activity, including physical education and school sport, leisure/community-based participation and competitive
sport at elite level. The contributors to this book come from fourteen countries:
Bahrain, Bosnia and Herzegovina, Denmark, Egypt, Germany, Iran, Iraq,
Morocco, Oman, South Africa, Syria, Turkey, the United Arab Emirates and the
United Kingdom. It is the first international publication in the field of physical
education and sport studies with an intersecting theme of women, sport and religion, set in a variety of cultural contexts.

'Women, Islam and sport' constitutes a contested area where issues of power
intersect: for example, in gender relations and politics; where tensions arise
between religious and secular values; and where answers need to be found
between universal human rights, which can deny the significance of cultural distinctiveness, and cultural relativity, which can unacceptably justify inhumane
activities on the grounds of long-held cultural traditions. In promoting understanding, the authors incorporate both Islamic studies and socio-cultural
approaches to the analysis and interpretation of data. By focusing on the experiences of Muslim women, the reader can gain insight into the differences of situations, histories and nuances of power relations that influence their lives.

The term 'Muslim women' is used to include all women who have committed
themselves to the Islamic faith. Although the use of 'Islamic women' is becoming popular in everyday usage, it is a term normally reserved for those who are
related to, empathetic with or belonging to political Islamic organisations. Therefore, the term 'Muslim women' is used in this book to be as inclusive of Islamic
faith followers as possible. The predominantly qualitative insights into women's

lives are not intended to be representative but to offer rich descriptions of the lives of people who are normally silent and of histories not previously written. In a world of multiple realities, this book offers a unique collection of narratives, including those from experienced leaders and practitioners in the field of sport and those from emerging and established researchers. Waljee (2008: 99), in her research on transitions in the lives of Muslim women in Tajikistan, critiques academia dominated by Western researchers who do not treat as equal the accounts of women already redefining their roles in complex political, economic and cultural contexts:

> Western (even feminist) conceptualisations of gender relations will always remain at best incomplete and at worst misguided. To gain a better under-standing of what is played out in such relations it is crucial to pay more attention to political, economic and cultural context so as to understand how communities have historically dealt with imposed ideologies that are dia-metrically opposed to their values.

This book provides an opportunity to learn from the experiences of Muslim women in different situations, and the insights gained have the capability to broaden worldviews that may challenge previously held certainties, whoever we are and wherever we live.

Muslim women are often marginalised in accounts of the Muslim world (Runnymede Trust 1997; Richardson 2004). Fears of radicalism and stereotypes of Muslim people as 'other' have accelerated in the West with the growth of Islamophobia following the terrorist attacks of September 11, 2001. This has resulted in a fruitless polarisation of values related to how people live their lives (Allen and Nielsen 2002; Commission on British Muslims and Islamophobia 2004; Esposito and Mogahed 2007; Fekete 2008). In this dialogue Muslim women are often positioned as oppressed, victimised and disadvantaged, a per-spective challenged many times in this book.

The authors do not intend to suggest that Muslim women are homogeneous, but religion is a defining and important aspect of identity to those who regard themselves as Muslim. Hargreaves (2000: 68) wrote of the 'progressive sense of global Islam in the international Muslim women's sports movement, which grows in strength and effectiveness'. For many, Islam is a way of life, a set of principles, values and beliefs, a shared frame of reference that gives meaning and purpose to everyday living. Research into life experiences of Muslim women in sporting contexts addresses the contested discourses and practices between religion and sport, but also between the diversity of personal, local and interna-tional contexts. This is where sporting and educational institutions are culturally constructed by subtle nuances of cultural and religious dynamics, as well as political, social and economic factors.

Body culture and Islamic concern for modesty is one theme that permeates the book. For example, the *hijab* (used predominantly to refer to head-covering here, see Chapter 2 for further explanation), adopted by some Muslim women in response to religious belief, has become a global symbol of religious identity with many meanings for both the wearer and the observer. The *hijab* is seen by some as essential to religious observance, by others as a political statement and by others as a repressive imposition. Body culture in the dominant sporting world often demands high visibility of men's and women's bodies in accordance with the dress code regulations of international sports federations. Some Muslim women may participate when the dress code is flexible but be excluded when flexibility does not exist. Similarly, in schools, particularly in Diaspora Muslim communities in Western countries, dependent on state political persuasions, school-based physical/sport education policy and practice can accommodate or deny religiously motivated requests concerning dress (see Benn *et al.* (in press) and Dagkas *et al.* (in press) for an English case study). There are countries that make the *hijab* compulsory and others that deny citizens the right to wear it in public. These positions remove individuals' freedom of choice. The relatively rare participation of Muslim women in sporting activities means they are often labelled as marginalised and they become the subjects of struggle for feminists with common aims and different worldviews, such as Western and Islamic feminists.

A group of feminists have viewed the exclusion from the Olympic Games of Muslim women from Islamic countries' teams as discriminatory (Hargreaves 2000). Such views certainly defend the rights of women who wish to compete in the mainstream sporting context but are barred politically or culturally from doing so. In such cases it is important to have somebody who pleads their case. On the other hand, viewing all Olympic non-attendance by women from Islamic countries as discriminatory also ignores, denies or fails to respect the rights of those Muslim women who have embodied their faith in ways that lead them to prefer participation in physical activity in more private ways. For example, some choose to participate in events organised to provide a more Islamically appropriate environment that manages their faith need for body modesty and women-only environments (Ehsani *et al.* 2005; see also Benn and Ahmed 2006 for an account of the British Muslim Women's Futsal team that attended the 2005 Women's Islamic Games in Tehran, and www.mwsf.org.uk/ for the work of Rimla Akhtar and the Muslim Women's Sport Foundation in England). Sport institutions are themselves socially constructed, contested and changeable.

Islamic feminism offers a way to understand and empower Muslim women from inside the religion by recognising that a faith-based approach is the *only* way forward for many women (and men). As described in Chapter 2, Islamic feminists counter the suppression, experienced by some Muslim women, that does not reflect gender relations in early Islam and has come about by an Islam 'interpreted for them by men' (Waljee 2008: 99). 'Islamic feminism ... explicates the perspective of women (and men) who, although committed to Islam as an essential part of their identity, don't hesitate to criticise and challenge the Islamic patriarchal authority' (Jawad 2009: 2). Through reinterpretation of Islamic texts from a female perspective, these feminists have helped Muslim women to re-enter a more public life, pursuing equality within an Islamic framework

(Wadud 2006; Jawad 2009). Such interrogation has also helped Muslim women in sport to distinguish religious from cultural barriers through understanding that nothing in Islam precludes participation in physical activity (Sfeir 1985; Daiman 1994; Al-Ansari 1999). Islamic feminists are giving legitimacy to social action by Muslim women who are creating new agendas, for example in living more public lives, entering the workplace and contributing more visibly in their communities.

Muslim scholars, practitioners and leaders are marginalised in the scientific community and this book offers them a forum to share their contributions with a wider international audience. Much of the research and academic writing in the field of women in sport and physical education is produced in the USA, some parts of Europe and Australia. This constitutes a problem of invisibility and marginalisation for people who are living on the periphery of expanding scientific knowledge. This is acknowledged by many writers; for example, Tinning (2006: 369, 373) recognises the risk of a 'distorted vision'. The dominance of English-language literature is one of the reasons for the distorted vision and why the voices of few are much more audible than the voices of the majority of the world's population. The dilemma is that Western academic frameworks are at risk of legitimising and generalising what counts as knowledge from an ethnocentric position that fails to recognise the lens through which such work is created. This is not to deny that all researchers have ethnocentric perspectives and particular lenses through which worldviews are formed, but it becomes problematic when other ways of seeking to know and understand the world in which we live are marginalised or treated as inferior. Increased sensitivities are required in a globalised world as researchers increasingly cross cultural boundaries in endeavours to increase knowledge and understanding. For example, the limitations in international studies on 'gender' are criticised by Waljee (2008: 87), who suggests that restricted models of gender analysis such as access, outcomes and performance can be misinterpreted by those 'outside' the situation in a way that can 'fail to address, or find wanting, cultural and religious specificity and economic realities of nations in transition, or different cultural norms that frame gender relations'.

This book is an attempt to increase dialogue across religious, cultural and national boundaries, and encourage readers to understand the world of 'others'. Authors have different religious and ideological orientations, different life histories and situations. These diversities are mirrored in their writings, which have different points of departure, aims and perspectives. In respect for the international collective effort represented in the book, and the diverse first languages of the authors, chapter headings are presented in the authors' first language in addition to the titles in English.

The concept of the book evolved during a study week, held in Oman in February 2008, when 15 women (and one man from Iraq) from 14 different countries met to discuss what could be done to 'improve opportunities for Muslim girls and women to take part in sport and physical education'. Tansin Benn won a Leverhulme Research Fellowship that enabled her to spend time in Oman, an

Islamic country in the Middle East, in 2008. Part of the Fellowship visit involved the coordination of this international study week (see Foreword), held under the aegis of the International Association of Physical Education and Sport for Girls and Women (IAPESGW) and with the generous support of Sultan Qaboos University, Muscat. Colleagues from Europe, the Middle East and the Far East had the chance to be together and learn from each other. The experience and leadership of co-authors Gertrud Pfister, Haifaa Jawad, with Margaret Talbot, and the memorable contributions of most contributors to this book, were essential to the successful outcomes of the week. These included reaching the final 'Accept and Respect' Declaration (www.iapesgw.org), and commitment to the production of this book.

The 'Accept and Respect' Declaration is as follows

1   Islam is an enabling religion that endorses women's participation in physical activity.
2   We affirm the importance of physical education and physical activity in the lives of *all* girls and boys, men and women.
3   We emphasise the importance of good-quality programmes of physical education and sport in school curriculum time, especially for girls.
4   We emphasise the desirability, in places where many children have limited access to school, of providing other ways of helping children to learn the physical skills and confidence they need to practise sport.
5   We recommend that people working in the sport and education systems accept and respect the diverse ways in which Muslim women and girls practise their religion and participate in sport and physical activity, for example, choices of activity, dress and gender grouping.
6   We urge international sport federations to show their commitment to inclusion by ensuring that their dress codes for competition embrace Islamic requirements, taking into account the principles of propriety, safety and integrity.
7   We recommend national governments and organisations include in their strategies for the development of sport and physical-education structures and systems that encourage women to take positions in teaching and research, coaching, administration and leadership.

Underpinning the Declaration was the intention of increasing awareness that women have different religious preferences for sporting participation. Significant to the process and outcome was the need to reaffirm the important distinctions between Islam, the religion, and cultural overlays that can damage life chances and understanding in the world.

The Declaration, and this book, are intended to reach people interested or engaged in the policy and practice of physical education, from schools to universities, in community provision and elite-level sport. It is a Declaration and publication created with and for Muslim women whose religious beliefs and situational realities may lead them to *choose* a path of modest dress codes and/or sex-segregation for sports participation, as well as for those who do not choose the *hijab*. It is for Muslim and non-Muslim people who live together in many countries of the world and want to understand each other's worldview more fully and to stand in solidarity for the right of personal choice. Simply the Declaration and this book are about 'Accepting and Respecting' the choices and voices of others.

Book structure

The book is organised into four parts. Each chapter has an Editors' Introduction, to enable readers to select chapters most relevant to their particular interests.

Part I examines underpinning perspectives, starting with Chapter 1, a reaffirmation of values stated in the Accept and Respect Declaration: 'We affirm the importance of physical education and physical activity in the lives of all girls and boys, men and women.' Chapter 2 expands on the first statement in the Declaration: 'Islam is an enabling religion that endorses women's participation in physical activity.' The chapter explores an important distinction between authentic Islam and cultural overlays that disadvantage women. The authors address religious belief, Islam and ways in which Islamic religious texts are being reinterpreted, empowering women's roles as positive, contributing and distinctive from within the faith. Women with confidence in their faith-based position can challenge cultural overlays that deny them life chances.

Chapter 3 illustrates some of the socio-cultural theoretical perspectives that can be used to understand the experiences of Muslim women in sport. It focuses on the specific situation of Muslim women in the Diaspora. The author uses the case study of Denmark to illustrate how the application of theory can inform interpretation and analysis of specific life situations. The chapter also provides abundant material for cross-cultural comparisons of the opportunities and challenges of Muslim people in Western countries.

Part II contains national perspectives from Bahrain, Germany, Iran, Oman, Syria and Turkey. These chapters have in common: information that provides contextual knowledge of the country; key socio-historical issues impacting on the lives of women today; and information on the contemporary position of Muslim girls and women in arenas of physical activity, specifically education, community and elite sport.

Part III contains four case studies, the first from German authors who undertook research into the Muslim/Christian Palestinian women's national football team. The second case study is from South Africa, authored by a Muslim woman working in the health profession in the Western Cape. The chapter explores the experiences of Muslim girls in school-based physical education and sport situations. Third is the story of the Turkish Muslim judo champion 'Zeynep' who shares moments of personal identity-conflict as a Muslim athlete. She lives and competes in a secular country with a majority Muslim population that has banned the wearing of *hijab* in sporting competitions. Finally, a glimpse into life in the United Arab Emirates is provided with a case study about women with learning difficulties and initiatives to improve their situation. Their lives are shaped by the intersecting areas of culture, disability and gender.

Part IV contains narratives that inform us about the lives and sporting activities of Muslim women with histories rarely discussed. The first and last chapters in this section focus on the effects of war on women and sport in predominantly Muslim countries. The author of the contribution about Bosnia and Herzegovina tells of the horrors of war, the fate of women as victims and the special place of sporting networks, during and after the war, in supporting girls and women through terrible human atrocities. The rebuilding of sport and the number of women champions today is a success story, but the wounds are not yet healed.

From Morocco, three Olympians, whose careers span from the 1970s to the present day, offer a positive account of their lives, efforts and achievements in a country more often remembered for hardline religious objection to Muslim women's participation in sporting activities (Hargreaves 2000). The courage of authors and participants in the final narrative from a war-torn Iraq offers the world outside the country some insight into the conditions, the position of women and the destruction of a previously strong 'women in sport' movement. The narratives are told through the personal reflections of five women leaders of sport and physical education.

In the Conclusion, the editors comment on what can be learned through the chapters in terms of understanding differences in the positions of Muslim girls and women regarding participation in physical activity. Recommendations are offered that use the principles of the 'Accept and Respect' Declaration, with the knowledge shared in this book, to increase opportunities in the field of physical activity for all, particularly girls and women.

The book focuses on the multiple realities of Muslim women, providing insider views of those who live and work in the countries about which they write. The situations in the various countries covered in the book are diverse, including countries that are Islamic, under Sharia law, and others which have Muslim majority or Muslim minority populations. There are experiences of women whose countries are just beginning to create sporting opportunities for women, and countries in the West that provide an abundance of opportunities that are not used by Muslim women for a variety of reasons. There are great contrasts between the countries in terms of wealth and resourcing possibilities for developing an infrastructure to support participation by women in sport. Also there are important variations in levels to which cultural acceptance of girls' and women's participation in sport and physical-education facilitates or limits their opportunities. A common theme of the book lies in the fact that the authors' lives have been devoted to increasing life-chances and empowerment of girls and women, through all arenas of sport, education and physicality. Although there is a broad consensus about the content of the book amongst the authors, each author is ultimately responsible for his or her contribution.

It was a privilege to share the experiences and insights of the study week in Oman 2008. Those present will never forget the poignant stories, histories and achievements, the sensitivities gained through listening and exchanging disparate viewpoints, and the many challenges encountered along the way. The tribute to the work of that week lies in the negotiated consensus captured in the principles of the 'Accept and Respect' Declaration, and the collective endeavour of this book. It is a fitting legacy.

Finally, for all the authors and participants in this book, the following quotation is a reiteration of a response from the floor of the IAPESGW World Congress 2009 in South Africa that followed the panel presentation on Oman 2008 and the 'Accept and Respect' Declaration. It was made by Professor Christine Shelton (Smith College Massachusetts, USA), a life-long advocate for women in sport:

> I think what you are doing is a great thing and I wish you courage because people in some parts of the world have suffered in speaking out on this topic. Remember we [Congress delegates] applaud and support you in this effort.

Bibliography

Al-Ansari, M. (1999) Women, Sport and Islam. Historical and Future Implications for the New Millennium, Unpublished paper, Department of Physical Education, University of Bahrain.

Allen, C. and Nielsen, J.S. (2002) *Summary Report on Islamophobia in the EU after 11 September 2001*, European Monitoring Centre on Racism and Xenophobia, Centre for the Study of Islam and Christian–Muslim Relations, Department of Theology, University of Birmingham, England.

Benn, T. and Ahmed, A. (2006) Alternative Visions: International Sporting Opportunities for Muslim Women and Implications for British Youth Sport. *Youth & Policy* 92, Summer 2006: 119–132.

Benn, T., Dagkas, S. and Jawad, H. (in press) Embodied Faith: Islam, Religious Freedom and Educational Practices in Physical Education. *Sport, Education and Society.*

Commission on British Muslims and Islamophobia (2004) Islamophobia, Issues, Challenges and Action. A report by the Commission on British Muslims and Islamophobia. Stoke-on-Trent, Trentham Books.

Daiman, S. (1994) Women, Sport and Islam. *Sport* 2, May/June 1994: 14–15.

Dagkas, S., Benn, T. and Jawad, H. (in press) Multiple Voices: Improving Participation of Muslim Girls in Physical Education and School Sport. *Sport, Education and Society.*

Denzin, N. and Lincoln, Y. (eds) (2000) *Handbook of Qualitative Research* (second edition). London: Sage.

Ehsani, Kouzechiyan, Honarvar, and Sharifryan (2005) Role of Professional Sport in Muslim Women's Sport Development, in *Toward the Future*, the 5th International Sports-Science Congress of the Islamic Federation of Women's Sport, 24–25 September, Tehran, (IFWS): 67–69.

Esposito, J.L. and Mogahed, D. (2007) *Who Speaks for Islam? What a Billion Muslims Really Think.* New York: Gallup Press.

Fekete, L. (2008) *Integration, Islamophobia and Civil Rights in Europe.* London: Institute of Race Relations.

Hargreaves, J. (2000) *Heroines of Sport: The Politics of Difference and Identity*. London: Routledge.

Jawad, H. (1998) *The Rights of Women in Islam: An Authentic Approach*. Basingstoke: Macmillan Press Ltd.

Jawad, H. (2009) Islamic Feminism: Leadership Roles and Public Representation, *HAWWA – Journal of Women of the Middle East and the Islamic World* 7, 1: 1–24.

Pfister, G. (2000) Contested Her-Story: The Historical Discourse on Women in the Olympic Movement, in *2000 Pre-Olympic Congress Sports Medicine and Physical Education*, International Congress on Sport Science, 7–13 September, Brisbane, Australia.

Pfister, G. (2003) Women and Sport in Iran: Keeping Goal in the *Hijab*? In I. Hartmann-Tews and G. Pfister (eds) *Sport and Women: Social Issues in International Perspective*. London: Routledge: 207–223.

Richardson, R. (2004) *Islamophobia: Issues, Challenges and Action*. Stoke-on-Trent: Trentham Books.

Runnymede Trust (1997) *Islamophobia, A Challenge For Us All*. Report of the Runnymede Trust Commission on British Muslims and Islamophobia. London: The Runnymede Trust.

Sfeir, L. (1985) The Status of Muslim Women in Sport: Conflict Between Cultural Tradition and Modernization, *International Review for the Sociology of Sport* 30: 283–306.

Tinning, R. (2006) Theoretical Orientations in Physical Education Teacher Education. In D. Kirk, D. Macdonald and M. O'Sullivan (eds) *The Handbook of Physical Education*. London: Sage: 369–385.

Wadud, A. (2006) *Inside the Gender Jihad: Women's Reform in Islam*. Oxford: Oneworld Publications.

Waljee, A. (2008) Researching Transitions: Gendered Education, Marketisation and Islam in Tajikistan. In S. Fennell and M. Arnot (eds) *Gender Education and Equality in a Global Context*. London: Routledge: 87–101.

Part I

Underlying concepts

1 Reaffirming the values of physical education, physical activity and sport in the lives of young Muslim women

Symeon Dagkas, Maryam Koushkie Jahromi and Margaret Talbot

Editors' introduction

The chapter reaffirms the values of physical education, physical activity and sport in the lives of young Muslim women by beginning with a review of macro support dimensions in the form of international declarations and government commitments that support the right of all people to participation in these areas. The disadvantaged position of women necessitated specific attention, as did the position of Muslim women. The authors move on to review the literature on physical activity and health, with particular attention to ethnic diversity and physical activity health issues. Issues of religiosity, as well as the interface of faith and arenas of physical activity for girls, are discussed, as are possible structural barriers to faith identity in Muslim minority contexts. It is recognised that positive or negative attitudes towards sport-related activities are shaped in micro situations, participation environments and interactions with teachers/coaches and peers. While, in Islamic countries such as Iran, sporting structures build in Islamic requirements for modesty in dress and sex segregation, Muslim women in more Westernised contexts can struggle to find conducive environments in which to practise physical activity. One case study that sought local solutions to parental withdrawal of Muslim girls from physical education in England is shared.

The international case for physical activity, physical education and sport

There have been many declarations and statements about the value of physical education, physical activity and sport during the last three decades (see Talbot 2000, 2006, 2010). They outline (and some provide evidence for) a range of physical, social, educational and health benefits; and, also, many claim positive intellectual outcomes (see Bailey 2004, 2010). Such documents provide useful levers for those wishing to influence policy, provision or investment at the national level, but their effectiveness is often limited because leaders can be unaware of the commitments which their own governments have made. However, declarations and statements do provide well-articulated cases for the values of participation, which allowed, for example, the 'Accept and Respect' declaration to 'affirm the importance of physical education and physical activity in the lives of *all* girls and boys, men and women'.

The Convention of the Rights of the Child (United Nations 1989) stipulates that all children have a right to: (1) the highest level of health; (2) free and compulsory primary education for both cognitive *and physical development* (authors' emphasis); (3) rest and leisure; play and recreation. These provisions are directly relevant when considering Muslim girls' access to sport and physical education, since the UN describes the Rights as 'Universal'. It is perhaps worth noting that the UK government has only very recently committed to it, 30 years after it was approved by the UN General Assembly. These Rights were quoted in the Berlin Agenda (ICSSPE 1999), issued as the outcome of the First World Summit on Physical Education, and endorsed as the Declaration of Punta del Este (MINEPS III, 1999). These Declarations on behalf of physical education were themselves developments of the International Charter on Physical Education and Sport, issued by UNESCO in 1978, whose Article 1 asserted: 'The practice of physical education and sport is a fundamental right for all.' The male-gendered language used in the Charter may be in conflict with the commitment for inclusion in its Articles; but it has been one of the benchmarks for those working to improve access to physical education and sport.

Following the international activities that promoted the values of physical education, especially to young people, the international women and sport movement adopted similar tactics, with the Brighton Declaration of 1994, arguably one of the most influential levers in securing government commitment to extending and improving access for women to sport and physical activity (Houlihan and White 2002; Kluka 2008). It has been followed by a range of associated statements and action programmes (for example, see Talbot 1997), and has led to concrete outcomes such as the formation of the Arab Association for Women and Sport in 1995, and a series of international conferences led by the Faculty of Physical Education for Girls of the University of Alexandria, Egypt. Muslim women working in physical education and sport used these, as well as other opportunities, to voice their concerns and frustrations about their marginalised position in many countries' sport policies, and their impatience with Western perceptions of Muslim women as being uninterested or unable to participate in sport and physical activity. It was within this context that in 1999, the International Association of Physical Education and Sport for Girls and Women adopted, as a strategic priority, the promotion of physical education and sport specifically with Muslim women. This commitment by IAPESGW's members and leaders, and determined networking and collaboration, eventually led to the study week in Oman, which established the 'Accept and Respect' Declaration. This was achievable because of the previous articulation of the values of physical activity, sport and physical education by international sport leaders and organisations; and the assertion of access to physical activity as a universal human right.

Physical activity and health

Recent social, environmental and technological changes, such as accessibility of high-calorie foods, computer games and transport, have contributed to increased sedentary behaviours in young people (Fairclough *et al.* 2002, cited in Dagkas and Stathi 2007: 369). Research supports the view that involvement in physical activity contributes to numerous health benefits (such as prevention of obesity, type II diabetes and cardiovascular diseases) and the well-being of people (Duncan *et al.* 2004; Hardman and Stensel 2003).

The health benefits of physical activity are well established, with regular participation in physical activity associated with better and longer quality of life. Hardman and Stensel (2003: 14) define physical activity as 'any bodily movement produced by contraction of skeletal muscle that substantially increases energy expenditure'. Physical activity is a comprehensive concept. It encompasses many other terms related to physical exertion, such as work, sports, exercise, recreation, play, training, workouts, physical education, athletics and gymnastics (Astrand *et al.* 2003).

Descriptive and experimental studies have suggested that regular physical exercise may be associated with reduced symptoms of depression and anxiety, and have consistently found that more active individuals report lower depression scores than more sedentary individuals (Faulkner and Taylor 2005). Depression is associated with increased risk of physical and functional decline, cognitive impairment, institutionalisation, frailty, life-threatening malnutrition and weight loss, psychological distress, low self-esteem, negative interpretation of everyday perceptions and non-adherence to pharmacotherapy for chronic disease (Faulkner and Taylor 2005). According to Taylor and Faulkner (2005), there is tentative support for the view that participating in exerice and physical activity is associated with alleviation of negative symptoms connected with depression and low self-esteem.

Hardman and Stensel (2003) document that physical inactivity has been linked to the increase in obesity levels amongst children and adults in Western societies. Technological changes are attributed to changes in behavioural patterns that are linked with increased levels of obesity. Cardiovascular disease accounts for almost one-third of global deaths, with incidents rising, too, in developing countries (Hardman and Stensel 2003). However, according to Boreham and Riddoch (2003) the research evidence for the life-long benefits of physical activity for health is weak, and no studies have adequately recorded birth-to-death information relating physical activity to health. Longitudinal research of this kind is challenging and expensive, but given the importance of the topic, this is a notable gap in the research. Several national and international organisations have supported the promotion of physical activity as an important health behaviour in policy documents (Biddle and Mutrie 2008) and government policies in the UK have targeted specific groups identified as 'sedentary'.

In multi-cultural societies in the West, ethnic minority groups and women head national tables on all-cause mortality and poor health. All-cause mortality is especially high amongst men of ethnic minority groups, and poor health and high morbidity and mortality rates have been identified among Muslim women of Bangladeshi and Pakistani descent in the UK. Inactivity and certain lifestyle choices are seen by epidemiologists (see Sallis and Owen 1999) as reasons for poor health among ethnic minority groups. The importance of learning to be active from an early age has also been documented. Many young ethnic-minority girls have been identified as sedentary in their everyday life. This is particularly true of Muslim girls, and is related to barriers that restrict their participation in physical activity. Research (see Benn 2002; Benn *et al.* 2010; Dagkas and Benn 2006) indicates that participation rates of young UK Muslim women in physical activity settings in and out of school are rising, but are still relatively low. Despite global advocacy for the importance of physical education and physical activity, Muslim girls and women have fewer opportunities to participate compared with their male counterparts.

Since the early 1990s, research has identified areas of tension between cultural practices of Islam and physical education in schools in Western contexts (Carroll and Hollinshead 1993). The voices of Muslim girls and women of diverse ethnicities remain relatively silent – or, perhaps more accurately, the impact of Muslim voices remains undetectable despite efforts from recent research to produce evidence of 'lived experiences' of Muslim girls (see Benn *et al.* 2010; Dagkas *et al.* 2010; Macdonald *et al.* 2009). It is imperative to explore the barriers to participation in physical activity settings and reaffirm the values of physical activity in the lives of young Muslim women.

'Religiosity', girls and physical activity

Religion is an under-researched domain as an influence on the social self and body cultures, particularly in the fields of education and sport. Islam has a global status and has been acknowledged as the second largest religion in the world. Specifically, Muslims make up approximately 4 per cent of Europe's population, with almost 9 per cent of the population in France (Green 2008). They remain the second largest religious group in Britain with almost 3 per cent of the population (Benn 1998). According to Dagkas and Benn (2006), Islam is the fastest-growing religion in the West and many Diaspora communities are growing in Western countries, with most of the increased ethnic-minority groups in the UK being Asian of Islamic heritage with their origins in Bangladesh or Pakistan. Demographic trends are significant. According to the 2001 UK census, the 'mixed-race' population 'category' contains 50 per cent of youngsters below 16 years of age (Green 2008: 172). The particular mixes and cultural identities constitute what Dagkas and Benn (2006) identify as 'cultures of hybridity', issues of fluid cultural and religious interpretation that contribute to the development of different cultures of physicality where movement and participation have different levels of significance and meaning.

Physical activity and sport have been neglected by many Islamic scholars, with the subject perceived as non-academic, non-serious; and for some, as

Amara (2008: 548) declares, 'a deviation from religious teaching'. Kay (2006) maintains that a Muslim family exerts a tremendous influence over its members, shaping customary behaviours and beliefs. Benn (2003) found that school and home lives for some women required switching consciousness of identity layers to accommodate needs to 'fit in' differently between the school and the home contexts (not only in terms of Islamic dress code, but in conscious attention to other aspects of communication). According to Amara (2008), Islam has been reduced to its strict religious domain and separated from its civilisational constituents of scientific innovation and artistic creativity (Fates 1994, cited in Amara 2008: 548). The 'lived religion' or the religiosity of a Muslim population, their degree of 'Islamisation' and interpretation of their social world and environment have to be considered. Diaspora groups constantly find ways to display difference in managing the dilemma of sustaining identities connected to traditions and cultures (Dagkas and Benn 2006), while trying to fit into the host society. Religiosity impacts on everyday life of young Muslims with pressure from their families to adopt, adhere to and retain cultural distinctiveness that will shape identities and everyday life choices. According to Benn *et al.* (2010), while most people in the world cover parts of their bodies for reasons of modesty, the religious symbolism is highly significant in Islam and in current discourse about Muslim women. For example, there are some Muslim girls who choose to adopt the *hijab* (headscarf) and Islamic dress; others do not. Recent evidence, however, (Mirza *et al.* 2007, cited in Green 2008: 176) suggests that an increasing number of young adolescent Muslim women decide to adopt the *hijab* to conform to religious requirements and Islamic values. Shilling (2008: 150) maintains that 'Islam has become Europe's second religion', alongside other religions such as new forms of Charismatic Christianity and New Age paths to spiritual fulfilment. One outcome of this has been the resurgence in adoption of the *hijab* by Muslim women as an affirmation of religious identity. For many, the *hijab* is a symbol of honour connected to faith and respect for the Islamic requirement to cover the hair. Conversely, for some who may be coerced into wearing the *hijab*, it could be a symbol of oppression or repression. Others see it as a symbol of rebellion against Western values (Benn *et al.* 2010; Fekete 2008). Whatever the reason, there is clear evidence that those women who adopt Islamic dress in the West suffer increased violence, discrimination, prejudice and exclusion (Dagkas and Benn 2006: 23). Finally, the degree of religiosity and the problems of deciphering religious requirements from pseudo-religious, culturally embedded practices add to the challenge for any research that intersects religion and physical activity (Benn 2003; Dagkas and Benn 2006).

Evidence of increasing victimisation of Muslims and Islamophobia in the West, as well as current concerns about social cohesion and lack of integration, demand that sensitivity to the wider context and a positive approach to seeking solutions be essential features of any study focusing on Muslim girls and their participation in physical-activity settings (Dagkas and Benn 2006). Rhetoric for religious freedom in Europe is challenged by Islamophobia fuelled by fear of terrorism perpetrated in the name of Islam (Fekete 2008). Prejudice and discrimination, centred notably on followers of Islam, has led to the 'racialisation of religion' and victimisation of all Muslims (Dunn *et al.* 2007). According to Benn *et al.* (2010), such realities increase the urgency for addressing any marginalisation of Muslim young people in education and, for the purposes of this chapter, physical activity, physical education and sport, since this is an arena in which young people may improve knowledge, understanding, skills and social cohesion (Bailey 2008). Distinguishing between scholarly attention to divinely inspired religious texts and cultures based on pseudo-religious overlays can be helpful in challenging negativity towards women's participation in physical activity (see Chapter 2 of this book).

Many scholars, including Islamic feminists, have asserted that Islam supports the participation of girls and women in physical activity, within religious requirements for body modesty (Pfister 2003; Dagkas *et al.* 2010), although Walseth (2006) maintained that some Muslim women and girls in Norway were sanctioned by members of their ethnic group to participate in physical-activity settings. Dagkas and Benn (2006) explored the lived experiences of Muslim girls and physical education, where some girls identified the environment as a barrier to participation, especially when activities were visible to members of the community (mainly taking place outdoors), in particular to men.

It is important to emphasise that Muslim females are not a homogeneous group, and that there are differences in how they choose to resolve religious and other cultural demands. Islam permits Muslims (male and female) to practise sports, as long as it does not lead to the neglect of religious and other duties (Jawad and Benn 2003; www.islamonline.net). Macdonald *et al.* (2009: 9) also believe that Muslim girls should not be perceived as a homogenous group and that research should 'acknowledge the different cultural backgrounds and varied interpretations of Islam' to avoid 'quick fix' solutions to problems.

In many Muslim communities, high value is placed on the role of women as wives and mothers. Conversely, participation in sport has been seen as a distraction from higher-order pursuits in religious and familial duties. Sport has been associated with 'play' and therefore not worthy of time, commitment and dedication (Benn 1998). Such views continue to affect the lives and choices of some young Muslim girls and women, and discourage them from taking up life-enhancing physical activity regimes or career options and higher-education study in the field of sport (Turner 2007). There has been a lack of general interest in some Muslim communities in what is called 'physical culture', centred around 'health' and 'ideal-bodies' discourses (Evans *et al.* 2004) – again, something which is more highly valued in 'Western contexts', although globalisation is having its effect on this. Recent findings (Dagkas *et al.* 2010) suggest that Muslim girls are aware of the benefits of physical activity in 'health' and 'body', yet participation is limited, whether in physical education, structured environments or unstructured community contexts. Family, cultural, religious and environmental reasons are given for limited participation. Even structures of physical education initial teacher training and education (ITTE) in the UK can discriminate against Muslim women who wish to adhere to religious preference for sex-segregated practical studies and to become specialists in the subjects (Benn and Dagkas 2006). These occurrences reinforce stereotypes of non-participation, and the lack of positive role models becomes a structural barrier which is self-perpetuating.

Muslim girls 'in' physical activity settings

Sport can empower women, but there can be structural barriers for Muslim women in sport, such as those relating to issues of modesty and use of public spaces, particularly when Muslim women are in minority situations (Benn 2000; Dagkas and Benn 2006; Walseth and Fasting 2003). The outcry against the banning of religious symbols in French state schools, and the *hijab* for Muslim girls in particular, raised awareness of tensions across Europe (Vaisse 2004). Wider global issues have been recognised for some Muslim women wishing to participate in sport at a serious international level (Hargreaves 2000). There are shared experiences for young Muslim women across national boundaries, in tensions at the interface of physical education, sporting activities and Islam, where political situations are similar, as recent comparative research has shown between the UK and Greece (Dagkas and Benn 2006).

Aspirations for improved inclusion of Muslim girls and sports are captured in the 2008 Declaration, 'Accept and Respect' (Benn and Koushkie 2008). This Declaration reaffirms the importance of physical activity in the lives of all people, including girls and young women, maintaining the importance of respecting the diverse ways in which Muslim women choose to participate in physical activity. It also emphasises the importance of respecting religious needs and creating an environment in which Muslim girls can learn new skills and develop physicalities without religious transgression. The Declaration urges government policies to address the inclusion of Muslim girls in sport (within and out of school hours) in the community and the elite sport arena. This includes those who prefer sex-segregated spaces, uncommon in Western models of sport participation, and more modest clothing than some international sports governing bodies currently allow or promote. The challenge of accommodating such views and personal choice, particularly in some secular countries where religion and state are firmly separated in policy, should not be underestimated.

Evidence of poor health in South Asian women in the West is an important signal indicating the crucial importance of developing appropriate knowledge, skills and understanding of physicality and health issues in schools (Sriskantharajah and Kai 2007). The significance of the school as the main, if not the only, environment in which some young Muslim girls will experience physical activity and understand its importance in a healthy lifestyle cannot be ignored. Where tensions arise between issues of religious freedom and statutory entitlement to physical education, negotiation is required to seek solutions. The challenges and dilemmas for schools have been documented in recent empirical research (see Dagkas *et al.* 2010), demonstrating the diversity of Muslim girls' experiences in physical education in the UK. It also showed a range of school strategies adopted to improve inclusion. Regardless of a school's efforts, in some cases Muslim girls were excluded on the grounds of a school's inability to meet their religious or cultural needs.

Research has shown that requests for particular dress codes and gender-organisation practices relate to preferences for 'safer environments' that meet Islamic requirements for modesty and preserve cultural heritage. Such requests can challenge teachers' normalised assumptions about appropriate policies, organisation systems and expectations (Carroll and Hollinshead 1993; Dagkas and Benn 2006). 'Bodies are both inscribed with and vehicles of culture' (Garrett 2004: 141), which means there are multiple ways in which both social and religious values are embodied. Cultural values legitimise appearance, actions and behaviours. Where these are challenged, as in issues of body covering or gender organisation for some Muslim girls, solutions need to be based on understanding difference (Benn *et al.* 2010). Eurocentric curricula, based on 'Western white male' values and approaches to teaching physical education, have created tensions between educators and Muslim girls. Macdonald *et al.* (2009: 14) stress the need for physical educators to engage more with young people and their families, and to understand their values, to avoid acts of separatism and 'othering'. This is more evident in novice and newly qualified teachers, who are ill-prepared to teach children of ethnic minority groups and, more specifically, meet the needs of Muslim girls (Dagkas 2007).

A UK case study on Muslim girls in physical education

One recent UK research project illustrates collective efforts to improve participation of Muslim girls in physical education in England. Here, Muslims are a minority population, but in one city parents started withdrawing their daughters when Islamic requirements could not be met (Benn *et al.* 2010; Dagkas *et al.* 2010). The study, which encouraged Muslim girls to voice their anxieties concerning participating in physical-activity settings, demonstrated that, where schools were committed to ensuring equal opportunities for all, participation was assured. Schools that celebrated cultural 'differences' and demonstrated commitment to educating youth about cultural diversity had a close relationship with parents in order to adopt practices that preserved religious and cultural 'identities'. These 'close' relationships strengthen parental views on the importance of physical education and sport in the lives of young women. On the other hand, tensions were recorded in cases where schools were unable to address religious requirements, either due to lack of staff (especially lack of staff representing the Muslim faith) or lack of infrastructure. These tensions resulted in parental withdrawal of Muslim girls from physical education, especially in settings that were accessible to the general public (such as local swimming pools) or those viewed as antithetical to Islamic values (for example, creative dance). To resolve these problems, the project initiated by the Birmingham Advisory Support Service

(BASS) was commissioned and funded by Birmingham City Council in England.

The choice of Birmingham as the site for the project was appropriate as the city is highly populated by Muslim families, mainly of Bangladeshi and Pakistani descent. The BASS project investigated the tensions at the interface of Islamic requirements and school-based provision of physical education. A key outcome was the publication of guidance for schools to promote inclusion of Muslim girls in physical education and school sport. The guidance centred mainly on issues of modesty and privacy of the body, the challenge of visibility and centrality of movement. It emphasised throughout respect for the diversity of lived experiences of being Muslim, avoiding stereotypes and assumptions, and meeting individual needs, wherever possible, to enable participation in physical education. The greatest support for physical education came from the children and young people themselves.

The importance of the political situation was essential to the problem and the solution in Birmingham. Such a study could not happen in neighbouring France, for example, because of the strict separation of religion from education, including the wearing of religious symbols (like the *hijab*). Such differences are illustrated more fully in other chapters.

In conclusion, the increasing flow of people between countries ensures that most societies are growing in cultural diversity, perhaps epitomised in the United Arab Emirates, where nationals represent a tiny proportion of the population (see Chapter 13). Consequently, teachers, coaches and sports leaders need appropriate knowledge, skills, understanding and resources to manage different needs if more people are to enjoy the values of participation in physical activity:

> It is becoming increasingly essential for those who manage [sporting opportunities for young people] ... to be able to critique dominant practices, assimilate difference, broaden frames of reference, avoid ethnocentrism and assumptions, and to engage in culturally sensitive pedagogical practices to equip global citizens to respect diversity.
>
> (Benn *et al.* 2010)

This chapter has reiterated claims for the valuable life-enhancing contribution of physical education, physical activity and sport to the lives of all people, including young Muslim women. In addition to the need for universal human rights and health-related research linked with participation in physical activity, it is the micro context in which sporting practice happens that can encourage or deny the participation of young women. For many Muslim women, adherence to religious preferences for modesty is crucial to participation; and in increasingly diverse cultures, especially where the Muslim community is in the minority, such requirements are unlikely to be met. In the UK, schools are trying to address the issue; and groups like the Muslim Women's Sport Foundation are springing up in the community to provide Islamically appropriate sporting spaces for fellow Muslims which they cannot find in mainstream community provision. If more young Muslim women are able to participate in physical activity as a result of such initiatives, then such advantages must outweigh potential disadvantages of separatist strategies. The accounts from other countries in this book will reveal a variety of contexts for Muslim women's participation in physical activity, many revealing high levels of success in sports leadership and other achievements in the field.

Bibliography

Amara, M. (2008) An introduction to the study of sport in the Muslim world. In B. Houlihan (ed.) *Sport and Society: A Student Introduction* (2nd edition). London, Sage: 532–553.

Astrand, P., Rodalh, K., Dahl, H.A. and Strome, S.B. (2003) *Textbook of Work Physiology: Physiological Bases of Exercise* (3rd edition). Champaign, Human Kinetics.

Bailey, R. (2004) *The Role of Physical Education and Sport in Education, Final Report.* Berlin, ICSSPE.

Bailey, R. (2008). Physical education and sport in schools: a review of benefits and outcomes. In R. Bailey and D. Kirk (eds) *The Routledge Physical Education Reader.* London, Routledge: 29–39.

Bailey, R. (2010) This is your brain in the gym: physical education and cognitive outcomes. In M. Talbot (ed.) *Three Decades of Progress for Physical Education.* Berlin, ICSSPE.

Benn, T. (1998) Exploring Experiences of a group of British Muslim women in initial teacher training and their early teaching careers, Doctoral Thesis, Loughborough University, England.

Benn, T. (2000) Towards inclusion in education and physical education. In A. Williams (ed.) *Primary School Physical Education, Research into Practice.* London, Routledge/Falmer: 118–135.

Benn, T. (2002) Muslim women in teacher training: issues of gender, 'race' and religion'. In D. Penney (ed.) *Gender and Physical Education: Contemporary Issues and Future Directions.* London, Routledge: 57–79.

Benn, T. (2003) Muslim women talking: experiences of their early teaching careers. In H. Jawad, and T. Benn (eds.) *Muslim Women in the United Kingdom and Beyond: Experiences and Images.* Leiden, Brill: 131–150.

Benn, T. (2005) 'Race' and physical education, sport and dance'. In K. Green and K. Hardman (eds) *Physical Education – Essential Issues.* London, Sage: 197–237.

Benn, T. and Dagkas, S. (2006) Incompatible? Compulsory mixed-sex Physical Education Initial Teacher Training (PEITT) and the inclusion of Muslim women: a case study on seeking solutions. *European Physical Education Review* 12, 2: 181–120.

Benn, T. and Koushkie, M. (2008) 'Accept and Respect' International Study Week – improving opportunities for Muslim girls and women to participate in physical education and sporting activity. *ICSEMIS 2008 International Convention on Science, Education and Medicine in Sport*, Guangzhou, China, August 1–4, 2008.

Benn, T., Dagkas, S. and Jawad, H. (2010, forthcoming) Embodied faith: Islam, religious freedom and educational practices in physical education. *Sport, Education and Society.*

Biddle, S. and Mutrie, N. (2008) *Psychology of Physical Activity: Determinants, Well-Being and Interventions.* Oxon, Routledge.

Boreham, C. and Riddoch, C. (2003) Physical activity and health through the lifespan. In

J. McKenna and C. Riddoch (eds) *Perspectives on Health and Exercise*. London, Palgrave Macmillan: 11–24.

Brighton Declaration on Women and Sport (1994) www.iwg-gti.org/index.php?id=11.

Carroll, B. and Hollinshead, G. (1993) Equal opportunities: race and gender in physical education: a case study. In J. Evans (ed.) *Equality, Education and Physical Education*. London, Falmer Press: 154–169.

Dagkas, S. (2007) Exploring teaching practices in physical education with cultural diverse classes: a cross-cultural study. *European Journal of Teacher Education* 30, 4: 431–443.

Dagkas, S. and Benn, T. (2006) Young Muslim women's experiences of Islam and physical education in Greece and Britain: a comparative study. *Sport, Education and Society* 11, 1: 21–38.

Dagkas, S. and Stathi, A. (2007) Exploring social and environmental factors affecting adolescents' participation in physical activity. *European Physical Education Review* 13, 3: 369–383.

Dagkas, S., Benn, T. and Jawad, H. (2010, forthcoming) Multiple voices: improving participation of Muslim Girls in physical education and school sport. *Sport, Education and Society*.

Duncan, J.M., Al-Nakeeb, Y., Nevill, A. and Jones, M.V. (2004) Body image and physical activity in British secondary school children. *European Physical Education Review* 10, 3: 243–260.

Dunn, K., Klocker, N. and Salabay, T. (2007) Contemporary racism and Islamophobia in Australia. *Ethnicities* 7, 4: 564–589.

Evans, J., Davies, B. and Wright, J. (2004) *Body, Knowledge and Control: Studies in the Sociology of Physical Education and Health*. London, Routledge.

Faulkner, G.E. and Taylor, A. (2005) *Exercise, Health and Mental Health: Emerging Relationships*. London, Routledge.

Fekete, L. (2008) *Integration, Islamophobia and Civil Rights in Europe*. London, Institute of Race Relations.

Garrett, R. (2004) Gendered bodies and physical identities. In J. Evans, B. Davies and J. Wright (eds) *Body, Knowledge and Control: Studies in the Sociology of Physical Education and Health*. London, Routledge: 140–156.

Green, K. (2008) *Understanding Physical Education*. London, SAGE: 167–187.

Hardman, E.A. and Stensel, D. (2003) *Physical Activity and Health: The Evidence Explained*. London, Routledge.

Hargreaves, J. (2000) The Muslim female heroic: shorts or veils? In J. Hargreaves (ed.) *Heroines of Sport*. London, Routledge: 46–77.

Houlihan, B. and White, A. (2002) *The Politics of Sport Development*. London, Routledge.

International Council of Sport Science and Physical Education (ICSSPE) (1999) *The World Summit in Physical Education: A Landmark Event*. Berlin, November 3–5.

Jawad, H. and Benn, T. (2003) *Muslim Women in the United Kingdom and Beyond: Experiences and Images*. Leiden, Brill.

Kay, T. (2006) Daughters of Islam: family influences on Muslim young women's participation in sport. *International Review for the Sociology of Sport* 41, 3–4: 357–373.

Kluka, D.A. (2008) *The Brighton Declaration on Women and Sport: A Management Audit of Process Quality*. DPhil thesis, University of Pretoria, Pretoria.

Macdonald, D., Abbott, R., Knez, K. and Nelson, A. (2009) Talking exercise: cultural diversity and physically active lifestyles. *Sport, Education and Society* 14, 1: 1–19.

Ministers of Physical Education and Sport III Conference (1999) *Declaration of Punta del Este*. Punta del Este, UNESCO.

Pfister, G. (2003) Women and sport in Iran: keeping goal in the *hijab*? In I. Hartmann-Tews and G. Pfister (eds) *Sport and Women: Social Issues in International Perspective*. London, Routledge: 207–223.

Sallis, J.E. and Owen, N. (1999) *Physical Activity and Behavioural Medicine*. Thousand Oaks, SAGE.

Shilling, C. (2008) *Changing Bodies: Habit, Crisis and Creativity*. London, Sage.

Sriskantharajah, J. and Kai, J. (2007) Promoting physical activity among South Asian women with coronary heart disease and diabetes: what might help? *Family Practice* 24, 1: 71–76.

Talbot, M. (1997) *Commonwealth Women and Sport: Opportunities and Barriers*. Commonwealth Secretaria.

Talbot, M. (2000) 'The case for physical education'. *Proceedings of the World Summit on Physical Education*. Berlin, International Council for Sport Science and Physical Education.

Talbot, M. (2006) 'Making the political case'. *Proceedings*, 2nd World Summit on Physical Education, Berlin, ICSSPE.

Talbot, M. (ed.) (2010, forthcoming) *Three Decades of Progress for Physical Education*. Berlin, ICSSPE, supported by UNESCO.

Taylor, A. and Faulkner, G. (2005) From emerging relationships to the future role of exercise in mental health promotion. In G. Faulkner and A. Taylor (eds) *Exercise Health and Mental Health: Emerging Relationships*. Oxon, Routledge.

Turner, D. (2007) Ethnic diversity in physical education teaching. *Physical Education Matters* 2, 2: 14–16.

United Nations (1989) *Convention on the Rights of the Child*. Geneva.

United Nations Educational, Scientific and Cultural Organisation (1978) *International Charter on Physical Education and Sport*, 21 November, Paris.

Vaisse, J. (2004) *Veiled Meaning: The French Law Banning Religious Symbols in Public Schools: U.S.–France Analysis Series*. Washington, DC, The Brookings Institution.

Walseth, K. (2006) Young Muslim women and sport: the impact of identity work. *Leisure Studies* 25, 1: 75–94.

Walseth, K. and Fasting, K. (2003) Islam's view on physical activity and sport: Egyptian women interpreting Islam. *International Review for the Sociology of Sport* 38, 1: 45–60.

2 الريـاضــة والمـرأة فـي الإسـلام

Islam, women and sport

Haifaa Jawad, Yousra Al-Sinani and Tansin Benn

Editors' introduction

The purpose of including a chapter on Islam, women and sport is to contribute a more theological dimension to the socio-cultural studies dialogue in other chapters. The chapter examines the reasoning behind the opening 'Accept and Respect'[1] statement: 'Islam is an enabling religion that endorses women's participation in physical activity.' In order to arrive at that statement, the authors examine: the origins and essential features of the faith; early Islam as a period of enlightenment for women; processes of acculturation and change that damaged the position of women in Islamic societies; and recent revivalist attempts to locate Muslim women more positively in an Islam previously interpreted by men.

Background to Islam, women and sport

Theological as well as sociological analysis of Islam and Islamic culture can contribute to understanding the religion and its manifestations in the lives of followers. It is important to examine the role of gender relations in Islam and the effects on Muslim girls' and women's participation in the field of physical activity because of the relative invisibility of Muslim women in major sporting competitions. This is due partly to social, political, economic and educational factors, but also to a small number of high-profile cases of women's admonishment by conservative clerics for participating in sport with apparent disregard to Islamic requirements for body modesty (Hargreaves 2000). For girls in school-level physical education and sport, tensions can also arise at the interface of religious requirements and physicality. These are often based on misunderstandings in the Diaspora (Carroll and Hollinshead 1993; Dagkas and Benn 2006; De Knop *et al.* 1996; Benn *et al.* 2010). In an attempt to add clarity to the contested domain of 'Islam, Women and Sport', the authors take a historical journey from early (authentic) Islam (Jawad 1998), through the period of disenfranchisement of Muslim women's role in many societies, to the recent revivalist era and the work of feminists – notably Islamic feminists. It is their use of theological (hermeneutic/discourse analysis) approaches to deepening insight into interpretations of religious texts from inside the faith that have made a difference to the lives of Muslim women, empowering many to take more active roles in contemporary societies (Jawad 2009a, 2009b).

A return to early Islam is important because it enables damaging overlays of pseudo-religious cultural beliefs and practice to be distanced from 'authentic Islam' (Jawad 1998: 99). Jawad uses the term 'authentic Islam' to refer to the principles of the holy texts, the Quran and Hadiths, that captured life and meaning at the time of the Prophet Mohammed in the seventh-century AD. Early Islam proclaimed the equal value of men and women as essential contributors to the private and public life of their society. Since that time, Islam has spread from its Arabian roots to become a global religion with 1.3 billion Muslims living in most countries of the world (Esposito and Mogahed 2007: 3). Factors including globalisation, politicisation, acculturation, conflict, migration and Diaspora, spanning many centuries, have led to Islam in the twenty-first century being experienced differently throughout the world. The treatment of women in Islamic communities now varies across the world, and in some places they are no longer treated equally or encouraged to contribute fully to life in their society.

Islamic tradition addresses many questions that continue to be asked in the search for meaning and understanding in life, such as the purpose of creation, existence and death. The importance of these questions cannot be underestimated even though they have not always been valued in academia, but Shilling (2008: 144) in his book *Changing Bodies: Habit, Crisis and Creativity* states: 'Debates about belief have become extraordinarily important in recent years.' He attributes this to issues of migration, cultural changes in the West, ways in which different religions are visible and the global spread of fundamentalism, justified in part by religious affiliation.

The increased visibility of Islam in the West has been demonised through the messages propagated by the media, spreading and popularising particular world-views. Extremist derogatory views such as those of Younus Shaikh (2007: 8) who claimed 'Islam is an organised crime against humanity' are not only offen-sive to many Muslims and non-Muslims, but are also a means of fuelling Islam-ophobia that impacts on the lives of all Muslims globally (Allen and Nielsen 2002; Jawad and Benn 2003; Fekete 2008). The degree of contention surround-ing Islam, particularly after the atrocities of September 11, 2001 and the inva-sions of Afghanistan and Iraq, cannot be ignored, but current tensions and conflicts regarding the polarisation of Muslims and the West are often based on a lack of knowledge and understanding about each other's lives. For example, in the Parliament of the World's Religions held in Australia, December 2009, a large segment of the Conference time was allocated to the discussion of issues of Islam in the West in order to:

> Talk about a tradition that is misunderstood, talk about a tradition that is maligned, talk about a tradition where one percent of the tradition has given the entire community a bad name, it is Islam. And so we want to give

reputable Islamic scholars and leaders the chance first of all to share what they believe Islam is all about.

(Ficca 2009)

A two-way learning process is vital, since damaging stereotypes of both Islam and the West, exacerbated by media hype, can be equally misunderstood and misused.

Tenets of Islam

Islam is a monotheistic Abrahamic religion that brought reaffirmation of the oneness of God through the last of the Prophets, Mohammed, in seventh-century Arabia. The word 'Islam' is an Arabic word which means to surrender or to resign oneself. In religious terms it means submission (*Taslim*); hence, a Muslim is someone who submits to God, or to God's will, to Allah (the Arabic word for God) as the creator, sustainer and the ultimate controller of the universe. Islam also means peace (*Salaam*) due to the very act of submission; as such, Islam means living in accordance to the will of God in order to achieve peace in this world and success in the hereafter.

Islam is also referred to as 'al Din', a comprehensive term that denotes the totality of life and implies a primary orientation towards the Divine as the source of final authority. Understanding the significance of faith in the lives of believers is helped by awareness of their fundamental allegiance to the Divine revelation of texts that underpins the religious value systems. This is the essence of religion and distinguishes religious belief from ideologies that are not Divinely inspired and that are, therefore, more easily challenged (Jawad 1997).

In committing oneself to faith, no other pursuit, such as work or sport, should take precedence over religious obligations in daily life. From the Islamic perspective, religion is not part of life but the whole of it. The first of the core five pillars of faith in Islam requires commitment to one eternal truth, *Tawhid*, or Unity: 'There is no God but God.' Muslims believe that Islam always existed and that Adam was the first Prophet. It is believed further messages were sent through prophets to remind people of the primordial religion (*al-din al-hanif*). As signs of their Prophethood, these special people were given the power to perform miracles. Mohammed's miracle was the Quran (Nasr 1993; Jawad 2010).

In addition to a belief in one God, the other pillars of faith require conformity to routines that capture, demonstrate and reaffirm commitment to God in the form of *Salat* – commitment to prayer five times a day, *Zakat* – giving of alms, fasting during Ramadan and pilgrimage to Mecca – *Hajj*. It is commitment to these five pillars of faith that unite Muslims globally. The manifestation of faith in adherence to the five pillars of faith remains the central unifying feature of acceptable practice. Adherence requires systematic habitual bodily actions as expressions of faith, making 'faith an embodied habit as much as a reflexive commitment' (Shilling 2008: 154). These 'five pillars' show the significance of bodily techniques to Muslim religiosity; to be a Muslim is to be oriented to such practices on the path to paradise, not only in terms of God-consciousness, but as a holistic dimension integrated within an individual's existence. The degree to which religion is 'embodied' is reflected in the terms 'religiosity' or 'religious-ness', which refer to how devout a person is in terms of their faith, for example in its cognisance (knowledge), affective (feeling) and behavioural (doing) components (Cornwall *et al.* 1986).

Another important factor in understanding Islam today is Sharia law. With the death of Mohammed and his companions and the expansion of Islam to other territories, the Islamic community developed a more formal system of governance in Sharia law. This covers both public and personal/family law, including matters of marriage, divorce, inheritance and custody, as well as guidance on matters of dress and conduct. In addition to the Quran and Hadith (the Divinely inspired principles), Islamic/Sharia law contains further jurists' interpretations (*fiqh*). With few exceptions, for example Iran, Saudi Arabia and Sudan, most Muslim countries are not strictly governed by Sharia law, but recognise and implement aspects of the personal/family law which covers issues mentioned above. It is differently interpreted in accordance with the various schools of law, determined by historical, social, political and legal situations. This is reflected in the differences of women's experiences recounted in this book.

Amara (2007: 534) calls for distinction between: 'Islam as a belief system and Islam as a cultural form, interpreted, conceived and manipulated by nation states, political movements and different interest groups to legitimate their political agenda, social conduct and (sometimes pre-Islamic) practices.'

While emphasis here is on increasing understanding of core values of Islam as a belief system, the fact that relative freedoms continue to exist in lived experiences of Islam and that the discussion of the realms of belief, cultural practices and critical expression of views can open contested and serious dialogue also need to be explored to increase understanding of diverse realities (Grinberg 2006).

Early Islam, equality for women and their disenfranchisement

Social, political, educational and economic factors impact differently on the lives of all girls and women across the world. Although the pre-Islamic position of women remains a contested issue, there is no doubt that in Arabia before Islam, women in general were poorly treated, female infanticide occurred and the lives of girls and women were often wretched (Badran 1995; Kandiyoti 1996; Jawad 1998; Rajavi 2004). This is not to suggest that all women were badly treated in that context. There were wealthy elites who escaped such derogatory treatment, but scholars claim such women were exceptions in their societies, as indicated by Stowasser (cited in Jawad 1998: 5) in the following:

> We hear of publicly visible, independently wealthy women who are active in their own right … aside from such rare figures of public visibility (such as Khajida, the Prophet's first wife) … the majority of pre-Islamic urban

women appear to have lived in a male-dominated society in which their status was low and their rights were neglected.

Central to becoming Muslim is the search for guidance on life matters through belief in the Quran, the divine word, delivered through the Prophet Mohammed and the Hadith, or record of the Prophet's sayings, and the principles and practices which guided his life. These Islamic texts deal with women's rights on two levels, spiritual and social. At the spiritual level and before God, the holy texts proclaimed man and woman as equals in all essential rights and duties; to be equally rewarded or punished for their good or bad deeds. The Quran (Quran 3: 195) says: 'Never will I suffer to be lost the work of any of you, be he male or female, you are members one of another.' Men and women were framed as interdependent, both needing and depending on each other to achieve a harmonious and prosperous life. In the Quranic vision,

> A normal and healthy society is one in which both men and women are given the possibilities to develop fully their natures (and potentials) and to contribute to that richness and diversity which characterize creation and reflect the Unity of the Divine Principle.
>
> (Nasr 1981: 213)

Islamic texts stress that women should be offered all opportunities to participate effectively in the development of society and to attain the highest ranks of progress, intellectually and spiritually (Jawad 2009a, 2009b).

As a result of the knowledge that can be gained from the Quran and authentic Hadith, in Islam women were granted broad social, political and economic rights, as well as education and marital rights (Jawad 1998). With time, the rights embedded in early Islam gradually underwent steady erosion due to complex historical, cultural and political factors. Women's rights deteriorated under circumstances such as increasing patriarchal domination and acculturation. Many women were prevented from leading public lives, obtaining an education and sharing equal status with men. Some were subjected to heavy veiling and excluded from places of worship (Ahmed 1992; Jawad 1998). Hence, religious principles became confused and intertwined with cultural overlays. The disadvantaged position of Muslim women was frequently attributed to Islam when, in reality, it bore no resemblance to the aspirations of authentic Islam. This situation prompted Muslim women (and some male scholars) to voice their concerns regarding patriarchal traditions and practices in their societies. It is recognised that at no time has Islam ever been totally free of patriarchy because men have largely claimed and retained the power of interpreting the holy texts (El-Fadl 2001). The hostile religious and political establishments, however, ensured that these early voices went largely unheard. Not until the 1980s would these efforts re-emerge, especially in the context of Islamic feminism.

According to Shilling (2008), as part of a renewed search for meaning and fulfilment in life in an increasingly technological age, there has been a revival of interest in religious and spiritual aspects of life globally, including Islam, charismatic forms of Christianity and Catholicism in Africa, Asia and South America, Buddhism, Judaism and Hinduism.

> In the case of Islam, for example, this revival has generally been an urban phenomenon appealing to people who are modern orientated, well-educated, and pursuing professional careers. The Islamic world is also growing, and Islam has become 'Europe's second religion'.
>
> (Huntingdon 2002, cited in Shilling 2008: 150)

Revivalist Islam brought both positive and negative consequences for women. Negatively, there is the issue of radical Islam, which denies and constrains women's rights (for example, the situation of women under the Taliban, and more recently in Iraq). Positively, there are Muslim women (and men) turning to the Islamic holy texts to find new meaning for the lives of women in the form of Islamic feminism.

Revivalist Islam and Islamic feminism

Islamic feminism is a movement located within the contemporary feminist reform movement operating globally. Scholars who work in the field aim to improve the position of women in many fields of life, while upholding respect for authentic Islam. They aim to achieve gender equality and social justice within an Islamic framework. The emergence of political Islam (Islamism),[2] and the attempt of the Islamists to enforce patriarchal notions in Islamic societies, provoked strong reactions among many Muslim women, and became a driving force for more activism. Hasan explains (1987: 2):

> Despite the fact that women such as Khadijah and A'ishah (wives of Prophet Muhammed) and Rabia al-Basri (the outstanding woman Sufi) figure significantly in early Islam, the Islamic tradition has, by and large, remained rigidly patriarchal until the present time, prohibiting the growth of scholarship among women particularly in the realm of religious thought. Thus the sources on which the Islamic tradition is based, mainly the Qur'an and Hadith literature ... and Fiqh (jurisprudence), have been only interpreted by Muslim men, who have arrogated to themselves the task of defining the ontological, theological, sociological and eschatological status of Muslim women.

In addition to a shift in the long-term exclusion of women from the interpretation of Islamic texts and literature, a variety of complex political and social developments have facilitated these feminists' attempts to gain support and popularity. In this context Jawad (2009a) highlights the significance of the role played by women in the Diaspora, Muslim scholars and writers living in the West. Other factors that contributed to the upsurge of the movement were: the policy of the war on terror; the increasing education of Muslim women, giving them critical skills and the opportunity to question and challenge traditional gender patterns; the United Nations decade of focus on women from 1975, raising international awareness of the gross injustices facing many Muslim women; and aspects of globalisation spreading ideas through new technologies such as the Internet. Arguments can be found in the work of Kandiyoti (1996) and Cook (2001) that acknowledge, among other factors, the role of education in enabling gender activists to reclaim some of their rights within an Islamic framework. For example, women in Kuwait, according to Mughni (2001: 169), 'have begun to speak for themselves, voicing a female model of an Islamic society that differs from the masculine hierarchical order in which women are disenfranchised and constrained to roles dictated by their biological constitution'.

It is important to understand that any attempt to make a scholarly reinterpretation of the Quran is challenged by the fact that the text loses its aura (pure essence of meaning) once translated from the Arabic. Difficulties are exacerbated by multiple translations of the texts which reflect different schools of thought. Some are judged more authentic than others by those in the academic field of Islamic studies. As in all religions, differences in interpretation of the holy texts shape particular views in the lives of followers. Simplistically, today there are Muslim conservatives who believe that Islamic scriptures laid down in the past should be literally adhered to, others who use modern values as a starting point for interpretation, and Islamic feminists who return to the original texts of the Quran and Hadith to explore interpretation for issues related to women's lives today.

Conservative interpretation of Islamic texts is increasingly challenged by the reinterpretation process. Efforts by various groups continue to focus on improving the position of Muslim women; for example, the United Nations Development Fund for Women (UNIFEM) continues to support improvements for Muslim women, as illustrated in the South-East Asia Regional Conference on Advancing Gender Equality and Women's Empowerment in Muslim Societies held in Jakarta, Indonesia, in March 2009 with the International Centre for Islam and Pluralism (ICIP). Similarly, a recent conference in Bahrain (2008) focused on raising awareness of the work of different agencies such as CEDAW (United Nations Convention on the Elimination of all forms of Discrimination Against Women). The outcome of the speeches was a call for women to be agents, active in development and change, not simply recipients, in order to be able to join as a force in the building of modern states. Leaders such as the wife of the King of Bahrain (current President of the Supreme Council for Women) spoke powerful words suggesting the 'negative views on women … lie in traditions rather than religion' and 'the Quran did not discriminate against us in rights and responsibilities … it concentrated on the values of justice and equality' (Bahrain 2008: 9–10).

In summary, Islamic feminism is a theological approach to the reinterpretation of Islamic religious texts from a woman-friendly perspective, seeking new meaning while upholding Islamic adherence and identity. The key approach is to focus on textual analysis of the Quran and Hadith and to use hermeneutic reinterpretation of the texts to establish a new understanding of women's rights in contemporary situations – for example their role in public life and participation in making fuller contributions to societal progress (Wadud 2006; Jawad 2009a, 2009b).

Feminist perspectives of Islam, women and sport

As evidenced in the chapters of this book, there are those Muslim women who choose to participate in sport-related activities with head, arms and legs covered, others in Western sporting outfits, and others who choose to participate only in sex-segregated environments. All regard themselves as Muslim, and most are satisfied with the private and public ways in which they adhere to their faith and resolve their faith/athlete identities. Can an Islamic perspective of women and sport help in understanding, accepting and respecting these differences?

There is nothing in the Quran or Hadith that explicitly precludes men's or women's participation in physical activities, provided it does not take precedence over faith (Daiman 1994). Hence, the 'Accept and Respect' declaration claims that 'Islam is an enabling religion that does not preclude women's participation in physical activities'. The Hadith text contains some examples from the Prophet's life that can be used to support the participation and equality of opportunity for girls and boys. Examples of the time described children pursuing swimming, shooting and horse-riding (Hadith – Caliph 634–44H, 20–21). There is a reference to the Prophet racing with his wife, Aisha, and evidence that some women fought alongside the men, which would require them to be physically fit warriors. Acclaiming the efforts of one woman in particular, Nusaiba bint Kab al-Mazinia, the Prophet said, 'Wherever I looked I saw her fighting before me' (Jawad 1998: 22). This demonstrates equality and support for women attaining and maintaining physical capability in early Islam.

Entitlement to a 'physical' education as part of a holistic education is also supported through religious texts and examples. Since all Muslims are called upon to seek knowledge from the cradle to the grave, girls and women are equally entitled to education in Islam as boys and men, and to the pursuit of a balanced and fulfilled life. This requirement of all Muslims supports the entitlement to physical education within the formal education of young people. The subject is the only one that provides the means by which children learn and develop through human movement and physical engagement with the world in which they live. As evidenced in Chapter 1 of this book, many studies confirm that physical activity is important for a balanced life and has a beneficial impact on the overall development and welfare of human beings. Physical activity can improve both the physical and mental health of people, and enhance intellectual and social development (Bailey and Dismore 2004). Everyone has a right to that life chance.

Islam is a way of life that calls for the holistic development of human beings with attention to spirituality, as well as intellectual and physical well-being. As such, both men and women are strongly encouraged to live healthily in body, mind and spirit. The Prophet Mohammed is reported to have said, 'Your Lord has a right on you, your own self has a right on you and your family has a right on you; so you should give the rights of all those who have rights on you' (Hadith–Bukhari: 452). In this context 'your own self' refers to the obligation or responsibility for each person to take care of all personal needs, spiritual, intellectual and physical, in order to maintain a healthy and balanced life; it applies to men and women equally because neither is singled out.

For some women, however, there can be issues regarding the culture of sports participation environments and Islamic codes of conduct requiring modesty in dress and gender relations. Modesty, as a concept in Islam, relates to moral values of what is right and wrong with regard to personal conduct, particularly with regard to sexual relations outside marriage. In the Quran requirements for such values are the same for both men and women, as is clear in the following verse from the Quran 33: 35:[3]

> For Muslim men and Muslim women, for believing men and women, for devout men and women, for true men and women, for men and women who are patient and constant, for men and women who humble themselves, for men and women who give in charity, for men and women who fast (and deny themselves), for men and women who guard their chastity, and for men and women who engage much in God's praise – for them has God prepared forgiveness and great reward.

Despite attention to equality in the verse above, in reality, many Muslim women continue to shoulder the responsibilities of sexual propriety and family honour related to social conduct in heterosexual relationships. The following verse is often used to bestow this responsibility, in addition to its central attention to covering:

> O Prophet! Tell the wives and daughters, and the believing women, that they should cast their outer garments over their persons (when abroad): That is most convenient, that they should be known (as such) and not molested. And God is oft-forgiving, most merciful.
>
> (Quran 33: 59)

Women's bodies and public visibility, then, are a central concern in Islamic culture. It follows that women's participation in the sporting arena is contested because the dominant (Western/secular) sporting culture can lead to high visibility of women's bodies and public mixed-sex arenas. Decisions by Muslim girls and women concerning the choice of their sports clothes can cause controversies and conflicts within families, communities and with religious leaders. Two main themes in the chapter will be examined in more detail to further understand the diversity of realities for the Muslim women represented in the chapters of this book: the question of *hijab* and the issue of gender segregation.

Hijab

The Islamic concept of *hijab* has a broad meaning but in this book it is predominantly used to indicate the practice of head covering, as well as the covering of arms and legs, which many Muslim women adopt in accordance with their commitment to religious adherence and the practice of modesty. Not all women who are Muslim wear the *hijab* or Islamic dress. Differences for Muslim women today in their choices, coercion to wear or denial from wearing the *hijab*, arise in and between diverse social, economic and political situations. Islamic cultures are dynamic, sharing constants such as adherence to the practices of the five pillars of faith, but also differences in the local context and lived interpretations of religious texts.

The concept of modesty applies to both men and women: 'Say to the believing men that they should lower their gaze and guard their modesty: that will make for greater purity for them: And God is well acquainted with all that they do' (Quran 24: 30). For women:

> And say to the believing women that they should lower their gaze and guard their modesty; that they should not display their beauty and ornaments except what must (ordinarily) appear thereof; that they should draw their veils over their bosoms and not display their beauty except to their husbands (and certain family members).
>
> (Quran 24: 31)

Justifications are related to protection from sexual objectification and temptation to sexual transgression.

Under (a strict interpretation of) Sharia law, women are required to cover all of their bodies except hands and face (men from waist to knee). In practice, this is interpreted in various ways dependent on the situation and attitudes towards public/private faith, the body, gender relations and responsibilities for sexual propriety. While public manifestation of faith is essential in the lives of some Muslim women, others choose a more private, internalised commitment that may link to the Quran verse about righteousness (interpreted in this context as inner commitment to Islamic principles for moral conduct, values and behaviour): 'O ye children of Adam! We have bestowed raiment upon you to cover your shame, as well as to be an adornment to you. But the raiment of righteousness – that is the best ...' (Quran 7: 26).

The verse can suggest that inner righteousness, avoidance of sin or transgression of religious or moral principle in everyday codes of conduct is more significant than dress or outward appearance. Differences in lived realities can be attributed to interpretation of literal (for example, 'raiment' as material) or metaphorical ('raiment' as present but internalised) meaning on commitment to Islamic principles.

There is no simplistic way in which Muslim people embody the idea of modesty as part of their faith. For some, faith is an internalised/private commitment to belief, for others the expression of faith is externalised as a consequence of their commitment in the practice of covering hair, arms and legs in public. For the latter group, dress becomes an essential part of their 'embodied faith', to the holistic private/public experience of their faith identity (Benn 2009; Benn *et al.* 2010; Pfister, Chapter 3 of this book).

An answer to a question about whether Muslim women *should* wear *hijab*, then, could be seen as equivocal. The Quran (2: 256) rejects coercion in faith: 'There be no compulsion in religion', since the decision to commit to faith can be the most significant in a person's life, it is possible to deduce that there should be no compulsion in how individuals choose to embody their faith identity. Others would point to literal interpretations regarding modesty from verses of the Quran as implying that there is no choice. It is a contested area but lived Islam shows that many Muslim women do adopt the *hijab* and many do not, yet all who call themselves Muslim have committed to Islam. Interestingly, with the recent revival of Islam worldwide, many more women are choosing to adopt the *hijab* in their everyday lives as a symbol of their faith. This can bring additional challenges to sporting cultures in which, through policy or regulation, the wearing of the *hijab* is not allowed, for example in some secular states and some international sports governing bodies.

Gender segregation

The issue of sex segregation is also pertinent to any exploration of Muslim women in sport. While some Muslim women choose to participate in international events with no special dress code requirements and others take part provided their dress code for modesty is met, there are women who prefer, or are required by political or socio-cultural pressures, to avoid mixed-sex environments and any kind of contact between the sexes after puberty. Islamically, appropriate sporting competitions do exist, for example the Women's Islamic Games in Iran and the Gulf Countries (GCC) Women's Games (see Chapters 6 and 7). These environments have provided 'safe' environments for those women who prefer sex-segregated spaces in which to participate. Other chapters, for example, Chapters 3 and 5, which involve Diaspora communities, show that the lack of such opportunities in structural sporting provision can be a barrier for those women who prefer sex-segregated sporting spaces. The issue of sex segregation is, then, a real concern for some Muslim women with regard to active participation in physical activity.

As in the case of the *hijab*, this is another contested site of religious and cultural conflation where there are different opinions, religious views and lived realities globally. From the Islamic perspective, there is nothing, either in the Quran or the authentic Hadith, that explicitly stresses that a strict segregation between the two sexes is required. Conservative interpretations of Islamic texts combined with cultural overlays continue to prevent or restrict women from taking part in many spheres of life including physical activity. Interpretation of a single verse is often wrongly used to constrain the lives of women: 'And stay [the wives of Mohammed] quietly in your houses, and make not a dazzling display, like that of the former times of ignorance; and establish regular prayer, and give regular charity; and obey God and His Apostle ...' (Quran 33: 33).

The specific reference here is to the wives of the Prophet, who enjoyed a special status; it was not intended to relate to the role of all women, but it has been used by some to apply to all women. Similarly, verse 33: 53 of the Quran makes reference to the Prophet's wives speaking with guests from behind a screen during social events: 'for greater purity for your hearts and for theirs.' This again has been applied more generally than the original address to the wives of the Prophet and is used to underpin social separation of women from men in some societies.

Different realities lie in the twenty-first-century studies recounted in this book and in wider international research, suggesting that lived cultures are fluid and dynamic, responsive to modernisation processes, as well as to social, political and economic pressures. Everyday life goes on in-between all of the subtle nuances of situation. It cannot be denied that some Muslim women prefer and need women-only spaces for freedom of participation, or that others who find themselves in such contexts may prefer the alternative. In response to the diversity of experiences that exist today, the international Declaration 'Accept and Respect' recommended:

- that people working in the sport and education systems accept and respect the diverse ways in which Muslim women and girls practise their religion and participate in sport and physical activity, for example, choices of activity, dress and gender grouping.
- that international sport federations show their commitment to inclusion by ensuring that their dress codes for competition embrace Islamic requirements, taking into account the principles of propriety, safety and integrity.

Adopting such recommendations would lead to more opportunities for more women, a shift in sporting culture towards more inclusive practices that acknowledge the power of religious belief, and its effects on preferred body practices, in the lives of many.

Conclusion

The focus on Islam in this chapter was to enter a discussion on the religion, the tenets of the faith, and the differences in lived realities in Islamic cultures globally. The significance of religious belief in people's lives should not be underestimated, and revivalist movements demonstrate increasing numbers of people searching for religious and spiritual fulfilment globally in the twenty-first century.

In response to Islamic feminists' interrogation of holy texts, it can be seen that women are not always treated in accordance with the equal rights bestowed in early Islam. Islam encourages women to make full contributions to society. Moral codes of conduct for control in sexual relations underpin modesty concerns related to the *hijab* and sex segregation. Reinterpretation and closer analysis of the use of language and interpretation of the Quran and Hadith by Islamic feminists is bringing women more space from inside the faith. There is nothing in these texts that precludes women's participation in physical activity; indeed, there is support for women's equal opportunities with men and for assuming responsibility for their own health and well-being as a life-long holistic endeavour to pursue physical, spiritual and intellectual development.

The challenges of a more theological approach to understanding Islam, women and sport are many. Translations of original texts are problematic in themselves in terms of authenticity. Interpretation and application to living faith are further influenced by many factors discussed here and in other chapters, such as cultural, political and economic conditions. All of these ensure contested positions and impact on the experiences of Muslim women. Examples of the challenges of interpreting verses from the Quran, and the difference in consequences for the lives of women, are examined. The question remains – whose voice counts? Some interpretations are considered more valid than others; this again may depend on the situation, and there is much more research to be done in this area. At least, in many countries, women's voices are entering the debate.

In many societies sport-related activities can be regarded as 'non-serious', low-status pursuits rather than serious, life- and health-enhancing pursuits for all people. Paradoxically, sport may also be considered a luxury activity reserved only for the rich, as access to fitness and sports clubs can be costly. It should also be remembered that sport is not high on the agenda in countries, for example, where there is risk to personal safety, or where poverty and illiteracy are widespread and basic human needs cannot be met (Esposito and Magahed 2007). These considerations apart, those who disregard physical activity fail to recognise its significance in holistic human development and the part that it plays in the physical, cognitive, social and affective development of the human being.

As illustrated in this book and in other research, sport-related experiences of Muslim girls and women range from those requiring sex-segregated spaces to those participating in shorts and tops. The approach adopted here and in the 'Accept and Respect' Declaration is that women's choices and voices should be heard, and provision made accordingly, to incorporate faith-based needs that will enhance participation. Barriers that can preclude the involvement of Muslim girls and women in sport and physical activity are normally related to situations where meeting needs for modesty in dress or gender segregation is problematic. This is more common in the Diaspora, where provision is structured and organised in line with Western, secular sporting frameworks, dress requirements, public changing facilities and predominantly open mixed-sex provision. There are patriarchal cultural beliefs and dogmatic uses of religious texts that are used in some places to exclude girls and women from life chances such as education, physical education and the fulfilment of physical, spiritual and intellectual capabilities. This is not in line with an 'enabling Islam' that is currently empowering women to take their place, claiming both religion and equality in their lives (Esposito and Mogahed 2007; Zebiri 2008).

Education and training for teachers, coaches, sport administrators and organisers (both in Muslim and non-Muslim settings) need to incorporate greater awareness of faith-based principles and multiple expressions of that religious belief. Efforts are required to raise the status of careers in the field, such as in teaching, coaching and leadership development for women in general and for Muslim women in particular. Encouragement is needed for the training and retention of interested Muslim women as role models who could influence future generations. There needs to be greater understanding and action from international sports federations to relax dress codes and provide resources to enable Muslim women to participate if, and as, they choose. By the same token, Muslim communities and especially religious leaders need to accept and respect the choices of women.

Notes

1 International declaration made at the IAPESGW 2008 study week in Sultan Qaboos University, Oman. See www.iapesgw.org.
2 Islamism is defined by Arkoun (1995, cited Amara 2007: 534) as 'a type of discourse or collective affirmation linked to a category of actors who share a strong will/determination to re-establish "religious" (Islamic) values, and exactly a "religious" model of societal organisation.'
3 The Quran used is: The Holy Qur'an (printed 1993), translation and commentary by A. Yusuf Ali, India: Islamic Propagation Centre.

Bibliography

Ahmed, L. (1992) *Women and Gender in Islam*, London: Yale University Press.
Allen, C. and Nielsen, J.S. (2002) *Summary Report on Islamophobia in the EU After 11 September 2001*, European Monitoring Centre on Racism and Xenophobia, Centre for the Study of Islam and Christian–Muslim Relations, Department of Theology, University of Birmingham, England.
Amara, M. (2007) An introduction to the study of sport in the Muslim world, in B. Houlihan (ed.) *Sport and Society: A Student Introduction* (2nd edition), London: Sage: 532–553.
Badran, M. (1995) *Feminists, Islam and Nation: Gender and the Making of Modern Egypt*, Princeton: Princeton University Press.
Bahrain (2008) *National Conference on Gender Mainstreaming in Development*, 9–10 June, Kingdom of Bahrain, General Secretariat – the Supreme Council for Women, Manama, Bahrain.
Bailey, R. and Dismore, H. (2004) Sport in Education (SpinEd) – the role of physical education and sport in education. *Project report to the 4th International Conference of Ministers and Senior Officials Responsible for Physical Education and Sport (MINEPS IV)*, December, Athens, Greece.
Benn, T. (1996) Muslim women in Physical Education In Initial Teacher Training. *Sport, Education and Society*, 1, 1: 5–21.
Benn, T. (2009) Muslim women in sport: a researcher's journey to understanding embodied faith. *International Council for Sports Science and Physical Education, Bulletin*, 55: 48–56.

Benn, T. and Ahmad, A. (2006) Alternative visions: international sporting opportunities for Muslim women and implications for British sport. *Youth and Policy*, 92: 119–132.

Benn, T.C. and Dagkas, S. (2006) Incompatible? Compulsory mixed-sex Physical Education Initial Teacher Training (PEITT) and the inclusion of Muslim women: a case-study on seeking solutions. *European Physical Education Review*, 12, 2: 181–200.

Benn, T. and Koushkie. M. (2008) Increasing global inclusion of Muslim girls and women in physical activity, presentation at *International* Convention of Science, Education and Medicine in Sport, Guangzhou, China, 1–4 August, *ICSSPE Bulletin* 54: 22–24.

Benn, T., Dagkas, S. and Jawad, H. (2010, forthcoming) Embodied faith: Islam, religious freedom and educational practices in physical education. *Sport, Education and Society*.

Carroll, B. and Hollinshead, G. (1993) Equal opportunities: race and gender in physical education: a case study, in J. Evans (ed.) *Equality, Educational and Physical Education*, London: Falmer Press: 154–169.

Cook, M. (2001) *Women Claim Islam: Creating Islamic Feminism Through Literature*. London: Routledge.

Cornwall, M., Albrecht, S.L., Cunningham, P.H. and Pitcher, B.L. (1986) The dimensions of religiosity: a conceptual model with an empirical test. *Review of Religious Research*, 27: 226–244.

Dagkas, S. and Benn, T. (2006) Young Muslim women's experiences of Islam and physical education in Greece and Britain: a comparative study. *Sport, Education and Society*, 11, 1: 21–38.

Dagkas, S., Benn, T. and Jawad, H. (2010, forthcoming) Multiple voices: improving participation of Muslim Girls in physical education and school sport. *Sport, Education and Society*.

Daiman, S. (1994) Women, sport and Islam. *Sport*, 2: 14–15.

De Knop, P., Theeboom, M., Wittock, H. and De Martelaer, K. (1996) Implications of Islam on Muslim girls' sports participation in Western Europe. *Sport, Education and Society*, 1, 2: 147–164.

El-Fadl, K.A. (2001) *Speaking in God's Name: Islamic Law, Authority and Women*, Oxford: One World.

Esposito, J.L. and Mogahed, D. (2007) *Who Speaks for Islam? What a Billion Muslims Really Think*, New York: Gallup Press.

Fekete, L. (2008) *Integration, Islamophobia and Civil Rights in Europe*. London: Institute of Race Relations.

Ficca, D. (2009) *Australia Welcomes Parliament of World's Religions*. Online, available at: www1.voanews.com/english/news/03dec09-australia-religion-meeting-78406997.html (accessed 4 December 2009).

Grinberg, M. (2006) Defamation of religions. Freedom of expression: finding the balance in a democratic society. *Sri Lanka Journal of International Law*, 18, July.

Hargreaves, J. (2000) *Heroines of Sport: The Politics of Difference and Identity*, Routledge: New York.

Hasan, R. (1987) Equal before Allah: women–man equality in the Islamic tradition. *Harvard Divinity Bulletin*, 7, 2, January–May.

Horne, G. (2007) *The Code of Hammurabi*. Online, available at: www.ancienttexs.org/librarymesopotamian/hammurabi/html (translated by L.W. King).

Jawad, H. (1997) Pan-Islamism and Pan-Arabism, in H. Jawad (ed.) *The Middle East in the New World Order*, Houndmills Macmillan: 140–161.

Jawad, H. (1998) *The Rights of Women in Islam*, London: Macmillan Press.

Jawad, H. (2009a) Islamic feminism: leadership roles and public representation. *HAWWA Journal of Women in the Middle East and the Muslim World*, 7, 1: 1–24.

Jawad, H. (2009b) Islamic spirituality and the feminine dimension, in G. Howie and J. Jobling (eds) *Women and the Divine: Touching Transcendence*, London: Palgrave Macmillan: 187–203.

Jawad, H. (2010) Muslim thought and practice, in Santanu K. Patro (ed.) *A Guide to Religious Thought and Practices*, SPCK international Study Guide, 45, London, September.

Jawad, H. and Benn, T. (2003) *Muslim Women in the United Kingdom and Beyond: Experiences and Images*, Leiden: Brill.

Kandiyoti, D. (1996) *Gendering in the Middle East: Emerging Perspectives*, London: I.B. Tauris and Co. Ltd.

Mughni, H. (2001) *Women in Kuwait: The Politics of Gender*, London: Saqi Books.

Nasr, S.H. (1981) *Islamic Life and Thought*, Albany: State University of New York Press.

Nasr, S.H. (1993) *A Young Muslim's Guide to the Modern World*, Cambridge: The Islamic Text Society.

Shilling, C. (2008) *Changing Bodies: Habits, Crisis and Creativity*, London: Sage.

Wadud, A. (2006) *Inside the Gender Jihad, Women's Reform in Islam*, Oxford: Oneworld Publications.

Younus, S. (2007) *Islam and Women*. Online, available at: www.rationalistinternational. net/article/2004/120_en.html. 24/09/2007.

Zebiri, K. (2008) *British Muslim Converts: Choosing Alternative Lives*, Oxford: Oneworld.

3 Muslimske kvinder og idræt i diasporaer

Teorier, diskurser og metoder – analyse af et dansk eksempel

Muslim women and sport in diasporas
Theories, discourses and practices – analysing the case of Denmark

Gertrud Pfister

Editors' introduction

With the spread of Islam in Europe this is an important chapter because it provides an exploration of: socio-cultural theories; discourses of religion, immigration and Islam; and practices related to faith, gender and sport. Theoretical dimensions are applied to a case study of Muslim women in Denmark in order to illustrate ways of increasing understanding through analysing and interpreting a complex and dynamic European situation.

Background

In Denmark, as in many other countries, global migration processes mean that we must take leave of notions of a 'uniform population'. Although toleration is preached, the degree of our acceptance of 'alien' values and behaviour rises and falls depending on how similar they are to, or how different they are from, the mainstream culture. Problems of living side-by-side and questions of interacting with each other, however, must not only be addressed by the majority population but equally by immigrants, who come from a great number of different countries and cultures and have varying opportunities, options and problems in their dealings with mainstream society. A major role here is played by religious orientations and views of the world, with orthodox Muslims, for example, finding it relatively difficult to reconcile the norms, values and practices anchored in their religion and culture with Western ways of life. Frequently they prefer segregation, a life in and with their own group.

In coming to terms with the respective 'other culture', Muslim women, for instance, play a significant role since they demonstrate sameness or otherness even by the way they dress. The role allocated to them in some traditional Islamic cultures prescribes them a specific position, and assigns to them tasks in the family, which have a special and often negative impact on their integration into mainstream society.

The aim of my contribution is to explore the participation of Muslim girls and women in sport and physical activity (PA), as well as the opportunities and challenges that they encounter in these areas.[1] In addition, I will focus on possible causes and cultural and economic factors that contribute to an (in)active lifestyle among immigrant women.

Important issues that will be dealt with in this chapter are: Danish immigration and sports policies, the 'immigrant discourses' in the Danish media and society, the requirements of Islam, concepts of the body and sport in traditional cultures and, finally, gender relations in immigrant communities. All these issues have a large influence on the body and movement cultures of Muslim women.

The situation of female immigrants in Denmark, and the degree to which they participate in sport, may be used as a case study that provides useful insights that are applicable for cross-cultural comparisons of Muslim women's roles both in Denmark and in other Western countries.

Many different terms are used in Western countries for the members of ethnic and religious minorities.

> There is no universally accepted terminology to describe immigrants and non-native ethnic groups and their offspring. According to historically and socially determined views on migration, the terms migrants, immigrants, ethnic minorities and ethnic communities may sound perfectly legitimate in one country and offensive or biased in another.
>
> (Bollini and Siem 1995: 819)

In this chapter I will use the term 'immigrant' for a person who has been born in a foreign country[2] and call a person 'Danish' whose parents are Danes. Where it is important for the context, when speaking of the descendants of immigrants, I will point out their ethnic origins. No judgement is implied with these designations. In addition, I will, as far as possible, inform the reader of an immigrant's country of origin so that the term 'immigrant' does not obscure the numerous and profound differences between the various groups. It must be borne in mind, however, that immigrants from the same country may also differ from each other fundamentally in respect of religion, culture and customs, depending on whether they come from rural areas or large towns, and which religious orientation they have or to which of the country's ethnic groups they belong. It must also be taken into consideration that, in the meantime, numerous immigrants and their descendants think of themselves as Danes or as 'hyphen Danes' – that is, for example, Turkish-Danish or Danish-Somali citizens. With such diversity, and particularly with the latter groups in mind, it is definitely important for more research to be carried out with and within these populations in order to develop knowledge that may be used to create strategies designed to support all these different groups.

Ethnicity is intertwined with religious orientation, social class and many other characteristics that leave their imprint on identity, culture and way of life. Of special significance in the lives of immigrant women is the gender order that prevails in a particular group, along with gender enactment ('doing gender'), which constitutes a further key issue in this contribution.

Denmark – the context

Denmark, a small country in northern Europe with around five million inhabitants, separates the Baltic Sea from the North Sea and consists of a large peninsula and many islands. Denmark is a constitutional monarchy, with the king or queen as the (formal) head of the state, and has a parliamentary system of government headed by a prime minister. Based as it is on a free-market economy, the Danish welfare state finances free healthcare, free education and other welfare benefits by means of taxes. High income tax, on average around 50 per cent but peaking at 63 per cent, makes Denmark the country with the lowest level of income differences worldwide. With a GDP per capita of $37,700 in 2007 and an unemployment rate of approximately 2.5 per cent, the country has a very high standard of living. Surveys have ranked Denmark among the most peaceful, most liveable and the 'happiest' places in the world (see www.cia.gov/library/publications/the-world-factbook/geos/da.html (accessed 29 November 2009)). Even in Denmark, however, not everyone shares in the prosperity. Members of the lowest social group (those without any vocational training, who make up approximately 20 per cent of the population, among them many immigrants) have significantly less access to economic, social and political resources than people with an academic education.[3]

Although more than 90 per cent of all ethnic Danes are Lutherans, religion plays a decisive role neither in people's individual lives nor in society as a whole. A European poll (2005) showed that only 31 per cent of Danish citizens believed in God, while 49 per cent believed in the existence of 'some sort of spirit' (see http://en.wikipedia.org/wiki/Denmark#Religion (accessed 29 November 2009)). Nevertheless, religious issues have found themselves at the centre of public attention and debate, although these are concerned not so much with Christianity as with Islam and Muslim behaviour and customs. Of the approximately 200,000 Muslims who live in Denmark, only a minority have dogmatic views. Around 60 per cent of Muslims in Denmark state that they never (or only on feast days) go to the mosque.[4] According to a recent survey, it is young Muslims, above all, who are religious: 67 per cent of 15-to-20-year-old and 58 per cent of 21-to-30-year-old Muslims reported that religion was of importance in and for their everyday lives.[5] Roughly 4,000 Danes have converted to Islam, two-thirds of whom are women, and two-thirds of these wear the *hijab*. Many converts take religion more seriously and adhere to religious rules more strictly than 'born Muslims' (Østergaard and Jensen 2007).

One of the major conflicts between the Muslim and the mainstream population concerns the role of women. Women have achieved a high standard of equality in Denmark. They are over-represented in higher education, may serve in the Danish army and they have 37.4 per cent of seats in the Danish parliament. Excellent childcare facilities enable women, even women with young children, to work outside the home. Denmark is amongst the Western countries with the highest birth rates and the highest women's employment rates (more than 70 per cent). Thanks to a 'women-friendly' state and a positive attitude towards working mothers, women are seemingly able to combine employment (at least part-time work) and family work (Lister 2006; Bergmann 2008). However, despite the Nordic welfare system and the emphasis on egalitarianism, women are under-represented in senior management in the private as well as the public sectors.[6] The percentage of women among the top executives of private companies is around 4 per cent (Hansen 2006: 14). Only 22 per cent of the 6,000 academic positions at Danish universities and less than 10 per cent of professorships are held by women (Henningsen 2004). Despite these inequalities, Danish men and women are convinced that gender differences are caused by the choices made by women and that gender equality has been achieved in Denmark, at least among the Danish population.

Denmark and its ethnic minorities

Until the second half of the twentieth century, Denmark was a country with a largely homogeneous population. This only changed in the 1960s, when, as a result of the economic upswing, the country opened its borders for 'guest workers' in order to fill large gaps in the labour force. In the wake of the oil crisis in the early 1970s, however, immigration was brought to a halt in 1973 (Karpantschof 2003).[7] Since then, foreigners from non-EU countries can only live and work in Denmark under certain conditions. In spite of these restrictions, the number of immigrants from non-Western countries and their descendants has grown steadily, due in part to family reunification and the relatively large number of children born to Muslim families. Today, roughly 6 per cent of the population has immigrated from non-Western countries and around 4 per cent from Islamic countries (with a majority of Muslims amongst their populations). Some 30 per cent of the Muslim immigrants and descendants come from Turkey (around 57,000), 15 per cent from Iraq, 12 per cent from Lebanon and 10 per cent from Pakistan. Smaller groups of immigrants come from Somalia, Iran, Afghanistan and Morocco.[8]

Legislation and policy

Responsibility for immigration policy lies with the Ministry of Refugees, Immigration and Integration Affairs, which drafts legislation and regulations, decides on residence permits and is responsible for the overall integration of immigrants and refugees in Danish society. The Ministry formulates the rules to be followed by the municipalities (see www.inm.dkb (accessed 29 November 2009)).

Today, individuals from countries outside of the EU are permitted to stay in Denmark as long as they are recognised as asylum-seekers or if they are close relatives of a person with a residence permit. Spouses are only entitled to a residence permit when their partner, living in Denmark, is over 24 years of age and fulfils numerous other requirements. This rule is intended, among other things, to hinder forced marriages. Immigrants are financially supported by the state, but it is expected that they learn the language and 'function' in the labour market. Indefinite residence permits are only granted after immigrants have passed an 'integration examination' in which they must demonstrate their knowledge of the Danish language and culture.[9]

The Danish government and the municipalities have implemented a wide variety of projects and measures to try to induce immigrants to become independent of state support and make them a 'constructive' segment of the population. The majority of these schemes aim at improving language proficiency, providing an insight into Danish culture and equipping them with vocational qualifications. Women are a specific target group of education and integration schemes, but, as a group, they are also difficult to reach because women's lives are frequently bound up with the life of the family (Christiansen and Nielsen 2005).

In spite of considerable efforts, the integration of various groups of immigrants has not been very successful. On the contrary, there are indicators that the difference between life in mainstream society and the situation of some immigrant groups is growing, and that the ideological rift between the Danes and orthodox Muslims is deepening.[10] In surveys, however, the majority of the Muslim population report that they are content to live in Denmark (see http://avisen.dk/muslimer-vilde-med-danmark_105375.aspx).

Immigrants in public discourses

As the above-mentioned immigration policies indicate, what is expected of immigrants is assimilation, as well as a commitment to democracy, human rights, equality and the secular welfare state. In addition, it is expected that immigrants adapt to Danish ways of life. Underlying these demands is the desire that immigrants strive to become 'normal' citizens, which on the one hand means holding onto Danish traditions perceived as appropriate and reasonable while, on the other, attempting to improve the lives of the 'newcomers'.

'Deviant' norms, rules, behaviour patterns and 'tastes' among immigrant groups have caused debates and controversy, largely addressed in the mass media. Occasionally controversy becomes conflict on the streets between 'immigrant gangs' and Danish youths. The perceived threat from immigrants is met by conservative politicians with anti-immigration policies, an area in which the Danish People's Party, particularly, can make its mark.

Relations between Danes and Muslims have been severely strained by the so-called 'cartoons controversy'. When a Danish newspaper printed 12 cartoons of the Prophet Muhammad in September 2005, there followed a storm of indignation and protest in the Muslim world, which was politically exploited by Islamic leaders in Denmark. In other countries, Muslims reacted to the alleged vilification of their religion with mass demonstrations, arson, death threats and a boycott of Danish goods. At the same time, the Danish, as well as many foreign media, were engulfed by debates on freedom of speech.[11] The 'cartoons controversy' is the visible expression of a battle for values, a struggle between liberal, Western secularism on the one side, and dogmatic Islam on the other. However, the majority of Muslims and the Danish population hold moderate views and did not transfer the tension to everyday inter-ethnic relations.

In the battle for values, women's bodies and roles are key issues, not least because equal rights and the roles of men and women count as essential achievements of modern Danish society. The media's interest, therefore, is focused quite sharply on women's appearance and behaviour, and here dress serves as a signal and the visible expression of the ideological orientation. It is for this reason, particularly, that the headscarf worn by Muslim women in public has been interpreted as a symbol of Islamism and has provoked heated debates in the media (Ericson Ryste 2008). In addition, numerous articles and reports, concerning forced marriages, genital mutilation, operations on the hymen and 'honour killings' appeared and further raised the temperature of the arguments (Borchgrevink 2004). The Danish media construct Muslim women often as victims of an inhuman ideology and symbols of a savage culture. There are also some articles and discussions, however, that refer to successful integration, for example on female Muslim students doing well at university.[12]

Through such discourses the media seize upon public opinion and reinforce it. More than 60 per cent of the Danish population, for example, believe that headscarves are an expression of the discrimination of women in Islamic society, with only 26 per cent not sharing this view.[13] However, this opinion is not mirrored in the actual relationships between ethnic Danes and Muslims. In an opinion poll, for instance, Danes (more than 80 per cent) did not identify working with colleagues wearing headscarves as a problem.[14] Only a small but eloquent minority of the Muslim population, albeit more men than women, take an active part in these debates. Some immigrants and their descendants may have become Danes and do not feel affected by the discussions, while others living for the most part in their ethnic communities may not be interested in the assessments of the mainstream population.

Sport for all in Denmark

Sport providers

Recreational physical activities and sport are regarded, currently, as important tools in the promotion of health, especially the prevention of obesity, and also in the socialisation and education of young people, the integration of immigrants and, in general, as an essential part of the 'good life' (Pfister 2010a). The hopes for, and beliefs in, the benefits of physical activities have a long tradition in Denmark. This is seen, for example, in the introduction of obligatory gymnastics lessons in boys' schools as long ago as 1814 and the participation of girls and women in various forms of gymnastics in the second half of the nineteenth century. It was during those years that clubs developed as the main providers of gymnastics, sport and physical activities in Denmark. Sports clubs and federations are supported, currently, by the Danish state, due in no small measure to the belief that they contribute towards resolving the above-mentioned social problems (Pfister 2010b).

Danish sports clubs are autonomous, non-profit organisations based on the principles of voluntary work, reciprocity and democratic leadership. Volunteering as instructors, administrators or leaders in sports associations has a long tradition and is widespread in Denmark. Some 14 per cent of all men and 9 per cent of all women carry out voluntary work in sports clubs (www.frivillighed. dk (accessed 29 November 2009); Pilgaard 2008). Clubs not only provide opportunities for playing sports but also for building up social networks, making friends and enjoying the company of others. In Denmark there are around 14,800 sports clubs, which means a club for every 400 inhabitants (Pilgaard 2008).[15]

The Danish municipalities also try to encourage informal physical activities, by providing, amongst other things, an environment that enables and encourages people to take part in physical activities such as hiking, jogging, biking and fitness exercises, swimming and skating. There are various funds that provide money for projects aimed at various target groups from senior citizens to children of Muslim immigrants (see p. 00). In addition, a large number and variety of commercial sport and fitness centres meet the needs of their customers with respect to opening hours, the physical activities provided and the appropriate apparatus (Kirkegaard 2007). In the context of an EU survey, around 90 per cent of Danes report having the opportunity of taking part in sport and PA close to their homes (European Commission 2006: 86). This survey also shows that Denmark is one of the few countries where sport has the potential to be 'sport for all'.

Sport and integration – politics and policies

According to the former Minister of Culture Brian Mikkelsen, foreigners ought to join in the work of running society to the same extent as Danes and share in discussions and decision-making in all aspects of society from politics to sports clubs (Mikkelsen 2002: 1). In keeping with Danish immigration policy, he considered sports participation and membership in Danish (sports) clubs to be an excellent way of introducing immigrants to Danish culture and integrating them into Danish society.

Since sport is looked upon as a means of socialisation and integration, the state provides significant financial support for the children and adolescents from migrant families to encourage them to become members of sports clubs. From 2007 to 2009, for example, 51 million Danish kroner (approximately $10m) has been earmarked for information about sports in Denmark, the payment of club fees and the provision of sports equipment, to be distributed to young people. In 2004 and 2005, 7,200 children and adolescents received financial support, 30 per cent of them girls.[16]

In addition, numerous and various sports and PA projects and courses are provided for immigrants, including immigrant girls and women (see, for example, Carlsen *et al.* 2002). Some of the most promising projects are described at the end of this chapter.

Sport and sports participation – the Danish population

Since the 1960s, participation in sport and PA has increased considerably among the Danish population. In a representative survey, conducted in 2007, only 9 per cent of the women and 13 per cent of the men polled reported that they never take part in physical activities; 80 per cent of the adult population, slightly more women than men, reported that they are physically active at least one hour per week (Pilgaard 2008: 38), while 56 per cent of the adult population participate frequently or regularly in sporting activities (Pilgaard 2008: 7ff.). Hiking, jogging, fitness and gymnastics, aerobics, swimming and cycling are the most popular activities of Danish adults (Pilgaard 2008: 49).

Gender, age and social class have a decisive influence on the amount and type of physical activities undertaken. The percentage of the population which is physically active, for example, increases with income and length of education (Pilgaard 2008: 56). Women form a majority among the physically active population when everyday recreational activities are included. More men than women, however, are involved in competitive sport. Women prefer hiking, gymnastics and aerobics, while men prefer cycling, football and badminton. Children and adolescents are the most active group in the population: 84 per cent of 7-to-15-year-olds regularly take part in sport or PA, with distinctly more boys than girls taking part from the age of 13 onwards.

Sports clubs are popular as well as important institutions in Denmark. Being a club member and participating in sporting and social activities is part of the Danish identity and lifestyle: 37 per cent of adult women and 46 per cent of men, but 84 per cent of 10-to-12-year-old boys and girls are members of a sports club (Pilgaard 2008: 34). A total of 52 per cent of all sporting activities (excluding everyday PA) takes place in clubs (Pilgaard 2008: 56).

The statistics presented above show clearly that sport and PA are an integral part of the lives of most Danes and an essential feature of Danish culture.

Not so positive is the situation in the Danish schools, where physical education is provided in mixed-sex classes. Qualitative research, using interviews and observations, revealed that physical education in high schools consists predominately of ball games that attracted the male students, whilst most girls were either unable or unwilling to become involved. As a consequence, girls participate less intensively in physical education, avoid exertion and physical contests or even refuse to participate at all. Statistics show that girls are much more frequently absent from PE lessons than boys. This is not surprising given the fact that PE is organised around the expectations of boys, and girls must not only adapt to but also balance contradictory demands (being good at sport and avoiding being labelled as a tomboy) if they want to be included (Jørgensen 2006; With-Nielsen and Pfister 2010, forthcoming).

Sport and physical activities among immigrants

Even though there may be differences in the issues under investigation, the samples and the ways of data gathering, all studies available reveal a distinct pattern. Adult immigrants are far less active in sport and PA than Danes, and this is especially true of women. Whereas Danish women are even more active in physical activities (in a broader sense) than men, immigrant women are not only physically less active than their Danish counterparts but also less active than immigrant men. They form only a very small minority of the physically active population.

A study published in 2000, for instance, found that more than 50 per cent of women and around one-third of men with immigrant backgrounds did not take part in any physical activities at all. There were, however, large differences between the various groups, for example, between Iranian and Lebanese immigrants. Only 20 per cent of male and 32 per cent of female Iranians, but 50 per cent of male and 60 per cent of female Lebanese, were physically inactive. The largest gender difference was found among Somalis, where 33 per cent of men and 52 per cent of women were not physically active at all (Ingerslev 2000; Schläger *et al.* 2005).

On the basis of a survey of immigrants, Mikkelsen noted great differences between men's and women's sporting activities. Men showed particular interest in football, weight training, jogging and fishing, whilst the few active women favoured swimming, gymnastics/aerobics and jogging (Mikkelsen 2002: 18). Studies of the lifestyles of adolescents likewise revealed large differences in relation to gender as well as religious and ethnic background. A survey of more than 6,000 adolescents aged between 16 and 20 years showed, for example, that, in their leisure time, 70 per cent of Protestant boys and 53 per cent of girls were at least moderately physically active for at least 3.5 hours per week, but only 59 per cent of Muslim boys and 44 per cent of girls (Ringgaard and Nielsen 2004: 40) were similarly active. Meanwhile, 10 per cent of the Protestant boys and 14 per cent of the girls, and 24 per cent of the Muslim boys and 45 per cent of the girls, reported having a sedentary lifestyle (Ringgaard and Nielsen 2004: 46).

Studies conducted in several Danish cities have shown that in younger age groups just as many boys (immigrants and descendants) take part in sport and PA as their Danish peers. There are large gender differences, however, as well as differences between Danish and immigrant girls (Henriksen 2002; Hjære and Mikkelsen 2003; Ringgaard and Nielsen 2004). A survey of 10-to-16-year-old students in Århus Vest revealed, for instance, that 87 per cent of the Danish boys and 82 per cent of the girls were active in sports. Among immigrants of the first generation, the corresponding figures were 94 per cent for the boys and 50 per cent for the girls; and among the descendants of immigrants, 89 per cent for the boys and 63 per cent for the girls (Agergaard 2008). A high percentage of boys from ethnic minorities participate in informal sporting activities, especially in games of football on the streets or in parks.

A survey of sports participation among children and adolescents (11-to-16 years of age) in four Danish municipalities showed that being active in sport varied according to the sporting habits of the parents, the age of the respondents and the community they lived in. Interest in sport decreased generally, among the girls in particular, with increasing age. Ethnic background played a decisive role in the case of the girls' sport participation. Nielsen and Ibsen (2008: 36) identified the group of 16-year-old girls with immigrant backgrounds as being especially threatened by inactivity. In general, children of immigrant families prefer different sports from their Danish peers. They are scarcely interested in activities which are popular in Denmark, such as badminton and team handball. Besides football, boys favour basketball, weight training and combat sports, which can be explained by the ideals of masculinity in immigrant groups. Dancing, gymnastics, badminton, horse riding and team handball are popular among Danish girls. Of these activities, only dancing attracts girls from ethnic-minority families (Ibsen 2007; see also Agergaard 2008).

As mentioned above, sport clubs are important sport providers. Immigrant women, however, form a small minority among their members. According to Dahl and Jakobsen (2005: 78), between 30 per cent and 38 per cent of immigrant men, but only 6 per cent to 12 per cent of women, are members of sports associations, although, here too, there are great differences between the various ethnic communities. According to Schmidt and Jakobsen (2000: 237–239), 12 per cent of immigrant women from the former Yugoslavia, but only 6 per cent of women with Turkish or Pakistani backgrounds, were members of a sports association around the millennium. A spot survey recently carried out in Copenhagen has shown that only 19 per cent of men and 10 per cent of women with immigrant backgrounds, and resident in the city, are members of a sports club (København Kommune 2009).

Similar tendencies are to be found in the results of studies on children and adolescents. A survey of 10-to-16-year-olds in Viborg revealed that 57 per cent of boys and 32 per cent of girls from immigrant families took part in sport organized by a club (Lykkegård 2001: 9). In the four municipalities studied by Ibsen (2004), 59 per cent of 15-year-old boys with immigrant parents and only 21 per cent of the girls were club members. An even lower figure is found in a survey conducted by Agergaard in Arhus among 10-to-16-year-olds. Here, only 20 per cent of immigrant girls, but 64 per cent of boys, belonged to a club. A rather higher figure, 30 per cent, is noted for girls of the second generation (Agergaard 2008: 13).

Physical education is an obligatory subject in all Danish schools, and children from ethnic minorities must also participate. As a rule, boys and girls are taught in mixed-sex classes. This raises numerous discussions and causes controversy, especially about sportswear, although Muslim pupils are allowed to cover their hair and wear loose-fitting clothes. Especially problematic is the participation of Muslim girls in swimming lessons and excursions. Often girls with an Islamic background are not allowed to participate in these activities, and parents use a doctor's certificate in order to get around the obligation of taking part in physical-education classes.[17]

It is not surprising, then, that schools have no success in encouraging girls from ethnic minorities to develop a close and lasting affinity with sport. An interview and observation study has revealed that many Muslim girls scarcely join in when they have physical education, particularly when no attention is paid either to them or their needs (With-Nielsen and Pfister 2010). School thus becomes an important place where girls adopt and enact the intersecting categories of gender and ethnicity and develop dispositions that include neither interest nor competence in sport and PA.

Muslim women in competitive sport

No data is available as yet on the participation of Muslim girls and women in Danish competitive sports. There are good reasons to assume that they represent only a tiny minority of competitive sportswomen in Denmark considering the family's lack of active engagement in sport and the low number of Muslim females taking part in sport in general. Amongst the numerous obstacles that Muslims face is the dress code in force in various sports which does not allow the head to be covered. The Danish Football Association, however, made an exception to this rule in 2008, permitting the 15-year-old football talent Zenab El-Khatib to play matches with a tight-fitting cap.[18] There is also another female football player, the Afghan born Nadia Nadim, who plays (without covering her hair) in the national team.

One of the Danish national sports for women is team handball. Fulfilling the wishes of Muslim players, and prompted by the example of Zenab El-Khatib, the Danish Handball Federation decided in 2009 that female players could ask for a dispensation from current regulations and wear a tight-fitting headdress. This rule does not include, however, women playing at the highest level, the first division. This may change when more talented Muslim handball players force the federation to revoke the rule on headdress for all levels of the game.[19] From looking at newspaper reports and the websites of sports clubs and federations, it seems that girls and women with names inferring an immigrant background are beginning to take up competitive sports, if only sporadically, in a variety of disciplines including martial arts such as taekwondo.

Theoretical considerations

Physical (in)activity and commitment to sport, choice of sport, duration and frequency of doing sport, experiences, motivations and emotions, aims and circumstances all depend on a complex set of interrelated parameters and on influences based on physical, psychological, societal and cultural conditions. German sociologist Klaus Heinemann (2007) has developed an intricate scheme for elucidating the aims and motives for becoming active (or inactive) in sport, which can be used to shed light on the gendered sporting activities of Muslim immigrants. He points, on the one hand, to individuals with their abilities, skills and knowledge, their experience, feelings and motives, their likes and dislikes, as well as their potentials, which are influenced by political, social and economic factors and, generally, by society and culture, both Muslim and Western. Both cultures are based on a gender order that provides different scripts for women and men, and shapes gendered attitudes to and demands for sport. On the other hand, he emphasises the significance of the 'sports on offer' and the property which sport, or a specific type of sport, has of tempting and challenging individuals. People will engage themselves in sporting (or other) activities when the properties and demands of the activity correspond to their aptitudes, tastes and expectations acquired during their lifelong socialisation processes.

According to Connell (2002), individuals are immersed in what he terms 'socialisation projects'. He understands socialisation as 'active learning' and self-training in and through cultural practices. Via interactions and encounters with the socio-ecological environment (family, peers, physical surroundings, for example), and also with the aid of formal education in schools, individuals acquire the norms, rules and expectations, that is, the pertinent discourses and scripts, of the respective group (mainstream or minority), as well as of the society in general in which they live. In doing so, they also develop ideas, conceptions, attitudes and (dis)interests, and perhaps also skills, relating to sport, which either encourage or hinder participation in physical activities.

Bourdieu describes these two sides of sports participation and differing sporting practices as:

> the result of relating two homologous spaces, a space of possible practices, the supply, and a space of dispositions to practise, the demand. On the supply side, there is a space of sports understood as a programme of sporting practices.... On the other hand, there is, on the demand side, a space of sporting dispositions which, as a dimension of the system of dispositions (*habitus*), are relationally and structurally determined ...
>
> (1988: 158)

The *habitus* is the hinge between the individual and society, and is formed by the system of dispositions, which depends on social and cultural conditions and determines thoughts, perceptions and actions, thus re-producing specific cultural practices in each social group. *Habitus*, and the tastes related to it, thus characterise social classes, ethnicities, (religious) groups and genders. A central role in this is played by the body, which assumes an important symbolic function, expressing values which are specific to an individual, group, ethnicity or class, and thus becoming the bearer of social distinction and cultural capital. It is the body *habitus*, that is, the socially structured system of dispositions, which determines not only individual attitudes to the body and its management but also physical activities and sporting habits (Bourdieu 1984).

As already outlined, considerable gender differences are observable with regard to participation in sport, and especially the choice of sporting activities. Gender is here equally understood as a social construction embedded in social institutions and acquired by individuals. According to Judith Lorber (2005: 6), societies are 'gendered', meaning that 'work, family and other major areas ... are organized by dividing people in two categories, "men" and "women".... Gender is a binary system of social organization that creates inequality.' At the same time, gender is embedded in identities, enacted in social situations and 'embodied' in all individuals. But gender is not something we are or have.

According to Rakow (1986: 19) and others, it is 'something we do and something we think with, both a set of social practices and a system of cultural meaning'. By doing gender and thinking in terms of gender, we re-produce gender differences, and 'once the differences have been constructed, they are used to reinforce the 'essentialness of gender' (West and Zimmermann 1991: 24). Like gender, ethnicity can be understood as a social construction which is inscribed in the individual bodies and 'done' in social interactions. It must be remembered here, though, that both ethnicity and gender are not predetermined entities; that they are of more, or less, relevance in varying contexts, they can be emphasised or downplayed, in spite of their 'embodiment'. Bourdieu's concept of the 'body *habitus*' complies with Connell's (2002: 47) notion of 'social embodiment': 'Bodies are both objects of social practice and agents in social practice.' Gender and ethnicities can be understood as 'body-reflective-practices' and specific forms of social embodiment.

The collective interpretations and meanings of the body and body cultures, and also the ideas, norms and scripts connected with bodies, differ in different historical periods and different cultures. They influence individual experiences of the body and the interpretations and emotions connected with these experiences because discourses, metaphors and collective symbols leave their imprints on the body and influence, or even determine, how we see our body, how we feel it and how we interpret these feelings (see, for example, Martin 1989). 'Bodies are both inscribed with and vehicles of culture' (Garrett 2004: 141).

Benn *et al.* (2010) draw our attention to the fact that 'religion is an underresearched domain in terms of its influence on the social self and body cultures'. Religion is enacted with the body, is felt and 'done' with, through and in the body. According to these authors,

> faith is embodied in the sense that presentation of the body, appearance, physicality, social interaction and behaviour are integral to religious identity, to lived reality of the daily embodiment of religious belief. Embodied faith reflects outward manifestations inseparably connected to internalised belief.
>
> (Benn *et al.* 2010)

Based on these theoretical approaches, numerous influences can be identified that provide an insight into, and understanding of, body and movement cultures, gender discourses and practices, and also the (lack of) participation in sporting activities among female immigrants. Sport and PA depend on and influence the intersections of gender, faith, ethnicity, social class and other categories (Ringgaard and Nielsen 2004: 46). Physical activities, opportunities as well as obstacles, and sport-related experiences and evaluations are closely interrelated with: the values and practices rooted in the cultures of their home countries; the social situation (which in turn is interrelated with education, employment and income); the environment and area of residence; the circumstances of life; religion and immigrant cultures; and, above all, with regard to culturally situated gender ideologies, constructions and relations. These issues will be addressed in the second part of this chapter.

Abstaining from sport – potential influences

Sport and physical activities in Islamic countries

In some immigrants' countries of origin, sport and recreational PA are not integrated into the daily lives of the people, and this is especially true of the numerous immigrants who lived in rural areas, in economic hardship and/or in religiously dominated communities (see Pfister 2010a; Chapters 9 and 16 in this book). Work and everyday life seem to have offered the majority of the population sufficient exercise. Meanwhile, in developing countries, boys could find a piece of spare land almost anywhere to play football, but, often, there were no opportunities for girls to do sport. For these reasons, few immigrants, and even fewer immigrant women, felt a close relationship to sport when they came to Denmark.

For most people in Islamic countries, sport is a media event and not an everyday-life activity. In these countries numerous inhabitants are fans of famous football teams, and in their new home countries they are, taking the Turks as an example, fans of teams such as Besiktas, Fenerbahçe or Galatasaray. In societies structured by extended families, moreover, clubs and sport clubs do not play any major role in people's social lives. Many immigrants are thus unfamiliar with voluntary work (done for strangers with no financial reward) and the life in a (sport) association (Waldhoff 1995).[20] To become a member of a sports club, or to send their children to such a club, may therefore not be an option for them. There are also signs that by being exposed to numerous other influences, however, including a Western 'supply' of sports, the children do begin to develop different interests (including sports interests) from their parents.

Marginalisation processes in Danish sport cultures

In Denmark sport is seemingly 'sport for all'; but this is not true for immigrants from Islamic countries because sport is not embodied and integrated into their *habitus*. Even if there may be no formal barriers preventing them from doing sport or becoming members of a sports club, it is not easy for individuals from ethnic minorities to take up sport, in part because they are familiar neither with Danish sports habits and sports clubs nor with the norms and rules governing them.[21] On their side, the Danish clubs have little experience of integrating immigrants, who for example have great difficulty in finding out information about the opportunities to join a club. Club membership and/or knowledge about sports clubs in Denmark are 'taken for granted' and a 'social inheritance'. Many clubs are largely 'closed societies' in which numerous unwritten laws and norms apply. It is frequently expected, for example, that parents who send their children to the club also take part in the club's activities.[22] A large number of sports offered by clubs, especially in the children and youth sections, are oriented towards competitions, which can be a problem for less well-trained boys and girls. The club fees, particularly when they have to be paid for several children, may also be an obstacle – although in recent years state allowances for immigrant families have become available.

Problems may also arise on account of the social life, which is an essential part of sports club culture. The highlights of club life are festivities at which both men and women are present and alcohol is drunk. As interviews with young Muslims have revealed, most of these women, especially from Lebanese, Pakistani and Somali families, never or seldom attend festivities when men are present (Seeberg 2002). As club members, they would thus not be able to join in an important part of club life. For religious girls and women, the absence of gender-segregated sports programmes can be a reason for not taking up sport. Even though it is now permitted by the football and handball associations to cover the head in sport competitions, sportswomen wearing a headscarf continue to be stigmatised in certain settings. In addition, some girls and women (or their families) may consider the covering of the head to be insufficient in mixed-gender groups and regard such physical activities as 'improper'. Especially with swimming, many Muslim women demand the exclusion of men. Misgivings about club activities, possible contact with boys and men, evening training sessions and concern about respectability are all reasons for women not joining a club, and families not allowing their girls to become members. Commercial providers of sport, in particular fitness centres, are better able to adapt to the needs of their clients in providing opportunities for gender-segregated training. The relatively high membership fees, however, have the effect of excluding groups with limited economic resources.

Living conditions

The social situation of immigrants is part of the above-mentioned 'supply side' of Bourdieu's concept. It has a decisive influence on the individual's ability and willingness to participate in sport and PA. The numerous data available indicate that immigrants from non-Western and Islamic countries are, in many ways, economically and socially disadvantaged. They live primarily in deprived neighbourhoods and have, on average, a lower level of education, a much higher risk of unemployment and a lower income than the 'Danish' population.

Ghettos and ethnic communities

With regard to the ethnic backgrounds and the social strata of their inhabitants, residential areas in Denmark are relatively homogeneous, even though municipal housing authorities make the attempt to counter tendencies of segregation. A large percentage of immigrants live in state-assisted housing blocks and are concentrated in a small number of municipalities, especially in Copenhagen. The attraction of ethnic communities for immigrants, particularly Turks, Arabs and

Somalis, and the simultaneous move of Danish residents away from areas with a large proportion of so-called 'New Danes', has had numerous adverse effects on such things as the quality of schools, recreational facilities or opportunities for sports (Andersen 2005; Børresen 2008). Nevertheless, immigrants are generally satisfied with their living conditions, for living in an ethnic community has certain advantages, amongst them the fact that it provides social networks and creates a sense of belonging (Mikkelsen 2002). On the other hand, living quarters of immigrants are threatened by 'ghettoisation' which furthers the formation of more or less violent groups of boys and young men, increases social control and compliance to traditional norms and rules. These are all processes that impede integration into Danish society.

It is not only the absence of sports facilities that makes participation in sports difficult or even impossible for girls and women, but also the social control by their ethnic community. Participation in sport creates situations in which girls and women are beyond the control of the family, which can lead to 'gossip' about a girl's respectability and that of her family as a whole (Børresen 2008). The potentially dangerous environment, the fear of losing their good name and generally the pressure of the Muslim community, may cause women to abstain from physical activities and/or families to prohibit female family members from participating in sport.

School and education

While the men of the first generation of immigrants from non-Western countries possess, on average, better educational qualifications than the women, the tables are turned in the second generation. Young women from immigrant families today have better qualifications than their male peers, not least because the latter drop out of education (school, vocational training) quite frequently. Today parents usually support their children's education irrespective of their gender. Further, the social control exerted on girls contributes to their success at school (Hummelgaard et al. 2002; Larsen 2004; Dahl and Jakobsen 2005: 17; Tranæs et al. 2008). Many girls from ethnic minorities experience school as something positive since they receive attention, are together with their girl friends and able to act without being under the control of their parents.[23]

Despite positive attitudes and experiences, members of ethnic minorities continue to have a level of education which is, generally, far below that of young Danes, of whom the majority successfully complete either vocational training or university study (64 per cent of young women and 67 per cent of young men). This level of qualification is only reached by 46 per cent of young men and 42 per cent of young women with immigrant backgrounds. However, there are considerable differences between immigrants according to their countries of origin: 60 per cent of Iranians have vocational qualifications, while the corresponding figure for Turks is only 11 per cent. Roughly half of immigrant children, more boys than girls, leave school without being able to read properly (Dahl and Jacobsen 2005: 29; Tranæs 2008).

As already stated, school is where all children and adolescents are (or ought to be) made familiar with games and sport. Generally, boys seem to thrive in physical education. They love to play sports and they get acknowledgement as good athletes/players (Mørk 2003). For some, physical education may be a compensation for problems in other subjects. Muslim girls, however, as described above, do not seem to benefit very much from the mixed-sex physical education lessons that are common in Danish schools. However, there are exceptions. Being a Muslim girl and an athlete is not a contradiction per se (With-Nielsen and Pfister 2010).

Contributing to the problems that the second generation of immigrants has at school are not only the low status which education has in many families but also the common practice of choosing marriage partners from the same country of origin (Schmidt and Jakobsen 2004). This leads, among other things, to the fact that Danish is not spoken in many immigrant families, which has a detrimental effect on language proficiency and success at school for the second and third generations.

According to Danish studies, there is a correlation between sports participation and level of education, whereby education is also an indicator of social class. Engagement in sport and higher education depend on and, at the same time, provide physical, social and cultural capital. The lack of capital may be one of the various intertwined factors that contribute to the lack of interest in sport. It must be taken into consideration, however, that education, gender, ethnicity and religion are interrelated, and that their intersections form the system of dispositions (*habitus*) which includes dispositions referring to PA and sport.

Employment and its ambiguous influence on physical activities

Women immigrants, especially of the first generation, go out to work much less frequently than either their male counterparts or Danish women, whose rate of employment is similar to that of men. The differences become smaller in the second and third generations (Dahl and Jacobsen 2005). In 2003, for example, 52 per cent of immigrant men and 38 per cent of women were in employment. By contrast, the employment rate for Danish men was 79 per cent and 72 per cent for Danish women (see www.statistikbanken.dk (accessed 29 November 2009)). The employment rate is lowest for 25-to-29-year-old immigrant women (35 per cent), which can be explained by the necessity of looking after their small children at this stage of life.

Women immigrants from non-Western countries are predominantly employed in low-paid and insecure jobs in the service sector. Their unemployment rate is much higher than among the Danish mainstream population (in 2004, 4 per cent of Danes were unemployed). Somalis had the highest unemployment rate in Denmark, with 25 per cent of Somali men and 27 per cent of Somali women looking for work (Dahl and Jacobsen 2005: 49). These data reflect the difficulties of immigrants in the Danish labour market, which are attributable, at least in part, to their lack of educational qualifications (see p. 56) and the disappearance of manual jobs, but also to prejudice and discrimination. On the other hand, there are also growing numbers of immigrants, especially women, with good qualifications who are able to, and wish to, embark on an academic career. Thus, one can observe a high measure of diversity in the conditions of immigrant women's social and working lives.[24]

Women's employment is closely linked to the intersections of gender roles and ethnic backgrounds. The disproportionately low employment rate among immigrant women compared with men of the same cultural origins is ascribable, not only to the traditional division of labour between the genders, but also to concerns about the respectability of women working in mixed-sex environments. Men frequently express reservations about female family members taking up employment outside the home (Dahl and Jacobsen 2005).

Going out to work can affect participation in sport and PA in different ways. On the one hand, it can be difficult or even impossible to reconcile employment, work in the household and leisure activities. On the other hand, paid work provides women with a certain self-reliance and independence, two important prerequisites for taking up sport (for all). Through work, women learn how to conduct themselves in Danish society. They have the opportunity to make the acquaintance of, or even make friends with, Danes, gain an insight into, and information about, the Danish way of life and leisure activities and earn their 'own' money, which is necessary for most sporting activities. Unemployment and consequent low incomes exclude women from many physical and sporting activities.

Taking up sport in Denmark depends on cultural, social and economic capital, which is closely intertwined with levels of education, social class and ethnicity. The lack of all forms of capital contributes to the barriers that prevent immigrants, particularly women, from becoming physically active.

Gender relations

Gender constructions have an influence on both aspects of sports participation: the 'supply side' ('programme of sporting practices') and the 'demand side' (sporting dispositions of individuals), as described by Bourdieu (1988) and Heinemann (2007).

Among Muslim minorities, a traditional understanding of gender and gender roles predominates, in keeping with the precepts of Islam. Gender is considered an essentially dichotomous category based on biology which defines the duties and rights of both sexes. The belief in the natural and unalterable nature of woman and man justifies the division of responsibilities, work and life according to gender. Gender differences are symbolised and emphasised by clothing, especially the *hijab*. A lessening of gender differences in appearance and responsibilities is perceived as a threat and rejected, at least in traditional cultures of Islamic countries. Thus, athletic and muscular girls and women are incompatible with the ideals of beauty and femininity prevailing in many ethnic communities. Although in Islamic countries and Diaspora communities, the trend (or even pressure) towards women's slimness is increasing, a certain plumpness is still considered a sign of fertility and beauty (Nasser 1997; see also the articles in Ruggiero 2003).

The deep-rooted, embodied and permanently enacted everyday theories about men and women have a strong influence on the opportunities as well as the limits of both genders in many areas, from their appearance in public to their responsibilities within the family and to their participation in sport. In traditional families, the men's sphere is the public space, and their role is that of the breadwinner. The women's sphere is the home, and her most important tasks are housework and looking after the children. In immigrant families, small children are cared for at home, mostly by the mothers (Dahl and Jacobsen 2005). The proposal that immigrant parents should be forced to send their small children to a crèche, in order to improve their Danish-language proficiency, met with great indignation and rejection among parents from ethnic minorities.[25] As a rule, children of immigrant families are sent to kindergarten from the age of three (Dahl and Jacobsen 2005). On average, immigrant families have more children than Danes, which means that the women spend many years looking after their offspring.[26] Problems in finding a job, unattractive and low-paid work, as well as time-consuming housework, make it easier for women to take on the role of housewife, especially as work in the family is experienced as very valuable and rewarding.

As a rule, however, housewives have no real control over their time but must adapt to the rhythms of their husbands and children. Housework thus provides only a little leisure time, which may be spent listening to music, knitting, making visits or preparing meals. These 'relative freedoms' (Talbot and Wimbush 1988) make it difficult for women to take part in sports or PA, and may even make it impossible for them to attend the scheduled programmes and activities of sport clubs (Mikkelsen 2002; Siim 2003).

Unlike sons, daughters of immigrant parents are made to help with the housework to quite a considerable degree. They are expected to take over numerous household chores, particularly the duty of looking after younger siblings. In a survey focusing on leisure activities, 47 per cent of Muslim girls, compared with only 33 per cent of Protestants, reported that they devoted less than two hours per week to recreational activities (Ringgaard and Nielsen 2004). A further study revealed that girls with an immigrant background spent a large part of their day with their family (Agergaard 2008).

Several interview studies, mostly Master's dissertations or pilot studies, on immigrants and their participation in physical activities have revealed that caring for the family is one of the most important reasons that girls and women give for not taking part in physical activities. The women interviewed reported that they have to take care of small children, and often old relatives, cook time-consuming traditional meals and be at home when the older children and their husbands come home from school or work (Mouridsen 2002). However, they did not complain, but considered their engagement for the family as 'normal' and often rewarding. Noreen, a woman from Pakistan, is a typical example. She took care of a household of five adults and two little children and told a Danish researcher:

'I do want to exercise but I don't have the time now. Because my little one is too much work now … in my spare time I just want to sit in the front of the TV. Don't want to move or do anything at all' (Juul 2003).

Culture and religion

Gendered norms and rules

Islamic precepts relating to the lives of girls and women and their participation in sport are described in Chapter 2 of this book. It must be borne in mind, here, that religion and culture are inextricably interwoven and that cultural norms are often legitimised by reference to religion. The combinations of culture and religion vary considerably, however, depending in part on the immigrants' country of origin. This is also true for discourses and practices referring to sport. Islam supports PA and sport for both men and women, at least as long as religious norms and rules are not infringed by them. These rules and norms, though, are largely a matter of interpretation (Pfister 2010a). In traditional families, norms, rules and behaviour are oriented towards the concept of honour, which is based on the regulation of sexual relations through the control of women. In many cases, the family's honour, especially that of the male members, derives from the moral integrity of its female members and above all from the virginity of the daughters (Khader 2006; Pfister 2010a). Loss of honour results in the loss of respect and standing within the Muslim community. The control of female sexuality is not ensured, as in Christianity, through the internalisation of norms, but through the 'modest' behaviour and clothing of the women. Early marriages, often arranged and mostly with members of the same ethnic group, relieve the father and the family of their responsibility for their daughters and sisters.[27]

Even for daughters of 'modern' families, virginity is a vital necessity and therefore a large number of girls with immigrant backgrounds scarcely ever go to mixed-gender festivities and rarely have boyfriends (Seeberg 2002). Young women with sexual experience sometimes have their hymen 'repaired', and thus their virginity restored with surgery, before marriage.[28]

The integrity of Muslim girls and women appears to be particularly at risk when they take up sport, as in Denmark sport is, as a rule, practised in a mixed-gender environment and because sport requires functional clothing which is scarcely compatible with the traditional rules of dress (see the literature in Nakamura 2002). Solutions are to be found either in headscarves and loosely fitting clothes, when boys and men are present, or withdrawal to areas where they are out of the view of males. The result of this is that many physical activities, especially outdoor sports, must be ruled out.

Yet solutions do appear to be in sight for those girls and women who wish to take part in sporting activities and still obey the rule that the body must be covered. These solutions are currently to be seen in the development of innovative and culturally 'correct' sportswear such as the 'burkini', a swimsuit covering the whole body. In spite of this, many parents are far from happy when their daughters wish to take up sport, some forbidding it outright, chiefly because the girls are no longer under their control and the parents can no longer ensure their moral integrity. Concern about the hymen, which can allegedly be torn when girls do sport, is a further problem which may cause parents to forbid their daughters from taking part in physical activities.[29] Conversely, there are also many parents who are proud of their sporting daughters and support them whole-heartedly. This is the case, for example, with Zenab El-Khatib, a football player whose aim is to play for the Danish national team whilst wearing a headscarf.

The scarf – a contested issue

In recent years the number of girls and women wearing the *hijab* in Denmark has increased dramatically. 'Doing Islam' has become a widespread habit, in some cases almost a fashion. In several districts of Copenhagen, artistically designed and wrapped scarves, often in vivid colours, are common sights in everyday street life. Numerous, often very young, girls combine the *hijab* with fashionable Western clothes and make-up. Others wear *abayas*, which at first glance may look like uniforms, but can signal, especially to insiders, a certain taste and a desire for distinction (see, among other sources, www.kvinfo.dk/side/266/tema/32/ (access 29 November 2009).

The scarf and the *hijab* are currently contested issues in Danish society, among immigrants as well as among the mainstream population (Ericson Ryste 2008). The Muslims living in Denmark do not agree among themselves about the necessity and the purpose of wearing the *hijab*. A survey of 1,700 Muslims living in Denmark revealed that only 23 per cent of the respondents were of the opinion that women should cover their hair. (The figure was 38 per cent of the Pakistanis and Somalis.) Among those against the wearing of headscarves, who made up 51 per cent of those surveyed, the men outnumbered the women by a small margin.[30]

As already mentioned, covering the hair is regarded as a sign of discrimination by the majority of the Danes. Women wearing the *hijab* are often stereotyped as being poor, uneducated and incompetent,[31] with some employees refusing to hire them. For years there have been public demands, and even demands by politicians, for a ban on the wearing of religious symbols, including headscarves, in various professions, such as teaching or working in a kindergarten. Such a ban was put into effect by the government in 2008 for judges.[32] Headscarves provoke opposition among the mainstream population more than any other Islamic precept or interdiction, although the question arises whether this opposition, as well as the stigmatisation of women with a *hijab*, may confer on them the status of martyrs and thus give them further encouragement.

Numerous religious Muslims are convinced that the rules on dress were made by Allah himself, and that to cover the body, including the hair, is an essential part of being a Muslim. In interview studies the overwhelming majority of 'veiled' girls and women reported that they had taken the decision for 'modest clothing' (that is, for the *hijab*) of their own free will, on religious grounds and in the knowledge that wearers of the *hijab* were frequently looked upon with suspicion and even openly discriminated against.[33] However, as with decisions of individuals and groups in general, the choices of Muslim women raise questions as to how such decisions are arrived at and on what information they are based. Drawing on Benn *et al.* (2010), we can assume that wearing the *hijab* means an embodiment of faith, and that religious women perceive and experience the covering of their bodies as the right way, maybe the only way, to be in the world.

As mentioned above, Danish mainstream society regards the *hijab* as a contested sign of 'otherness', but the scarf issue demonstrates how different and ambiguous the meanings of cultural symbols are. Not all scarves are the same, there are different styles, and they can have different meanings depending on the woman wearing it, as well as on the context and the environment.

Some women wear Islamic dress as protection against the male gaze, both literally and figuratively. They assume that, by doing so, they gain respect, feel protected and believe they have eluded the 'beauty trap' by not having to struggle to conform to unattainable ideals of beauty (Nasser 1997). Girls may use the scarf as a strategy. Wearing a scarf signals that they are 'moral' and thus do not endanger the 'honour' of their families. As a result, they can demand, and receive, more freedom than their sisters who do not cover their hair. For young girls, adopting the *hijab* may be a sign of growing up.

A scarf can also be used as a political signal, expressing opposition to Westernisation, the politics, norms and values as well as the gender order and the sexualisation in Western countries. By wearing the scarf, women take part in a (religious) movement which seems to provide aims, orientation and meaning in the modern world with ambiguous and unpredictable demands.[34] In recent years, a growing number of girls and young women in Denmark have started to discover religion as a project and to interpret Islam as relevant to their own lives. For them, the *hijab* is also a symbol, a signal to their environment that the wearer is proud of her faith and identifies with Islam. The scarf is used both as a symbol and as an instrument of individual identity politics.

Mervat Nasser has interpreted the veiling phenomenon as an 'equivalent' of the increasing incidence of anorexia in Western countries. According to Nasser, wearing Islamic dress responds to 'conflicting cultural messages and contradictory cultural expectations experienced by women globally' (quoted in Pedwell 2007: 1). However, it must be pointed out again that only 28 per cent of Muslims living in Denmark agree with the wearing of headscarves and that attitudes depend, to a considerable extent, on the culture of the home country. There are also groups of immigrants, for example the *Frie Iranske Kvinder* (Free Iranian Women), who fight against the compulsory wearing of the *hijab* (see www.kvinfo.dk/side/560/article/629/ (accessed 29 November 2009)). Many girls and women, even some declaring themselves as 'religious', do not accept the law of covering the body and the hair; however, much modern, Western fashion is considered 'immoral' and widely rejected in Islamic communities.

Playing sport in a headscarf?

The rule of covering the body has a decisive influence on sports participation, even though women and girls are able to take part in various sports and PA if they wear loose-fitting clothes and a headscarf. Here, though, it might be asked how such clothing affects the experience of the body and movement in sport, whether it prevents motor activities and/or exercises and games, and how it generally influences the women's relation to, and experiences of, their body. The first 'veiled' Muslim woman to be elected to the city council of Odense and to take part in meetings wearing a headscarf, Asmaa Abdol-Hamid,[35] reported to newspapers that the scarf did not influence her life. She had to stop playing handball, however, because she felt uncomfortable with her 'modest' dress on the handball field.[36]

The participation of girls and women in sport can also mean violating the culturally rooted concepts of the body and norms of femininity, even if they fulfil the rule of modest clothing. Strength (physical and mental), assertiveness and the willingness to compete, the public presentation of the body, bodily skills and a muscular body may not be in keeping with traditional ideals of Somali or Pakistani femininity, and may also fail to suit the 'taste' of the 'Danish-Somali' population. It can be assumed that girls' and women's concepts of the self and their physicality are influenced by their embodiment of faith, but also by the fact that their bodies are an outward symbol of ethnicity and religion. Thus participation in sport and embodied Muslim identity may produce ambiguities and contradictions.

Living as immigrants

Immigrants bring their cultures with them to their new countries of residence. This includes the gender order with gender ideologies and arrangements, which they pass on to the next generations, not least because they tend to marry partners of the same ethnic group, often from their home countries. For example, 78 per cent of female and 88 per cent of male Pakistani immigrants married partners with the same background, and the same is true of 91 per cent of immigrants from Turkey (Seeberg 2002). A survey conducted with more than 1,700 participants has revealed that immigrants of the first and second generations report similar attitudes and opinions.[37] This means that many characteristics of the gender relations and sports 'tastes', shaped by Islamic laws and the cultures of the countries of origin, are reproduced in ethnic communities across Denmark.

Life as an immigrant, therefore, can be seen as offering both specific opportunities and challenges. Immigrants have to live and to 'function' in a new society with certain demands, rules and values with the various groups differing in the way they develop their relations with mainstream society, also with regard to gender arrangements. Thus the threat posed to traditional gender roles by a Danish society based on the ideals of gender equality can either lead to a more rigid observance of traditional gender roles or to opportunities seized by men, as well as women, to change the status quo. Here, it must be taken into consideration that immigrants living in foreign countries have to form new self-concepts and identities since they are the 'others', and this can give rise to ambivalences and conflicts (e.g. Massey and Jess 1995; Jeldtoft 2008). In addition, the first generation of immigrants is confronted with new, often inscrutable and sometimes contradictory values, rules and demands, and may react by withdrawing to their traditional roles and patterns of behaviour, and also by adhering to the rules and prohibitions regulating girls' and women's lives, which may relate to participation in sport and PA.

In their new country, however, traditional rules and family arrangements are often no longer in force, partly due to the fact that children have an advantage over their parents as far as their proficiency in the new language is concerned. Parents frequently react to the imagined loss of their children to the Danish society by attempting to shield them from the influences of an alien culture and to maintain their superior position in the family. Daughters, particularly, have to be protected from the dangerous influence of the Danish culture, and this often happens via supervision and control. Since, for instance, many immigrants consider sport, especially in mixed-sex settings, to be a hazard for the integrity of girls and women, they are forbidden either from taking part in sport outright or their sporting activities are supervised. In fact, some families adhere to traditional values even more strictly than they would have done in their home country.

Widespread among certain groups of immigrants, moreover, is the opinion that it is more important for girls to learn to cook traditional food and to look after their smaller brothers and sisters than to take up sport (Dahl and Jacobsen 2005). Helping with the housework and looking after siblings is even more important in the immigrant communities than it is in the countries of origin, where children frequently grow up in extended families with grandmothers and aunts helping in the house. Islamic communities in Western countries seem to demand a high degree of conformity of their members and, as already mentioned, 'gossip' about the inappropriate behaviour of girls, within as well as outside a sporting environment, is a threat to families in a situation where they are, in many ways, dependent on their neighbourhoods and networks. Parents may therefore forbid their daughters from taking part in sporting activities in public out of concern for their 'good reputation'. However, individuals and groups, especially those with a higher level of education and/or who come from large towns, try, often successfully, to combine their different cultural heritages and become part of the mainstream population.

Examples of negotiations and balances in everyday life

Several Danish scholars have explored the lives of immigrants by listening to the narratives of girls and women. Some of these qualitative studies, often following a post-structuralist approach, reveal how immigrants have developed competences in order to adapt to different cultures, how they have negotiated (relative) freedoms and have achieved a balance in their lives between the expectations of their families and their respective ethnic communities on the one hand, and the expectations of schools, employers and of Danish society as a whole on the other.[38] Immigrants of the second generation have learned to speak and understand the 'texts' (that is, rules, values, codes of behaviour) in both cultures and can use different 'languages', depending on where and with whom they interact. In this way, girls may signal their respectability by means of the head-scarf and thus gain permission to visit school friends or take part in sporting activities (Mørck 1998).

In interviews, most girls and women with immigrant backgrounds express similar expectations for their futures to those of Danish girls and women – that is, vocational training, a good marriage, children and achieving a balance between family life and work. Here, education plays a major role. Many young educated Muslim women, even those who have chosen to wear a headscarf, have a fair amount of self-confidence. They take vocational training and their work seriously and seek partnerships modelled on equality. In this regard they resemble, to a large degree, the emancipated women of the Danish majority population (Schmidt 2007).[39]

For a number of girls and women, vocational training and independence lead to conflict with their families. As a rule, though, in negotiating certain freedoms they manage to reconcile the expectations of the family with their own plans for the future and their wishes with regard to qualifications and career.[40] A young Turkish woman, for example, who had just finished upper-secondary education, reported in an interview that she obeyed her parents and spent lots of time with them and therefore was given permission to study 'without the threat of marriage hanging over my head'.[41]

Many immigrants, especially those of the second and the third generations, no longer identify with the home country of their (grand)parents. It can be assumed that immigrants develop new types of cultural identification. Mørck (1998) defines these new identities as 'hyphenated identities' and the new cultures as 'hybrid cultures', which represent a balance between several identities and a mixture of various cultural traditions. She shows how individuals regard themselves, for example, as 'Danish-Pakistani' and how they are able to behave in either a Danish or a Pakistani way depending on the setting (see also Papastergiadis 1997). Educated young women, in particular, tend to create a hybrid culture in which they combine emancipation and Islam, wear a headscarf and high heels, and demand that women themselves should decide what to wear and how to behave.[42] These 'new women' are also active in a number of Islamic associations, which are looking for new paths for their religion in Diaspora communities or simply claiming equal rights. Some women even have leading positions in Islamic associations. Amani Hassani, an anthropologist, is, for instance, head of the Muslim students' union at Copenhagen University.[43] New Muslim women, however, are frequently not only self-confident but also have a mission, often exerting great pressure on other girls or women to dress and behave in the 'correct' manner.[44]

Typical of new Muslim women is 28-year-old Asmaa Abdol-Hamid, mentioned earlier, who used to work as a social counsellor and television presenter and whose parents came to Denmark as asylum-seekers from Palestine. At the age of 14 years, Asmaa decided, of her own free will, to wear the *hajib*. While she was still at school, she set up a club for girls in her home town and became active in various projects. In 2005 she won a seat on the municipal council of Odense in a by-election, and in the following year she founded the 'Green Veil', a network of Muslim women in Denmark. In the 2007 Danish parliamentary elections she stood as a candidate for the *Enhedslisten* (Danish socialist party). This provoked heated debates even in her own party about the *hijab* worn in public and also, generally, about her attitude towards Sharia, homosexuality and the war in Iraq. In April 2009 she attended a meeting of Odense municipal council, the first woman wearing a *hijab* in such a committee (see http://avisen. dk/abdol-hamid-indtager-raadhuset_106803.aspx). Despite her achievements and her assertiveness, Asmaa does not fight for gender equality; on the contrary, she emphasises the biological differences between the two sexes and accepts the superiority of men.[45]

Among the new and self-confident Muslim women are also groups such as the Association of Young 'New Danish' Women ('New Danes' is a popular term for immigrants from non-Western countries). They do not focus on religion, do not wear the *hijab* but work for an improvement of the situation of ethnic minorities and the integration of immigrants in the Danish society (see www.f-unk.dk/ (accessed 29 November 2009)).

New Muslim women and sport – narratives and observations

Opportunities and barriers in sport and PA do not seem to be an important concern of Muslim women in Denmark (with a secular or a religious orientation). The topic does not play any role in current debates that focus on religion, dress code, opportunities and barriers in the Danish society. In the collection of 'success stories' told by ethnic minority women on the website of Kvinfo (Centre for Information on Women and Gender), only three of the 30 women portrayed mentioned sporting activities briefly (www.kvinfo.dk/side/674/ article/87/ (accessed 29 November 2009)). The reasons for this can be found in the culture, traditions and everyday lives of Muslim girls and women, which have been described above. However, there are several interview studies that provide a foundation for further exploration of the perspectives of girls and women who are interested in playing sport.

Juul (2003) interviewed ten women of Pakistani origin, five of whom she had made the acquaintance of during a swimming course for immigrant women. Three of them were still swimming at the time of the interview, one woman went to an aerobic course and the other six were not physically active in their leisure time. Those women who took part in physical activities did this, with one exception, either to lose weight, to help deal with health problems or to get back a 'good figure' after giving birth. The exception was 44-year-old Sirin. She went swimming, attended water gymnastics classes and played badminton, even though she had trouble with her knees. In Pakistan she had played basketball at school and had even participated in competitions. Her wish to become a physical-education teacher was impossible to fulfil because of her parents' opposition. Even cycling was forbidden to women in her home country. In Denmark, Sirin could fulfil her dream of an active lifestyle. The narratives of the interviewed women show the wide spectrum of possibilities that exist, but also the limits that women are faced with and which are (almost) insurmountable for women with small children.

Interviews and observations in a Master's thesis on immigrant girls and their 'doing gender' in physical education revealed that, even if they are good at sports, Muslim girls do not take part in games in a mixed-sex setting. They justified their behaviour by pointing to their religion and their identity as Muslims. However, these interviews also showed that Muslim girls do have opportunities to take up sport. A good example is that of Iram, who plays basketball and practises Thai boxing and swimming in a gender-separated environment with both 'immigrant' and Danish girls. Iram is proud of her sporting abilities and describes how she surprises the Danish girls when, after training, she puts on her *hijab*. The interviews with other Muslim girls in her physical-education class reveal that they admire Iram, although she does not show her skills in PE because she avoids encounters with boys (With-Nielsen and Pfister 2010).

Currently Muslim girls and women are beginning to see the benefits of sport and games, even at the competition level. In dealing with the Islamic dress code, they have developed various strategies. Some sportswomen decide to wear religiously 'correct' clothing, but adapted to their sport, while others opt for the official sportswear.

The already mentioned Zenab El-Khatib is the idol of numerous Muslim girls. A football player and a member of the Danish national under-16 team, she plays matches wearing a tight-fitting cap and is almost a media star in Denmark as a result (www.fyens.dk/article/1005907:Sport–Zenab-bryder-barrierer (accessed 29 November 2009)). Zenab is ambitious and eloquent and emphasises that she covers her hair when playing matches of her own free will.

Nadia Nadim has reached her goal. The 21-year-old football player, a refugee from Afghanistan, is the first female immigrant playing on the Danish national team. Her father, a general in the Afghan army, taught her to play football in a garden surrounded by walls, where nobody could see her inappropriate behaviour. After the execution of her father by the Taliban, the family left the country for Europe. In Denmark, Nadia started to play football in a club, where her talent was detected and supported. She adapted quickly to the new environment, including the official dress code, adopting the motto: 'No risk, no fun.' This motto expresses the way she lives and competes. In a newspaper report, Nadia explains that she is Muslim and religious, but not fanatical: 'My faith helps me with my play.' Besides a football career she plans to study law or journalism.[46]

Arezu Kamali-Rousta is another immigrant sportswoman who does not wear the *hijab*. In interviews about her political work, she does not even mention her religious orientation. She came with her parents from Iran when she was 12, and today attends a commercial college and is active in the Free Iranian Women Association. At the age of 14, Arezu began to practise taekwondo and is now a holder of the red belt. Her hobbies are sport and music (see www.kvinfo.dk/side/560/article/629/ (accessed 29 November 2009)).

These and many other women with an immigrant background are role model for girls and other women. Whereas boys of ethnic minorities have numerous sporting heroes, girls have difficulty in finding women who successfully combine sporting activities and being a Muslim. This may contribute to their lack of interest in sport. The stories of Zenab, Nadia and Arezu can encourage them to follow their examples and dare to venture out and prove their skills in sporting arenas. A comparison of these three women and their biographies reveals the whole gamut of situations in which Muslim women may live and do sport.

Sport and physical activity – projects

Instead of a summary, I would like to present a few of the numerous projects on sport and PA in Denmark. They are designed with girls and women of immigrant families in mind in order to encourage them and provide them with competences to take up sporting activities. The key principle of these schemes, which receive financial backing from the ministry responsible for immigration or the municipalities, is to take seriously the wishes and needs of participants of different ages and with different ethnic and religious backgrounds. This means that some of the courses take place in a 'women-only' environment.

Popular among immigrant women, but problematic because of propriety, is swimming. There are several initiatives to offer women opportunities to swim. A Copenhagen sports club, for example, has reserved special hours for women at the indoor swimming pool in the centre of Copenhagen. Men are not allowed access, and the pool area cannot be viewed from the outside. It has a huge oval-shaped pool and is equipped with a whirlpool as well as diving and water sports facilities. The swimming courses for Muslim women have proved so popular that waiting lists have had to be introduced.[47]

A project named 'She-zone' provides an opportunity, for girls only, to play ball games and do gymnastics as well as dancing. In Nørrebro, a district of Copenhagen, a taekwondo club has opened, again only for girls and women (Rasmussen 2004). Both girls and boys can take part in 'container sport', a scheme which provides sports and games locally in several socially deprived neighbourhoods. A container houses lots of different games and sports apparatus, which can be borrowed and used by the children living in the area. The majority of users are boys, but there are also quite a few girls who use, among other things, roller blades, balls or skipping ropes. Parents are willing to let their children take part in this scheme because it is not far from home, which makes it easier to supervise the children to a satisfactory degree.[48]

Projects like Get2sport and ClubGuides do not themselves provide any sports for immigrants and their descendants, but try to get children and adolescents to join sports clubs, among other things by giving advice to parents. Girls are an especially important target group in these schemes.[49]

Several projects have also been initiated for immigrants by immigrants themselves. A group of Somali women with small children, for example, tried to start up a fitness class in the basement rooms of a block of flats. This initiative unfortunately suffered from the irregular attendance of the women, who all had small children, and was discontinued when the initiator moved away (Mouridsen 2002).

The initiatives of Iman Ahmad have had more impact and been more long-term. I met Iman Ahmad during a running event for women organised by a women's magazine. After working for many years with immigrants, especially immigrant families and women, she succeeded in creating and filling a post as Commissioner for the Environment and Integration in Amager, a district of Copenhagen. Besides health and nutrition counselling, she organises sporting activities such as cycling and swimming courses for women. For the swimming courses she had to find a swimming pool in Amager where the women could not be observed by men. On account of the great demand for her swimming courses, she decided to train immigrant women as swimming instructors so that the courses were not entirely dependent on her. In addition, she founded a women's swimming club whose members are of many different nationalities.[50] It can only be hoped that others follow her example and that more and more women with immigrant backgrounds take their sporting life in their own hands.

Conclusion

The conditions of life, as well as the body and movement cultures of Muslim women in Western countries, are in many ways shaped by life as Diasporas. This is just as true of Muslims in Denmark as it is of migrants from non-Western countries in other European societies. For this reason the theoretical approaches presented in this contribution, along with the analyses based on empirical material and the biographical narratives of the girls and women, may serve studies in other countries both as points of departure and as templates for drawing comparisons.

The empirical studies undertaken in Denmark have provided a clear picture. Muslim girls and women are significantly under-represented among the physically active population. Many of them do not give any priority or even any place in their lives at all to sport. Nevertheless, there are clear signals that some girls and women are taking up sport and PA at the recreational and even elite levels. Narratives of Muslim sportswomen have revealed different body 'projects', multiple ways of practising their faith and a diversity of sports practices, opportunities and barriers. They have also demonstrated the active roles of these women, as witnessed by their efforts and negotiations in striving to position themselves in their social environments. Participation in sport and PA can be part of these negotiations. Some women succeed in balancing the demands of sport and the demands of their families and ethnic communities.

Despite such successes, the question of why the majority of women with migrant backgrounds are not interested in sport remains. This issue has to be addressed from theoretical perspectives. My theoretical considerations focus on the interplay between individuals and society, as well as on the mutual dependencies of identities and cultures on the one hand, and social fields, dispositions and tastes on the other. From this perspective, gender, ethnicity and faith are socially constructed and embodied, but at the same time are dependent on the discourses, practices and actual conditions of life in both Danish society and the ethnic communities.

The analysis of various studies and sources has shown that the aim of integrating or even assimilating the Muslim population has been achieved only to a certain degree, if at all, and that the difficult social situation of Muslim families has also had an adverse effect on sports participation among Muslim girls and women. Furthermore, the influence of the ethnic community may also make it even more difficult, or indeed impossible, for girls and women to take up sport.

The growing self-confidence of young female Muslims, along with numerous schemes initiated by the state and municipalities to further and support Muslim women, have led, in recent years, to positive development, amongst other things, in the participation of this target group in sporting activities. With the right kind of support, and in the right environment, Muslim girls and women are willing and able to achieve great things, with or without headscarves and in both 'women's' and 'men's' sports, as is demonstrated through the examples and projects presented in this chapter.

Notes

The author of this chapter, Gertrud Pfister, would like to thank the graduate student Kasper Pedersen for his support.

1 The term 'Muslim' refers to religion. However, in the available studies this term is often used for individuals coming from Islamic countries. The situation of Muslim and non-Muslim immigrants from non-Western countries is in many ways similar. Therefore the data also refer to Muslims. Information about religiosity of individuals and groups is not available.

2 Available statistics and studies about 'immigrants' as a rule refer to individuals coming from non-Western countries. There is very often no indication from which countries they came.

3 www.leksikon.org/art.php?n=4940 (accessed 29 November 2009).

4 www.dr.dk/Nyheder/Temaer/Oevrige_temaer/2009/Naboer/index   (accessed   29 November 2009).

5 www.information.dk/131700 (accessed 29 November 2009).

6 IFKA 2007. There are numerous studies available which all confirm the existence of a gender hierarchy in Danish society. See, among others, Borchorst 2002; Tienari *et al.* 2005; Holt 2006; Lister 2006; Bloksgaard 2008; Emerek and Holt 2008. On the limited representation of women on company boards, see: www.eurofound.europa.eu/eiro/2007/02/articles/dk0702029i.htm (accessed 29 November 2009).

7 www.religion.dk/artikel/248459:Islam–Islam-i-Danmark (accessed 29 November 2009).

8 See 'New in Danmark', information of the ministry of refugees, immigrants and integration, www.nyidanmark.dk/da-dk. Source: Danmarks Statistik (www.statistik-

banken.dk); for the percentage of Muslims in the various Islamic countries see http://en.wikipedia.org/wiki/State_religion#Islamic_countries (accessed 29 November 2009).

9 www.nyidanmark.dk/da-dk/ministeren/regeringens_integrationspolitik/Integration-sindsatsen+_nyankomne_udlaendinge.htm (accessed 29 November 2009).

10 Tranæs and Zimmermann 2004; to the ideological conflicts, see also www.euro-islam. info/country- profiles/denmark/ (accessed 29 November 2009).

11 On the events, but particularly on the political background in the various Islamic countries, see: http://jp.dk/udland/article1292552.ece (accessed 29 November 2009).

12 The debates about Muslims in Denmark can be accessed via the websites of the Danish newspapers (e.g. *Politiken*, *BT*, *Extra Bladet*) and TV stations.

13 http://nyhederne-dyn.tv2.dk/politik/article.php/id-6974377.html (accessed 29 November 2009).

14 http://nyhederne.tv2.dk/politik/article.php/id-12194666.html (accessed 29 November 2009).

15 See also the overview about the Danish Sport Federations (foreningsidrættens vilkår) 2004 on the webpage of the Danish Sport Federation, www.dif.dk/OmDIF/Forside/ Idraetten per cent20i per cent20tal/Undersoegelser/Foreningsidraettens per cent20vilkaar.aspx (accessed 29 November 2009).

16 See the report of LG Insight https://www.nyidanmark.dk/resources.ashx/Resources/ Publikationer/Rapporter/2006/eval_idraet.pdf (accessed 29 November 2009).

17 See, for example, the discussion of politicians and Arhus in DOKUMENT. NO. February 27, 2007. www.document.no/2007/02/forslag_om_en_mer_religios_hve.html (accessed 29 November 2009).

18 www.nordjyske.dk/indland/forside.aspx?ctrl=10anddata=2 per cent2c2825937 per cent2c5 per cent2c4andcount=1 (accessed 29 November 2009).

19 www.haandboldspiller.dk/viewnewsitem.jsp?id=486 (accessed 29 November 2009).

20 A long article in the newspaper *BT* focused on the lack of knowledge about clubs among young immigrants: www.bt.dk/danmark/foreninger-er-ukendt-land-etniske-unge (accessed 29 November 2009). See also the report in the journal *Ny i Danmark* 2, 12, 2009; Bøskov and Ilkjær 2005.

21 For an overview of barriers that prevent (female) immigrants from joining a sports club, see Bøskov and Ilkjær 2005.

22 See Mikkelsen 2003; and the report in the journal *Ny i Danmark* 2, 13, 2009.

23 See several contributions in the journal *Ung trivsel. Socialmagasinet om unge, udgivet af Ventilen Danmark* 5, October 2006.

24 See, for example, the stories of successful women of ethnic minorities on the website of the Danish Centre for Research on Women and Gender, Kvinfo, www.kvinfo.dk/ side/539/ (accessed 29 November 2009).

25 *Politikken*, 31 January 2009, 4.

26 The differences in the birth rates between Danish women and non-Western immigrants is diminishing. In 1998, immigrant women had a birth rate of 3.04 children, in 2008 this figure has been reduced to 1.94; http://islamineurope.blogspot.com/2009/05/ denmark-immigrantsdanes-have-same.html (accessed 29 November 2009).

27 www.dr.dk/islam/index.asp?ID=aegtefaelle.htmandM=m_familien.htm (accessed 29 November 2009).

28 See, e.g., the website of the organisation kvinder for frihed (women for freedom): www.blog.kvinderforfrihed.dk/?p=411 (accessed 29 November 2009).

29 www.bt.dk/article/20021210/nyheder/112100341/ (accessed 29 November 2009).

30 www.dr.dk/Nyheder/Indland/2009/04/30/232405.htm (accessed 29 November 2009).

31 See, for example, the experiences of Asmaa Abdol-Hamid and her sister at school: www.kvinfo.dk/side/539/?personId=25 (accessed 29 November 2009).

32 http://en.wikipedia.org/wiki/Islamic_dress_controversy_in_Europe#cite_note-18 (accessed 29 November 2009).

33 Schmidt 2007; see the studies quoted on the website of Kvinfo with the topic 'head-scarf'; www.kvinfo.dk/side/266/tema/32/ (accessed 29 November 2009); Ericsson Ryste 2008.
34 On identity constructions of Muslim immigrants, new interpretations of Islam and women's roles in the new Islamic movements, see Schmidt 2007.
35 www.bt.dk/politik/asmaa-med-toerklaede-i-odense-byraad; see also: http://da.wikipedia.org/wiki/Asmaa_Abdol-Hamid (accessed 29 November 2009).
36 www.kvinfo.dk/side/539/?personId=25 (accessed 29 November 2009).
37 www.dr.dk/Nyheder/Indland/2009/04/30/232405.htm (accessed 29 November 2009).
38 For the report about successful Muslim women with and without scarves, see: www.kvinfo.dk/side/864/ (accessed 29 November 2009).
39 See the article 'Muslim women share the dream with other women' (18 March 2009); http://videnskab.dk/content/dk/samfund/muslimske_kvinder_deler_dromme_med_andre_kvinderwww.videnskab.dk (accessed 29 November 2009) and the studies quoted in *Ung trivsel Socialmagasinet om unge, udgivet af Ventilen Danmark* 5, October 2006.
40 Mørck 1998; Knocke and Hertzberg 2000; Larsen 2004; Dahl and Jacobsen 2005; see also http://jp.dk/nyviden/article1636649.ece?page=2 (accessed 29 November 2009).
41 See the article 'How to be a Muslim woman in Denmark' (21 March 2009): www.lige.dk/files/PDF/at_vaere_muslimsk_kvinde_i_dk.pdf (accessed 29 November 2009).
42 Caglar 1997; see also www.dr.dk/Nyheder/Indland/2009/04/30/232405.htm www.berlingske.dk/article/20080101/kronikker/80101026/ (accessed 29 November 2009).
43 www.islamonline.net/servlet/Satellite?c=Article_C&cid=1233567733671&pagename=Zone-English-Euro_Muslims%2FEMELayout (accessed 29 November 2009).
44 For the report about the lives of Muslim women in Denmark, see: www.lige.dk/Default.asp?Id=134andAjrNws=1081 (accessed 29 November 2009).
45 http://da.wikipedia.org/wiki/Asmaa_Abdol-Hamid#Syn_p.C3.A5_ligestilling (accessed 29 November 2009).
46 www.e-pages.dk/3f/142/4; see also *Ny i Danmark* 2, 2009: 10–11 (accessed 29 November 2009).
47 www.kobenhavn.dk/Borger/KulturOgFritid/FritidOgIdraet/IntegrationOgForeningsliv/-Projekter/Pige-%20og%20kvindesv%C3%B8mning/SvoemmetilbudTilPigerOgKvinder.aspx (accessed 29 November 2009).
48 Several projects are described in Hansen and Dreier 2007.
49 www.get2sport.dk/; www.foreningsguiderne.dk/ (accessed 29 November 2009).
50 www.kristeligt-dagblad.dk/artikel/39838:Danmark–Indvandrerkvinder-svoemmer-sig-danske?page=2; www.berlingske.dk/article/20090530/danmark/705290089/ (accessed 29 November 2009). I also included information from an interview with Iman Ahmad.

Bibliography

Agergaard, S. (2008) *Unges idrætsdeltagelse* og *integration i idrætsforeninger i Århus Vest*, Århus: Institut for Idræt, Århus Universitet.
Andersen, H.S. (2005) *Den Sociale og etniske udvikling i almene boligafdelinger*, Hørsholm: Statens Byggeforskningsinstitut.
Benn, T., Dagkas, S. and Jawad, H. (2010, in press) 'Embodied faith: Islam, religious freedom and educational practices in physical education', *Sport, Education and Society*.
Bergman, S. (2008) 'Women-friendly Nordic societies?' *Eurotopics*. Online, available at: www.eurotopics.net/en/magazin/gesellschaft-verteilerseite/frauen-2008–3/artikel_bergman_frauen_norden/2 (accessed 29 November 2009).
Bloksgaard, L. (2008) 'Kompetencekrav, familiepolitikker og køn i modern arbejdspladskontekster', in R. Emerek and H. Holt (eds) *Lige muligheder – Frie valg? Om det*

kønspolitiske arbejdsmarked gennem et årti, København: SFL 317–340. Online, available at: www.sfi.dk/sw61815asp (accessed 29 November 2009).

Bollini, P. and Siem, H. (1995) 'No real progress towards equity: health of migrants and ethnic minorities on the eve of the year 2000', *Social Science & Medicine*, 41, 6: 819–828.

Borchgrevink, T. (2004) *Dishonourable Integration: Between Honour and Shame*, Oslo: Institut for Samfunnsforskning, AMID, Working Paper series.

Borchorst, A. (ed.) (2002) *Kønsmagt under forandring*, Copenhagen: Hans Reitzels Forlag.

Børresen, S.K. (2008) *Konflikter i boligområder: Opfattelser og håndtering*, Hørsholm: Statens Byggeforskningsinstitut.

Bøskov, S. and Ilkjær, T. (2005) *Integration og det frivillige foreningsliv*, København: Institut for Idræt, Københavns Universitet.

Bourdieu, P. (1984) *Distinction: A Social Critique of the Judgment of Taste*, Cambridge: Harvard University Press.

Bourdieu, P. (1988) 'Program for a sociology of sport', *Sociology of Sport Journal*, 5: 153–161.

Caglar, A.S. (1997) 'Hyphenated identities and the limits of "culture"', in T. Modood and P. Werbner (eds) *The Politics of Multiculturalism in the New Europe: Racism, Identity and Community*, London: Zed Books: 169–186.

Carlsen, H, Kruse, L. and Astrup, P. (2002) *Idrættens rummelighed. 14 integrationsprojekter om foreningslivets muligheder og begrænsinger*, Brøndby: Danmarks Idræts-Forbund.

Christiansen, M. and Nielsen, A.M. (2005) *Kortlægning af aktiviteter om forebyggelse og sundhedsfremme tilrettelagt for etniske minoriteter i Danmark*, København: Sundhedsstyrelsen.

Connell, R.W. (2002) *Gender*, Cambridge: Polity.

Dahl, K.M. and Jakobsen, V. (2005) *Køn, etnicitet og barrierer for integration*, København: Socialforskningsinstituttet.

Emerek, R. and Holt, H. (2008) 'Indledning', in R. Emerek and H. Holt (eds) *Lige muligheder – Frie valg? Om det kønspolitiske arbejdsmarked gennem et årti*, Copenhagen: SFI. 13–26. Online, available at: www.sfi.dk/sw61815.asp (accessed 8 October 2008).

Ericson Ryste, M. (2008) 'Askepott i *hijab*', Kilden: Informatjonssenter for Kjønsforskning. Online, available at: http://kilden.forskningsradet.no/c16880/artikkel/vis.html?tid=54131 (accessed 29 November 2009).

European Commission (2006) *Eurobarometer: Health and Food*, Brussels. Online, available at: http://ec.europa.eu/health/ph_publication/eb_food_en.pdf (accessed 29 November 2009).

Garrett, R. (2004) 'Gendered bodies and physical identities', in J. Evans, B. Davies and J. Wright (eds) *Body, Knowledge and Control: Studies in the Sociology of Physical Education and* Health, London: Routledge: 140–156.

Hansen, E.K. (2006) *2005 Report and 2006 Perspective and Action Plan for Gender Equality*. Submitted to the Danish Parliament on 28 February 2006. Online, available at: http://ligeuk.itide.dk/files/PDF/Perspective_actionplan_2006.pdf (accessed 29 November 2009).

Hansen, V.H. and Dreier, M.B. (2007) 'Integration gennem idræt', Master's Thesis, University of Copenhagen.

Heinemann, K. (2007) *Einführung in die Soziologie des Sports*, Schorndorf: Hofmann.

Henningsen, I. (2004) 'Underrekruttering af kvinder på danske universiteter', *Kvinden og Samfundet*, 120, 1: 20–21.

Henriksen, C.S. (2002) *Børn og unges fritid i Hoje Taastrups Kommune*, Hoje Taastrup: Casa.

Hjære, M. and Mikkelsen, F. (2003) 'Den frivillige sektors bidrag til integration af flygtninge og indvandrere i Norden', paper presented at a conference in Oslo, 29 November 2002.

Holt, H., Geerdsen, L.P. Christensen, G., Klitgaard, C. and Lind, M.L. (2006) *Det kønsopdelte arbejdsmarked: En kvantitativ og kvalitativ belysning*, Copenhagen: SFI.

Hummelgaard, H., Husted, L., Nielsen, H.S., Rosholm, M. and Smith, N. (2002) *Uddannelse og arbejde for andengenerationsindvandrere*, København: AKF-forlaget.

Ibsen, B. (2004) 'Idrætsdeltagelse hos børn med anden kulturel baggrund end dansk', *Focus Idræt*, 38, 4: 20–24.

Ibsen, B. (2007) *Børns idrætsdeltagelse i Københavns Kommune*, Odense: Syddansk Universitet, Institut for Idræt og Biomekanik.

Ingerslev, O. (2000) 'Sundhedsforhold blandt indvandrere', in G.V. Mogensen and P.C. Matthiesen (eds) *Integration i Danmark omkring årtusindskiftet*, Aarhus: Aarhus Universitetsforlag: 222–251.

Jeldtoft, N. (2008) 'Andre muslimske identiteter: et studie af ikke-organiserede muslimer i Danmark', *Tidsskrift for Islamforskning*, 1.

Jørgensen, P. (2006) 'Drengene, pigerne og gymnasieidrætten i det 20. århundrede', in A.L. Poulsen and E. Trangbæk (eds) *Kvinder, køn og krop – Kulturelle fortællinger: Idrætshistorisk årbog 2006*, Odense: Syddansk Universitetsforlag: 33–44.

Juul, J. (2003) 'Muslimske kvinder i Danmark og deres relationer til idrætten', Master's Thesis, Institut for Idræt, Københavns Universitet.

Karpantschof, R. (2003) 'Højreradikalismen I Danmark – en politik model på historisk-sociologisk grund', *Dansk Sociologi*, 13: 3.

Khader, N. (2006) *Ære og skam*, 3rd edn, Valby: Borgen.

Kirkegaard, K.L. (2007) *Overblik over den danske fitness-sektor – en undersøgelse af danske fitnesscentre*, København: IDAN.

Knocke, W. and Hertzberg, F. (2000) *Mångfaldens barn söker sin plats: En studie om arbetsmarknadschanser för ungdomar med invandrarbakgrund*, Stockholm: Svartvitts Forläg.

København Kommune (2009) *Kortlægning af ligestilling mellem kønnene blandt etniske minoriteter i Københavns Kommune*, København: Københavns Kommune, Beskæftigelses- og integrationsforvaltningen.

Larsen, M.N. (2004) *De små oprør – tanker og metoder i arbejdet med minoritetspiger*, Århus: Århus Universitetsforlag.

Lister, R. (2006) 'Gender, citizenship and social justice in the Nordic welfare states: a view from the outside', *NIKK Magasin*, 3: 28–33.

Lorber, J. (2005) *Breaking the Bowls, Degendering and Feminist Change*, New York: W.W. Norton.

Lykkegård, L. (2001) 'Integration af flygtninge- og indvandrerbørn i foreningslivet', Viborg: Viborg Kommune.

Martin, E. (1989) *Die Frau im Körper*, Frankfurt: Campus.

Massey, D. and Jess, P. (1995) *A Place in the World*, Oxford: Oxford University Press.

Mikkelsen, C.L. (2003) *Foreninger fremmer forståelsen – inddragelse af etniske minoriteter i foreningerne og mangfoldighedsledelse*, København: Dansk Ungdoms fællesråd.

Mikkelsen, F. (2002) *Indvandrere og civilsamfund. En forskningsoversigt vedrørende etniske minoriteters deltagelse i civilsamfundet samt kulturmøder mellem minoriteter og danskere på arbejdspladsen, i boligområder og i foreninger*, Ålborg: AMID, Ålborg Universitet.

Mørck, Y. (1998) *Bindestregsdanskere: Fortællinger om køn, generationer og etnicitet*, Frederiksberg: Forlaget Sociologi.

Mørk, I. (2003) 'Narratives of the intersections of masculinities and ethnicities in a Danish high school class', *NORA: Nordic Journal of Women's Studies*, 2: 11.

Mouridsen, M. (2002) 'Respekt – idrættens rolle i integrationsprocessen hos somaliske kvinder', Bachelor's Thesis, Institut for Idræt, Københavns Universitet.

Nakamura, Y. (2002) 'Beyond the *hijab*: female Muslims and physical activity', *Women in Sport & Physical Activity Journal*, 11, 1: 21–48.

Nasser, M. (1997) *Culture and Weight Consciousness*, London, New York: Routledge.

Nielsen, G. and Ibsen, B. (2008) *Kommunale forskelle på børns idrætsdeltagelse – En undersøgelse af fire kommuner*, København: Idrættens Analyseinstitut.

Østergaard, K. and Jensen, T.G. (2007) *Nye muslimer i Danmark. Møder og omvendelser*, Højbjerg: Forlaget Univers.

Papastergiadis, N. (1997) 'Tracing hybridity in theory', in P. Werbner and T. Modood (eds) *Debating Cultural Hybridity: Multi-Cultural Identities and the Politics of Anti-Racism*, London: Zed Books: 257–281.

Pedwell, C. (2007) 'Tracing "the anorexic" and "the veiled woman": towards a relational approach', *New Working Paper series*, 20, London: LSE.

Pfister, G. (2010a) 'Women and sport in Islamic countries', *Forum for Idræt*, 1: 35–50.

Pfister, G. (2010b) 'Denmark', in C. Sobry (ed.) *Governance of Sport in European Countries*, London: Routledge.

Pilgaard, M. (2008) *Danskernes motions- og sportsvaner 2007 – nøgletal og tendenser*, København: Idrættens Analyseinstitut.

Rakow, L. (1986) 'Rethinking gender research in communication', *Journal of Communication*, 36: 18–34.

Rasmussen, A. (2004) 'She Zone – en ren pigeforening', Bachelor's Thesis, Copenhagen: Institut for Idræt.

Rheinländer, T. and Nielsen, G.A. (2007) *Unges livsstil og dagligdag 2006*, København: Kræftens Bekæmpelse & Sundhedsstyrelsen.

Ringgaard, L.W. and Nielsen, G.A. (2004) *Fysisk aktivitet i dagligdagen blandt 16–20-årige i Danmark*, København: Kræftens Bekæmpelse & Sundhedsstyrelsen.

Ruggiero, G.M. (2003) *Eating Disorders in the Mediterranean Area: An Exploration in Transcultural Psychology*, New York: Nova Biomedichal Books.

Schläger, D., Rasmussen, N.K. and Kjøller, M. (2005) *Sundhedsforhold blandt etniske minoriteter – en litteraturgennemgang*, København: Statens Institut for Folkesundhed.

Schmidt, G. (2007) *Muslim i Danmark, muslim i verden*, Uppsala: Swedish Science Press.

Schmidt, G. and Jakobsen, V. (2000) *20 år i Danmark: En undersøgelse af nydanskeres situationer og erfaringer*, København: Socialforskningsinstituttet.

Schmidt, G. and Jakobsen, V. (2004) *Pardannelse blandt etniske minoriteter i Danmark*, København: Socialforskningsinstituttet.

Seeberg, P. (2002) *Unge indvandreres integration, herunder integration gennem gymnasiet, fritidsaktiviteter, kærester mv*, Ålborg: AMID, Ålborg Universitet.

Siim, B. (2003) *Medborgerskabets udfordringer – etniske minoritetskvinders politiske myndiggørelse*, Århus: Århus Universitetsforlag.

Talbot, M and Wimbush, E. (1988) *Relative Freedoms: Women and Leisure*, Philadelphia: Open University Press.

Tienari, J., Søderberg, A.-M., Holgersson, C. and Vaara, E. (2005) 'Gender and national identity constructions in the cross-border merger context', *Gender, Work & Organization*, 12, 3: 217–224.

Tranæs, T. and Zimmermann, K.F. (2004). *Migrants, Work, and the Welfare State*, Odense: University Press of Southern Denmark.

Tranæs, T. (ed.) (2008) *Indvandrerne og det danske uddannelsessystem*, København: Gyldendal.

Waldhoff, H. P. (1995) *Fremde und Zivilisierung: Wissenssoziologische Studien über das Verarbeiten von Gefühlen der Fremdheit. Probleme der modernen Peripherie-Zentrums-Migration am türkisch-deutschen Beispiel*, Frankfurt am Main: Suhrkamp.

West, C. and Zimmermann, D.H. (1991) 'Doing gender', in J. Lorber and S.A. Farrell (eds) *The Social Construction of Gender*, California: Sage Publications: 13–37.

With-Nielsen, N. and Pfister, G. (2010, in press) 'Gender constructions and negotiations in PE – case studies', *Sport, Education and Society*.

Part II
National perspectives

4 والقيـــادة فـــي المجـــال الرياضـــي المـــراة البحرينيـــة

Women in sports leadership in Bahrain

Mona Al-Ansari

Editors' introduction

This chapter is the first to be written on women in sports leadership in Bahrain. An overview of the socio-historical, political, economic and religious background of the country will provide a context within which the status and role of women may be recognised and defined in order that the opportunities and challenges for women, as they strive to become leaders in sport, can be identified.

Context

The Kingdom of Bahrain is an archipelago located in the Arabian Gulf between the Qatar Peninsula and Saudi Arabia. It covers an area of 676 km² and has a population of 754,000 (Statistical Abstract 2006). Whilst it has a constitutional monarchy, Bahrain is an Islamic country, governed by Sharia law. Over 80 per cent of the population is Muslim but other faiths do co-exist in a spirit of mutual acceptance. The country's official language is Arabic, and Bahrain is a member of the Arabian Gulf Cooperation Council (GCC), which consists of the six Arabian Gulf countries, the Kingdom of Bahrain, Qatar, Kuwait, Oman, the Kingdom of Saudi Arabia and the United Arab Emirates.

Bahrain was a British Protectorate from the early nineteenth century until independence in 1972. Although small, its strategic geographical location at a trading crossroads brought cosmopolitan influences from passing traders. Since the discovery of oil in 1932, Bahrain has experienced rapid modernisation. The twentieth century saw periods of reform, with ethnic diversity growing in the population as a consequence of the influx of migrant workers, especially those from Asia and the Far East.

More recent change in the socio-political direction of the country came with the succession of the current king in 1999, arguably the most influential being the move to 'Kingdom' status in 2002 and to political liberalisation with democratic elections to government positions. Significantly, women received voting rights for the first time in that year.

Women in Bahrain

Women represent around 30 per cent of the total workforce in Bahrain and are employed in almost every work sector. Indeed, many women work with the support of their families, including the male members. This is particularly the case in lower-class families where women are employed, for example, as water suppliers, housemaids, dressmakers and nurses. Women are actively engaged in public and private economic sectors and compete with men to occupy higher and decision-making positions. For example, there are women ministers, bank directors, university presidents and college deans, judges, prosecutors and ambassadors, although their numbers do not equal those of men. At present, of 24 members of the cabinet, only two are women. In 2001, a Supreme Council for Women (an advisory body to the government on women's issues) was established to assist the government in drawing up policies on women's issues and to encourage women's participation in commercial and public life. The Council is chaired by Her Highness Sheikha Sabeeka Bint Ibrahim Alkhalifa, wife of His Majesty the King of Bahrain. Starting in 2001, women also engaged in Bahrain's reform and development alongside their male counterparts. They took part in the preparation of the National Action Charter (2001) and the referendum process that validated it.

Since their inclusion in the political arena in 2002, Bahraini women have entered the upper chamber of parliament, the Shura Council, and the Chamber of Deputies. The Shura Council is appointed by the government and has 40 members, ten of whom are women (www.shura.bh/En/Council/MPs/Pages/default.aspx). The Chamber of Deputies also has 40 members, only one of whom is a woman, Lateefa Al Gaood, who was elected in 2006 (www.nuwab.gov.bh/ServicesCenter/Members/Search.aspx). In 2006, a Bahraini woman, Haya Rashed Al-Khalifa, was voted President of the UN General Assembly, the first Middle Eastern woman and only the third woman in history to take over the post. Women's Day was designated as 1 December 2008, during which acknowledgements were paid to women in every workplace.

It must be noted that Islam does not prohibit women from working, being educated or becoming involved in government, and under Sharia law working women must enjoy the same rights as men. This includes equal pay for equivalent work. In Bahrain, women are now competing with men to complete their education and work alongside them with no gender discrimination. Recent attitudinal changes in Bahrain have opened doors for women to step forward and be part of national development. They are beginning to take their place in planning, policy-making and government. In many ways, Bahrain led the way in the Gulf region for the education and advancement of women; however, the inclusion process is slow and the proportion of women in policy- and decision-making positions is still small.

Education, physical education and women's sport in Bahrain

Due to the relatively recent history of sport in the region, there is a shortage of literature about sport in general and about women's sport in particular across the Gulf countries. For the purpose of this chapter, the author has used the limited sources available, which consist of government documents, symposium or conference papers, unpublished reports/booklets and personal life experience.

Author's professional biography

I am a Bahraini woman with over 25 years of experience in sports leadership. Being an active sports participant at school during my childhood and teens, representing my school in school tournaments in different activities, for example handball and gymnastics, gave me the inspiration and desire to carve out a career in sport, later specialising in sports sciences. I trained at the High Institute of Teacher Training, where I gained my diploma in teaching and began my career as a teacher of physical education. This institute was closed in the 1970s and replaced by the College of Education in the University of Bahrain, where I later gained my Bachelor's degree. After gaining my degree, I took on managerial roles, first as a specialist in physical education and then as a specialist in women's sport and a director of the sports programme section at the General Organisation for Youth and Sport (GOYS). When I gained my doctorate, I returned to teaching at the university and finally became Head of the Physical Education Department at the University of Bahrain.

To collect more specific information for this chapter, questionnaires were sent to 35 Bahraini women, previously or currently involved in school and in sports leadership at local, national or international levels. The consultative sample was made up of physical educators, coaches, officials, physical-education specialists, heads of different departments at the Ministry of Education and the GOYS, as well as members of committees in different Bahraini sports clubs and associations. Questions were asked concerning their roles and experiences during their careers. Finally, interviews were conducted with six women engaged in sports management. These were directors of sports associations, board members of sports associations and the Bahrain Olympic Committee or Head of a Department at GOYS.

The histories of physical education and sport for girls and women are interwoven in Bahrain. The education system in governmental schools is currently a total of 12 years of basic education, divided into three levels: the first six years is the primary level, the next is the intermediate level (three years) and the last is the secondary level (three years).

Historically, education was provided in Bahrain for boys from 1919 and for girls from 1928. Both genders were treated equally and much early attention was given to combating illiteracy. Physical education was one of the main subjects taught to students at that time. Teachers were recruited from other Arab countries such as Egypt, Jordan and Palestine, although their approach to teaching the subject laid great emphasis on rhythmic exercise patterns similar to that of Swedish gymnastics of the time. Girls participated in sports kit (shorts and shirts) in gender-separated schools at all levels, showing that the subject was taken seriously by school authorities at that time. There is evidence that in the 1940s female students were actively engaged in extra-curricular activities, and competitions were arranged between schools (Al-Jeeb 1990).

Bahraini women first entered the field of sports through interest generated in the schools' physical-education programmes as pure exercise gave way to familiar sports. From the early days of education, Bahrain's governmental and some of the private schools were gender-segregated, with girls taught by female teachers and boys taught by male teachers. However, during the last three decades, the first stage of primary education has been administered and taught by all-female staff and teachers. Girls and boys in Bahrain attend separate schools, with separate facilities. The condition of schools and their facilities is similar for both sexes and the curriculum is the same. Culture and traditional values require that boys and girls are separately educated. However, at university level male and female students attend lectures together, although practical lectures, such as in physical education, are sex-segregated. Male and female students learn different skills and sports, and are taught by same-sex staff. The sport-dominated curriculum meant that many of the leaders of women's sport were initially trained as physical educators at university.

By the 1970s there was a well-established arena of women's sports in Bahrain. Several sports federations began to accept women as members, and in addition, a number of women's societies catered for sportswomen, providing them with support in order to practise their favourite sports (Al-Khaja 2001). At that time, the most popular sports for girls were table tennis, volleyball and basketball. It is worth mentioning that the Bahraini federations of these sports are the most active in encouraging girls to become members. Men and women used the same training facilities, although the coaches were invariably men. Physical-education teachers as well as popular male athletes became role models for girls as well as boys. Women's teams were able to compete against each other in these popular sports within Bahrain and against other countries in the Arabian Gulf region. These championships were held at the national sports halls in Bahrain, where spectators (men and women) were allowed to watch and support their teams.

This development in women's sport did not continue as Bahraini society, like other Gulf societies, has experienced a resurgence in social and conservative religious values since the 1970s. Conservative religious activists and sympathetic politicians led the way, and men and women began to identify more closely with religious norms and rules and began to follow Islamic rules with regard to lifestyle and dress. Accordingly, some women in Bahrain changed from a Western style of dress to that required by a strict adherence to Islamic laws and customs. During this transformation, some female athletes followed this trend and gave up their sporting activities, while others continued with their previous lifestyle, training and wearing normal sportswear. From the mid-1970s, female athletes were more and more discouraged, largely by their families, from practising their sports if men were present during their competitions. Thus, those women who chose to continue their sporting life were pressurised to participate in separate facilities with all-women spectators (Al-Ansari 2008). Despite this discouragement of women's participation in sports, female table tennis players swam against the tide of social pressure and did not stop training and competing. Table tennis was a highly developed sport, and some female players had been trained by the association to a very advanced stage with many opportunities to compete at a high level in Arab and Asian tournaments, Islamic and non-Islamic events. Moreover, the table tennis association did not provide special separate facilities for girls and women, who continued to train and compete alongside the men. Players of other games such as basketball did not get the same attention or preparation, and did not have an equivalent performance standard. Among the table tennis players was a Bahraini champion, Sh. Hayat Al-Khalifa, who started playing at school and continued until she became a star in this sport during the 1970s and the early 1980s. Trained by a male coach, she and her colleagues participated in many national and international tournaments (Al-Khalifa and Al-Enzoor 2005). In 2000 she was elected President of the Bahraini Table Tennis Federation.

Through all of this change, physical education and sports in schools continued, and girls retained their opportunities to participate in sport both within the curricular and in extra-curricular time. Despite strict segregation of the sexes, there were still opportunities for children to compete (Al-Jeeb 1990, 2004).

The Department of Physical Education (DPE) at the Ministry of Education (MoE) continues to recognise the value of physical education and constantly strives to improve the status of the subject in the schools. The influence of school-based physical education on the contribution women make in sport and leadership positions today cannot be underestimated. The university programme, established in 1982 to train specialist teachers of physical education, became a major source of future leaders in women's sport. The next section focuses more specifically on the issue of higher education and its influence on sports careers for women in Bahrain.

Higher education and sports careers for women

The physical-education profession established itself in Bahrain prior to any other state in the Arabian Gulf region. As mentioned earlier, opportunities for girls in school sports and physical education started with the development of education for all during the 1920s, with physical-education/sport teachers coming from other Arab countries such as Egypt and Jordan. It was not until the 1960s that opportunities arose for men and women interested in sport-related careers as physical educators to undergo training in Bahrain. The Higher Institute for Teachers was established, and successful students graduated with teaching diplomas. Physical education was one of the main areas of specialisation at the institution. Students wishing to pursue their higher education, however, had to travel abroad, mainly to one of the Middle Eastern universities in order to gain a degree.

During the early 1970s, the first two Bahraini women[1] to gain degrees in physical education – Layla Al-Anzoor and Seham Hijres, from Iraq and Egypt respectively – were appointed physical-education teachers before moving into the Ministry of Education as advisors. During their time as teachers and Ministry advisors, they were also involved in sport as supervisors or team directors. With these two role models leading the way, many more women with diplomas followed suit, gaining their degrees abroad and returning to teach physical education in Bahrain.

In 1982, the University of Bahrain established a Physical Education Department (PED) in its College of Education. It was now possible for Bahraini people to study for a degree in the teaching of physical education without having to travel abroad. Although the programme offered by the PED was targeted at both men and women, the majority of the graduates, especially in recent years, have been women, as the profession appears to appeal more to women than to men. Male and female professors, associate and assistant professors are responsible for teaching the programme. Islamic requirements are met and, as mentioned earlier, the practical modules of the course are sex-segregated although the theoretical modules are not. At the present time, the department has 11 Bahraini staff, seven men and four women, and four non-Bahraini staff (one man and three women). While student numbers vary, the average is around 38 per year. The 2008 group of students who enrolled at the department numbered 32, of which 21 were women.

In 1999, the Physical Education Department started its postgraduate programmes (for Master's and Doctoral degrees). Prior to this, as was noted earlier, women wishing to advance their studies had to travel abroad. As opportunities developed for Bahraini women to fulfil careers in physical education, other Gulf states were still relying on teachers from other Arab countries like Egypt, Jordan, Tunisia and Iraq.

It was the advancements in physical education and sport in the university sector that gave Bahraini women the confidence and skills to become sports leaders, officials and coaches. Today, women with high educational qualifications in the subject of physical education and sport work as university professors, sports administrators at government establishments, chairpersons and board members of national and international federations. From their positions, these leaders are able to contribute to advancing and developing sporting opportunities for women in and beyond Bahrain.

Bahraini women in managerial positions in sport

The management of sports in the Kingdom of Bahrain is the task of different governmental and non-governmental institutions. These are:

1   the Supreme Council for Youth and Sports (SCYS);
2   the General Organisation for Youth and Sports (GOYS);

3   the Directorate of Physical Education at the Ministry of Education (DPE);
4   the Bahrain Olympic Committee (BOC);
5   the Physical Education Department at the University of Bahrain (PED); and
6   sports committees within various companies and government ministries.

The SCYS is the highest sports authority in Bahrain with the task of drawing up policies on sport and youth issues. The SCYS is chaired by HH the Crown Prince, with board members who represent the government and the private sectors. The first female board member, Professor Huda Al-Khaja,[2] was appointed to the Council in 2000. This appointment was seen as a breakthrough by the women's movement. The Supreme Council, as mentioned earlier, is chaired by the First Lady, who is proactive in relation to women's activities. The success of the appointment has led to a desire for more women to be involved in the SCYS.

GOYS is an operational governmental organisation for youth and sports and sits under the SCYS umbrella. It encompasses various departments and sections that manage sports. Women are not involved at the top rank of the managerial hierarchy of GOYS. In other words, they are not part of the decision-making process, but are only involved in administrative work. The issue of promoting women's involvement in sport is managed through different unspecialised sections at GOYS, for example in the division of training or the public relations section. Unfortunately, there is no longer any unit dedicated to the provision and development of sport/physical activity for women.

In the 1980s, GOYS had a specialised section for women's sport led by a female specialist, Dr Mona Al-Ansari (this chapter's author). This section introduced sports and exercise to women from different backgrounds. The women attending the programmes organised by this section were from rural as well as urban areas and also represented different religious backgrounds. Several indoor sports activities were offered, including aerobics, fitness training and squash. The classes took place in female-only environments and, consequently, the women were able to wear light sporting clothes of their choice. Some outdoor activities such as running and tennis were also offered. For these activities, the women dressed modestly and many wore head coverings.

The education of women on the importance of exercise in their lives was also a responsibility of the special section of GOYS and, apart from the sports activity programmes, seminars were organised to spread the healthy lifestyle message. It was due to this activity that the 1980s witnessed the development of women's sports in Bahrain. During the 1990s, GOYS was reorganised and many of the sections were designated new roles, including the section looking after women's sport.

As members of the management boards and committees of sports clubs and national federations, women have gradually increased their numbers since the 1980s. Most notably the table tennis[3] and gymnastics[4] federations both appointed women as their presidents, with the gymnastics federation also appointing a woman vice-president.

Women were members of the boards of other Bahraini sports federations between 2004 and 2008.[5] However, despite the IOC recommendation that 20 per cent of the membership of each National Olympic Committee should be female, since 1996 Bahrain has appointed only one woman member to its board.

Women do chair and act as board members on different sub-committees of various sports clubs and sports federations in Bahrain, but these are invariably women's committees within the overall management structure of the particular sports organisation. Whilst this is essential in protecting and developing sports participation for women, it does not address the imbalance in gender equity and the very much higher representation, funding and control positions held by men in sports structures. Bahraini women are representatives in some regional and international sports agencies such as the Asian Sports Federations (football, Olympic Committee), the Arab Volleyball Federation, the West Asian Sports Association, the Asian Olympic Committee, the Arab Table Tennis, Volleyball and Physical Education Federations and the Committee of Physical Education in the Arabian Gulf Countries. Involvement of Bahraini women in the above-mentioned sports sectors gave support for the participation of women as competitors, officials and contributors at various sporting events such as the Olympic Games and international symposia and conferences.

Two Bahraini women, including the author, were delegates at the First International Conference on Women in Sport which took place in Brighton, England, in 1994. Some 280 delegates from 82 countries, representing governmental and non-governmental organisations, national Olympic committees, international and national sports federations and educational and research institutions, endorsed an important declaration. The Brighton Declaration provided the principles that were to guide action intended to increase the involvement of women in sport at all levels and in all functions and roles.

Whilst the Bahrain Olympic teams have always been small in number, from two to 15 competitors since 1984, women have featured in the teams from 2000. Bahrain sent its largest ever team to the last Olympic Games in Beijing: 15 competitors, of whom three were women. This almost matched participation in the previous games in Athens when, again, three women were included in a team of 14.

The two most famous Bahraini women athletes, both Olympians, are Ruqaya Al-Ghasara and Mariam Jamal. Ruqaya Al-Ghasara is considered a role model in Bahrain, where she visits schools, gives interviews and addresses symposia. Ruqaya made history when she ran in the 2008 Olympic Games, Beijing, fully covered and wearing the *hijab*. She is regarded as a devoted Muslim athlete who competes at the top level of her sport without giving up her Islamic faith, represented through her dress. Mariam Jamal, however, is not hailed as a role model. Originally from Ethiopia, Mariam has represented Bahrain many times at the international level, winning gold in the 200 m at the Fifteenth Asian Games in 2007. She was condemned by a high-profile Bahraini MP for competing in athletics clothing which left her legs, midriff and arms uncovered. Consequently, she is not considered by some people a good role model for Muslim girls.

The various national federations, supported by GOYS and the Ministry of Education in the training of physical-education teachers, encourage and manage the training and supply of referees and officials. In general, women officiate in women's sports only, although some do have the chance to officiate in men's events, such as in volleyball and table tennis, where there is no body contact.

Finally, it is important to return to the role of education in the development of sporting opportunities for girls and women in Bahrain. It can be observed that training for the profession of physical-education teaching has acted as a catalyst for most Bahraini women now contributing to the development of women's sport. The Directorate of Physical Education (DPE) at the Ministry of Education is responsible for the management of sports at public (state-funded) schools according to the following divisions:

1   teaching physical education;
2   inter-school sports activities;
3   extra-curricular activities;
4   Girl Scouts;
5   Boy Scouts.

The DPE organises sports for both boys and girls in governmental schools and has been chaired by a woman since 2001. Large numbers of women continue to be employed in ongoing administrative capacities, including those of supervisors and inspectors. The director of the DPE, Dr Shaikha Al-Jeeb,[6] initially graduated as a physical-education teacher, before continuing in higher education to be awarded a PhD in sports management. The contribution of a woman leader, with the assistance of women co-leaders, at the DPE was recognised through their efforts in the development of physical education at schools for both boys and girls. The subject continued, for example, as a main curriculum subject offered to both sexes in schools during and after the resurgence of Islamic codes of behaviour and dress in the late 1970s. Girls at schools were given the opportunity to participate in school tournaments at regional and national levels. What is more, physical educators, both male and female, were given the same opportunities for career improvement, such as attendance at workshops, courses and conferences.

From the earliest days of school-based physical education and sport in Bahrain, girls were encouraged to practise their favourite sports through extra-curricular activities. From the 1970s, beyond the school environment, girls were advised to create their own sports teams in sports clubs, associations and women's societies, where doors were opened to them to practise sports in these establishments. Whilst most clubs were male domains with male administrators, some sports clubs, particularly those offering basketball, volleyball and table tennis, did begin to open their doors to women members. At certain times of the year, for example the summer, clubs organise activities for boys and girls or/and special sessions for women to practise their sport. Many clubs now have a women's committee, albeit largely ad hoc, in order to organise activities for women and encourage more involvement. Today, the DPE is creating better connections with sports associations, clubs and training centres in order to supply the national federations with talented players (girls and boys). In addition to heading the DPE at the Ministry of Education, Dr Shaikha Al-Jeeb is also a member of different sports federations (national and international). From these positions, her contribution to women's sport in Bahrain is recognised at government level.

The Ministry of Education and GOYS have worked together, through school sports tournaments, in recruiting and training young girls and boys as athletes. Young athletes practise at schools until they reach a high standard of performance. At this point, they may be transferred to sports clubs and federations, where they receive advanced training. This arrangement between the two governmental bodies (DPE and GOYS) is very important in supporting young athletes. While at school, girls and boys receive similar attention with regard to sporting opportunities. Beyond school, however, boys become the main focus of attention.

When promising boys and girls become members of clubs and associations, it is the boys who receive the most support and are offered greater opportunities to pursue their training to national and international levels of performance. The general sport system in Bahrain (mainly GOYS), through its operational system (clubs, centres and federations), is meant to support the involvement of talented youngsters in sports. It is at club and federation level that a large proportion of this support flows towards the male athletes. The sports clubs and federations do not deny their preference of supporting male athletes. Officials responsible for the allocation of resources argue that female athletes do not represent a good investment as they are much less likely to continue their sporting careers and fulfil their potential. Cultural discouragements, early marriage, family responsibilities and childcare are cited as reasons for this decline in female participation. Men, on the other hand, are better able to pursue their sporting careers, unsaddled as they are with childcare and homebuilding. As visible sporting success leads to continued support for clubs and federations, it is understandable, if not morally justifiable, that support is given where success can be maximised.

The DPE has a programme of professional development and organises a variety of managerial courses annually for female physical educators. Apart from making the teachers more effective in their delivery of physical education by including training in coaching and officiating, these programmes help to produce the managers needed within the sport provision system both in and beyond the school environment. These courses are considered to be of such importance that a teacher's career prospects are often dependent upon their attendance and progress made on the courses.

Conclusion

Despite the fact that women in Bahrain appear to have the opportunity of becoming part of the sporting system as performers, officials and managers at all levels, they do not occupy the positions of influence and status, or achieve the high performance profiles that might be expected. This may be due to several factors, not the least of which is the culturally accepted dominance of men. The deep-rooted acceptance of this means that women rarely get the support of their female counterparts when it comes to elections for higher managerial positions, and this is reflected in the number and type of managerial positions held by women in the sporting context. It could be argued, with this attitude prevailing, that women collude in maintaining a low level of involvement in sports leadership and need to make a greater effort to occupy decision-making positions in sport.

Women's sports in Bahrain have been influential in the Gulf region, especially through the pioneering teacher-training programme at the university and the success of the women teachers of physical education and sport, influencing the provision of sporting opportunities inside and outside the school environment. Directives from the IOC and recommendations of international conferences have been of some, if limited, support for women in Bahrain, but for significant further progress to be made, there needs to be more equal recognition in positions of decision-making and funding allocation between men and women – even, perhaps, the provision of women-only sports spaces.

Despite relatively small numbers compared to men's involvement in sport and sports leadership – for example, the Bahrain Olympic Committee and the Swimming Association each have only one female member of their eleven and nine member committees respectively – it is fair to say that the Bahraini government gives women the opportunity to be actively involved in sport both in the participation and management sectors. Also, the community has been well-educated in the importance and the role of sports in the lives of girls and women. Bahraini women have demonstrated their potential and abilities as managers and performers, although the level and nature of their involvement in sport will continue to be determined by the social and cultural behaviours accepted and required by an adherence to Islam and the traditional values of an Islamic society.

Notes

1 Mrs Layla Al-Enzoor, retired, formerly worked as a leader in PE curriculum at the Ministry of Education, Bahrain; a member of different national and international sports committees. Mrs Seham Hijres, retired, formerly worked as a leader at GOYS, Bahrain; a member of different national and international sports committees.
2 Professor Huda Al-Khaja, former dean for students affairs, University of Bahrain; a member of SCYS; a president of the Bahraini Gymnastics Federation; a member of different national and international sports committees.
3 Hayat Bint Abdulaziz Al Khalifa, former president of the Bahraini Table Tennis Association (2000); former member of BOC; vice-president of the Arab Association of Table Tennis; a member of different national and international sports committees; a board member of the West Asian Sports Association; chairperson of women's sport at the West Asian Sports Association; a member of the women's sport committee at the Asian Olympic Committee.
4 Professor Huda Alkhaja, former Dean for Students Affairs, University of Bahrain;

a member of SCYS; a president of the Bahraini Gymnastic Federation; a member of different national and international sports committees.

5 Dr Samya Al-Gatan, board member of the Bahraini Swimming Federation; former board member of the Bahraini Badminton Federation; a member of different committees.

Dr Aysha Al-Amer, board member of the Bahraini Gymnastics Federation (2004); a member of different committees.

Dr Amal Al-Jouder, former board member of the Bahraini Tennis Federation; a member of different committees.

Lubna Alnayem, former board member of the Bahraini Athletic Federation.

Nahed Al-Afnan, board member of the Bahraini Fencing Federation.

Sameera Asiri, former board member of the Bahraini Badminton Federation.

Lateefa Sharaf Aldeen, board member of the Bahraini Cycling Federation.

Reem Mansory, Women's Committee, Bahrain Volleyball Federation.

Wafa Al-Jazaf, Women's Committee, Bahrain Table Tennis Federation.

Wafa Al-Mula, Women's Committee, Bahrain Table Tennis Federation.

Fatima Al-Shekar, Women's Committee, Bahrain Water Sports Federation.

Fatima Hasan, a leader at DPA; table tennis referee; a member of different national federations.

Kulood Al-Mugla, a leader at DPA; table tennis referee; a member in different national federations.

Nabeela Al-Dosari, a leader at DPA; table tennis referee; a member of different national federations.

Rania Shawkat, a leader at DPA; table tennis referee; a member of different national federations.

Manal Hassan, a leader at DPA; table tennis referee; a member of different national federations.

SH. Hisa Bint Khalid Al-Khalifa, head of Women Sports in Rifaa Club.

Hayfa Malalla, former member of the Women's Committee, BOC.

6 Dr Shaikh Al-Jeeb, Director of the DPE, Ministry of Education, Bahrain; former member of BOC; a member of different national and international sports and physical-education committees, e.g. a member of the Women's Committee in a number of the Arab federations for physical education; vice-president of the Organising Committee of Physical Education of the Arabian Gulf countries.

References

Al-Ansari, M. (2008) *Women's Sport: a Future Direction*, Paper presented at the First International Conference in Physical Education and Sports Science, Kuwait, College of Basic Education (in Arabic).

Al-Jeeb, S. (1990) Non-Participation of Secondary School Girls in the Competitive Sports Programmes in Bahrain, unpublished Master's dissertation: 18–19, Cairo: Helwan University (in Arabic).

Al-Jeeb, S. (2004) *The Status of Physical Education and Sports for Girls in Bahraini Schools*, Paper presented at the Second Arabic Symposium for Women's Sports, Arab Countries University, Cairo (in Arabic).

Al-Khaja, H. (2001) *Women & Sport in the Kingdom of Bahrain*, Paper presented at the IOC's Regional Seminar on Women and Sports, Bahrain.

Al-Khaja, H. (2002) Woman and Sports in the State of Bahrain, *Bulletin of IAPESGW, International Association of Physical Education and Sport for Girls and Women*, 11: 7–10.

Al-Khalifa, H. and Al-Enzoor, L. (2005) *Women's Competitive Sport in Bahrain*, Women Sport Committee, Bahrain Olympic Committee (in Arabic).

Statistical Abstract (2006) Central Informative Organization, Directorate of Statistics, Bahrain.
http://multimedia.olympic.org/pdf/en_report_756.pdf (accessed 3 December 2008).
http://multimedia.olympic.org/pdf/en_report_757.pdf (accessed 3 December 2008).
www.scw.gov.bh//media/pp-may08.ppt#265,9 (accessed 7 September 2009).
www.shura.bh/En/Council/MPs/Pages/default.aspx (accessed 7 September 2009).
www.nuwab.gov.bh/ServicesCenter/Members/Search.aspx (accessed 7 September 2009).
www.olympic.org/uk/organisation/noc/noc_uk.asp?noc_initials=BRN.

5 'Ich tänzele so zwischen den Kulturen ...'

Bewegung, Spiel und Sport muslimischer Mädchen und Frauen in Deutschland

'Balancing between the cultures ...'
Sports and physical activities of Muslim girls and women in Germany

Christa Kleindienst-Cachay

Editors' introduction

The situation for Muslim women in sport in Germany is important because of the large immigrant population of this European country. The discourse of integration and the role of sport are explored, indicating that only small numbers of Muslim girls and women participate in sport. There are multiple reasons for this, as should be expected given the heterogeneity of the group. The greatest problems are for those Muslim women seeking accommodation of religious requirements for sex-segregation, privacy in changing and formal approval to cover the hair after puberty. Recent research indicates changes in the arena of elite sport as some Muslim women are becoming agents of change, using sport to challenge cultural and family restrictions while retaining important aspects of religious observance.

Muslims in Germany

Like many other European countries, Germany has long been a destination for immigrants, even if this may not be the accepted view in official German politics. Considering the fact that of the 82 million people living in Germany, over 15 million have a background of migration, this is something that can no longer be denied. It means that almost one-fifth of the German population comes from abroad or has parents or grandparents who originally came here as immigrants (cf. Statistisches Bundesamt 2006). In the large towns of western Germany, for example Hamburg, children and adolescents with a migration background already make up 50 per cent of young age groups (Stadt Hamburg 2006). Among these are some 3.5 to four million Muslims, the majority of whom are of Turkish origin (52 per cent). Besides the Turkish Muslims living in Germany, there are also Muslims from ex-Yugoslavia (Bosnia-Herzegovina), Iran, Morocco and Afghanistan. The largest faith group among the Muslims, in terms of numbers, is that of the Sunnis, who make up 80 per cent of all Muslims in Germany, followed by the Alevites and the Shiites (17 per cent and 3 per cent respectively) (Bundesministerium des Innern 2006).

Observable in recent years among some of the Turkish economic migrants has been a strong resurgence of interest in religion and in the culture and traditions of their country of origin (Gesemann 2006: 9–10). By contrast, there are also groups that can be considered religiously indifferent and these have come to resemble German mainstream society as far as educational levels, career and way of life are concerned (Gesemann 2006: 8–9).

The discourse on integration in Germany

Until recently, German politicians have largely ignored the potentially explosive problem of integration, partly because it was widely assumed that the migrants would automatically assimilate over a period of time. Although there are dedicated bodies with so-called commissioners for foreign citizens (as well as several migrant support schemes[1] at national and regional levels) who are required to draw up reports on their activities,[2] it is only since 2006 that intensive efforts have been made at the national political level to improve the integration of migrants in society. This is particularly the case for the migrant population with a Muslim background since it is mainly this group that is considered to be farthest removed from the mainstream of German society (Berlin-Institut für Bevölkerung und Entwicklung 2009: 7ff).

Since 2006, for example, several 'integration summits' and two 'Islam Conferences' have been convened by the German government (Bundesministerium des Innern 2006). The reason for these intensified efforts to improve integration is that, in spite of guaranteed equal rights in principle, the migrant population in Germany continues to suffer considerably from social inequality and discrimination. It is true, for instance, that migrants have the same opportunities in education and careers, but in reality this population is disadvantaged in many areas of society. This applies especially to educational qualifications, access to the labour market, career advancement and participation in the political life of the country (Deutsches PISA Konsortium 2002; Beauftragte der Bundesregierung 2007; Berlin-Institut für Bevölkerung und Entwicklung 2009).

Sports clubs and associations were among the first social areas to establish initiatives to improve integration. As early as the 1980s, a federal programme called 'Integration Through Sport' was introduced, which was designed to encourage migrants to join German sports clubs and, since the beginning of the 1990s, has received funding amounting to over 90 million euros. From the 1980s, moreover, numerous ethnic sports clubs have been founded by immigrants themselves, which belong to the network of ethnic, mainly Turkish, communities but at the same time are members of German sports federations. These ethnic sports clubs, though, mainly attract male migrants since their activity is largely restricted to football. Up to the present, they have seldom provided sports for girls and women (Halm 2003).

Participation of Muslim girls and women in sports and physical activities

Although in recent years the German media have drawn attention to increasing numbers of successful sportswomen with a Muslim background, such as Fatmire Bajramaj, who plays in the German national football team, Sümeye Gülec, Olympic participant in taekwondo, or the boxer Julia Sahin, the proportion of Muslim women who are active either in club sports or in more informal sporting activities is very small compared with the German population as a whole. This is especially true of adult women who, according to estimates of the sports federations, account for a mere 5 per cent of club members (Landessportbund Nordrhein-Westfalen 2004: 15; cf. Halm 2007: 105).

By contrast, according to the 2008/2009 *Sports Yearbook*, the overall proportion of German women active in sport amounts to 22.27 per cent (Deutscher Olympischer Sportbund 2008: 89). Since German sport is mainly organised around sports clubs (in contrast to Anglo-American countries, university sports play only a very subordinate role in Germany), the membership figures of sports clubs can be seen as a significant indicator of the participation in sports by particular social groups.

As is to be expected, significantly higher figures of female Muslims participating in sports are to be found in children's and adolescent age groups. A study undertaken by the German Youth Institute in the year 2000, for example, in which five-to-eleven-year-olds were surveyed, 21 per cent of girls from migrant backgrounds reported that they took part in club sports, especially football and combat sports/martial arts, but also in gymnastics, swimming and track-and-field athletics. This study, which included sports provided not only by clubs but also by cultural societies and youth clubs, also shows that the proportion of German girls active in sports clubs remains much higher, namely 58 per cent. Similar differences are manifest in two new studies, the World Vision Children's Study (Hurrelmann and Andresen 2007: 175) and the Child and Youth Health Survey (KiGGS) carried out by the Robert Koch Institute. These reveal that girls from migrant backgrounds have up to three times less chance of being able to take part in club sports than girls in the mainstream of society. Within the category of female migrants, Muslims (meaning, in Germany, especially Turkish girls) form the group that is farthest removed from sports (Kleindienst-Cachay 1993: 205f., Mutz 2009: 110). Only 20 per cent of 15-year-old Turkish girls are members of organised sports clubs, whereas the corresponding figure for German girls is 42 per cent (Mutz 2009: 108 f.).

Finally, the extent to which girls and women from migration backgrounds do sports in the commercial sector, for example fitness centres and sports schools, is still largely unknown. It is known that many girls and women from migration backgrounds who are interested in combat sports, especially many young

Muslim women, join commercial combat sports schools rather than sports clubs. Drawing on an older study, Brinkhoff and Sack (1999) conclude that as many as 22.2 per cent of the Turkish girls surveyed and 21 per cent of women 'reset-tlers',[3] predominantly from the former Soviet Union and Poland, do sports in commercial sports facilities. Again, though, the number of German girls engaged in sporting activities at private sports schools is almost double (40 per cent).

The extent to which immigrant girls take part in extra-curricular sporting activities at school, however, should not be underestimated. For example, *Haupt-schulen*, schools with the lowest educational standards in Germany's three-tier secondary education system, tend to have the highest numbers of pupils with migration backgrounds.[4] The results of a survey conducted in these schools indi-cated that as many as 34 per cent of the girls reported that they took part in after-school sports groups, whereas the corresponding figure for German girls is only 17 per cent (although they do a little more sport at sports clubs – see Frohn 2006: 178). These extracurricular sports activities differ from ordinary sports lessons in that only girls take part whilst compulsory physical education in German schools is co-educational. In only two of the 16 federal states of Germany (Bavaria and Baden-Wurttemberg) is it mandatory to separate boys and girls from the age of 14 in sports lessons. The other federal states schools are free to choose themselves whether or not to separate the sexes, but it is seldom practised.

Despite the lower participation level of girls from migrant backgrounds in sport that has been diagnosed, it would be a mistake to draw the conclusion that they are not at all interested in sport. This is reflected in the fact that as many as 45 per cent of the young migrant women surveyed express the wish to do more sport in their leisure time. Especially prominent is the wish to learn self-defence (Boos-Nünning and Karakasoglu 2005: 5).

In summary, it can be stated that, as a group, Muslim girls and women in Germany participate in sport to only a very small degree. Above all, few of them have so far taken the opportunity to join German sports clubs. Ethnic sports clubs, however, which would be expected to have a greater attraction for these girls and women on account of the cultural and religious customs practised there, have so far failed to provide virtually any sports for women.

Causes of the limited participation of Muslim girls and women in sport

When examining these migrant background-related data on the participation of girls and women in sports, it must be taken into account that there is consider-able overlap between the categories of 'gender', 'ethnicity' and 'social stratum'. As various empirical studies have demonstrated, the numbers of German girls as well as young German males from the lower social strata who take up sport are much smaller, proportionally, than those of higher socio-economic groups (Hur-relmann and Andresen 2007: 175; Lampert *et al.* 2007: 638). Since a large section of the migrant population (of whom the majority are Muslims) belongs to the two lowest social strata,[5] the question arises whether (and, if so, to what extent) social class is a determining factor in levels of participation in sport; in other words, whether effects of intersectionality arise from the different categories of gender, ethnicity and social stratum, and what these effects are.

That a lack of education is at least partly responsible for non-participation in sport is corroborated by many empirical studies which have established a link between low levels of education and sports inactivity. With rising levels of education, the number of young female migrants active in club sports increases considerably (Kleindienst-Cachay 2007: 23). Similarly, the higher the aspirations of young people are with regard to educational qualifications, the greater their willingness to take part in sports. These two attitudes, the desire for a good education on the one hand and to take part in sport (with success) on the other, correspond to a willingness to develop ties with the host society, make an effort to live in the country permanently and be able to work there.

These considerations are an indication that, in searching for reasons for the widespread lack of participation in sport among women Muslims, ethnic background and adherence to the Islamic faith are not the only deterring factors. There is also a wide range of chiefly socio-economic, educational and social-class-related factors.

At the same time, it must be said that amongst migrant families, especially of Turkish-Muslim origin, in many cases it is also religio-culturally motivated values and norms that, if not prevent, then at least restrict sports activity amongst girls from adolescence onwards and amongst adult women. This is not only discussed in the pertinent literature on matters of Islam (see, for example, Rohe 2001; Boos-Nünning 2007), but is also reflected in interviews with experts and Muslim sportswomen (Kleindienst-Cachay 2007: 25ff).

Religio-cultural rules, which apply to many Muslim girls in Germany from their first menstruation, can make participation in sporting activities very difficult. Family preferences at this life stage sometimes lead to gender segregation, supervision of (unmarried) daughters by adult family members that limits movement outside the home, and covering of the body to ensure modesty of appearance, including in sporting contexts. Since public nudity, even in same-sex groups, is not allowed, changing and showering arrangements in German sports clubs can be difficult for Muslim women because private spaces are rarely available. The Western sport culture related to dress and mixed-sex environments consequently sometimes conflicts with religious requirements and the moral preferences of Muslim families.

There can be parental reluctance to allow daughters to participate in sport, unless there are changes in the nature of current provision, to accommodate religious requirements. Some Muslim girls give up certain sports on reaching puberty. Although in German organised sport there is no formal ban on wearing the *hijab* (or headscarf), wider norms of sports dress and organisation in clubs and competitions are reasons why some Muslim girls either give up sport altogether or move to a more 'covered' sport such as martial arts. A karate sportswoman reported, for example, that at the onset of puberty she had given up swimming as a sport because of her father's wishes and instead moved into

martial arts on account of the more modest clothing. A friend of hers had suggested: 'Well, why not do karate [...]? There you've got to wear a long coat and
long trousers. Your father won't say anything to that, I'm sure' (Kleindienst-
Cachay 2007: 29). Karate and taekwondo are popular amongst Muslim young
women. In addition to dress code, another reason for their popularity is that, like
boxing and kickboxing, they are widely popular in Germany's Turkish communities. With large numbers of family and acquaintances attending from the local
community, parents are often reassured about the supervision of their daughters.

Although the wearing of the *hijab*, or headscarf, is not formally forbidden,[6]
they are seldom worn in German competitive sports. In physical-education
lessons in schools, however, the *hijab* is commonly worn by Muslim girls. Currently, newly designed swimwear, the so-called 'Burkini', or other long-sleeved
and long-legged clothes, which conform with Muslim codes of modesty, are
worn during swimming lessons. Physical-education teachers favour this type of
clothing because it allows Muslim girls to participate in swimming lessons.

The great importance that is attached to the observance of the faith-based
rules in many Muslim families in Germany, even those which may, to all
outward appearances, seem assimilated, is founded on the tenets of women's
chastity and virginity, on which the honour of the family is based. This 'honour'
is of great significance, particularly to fathers, within the Turkish migrant society
in which the family is embedded. The 'protection' of daughters is part of safe-
guarding family honour.

Religiosity, or the intensity with which the family observes the rules of its
faith, was found to be a contributory factor to women's non-participation in sport
in an empirical quantitative study undertaken by Boos-Nünning and Karakasoglu
(2005b: 25ff.). When Muslim girls in this German representative survey were
asked whether or not they participated in sport in their leisure time, 100 per cent
of the girls who wore a *hijab* and reported that they were not allowed to leave
the home unsupervised, replied in the negative, whereas 15 per cent of the
Muslim girls who did not wear a headscarf answered in the affirmative.[7]

The socialising effects of participating in sports: 'I think of it as balancing between the cultures'

Sport as a catalyst for development processes in youth

In recent years a development has been observable in German sport that seems
to contradict the research results presented above. From the very group of girls
and women with migration backgrounds that are regarded as being the farthest
removed from sport, namely those of the daughters of Turkish-Muslim economic
migrants, there are suddenly appearing successful top-level sportswomen.
Success is being achieved notably in the martial arts and combat sports like
karate, taekwondo and boxing, but also in football and in other sports too.

How can it be explained that some Muslim girls and young women have
crossed the boundaries of their culture, and what consequences do long years of

commitment to sport and intensive training for competitions have for the socialisation of these young women? Tentative answers to these questions are provided by
a number of recent academic studies carried out with young Muslim sportswomen,
in which they have given information about themselves in semi-structured, qualitative interviews.[8] The statements made in the interviews reveal that sport frequently
acts as a catalyst in the processes of young people's development.

Influenced by their interaction and communication with others in sport, for
example within a team or in the club, the young women go through an intense
process in which they encounter, or are confronted with, the different norms and
values of various cultures. This, in turn, has a positive effect on important tasks
required of adolescents, which include processes of developing a self-concept as
well as a capacity for decision-making in the areas of education and career, the
body and sexuality, friendships and partnerships. It is likely, moreover, that
intergenerational transmission processes occur with regard to norms and practices (Nauck 2001), meaning that all this has an effect on the parent generation.
Ultimately, younger brothers and sisters benefit from these intergenerational
changes.

Influences on education and career

Young Muslim women in the sporting context speak of positive changes in self-
confidence, esteem and of feeling good, as well as the spin-off in motivation and
drive to 'go to the limit' (Kleindienst-Cachay 2000: 498). In some cases this has
influenced their behaviour and ambitions in the field of education. Several of the
sportswomen interviewed reported that at some time in their sporting careers
they had made the decision either to continue or resume their education, or to
start improving their vocational qualifications:

> When you go to training three or four times a week, and then have the
> chance four or five times a year to compare yourself with others, and you're
> still right at the top, then that really gets the adrenalin pumping, and you say
> to yourself: 'You can do more, you can do better'.... So, if I hadn't been so
> successful in sport, I don't think it would have entered my head to go on
> with my education, to do my *Abitur* [university entrance examination] and
> to study.

(Kleindienst-Cachay 2007: 45)[9]

Out of the 18 adult sportswomen surveyed (all with working-class backgrounds),
nine have passed the *Abitur*, entitling them without restriction to a place at university, and a further four have qualifications that enable them to study a
restricted range of subjects at a college of higher education. Thus, 13 out of the
18 women (more than 72 per cent!) are in possession of the two highest school-
leaving qualifications in Germany. A further four women have a school-leaving
certificate from a *Realschule* while one of them has a school-leaving certificate
from a *Hauptschule* (the second and third types of school respectively, below the

Gymnasium, in the German secondary school hierarchy). These figures are above the average level of education among young Turkish Muslim women. In comparison, according to the latest report of the Federal Government's Commissioner for Integration, only 11.3 per cent of all non-German female school leavers in 2005 were in possession of the *Abitur*, and 17.5 per cent of the girls belonging to this group left school without any qualifications whatsoever (Beauftragte der Bundesregierung für Migration, Flüchtlinge und Integration 2007: 59).[10]

The question arises how this conspicuous cluster of high-educational qualifications among the elite Muslim sportswomen surveyed can be explained, and how the level of education and the unusually intensive involvement in sport of this group may be linked. Empirical surveys have shown that sports participation among both men and women correlates with levels of education in terms of school-leaving qualifications, and that this equally applies to migrants (Halm 2003).[11] In addition, the 2000 OECD PISA study revealed that active recreational pastimes, such as a sport, correlate to a large degree with good academic achievement (Deutsches PISA Konsortium *et al.* 2002: 31–32). This means, on the one hand, that certain pre-selection processes can be assumed to have taken place among the elite sportswomen surveyed; that is to say, they are active in sport because they are also achievement-oriented in other spheres, for example education. On the other hand, the statements made by the women in the interviews (namely their own assessment of themselves) clearly point in the opposite direction of their educational aspirations having been influenced by sport, signifying a positive socialising effect through sports activity:

> My development moved steadily forwards; it grew and grew.... Because of the fact that you were fairly successful in sport, you hoped for other things in life, too, and because you got to know different points of view ..., different orientations, different aspects which were worth thinking over and which you kept in mind when thinking about things [...]. Life at home and life at school and at the club were worlds apart.
>
> (Kleindienst-Cachay 2007: 47)

This Muslim sportswoman emphasised that, along with her sporting success, her self-assurance grew and grew, so that the idea of extending this striving for achievement to other areas besides sport seemed only natural:

> When it became clear to me that, with lots of ambition, I could achieve nearly everything in life, I wanted to have success not just in sport but in my career, too. I had no wish to follow this typical picture of Turkish women. I wanted more from my life, and I began systematically to develop my style.... I've always thought: 'I want to do it, and if I put all my energy into it, I'll manage it' – and I've managed it.
>
> (Kleindienst-Cachay 2007: 47)

Besides the increased incentive as a result of sporting success, there is also the motivating effect of contact and conversations with fellow sportswomen and sportsmen, the majority of whom are studying for a profession, as well as with teachers, coaches and trainers:

> Well, it was mainly people or friends who also studied or had got their *Abitur* and sometimes talked about things, where you sat there and asked yourself: 'What are they talking about?' And you couldn't join in, and you thought you'd also like to be able to make a contribution, or express your view of things.
>
> (Kleindienst-Cachay 2007: 47)

It would be wrong to assume a simple causality between doing sport in the domain of elite sports and educational ambition and success. What is plausible, however, is the transmission of certain elements of achievement motivation, for example the concept of 'hope for success'. If, as a result of repeated success in competitions, young people acquire a 'hope for success' orientation (in contrast to a 'fear of failure' orientation) in the course of their socialisation in sport, it appears plausible to assume that transfer effects have taken place between the area of sport and the area of school education.

Body practices and greater acceptance of the body

With regard to attitudes towards one's own body and the system of values connected with it, it can be observed that all the Muslim sportswomen interviewed have made the effort to come to terms with the different body practices in the various cultures. In sports teams, the significance of various rules in the use and management of the body are frequent topics of conversation, as are diverging norms of sexual behaviour. Such interactions can lead to reflection on personal stances concerning identity and living in two cultures – for example, over issues such as dress codes and sex-segregation in a predominantly non-Muslim country. Personal struggles, including negotiating the space between cultures, can lead to decision-making that reasserts or rejects commitment to certain practices and modifies others. Central to the experiences of the women was their self-determination in defining ways to accommodate their position, a sense of having the confidence to make personal choices. In the study, for example, some rejected the wearing of the *hijab* when playing sport but insisted on observance of other rules regarding alcohol or the eating of pork. Others wanted longer shorts in football to cover the legs more fully and acceptance of fasting in Ramadan. Their own ways of managing this were understood (Kleindienst-Cachay 2007: 29). In the interviews it was clear that the young women wanted the observance or non-observance of such rules to be understood as decisions they had reached themselves, individually, after giving the questions much thought and not just as a matter of adapting to prescribed norms.

A positive body image was another outcome of Muslim women's experiences of sport. They described their increasingly athletic bodies as 'strong', 'determined' and 'reliable', as well as 'beautiful' and 'desirable'. Many had also received complements on their skill levels and competence in male-dominated sporting environments:

> Training makes you very strong, as a woman, too ... you notice that you get a beautiful body, you don't get fat ... and that is always noticeable; people look at you, you get recognition from outside. You feel good as a woman ... my father was always strict and stern about things ... and you always had to hide yourself, like. That wasn't so nice. When you could show yourself, that was always good. You got recognition, ... you felt so self-confident.
>
> (Kleindienst-Cachay 2007: 45)

Such public reference to beauty, strength and bodies contrasts with the women's experiences at home and also with views of some other Muslim women whose concept of bodies and beauty is private and for sharing only with family.

Forming a separate, mixed-ethnicity circle of friends and acquaintances

Sport provides the opportunity to communicate and interact in groups that are heterogeneous in terms of age, sex and ethnicity. Especially for Muslim girls and young women, who beyond the school gates often have little contact with children or adolescents of the same age, and even less with German children or adolescents (Dollase *et al.* 1999; Fischer and Münchmeier 2000), developing friendly relationships through sport means an enormous enrichment to their lives. It is not surprising, then, that adolescents from migration backgrounds who belong to sports clubs attach significantly more importance to their friends and networks of friendly contacts than peer groups who are not members of sports clubs (Fussan 2007: 304). The Turkish sportswomen who were interviewed valued and took the opportunity to find friends and acquaintances in sport. This is shown especially among the 15-to-16-year-old Muslim girls from the mixed-ethnicity football team that was studied:

> Yes, well, it was because of that [the social contact] that I did it ... because I don't go anywhere much, always at home. I thought it would be a chance to meet friends. We talk there, we don't just do sport, after training we talk ... like, once a week, and other than that there's no possibility.
>
> (Kuzmik 1998: 35)

In educational studies and development psychology, the peer group in sport is regarded as an important moderator variable in necessary youth development processes, for example in accepting one's own biological body, in developing one's own norms and values, or in coping successfully with school and work

(Brinkhoff 1998; Fend 2003: 22ff.). This is especially true of the young football players interviewed, who relate the group at the sports club to social resources such as 'solidarity', 'trust' and 'support', and look upon their team as 'almost something like a family' (Kuzmik 1998: 64). As the interviews with adult top-level Muslim sportswomen show, when looking back at their own life history, they regard the readiness to talk amongst sports friends as a significant social resource which they also made use of in everyday conflicts, for instance with their parents or at school:

> My sports mates really did help me. And I had someone I was especially attached to – my coach.... I could sit down with him and sort of talk about myself and [about a difficult personal problem] ... they all gave me strength ...
>
> (Kleindienst-Cachay 2007: 48)

Sport makes it possible to 'balance' between different cultures

This study on Muslim women in sport in Germany shows how they negotiated their way between two cultures and provides useful insights for those interested in the experiences of Muslim women in diaspora situations. With the women's decision to go on doing sport at the onset of puberty, often in spite of their parents' initial opposition, and to tie themselves to the German system of sport and education, the girls made a conscious decision in favour of working towards excellence in sport, and becoming totally different types of role models than their families could have anticipated. They are studying (at school or university) or working in their profession, often as a teacher, or as a clerk in commercial or industrial companies, or as a doctor's medical assistant. Empowerment, through sport, has enabled these young women with migrant backgrounds to re-define the relationship of gender, bodies and faith for themselves. This new image of themselves as young women who live, work and do sport in Germany and have a Turkish background is determined by their 'own modernisation project', which by no means corresponds to Western ideas of modernisation in all respects (Herwartz-Emden and Westphal 1997). It may be conceived of, rather, as an attempt to create a viable, albeit tension-filled, balance between the different cultures. It offers, furthermore, the opportunity of constructing a 'unique' identity, namely that of the Turkish Muslim woman who may live according to certain traditions, but who at the same time is successful in top-level sports in groups that are largely German and, what is more, in a 'male preserve' such as a combat sport or football. A boxer sums up this construction of a special identity in a passage of the interview in which she reports on her social standing and the recognition she gained among male adolescents of the same age, also of Turkish origin, who trained alongside her at the boxing club:

> They said: 'Hey, she's cool. She does all that, and she's a girl and ... she trains with us; but she still has her rules, and her values, and she still keeps up with her school work ...; and she's ambitious and successful.' ... They

were proud of me. And also that I never neglected the religious bit, that I had clear principles.

(Kleindienst-Cachay 2007: 49)

Asked what she felt about this way of life with, and in, two different cultures, this sportswoman said without hesitation:

> Really, I think of it as balancing between the cultures, but it isn't as though you fall between them. You know where you belong. You've got definite roots, where you come from, what you are. But in both cultures there are positive things.

(Kleindienst-Cachay 2007: 49)

Perceptible, too, are the efforts of the young women to fulfil the different, often ambivalent, demands made of them in spite of sometimes enormous difficulty. This is frequently noticeable from the very beginning because of the sports they choose, but also because of the way they dress for their particular sport, the way they perform certain body techniques, what they eat, the way they observe fasting during Ramadan, and especially because of the partners they choose and the way they observe the rule on virginity (Kleindienst-Cachay 2007: 28ff.). Thus, the process of getting to know people, reflecting on new ideas and re-defining norms and values in the course of their sporting careers results in a tension-filled balance of different cultural practices and the opportunity of 'living in many worlds', something which Boos-Nünning and Karakasoglu (2005a) regard as typical today for many young female migrants. An important, exoge-nous prerequisite for the success of each individual correlation, however, is that the parents are to some degree willing to discuss these issues, even though this willingness in some families was, at first, in a rudimentary stage of development and, in effect, had to be nurtured by their daughters' actions.[12] Of the 18 families with daughters interested in sport in the study, eight supported their daughters' interest, six were indifferent and four had experienced conflicts (Kleindienst-Cachay 2007: 32ff.). Sport became a source of empowerment for those facing the greatest problems, and today the families are reconciled.

The range of experiences encountered amongst this small group indicates how distinctive each family situation is, and that multiple influences impact on the life experiences of Muslim women in sport, as for all women. It would be wrong to conclude from the 'successful' examples of socialisation depicted that a life 'in many worlds' is free of risk (Boos-Nünning and Karakasoglu 2005a). Indeed, the strategies described for balancing between the world of Muslim culture on the one side, and the sports world of the majority society on the other, may not only lead to both external and internal conflicts. The risk of failing to construct one's own identity or merely of giving up sport out of a sense of resig-nation, causing possible later recriminations directed towards oneself, are courses of development that cannot be ruled out. Whilst the structures of sport, in some cases, have to change to accommodate the needs of some Muslim women, the cultural beliefs that associate sport with negative influences in women's lives also need to be challenged and changed.

How many 'drop-outs' there are in the field of sport among Muslim girls and women has so far not been established. The women we interviewed, all of them successful sportswomen, would appear to have emerged stronger from the conflicts they described. In the interviews, they give themselves the credit of having solved their problems. This can be viewed as an indicator for experiencing a sense of 'self-effectiveness', which in turn is a major prerequisite for preserving one's identity.

Notes

1 See, for example, 'Integration Through Sport', a programme funded by the Federal Ministry of the Interior that was originally planned for only the group of resettlers from eastern European countries: www.integration-durch-sport.de.

2 See the annual reports (since 2001) of the Beauftragte der Bundesregierung.

3 'Resettlers' is a term used for ethnic Germans who have resettled in Germany from former German settlements, mainly in eastern Europe.

4 In terms of income, education and occupation, the overwhelming majority of migrants living in Germany belong to the two lowest social strata (Beauftragte der Bundesregierung für Migration, Flüchtlinge und Integration 2007: 115ff.); by far the largest group in the lowest stratum is made up the population of Turkish origin (cf. Alt 2006: 11). In addition, migrants are significantly more prone to poverty than the German population, the ratio being 34 per cent to 25 per cent (cf. Beauftragte der Bundesregierung 2007: 117).

5 A comparison of the different school types in Germany's three-tier secondary school system shows that 25 per cent of girls with a migration background who attend the *Realschule* (the intermediate educational level) are active in club sports while the corresponding figure for girls with a migration background attending the *Hauptschule* (the lower educational level) is only 14 per cent (cf. Kleindienst-Cachay 1993). This correlation is corroborated by the results of the Shell Youth Study of 2000, as well as by data of the Socio-economic Panel of 2001. Cf. the reanalyses of Fussan and Nobis (2007: 277ff.) and the research of Mutz (2009).

6 Muslim women teachers are not allowed to wear the *hijab* or headscarves in school, whilst pupils are.

7 A similar interpretation of the correlation between little sports activity and strict observance of traditional religious rules among Muslim women in Egypt is to be found in Walseth and Fasting (2003: 56ff.)

8 For a discussion of the paradigm shift in Educational Studies, see Diehm (1999); for the corresponding discourse in the Social Sciences, see Beck-Gernsheim (2004: 52ff.).

9 The results presented in the following are from the project 'Sport Socialisation and Identity Development Among Muslim Girls and Women in Germany Who Are Highly Active in Sport', for which 18 top-level sportswomen, among them world champions and Olympic participants (mainly active in football and martial arts, but one or two of them in volleyball, handball, American football, gymnastics and dance, as well as six adolescent football players), all of them daughters of economic migrants, were studied (Kleindienst-Cachay 2000, 2007; Kleindienst-Cachay and Kuzmik 2006; Linneweh 2007).

10 In the same year, 31.1 per cent of young German women and 23.1 per cent of young German men passed the *Abitur* exam (cf. Beauftragte der Bundesregierung für Migration, Flüchtlinge und Integration 2007: 59).

11 According to Halm, 81 per cent of the non-German males with no educational qualifi-

cations who were surveyed did no sport at all, while among non-German males with *Abitur*, the figure was only 54 per cent (Halm 2003). See also Boos-Nünning and Karakasoglu 2005b and, with regard to pupils at *Hauptschulen* and *Realschulen*, see Kleindienst-Cachay 1993.

12 Cf. Ofner, who, with regard to the educational careers of Turkish women academics in Germany, established that both sides, for example parents and daughters, managed to reach a compromise and find a modus vivendi during the daughters' process of emancipation from the family, irrespective of how liberal or strict the methods were in the individual families of bringing up the children (Ofner 2003: 239).

References

Alt, C. (2006) Milieu oder Migration – was zählt mehr? [Milieu or Migration – What Counts More?] *DJI Bulletin* 76, 3: 10–11.

Beauftragte der Bundesregierung für Migration, Flüchtlinge und Integration [The Federal Commissioner for Migration, Refugees and Integration] (2007) *Siebter Bericht über die Lage der Ausländerinnen und Ausländer in Deutschland.* [*Seventh Report on the Situation of Foreigners in Germany.*] Berlin.

Beck-Gernsheim, E. (2004) *Wir und die anderen.* [*We and the Others.*] Frankfurt: Suhrkamp.

Berlin-Institut für Bevölkerung und Entwicklung [Berlin Institute for Population and Development] (2009) *Ungenutzte Potentiale: Zur Lage der Integration in Deutschland.* [*Unused Potential: On the State of Integration in Germany.*] Online, available at: www.berlin-institut.org (accessed 27 January 2009).

Boos-Nünning, U. (2007) Religiosität junger Musliminnen im Einwandererkontext. [Religiousness Among Young Female Muslims in a Migration Context.] In H.J. Wensierski and C. Lübcke (eds) *Junge Muslime in Deutschland.* [*Young Muslims in Germany.*] Opladen: Verlag Barbara Budrich: 117–134.

Boos-Nünning, U. and Karakasoglu, Y. (2005a) *Viele Welten leben: Zur Lebenssituation von Mädchen und jungen Frauen mit Migrationshintergrund.* [*Living in Many Worlds: On the Situation of Girls and Young Women from Migrant Backgrounds.*] Münster: Waxmann Verlag.

Boos-Nünning, U. and Karakasoglu, Y. (2005b) *Viele Welten leben: Zur Lebenssituation von Mädchen und jungen Frauen mit Migrationshintergrund.* [*Living in Many Worlds: On the Situation of Girls and Young Women from Migrant Backgrounds.*] Sonderauswertung 'Sport' Quelle: www.bmfsfj.bund.de.

Brinkhoff, K.-P. (1998) *Sport und Sozialisation im Jugendalter: Entwicklung, soziale Unterstützung und Gesundheit.* [*Sport and Socialisation in Adolescence: Development, Social Support and Health.*] Weinheim: Juventa.

Brinkhoff, K.P. and Sack, H.G. (1999) *Sport und Gesundheit im Kindesalter: Der Sportverein im Bewegungsleben der Kinder.* [*Sport and Health in Childhood: The Sports Club in Children's Active Lives.*] Weinheim und München: Juventa.

Bröskamp, B. (1994) *Körperliche Fremdheit: Zum Problem der interkulturellen Begegnung im Sport.* [*Bodily 'Otherness': On the Problem of Cross-Cultural Encounters in Sport.*] St. Augustin: Academia Verlag.

Bundesministerium des Innern [Federal Ministry of the Interior] (2006) Deutsche Islamkonferenz. [German Islam Conference.] Online, available at: www.bmi.bund.de//nn_1018358/Internet/Content/Nachrichten/Pressemitteilungen/2006/Einzelseiten/Islamkonferenz (accessed 18 December 2008).

Deutscher Olympischer Sportbund [German Olympic Sports Confederation] (2008) *Jahrbuch des Sports 2008/2009*. [*Sports Yearbook 2008/2009*.] Niedernhausen: Schors.

Deutscher Olympischer Sportbund (2008) www.integration-durch-sport.de.

Deutsches PISA Konsortium [German PISA Consortium] *et al.* (2002) *Sonderauswertung: Soziale Bedingungen von Schulleistungen: Zur Erfassung von Kontextmerkmalen durch Schüler-, Schul- und Elternfragebögen.* [*The Social Conditions of School Achievement: Gaining Relevant Data by Means of Pupils', Schools' and Parents' Questionnaires.*] Online, available at: www.mpib-berlin.mpg.de/pisa/kontextmerkmale. pdf (accessed 8 December 2008).

Diehm, I. (1999) Pädagogische Ent-Fremdung: Die Verdichtung von Differenz in der Figur 'fremder' Frauen und Mädchen. [Educational Alienation: The Consolidation of Differences in the Form of 'Other' Women and Girls.] In B. Rendtorff and V. Moser (eds) *Geschlecht und Geschlechterverhältnisse in der Erziehungswissenschaft: Eine Einführung* [*Gender and Gender Relations in Educational Science.*] Opladen: Leske und Budrich: 181–200.

Dollase, R. *et al.* (1999) Sind hohe Anteile ausländischer Schülerinnen in Schulklassen problematisch? [Do Large Percentages of Foreign Girls in School Classes Cause Problems?] *Journal für Konflikt- und Gewaltforschung* [*Conflict and Violence Research Journal*] 1: 56–83.

Fend, H. (2003) *Entwicklungspsychologie des Jugendalters*. [*Adolescent Development Psychology.*] Opladen: Leske und Budrich.

Fischer, A. and Münchmeier, R. (2000) *Jugend 2000.* [*Youth 2000.*] 13th Shell Jugendstudie. [13th Shell Youth Study.] Opladen.

Frohn, J. (2006) *Mädchen und Sport an der Hauptschule*. [*Girls and Sport at German Hauptschulen.*] Hohengehren: Schneider.

Fussan, N. (2007) Integration von Jugendlichen mit Migrationshintergrund in Peer Netzwerke: Sozialisationsvorteile sportvereinsorganisierter Jugendlicher. [Integration of Adolescents from Migration Backgrounds in Peer Networks: Advantages of Sports Club Membership in Adolescent Socialisation.] In T. Nobis and J. Baur (eds) *Soziale Integration vereinsorganisierter Jugendlicher* [*The Social Integration of Adolescent Members of Clubs.*] Köln: Strauß: 298–317.

Fussan, N. and Nobis, T. (2007) Zur Partizipation von Jugendlichen mit Migrationshintergrund in Sportvereinen. [On the Participation of Adolescents from a Migration Background in Sports Clubs.] In T. Nobis and J. Baur (eds) *Soziale Integration vereinsorganisierter Jugendlicher.* [*The Social Integration of Adolescent Members of Clubs.*] Köln: Strauß: 277–297.

Gesemann, F. (2006) *Die Integration junger Muslime in Deutschland: Bildung und Ausbildung als Schlüsselbereiche sozialer Integration.* [*The Integration of Young Muslims in Germany.*] Berlin: Friedrich-Ebert-Stiftung. Politische Akademie. Referat Interkultureller Dialog. Islam und Gesellschaft Nr. 5.

Halm, D. (2003) Türkische Zuwanderer im Deutschen Amateurfußball – Situation, Probleme und Perspektiven. [Turkish Migrants in German Amateur Football – Situation, Problems and Perspectives.] In A. Goldberg, D. Halm and M. Sauer (eds) *Migrationsbericht der Stiftung Zentrum für Türkeistudien. [Migration Report of the Centre of Turkish Studies Foundation.*] Münster: LIT: 9–62.

Halm, D. (2007) Freizeit, Medien und kulturelle Orientierungen junger Türkeistämmiger in Deutschland. [Leisure, Media and Cultural Orientations of Young People of Turkish Origin in Germany.] In H.J. Wensierski, and C. Lübcke (eds) *Junge Muslime in Deutschland. [Young Muslims in Germany.*] Opladen: Verlag Barbara Budrich: 101–113.

Herwartz-Emden, L. and Westphal, M. (1997) *Arbeitsmigrantinnen aus der Türkei in der Bundesrepublik Deutschland: Zwischen Emanzipation und Unterdrückung.* [*Women Migrants from Turkey in the Federal Republic of Germany: Between Emancipation and Oppression.*] Hannover: Niedersächsische Landeszentrale für Politik.

Hurrelmann, K. and Andresen, S. (2007) *Kinder in Deutschland. 1. World Vision Kinderstudie.* [*Children in Germany. 1st World Vision Children's Study.*] Frankfurt: Fischer.

Kleindienst-Cachay, C. (1993) *Forschungsprojekt: Sportengagement von Hauptschülerinnen. Abschlussbericht des 1. Teils: Fragebogenuntersuchung zur sportiven Praxis und zum Sportengagement von Hauptschülerinnen und Realschülerinnen sowie Hauptschülern und Realschülern.* [*Research Project: Sports Participation of Girls at the German* Hauptschule. *Concluding Report of Part I: Questionnaire-Based Study of the Sporting Activity and Sports Participation of Girls and Boys at the German* Hauptschule *and* Realschule.] Pädagogische Hochschule Ludwigsburg, Maschinenschriftliches Manuskript.

Kleindienst-Cachay, C. (2000) *Forschungsprojekt Sportsozialisation und Identitätsentwicklung hochsportiver muslimischer Frauen in Deutschland: Abschlussbericht zum 31.3.2000.* [*Research Project: Socialisation in Sports and Identity Development of Muslim Women in Germany Who Are Highly Active in Sport: Concluding Report of 31 March 2000.*] Universität Bielefeld, Maschinenschriftliches Manuskript.

Kleindienst-Cachay, C. (2007) *Mädchen und Frauen mit Migrationshintergrund im organisierten Sport.* [*Girls and Women from a Migration Background in Club Sports.*] Baltmannsweiler: Schneider-Verlag Hohengehren.

Kleindienst-Cachay, C. and Kuzmik, C. (2006) Fußballspielen und psychosoziale Entwicklung türkisch-muslimischer Mädchen: Ergebnisse einer Interviewstudie. [Playing Football and the Psychosocial Development of Turkish-Muslim Women: Results of an Interview Study.] *Zeitschrift 'Mädchen'* 4: 159–164.

Kuzmik, C. (1998) *Die Bedeutung des Sports für die Identitätsentwicklung weiblicher muslimischer Jugendlicher in der Bundesrepublik Deutschland.* [*The Significance of Sport in the Identity Development of Female Muslim Adolescents in the Federal Republic of Germany.*] Hausarbeit im Rahmen der Ersten Staatsprüfung für das Lehramt an Grund- und Hauptschulen. Universität Hannover.

Lampert, T., Mensink, G.B.M., Romahn, N. and Woll, A. (2007) Körperlich sportliche Aktivität von Kindern und Jugendlichen in Deutschland: Ergebnisse des Kinder- und Jugendgesundheitssurveys (KiGGS). [Physical/Sporting Activity of Children and Adolescents in Germany: Results of the Child and Youth Health Survey.] *Bundesgesundheitsblatt* 50, 5/6: 634–642.

Landessportbund Nordrhein-Westfalen [Regional Sports Association of North Rhine Westphalia] (2004) *Ein Leitfaden durch das Programm 'Integration durch Sport' der Sportjugend im Landessportbund Nordrhein-Westfalen e.V.* [*A Guide to the 'Integration Through Sport' Project of the Youth Section of the Regional Sports Association of North Rhine-Westphalia.*] Duisburg: o.V.

Linneweh, M. (2007) *Sportsozialisation muslimischer Mädchen am Beispiel Geräteturnen- Theoretische Begründung und empirische Validierung an Hand eines Fallbeispiels.* [*Socialisation in Sport of Muslim Girls Exemplified by Gymnastics on Apparatus – Theoretical Foundation and Empirical Validation by Means of a Case Study.*] Bielefeld: Masterarbeit in Sportwissenschaft.

Mutz, Michael (2009) Sportbegeisterte Jungen, sportabstinente Mädchen? – Eine quantitative Analyse der Sportvereinszugehörigkeit von Jungen und Mädchen mit ausländischer Herkunft. [Boys Who Love Sports, Girls Who Don't? A Quantitative Study of Sports Club Participation Among Immigrant Boys and Girls.] *Sport und Gesellschaft* [*Sport and Society*] 6: 95–121.

Nauck, B. (2001) Social Capital, Intergenerational Transmission and Intercultural Contact in Immigrant Families. In B. Nauck, and B. Settles (eds) *Immigrant and Ethnic Minority Families*. Special Issue of *Journal of Comparative Family Studies* 3: 465–488.

Ofner, U. (2003) *Akademikerinnen türkischer Herkunft: Narrative Interviews mit Töchtern aus zugewanderten Familien*. [*Female Academics of Turkish Origin: Narrative Interviews with Daughters of Migrant Families*.] (Berliner Beiträge zur Ethnologie. Band 3). Berlin: Weißensee.

Robert-Koch-Institut (ed.) (2007) Ergebnisse des Kinder- und Jugendgesundheitssurveys. [Results of the Child and Youth Health Survey.] *Bundesgesundheitsblatt* 50, 5/6.

Rohe, M. (2001) *Der Islam – Alltagskonflikte und Lösungen*. [*Islam – Everyday Conflicts and Solutions*.] Freiburg: Herder.

Stadt Hamburg [City of Hamburg] (2006) *Handlungskonzept zur Integration von Zuwanderern*. [*Strategy for Managing Migrant Integration*.] Online, available at: http://fhh. hamburg.de/stadt/Aktuell/behoerden/soziales   familie/zuwanderung/service/kon-zept, property=source.pdf.

Statistisches Bundesamt [German Federal Statistics Office] (2006) *Leben in Deutschland*. [*Life in Germany*.] www.destatis.de/presse/deutsch/pk/2006/mikrozensus2005i.pdf (accessed 22 February 2007).

Walseth, K. and Fasting, K. (2003) Islam's View on Physical Activity and Sport: Egyptian Women Interpreting Islam. *International Review for the Sociology of Sport* 38: 45–60.

6 ورزش و فعالیت بدنی زنان در ایران

Physical activities and sport for women in Iran

Maryam Koushkie Jahromi

Editors' introduction

In this chapter, the author offers a brief history of Iran, its political, religious and cultural dimensions, and the position of women in contemporary Iranian society. A detailed history of the development of sport, physical education and physical activity for girls and women is followed by insights into the organisational sporting structures of the country. The return of sporting arenas to stricter Islamic regulations after the Revolution is discussed and, although contested by some, sex-segregation in sports competitions has led to a growth in opportunities for women to gain qualifications, responsibilities and employment at all levels of sports participation, organisation and management. An overview of research available on physical-activity levels in Iran is discussed, and illustrates opportunities and barriers to participation. Finally, the author's narrative tells of her life growing up in Iran and pursuing her career interests in physical education through school, university and into her current career as Head of the Department of Physical Education at Shiraz University.

Iran – an introduction

Iran, formerly Persia, is located in the Middle East between the Persian Gulf, the Gulf of Oman and the Caspian Sea, bordering on Afghanistan, Armenia, Azerbaijan, Iraq, Pakistan, Turkey and Turkmenistan. The population of almost 70 million is extremely diverse, reflecting distinct waves of migration into the country, as well as its conquest by numerous powers through the ages. The main ethnic groups in Iran are Persians (65 per cent), Azerbaijani Turks (16 per cent), Kurds (7 per cent), Lurs (6 per cent), Arabs (2 per cent), Baluchis (2 per cent), Turkmens (1 per cent), Turkish tribal groups such as the Qashqai (1 per cent), and non-Persian, non-Turkic groups such as Armenians, Assyrians and Georgians (less than 1 per cent). Persian is the official language spoken as a mother tongue by at least 65 per cent of the population and as a second language by a large proportion of the remaining 35 per cent. The state religion is Shiite Islam, practised by 90 per cent of the population, and most of the remainder (8 per cent) are Sunni Muslims. A minority of about 2 per cent are adherents of non-Muslim religions, including Christians, Bahá'ís, Mandeans, Hindus, Sikhs, Yezidis, Yarsanis, Zoroastrians and Jews (Library of Congress 2008).

Iran – a historical perspective

Once established, circa 550 BC, ancient Persia developed a significant world position and a sophisticated civilisation. From the seventh-century AD it became part of the Islamic world and has experienced periods of peace and turmoil, with social, cultural and religious struggles throughout its history under various Islamic dynasties. Shia religion has dominated since the fifteenth century (Library of Congress 2008). Over the last 200 years, Russian and British powers have vied for influence in Iran, particularly after the discovery of oil in the early 1900s (Zarrinkoob 1998).

From 1921, the Pahlavi dynasty became highly influential with the establishment of a military dictatorship, Reza Pahlavi becoming Shah of Iran from 1925, followed by his son (1941–1979). In the 1960s, an ambitious development plan for modernisation and Westernisation was introduced, which is often labelled the White Revolution. Women were encouraged to gain education, take wider public opportunities and adopt modern (Western) values. Dress codes for men and women played a part in this process, with Iranians being encouraged to abandon the *hijab* and traditional dress codes. Although a referendum, disputed by some, showed approval for the changes by the population (Khalaji 2002), with time criticisms emerged, particularly amongst religious leaders, about the increasing autocracy of the Shah, the enforcement of Western values and alliances, the abuse of power by the military and the violation of Islamic laws (Jaafari 1991).

Religious leaders such as Ayatollah Khomeini led a nation-wide uprising that included opponents from different political persuasions. This uprising paved the way for the downfall of the Shah and brought to power a theocratic government in 1977. The Islamic Revolution of 1979 saw the return of the exiled leader Ayatollah Khomeini to become the spiritual leader of the officially renamed 'Islamic Republic of Iran'. At the time, 98.2 per cent of Iranian people voted for an Islamic Republic and a theocratic government, based on the Sharia (Islamic laws) with the Supreme (religious) Leader as the highest authority. After the revolution, dress and behaviour, duties and rights of women and men, as well as the relations between them, were strictly regulated by laws. To this day, women have to follow the Islamic dress code and to wear a *hijab* or at least long clothes and a headscarf in public places (Paidar 1995), and sex-segregation is enforced in schools and some public places (Rovshan nia 2005). Great instability followed between 1980 and 1988, with the Iraq–Iran war, in which over one million Iranians died or were injured. Social and economic life was disrupted and much infrastructure and industry were destroyed. It took many years to recover.

The status of women in Iran

Iranian women today constitute about half of the population but do not form a monolithic group (CWS 2009). They lead varied lives determined by their location, socio-economic class, livelihood and specific culture. Iranian women have diverse views and life experiences. They enjoy relative freedoms, and perceive and experience these freedoms in various ways (Pfister 2002).

Socially, there is evidence from pre-Islamic times through to the creation and establishment of the Islamic Republic that many women played vital roles in different areas of Iranian society and in their families and communities, despite the exclusion of some from public life (Nashat and Beck 2003). The family constitutes the basis of society, women having their main responsibility as mothers and transmitters of values to the next generation (Paidar 1995), and men for providing financially for the family. Where women do work, they can choose whether to keep their money separate or contribute to the household. In practice, it depends on family needs and agreement between a woman and her husband. Klett observed that 'Traditionally, women have always had a great deal of power not only in family, where nothing happens against their will, but also in social and community affairs'. She concluded: 'I have never seen so many self-confident, impressive and strong women. Neither in the orient, nor anywhere else' (2001, cited in Pfister 2002: 210).

Since 1997 pre-marriage contracts have been introduced which outline the couple's decisions on important issues in their lives, for example that the husband gives up his right to polygamy or that the woman has the right to work outside the house or to divorce her husband. Other family negotiations include where they will live, the schooling of the children and the marriage of the daughters. Differences in family culture and tradition can influence such decisions. Islamic feminists inform women about their rights and encourage them to negotiate the conditions of their marriage and contract. Another indicator of changes in favour of women's choices is seen in the rise of the mean age of marriage to 23.7 years in 2001 (CWS 2009).

Politically, throughout the twentieth century, there has been a women's movement in Iran with groups campaigning for women's rights and changes in the hierarchical gender order. Iranian women played important roles in the Islamic Revolution of 1979 (Pfister 2002), and a strong women's movement continues to advocate reforms of laws and customs, and for the rights of women and children (Paidar 1995). Although always under-represented in political decision-making positions, in 1963 Iranian women took part for the first time as candidates in the twenty-first parliamentary elections, and they gained six of the 198 seats. In the first *Majles* (Iranian Parliament) after the Revolution in 1981, 1.4 per cent of the members were women. This increased to only 4.4 per cent in the seventh *Majles* in 2004, 28 years after the Revolution (Amoli 2004).

Education is a symbol of social progress in every country. In line with Islamic teaching, all women have the right to education (Motahhari 1988), but a minority are still prevented from education and work, a product of traditional cultural values and not Islam or current law. Education for all, particularly the eradication of illiteracy, has been among the most important goals of the Iranian government since the Revolution. The numbers of illiterate adults, especially women, decreased, dropping between the years 1988 and 2006 from 640,000 to 115,000. These figures compared with from 316,000 to 205,000 for men (CWS 2009).

The increasing level of education in Iran is also reflected by the continuously increasing numbers of college and university students, particularly women, who currently make up over half the number of students in Iranian universities (Figure 6.1). At present, male and female undergraduate and postgraduate students study physical education and sport science in about 34 governmental and 70 non-governmental universities at undergraduate and postgraduate levels across Iran. The gender balance in favour of women is also visible in this field (CWS 2009).

Given the social status and education opportunities of women in Iran, it is surprising that in employment women remain largely excluded (Figure 6.2). Although about 90 per cent of other women include housewives, farmers and students, they are not regarded as employed people (Mehdizadeh 2006). Perhaps traditional family values, rights and responsibilities persuade women to stay in the home once married, or perhaps the husband's income is sufficient to meet the financial needs of the household. There may also be prejudice and discrimination against women entering the workforce. CWS (2009) reported an increase in the last decade of women taking up senior management positions, although a woman's promotion is also likely to be hindered by traditional male values, where the dominant view amongst the powerful male directors and managers is that a woman's place is in the home, especially if she is married and has children. Justifications for the 'glass ceiling' include the risk of absenteeism of women and their inability to travel to work (Amoli 2004). It might also be that

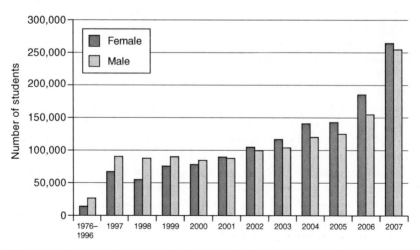

Figure 6.1 Number of male and female students entering universities or higher
education.

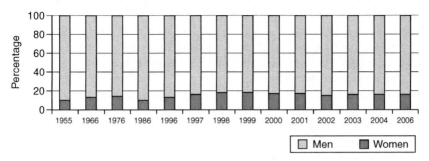

Figure 6.2 Relative distribution of employed population.

women do not put themselves forward for such positions. Further research is necessary.

In the last 30 years, the number of female teachers in schools has increased by 285.3 per cent, currently amounting to 51 per cent of the total teaching profession. This is not matched in universities. Although the numbers of female teaching staff in universities has increased from around 2,000 in 1976 to 16,000 in 2007, male teachers are still in the majority, with their numbers increasing during the same years from 12,000 to 66,000 (CWS 2009).

In summary, over the last decades many aspects of the lives of women in Iran have improved, such as conditions of marriage and education, and small inroads have been made with regard to political and career opportunities. Cultural traditions regarding the familial role of women remain strong, but the power and potential of women in building a prosperous Iran is recognised and encouraged by the Islamic government. There is commitment to the provision of all necessary means, including appropriate legislation for marriage, divorce, education and having a job outside the home, to enhance women's scientific, educational, social, political, health and welfare capacities to enable their contribution to societal progress (Motahhari 1988; Mehdizadeh 2006). Given the struggles of Iranian women in some spheres, their success in participation levels in sporting physical activities is remarkable.

Sport, physical education and physical activities in Iran

Historically, the development of sporting physical activities in Iran has been influenced by various factors: geography, politics and policies, religion and culture. Because of its turbulent history and a string of foreign occupations, emphasis has traditionally been placed on physical training and fitness for war. Religion has been influential on sporting practice in many historical eras, with a positive Islamic emphasis on the 'necessity for physical training and sports activities' (*Encyclopedia of Iran and Islam* 2006).

Modern sport and physical education developed in Iran from the 1850s with the increase in travel and the spread of ideas as a result of international labour migration. It is interesting that the major influences of physical education in European schools returned with scholars to Iran. The gymnastics system of German *Turnen* (founded by Friedrich Ludwig Jahn) was introduced in 1915, but the Swedish gymnastics system developed by Pehr Henrik Ling, with its promise of health and its scientific basis, became the officially adopted model for schools in Iran in 1919. Education was seen as desirable by the rising middle classes, and physical education for girls was supported because healthy bodies were required for successful motherhood (Koyagi 2008). Although a daily compulsory lesson of physical education in schools for girls and boys was approved by the *Majlis* in 1927 (Chehabi 2003), the reality was quite different because of the shortage of qualified teachers and inadequate facilities. Today Iran's education constitution guarantees 'free education and physical training for everyone at all levels, and physical-education lessons are compulsory for all students at all levels in schools and universities' (cited in Pfister 2002: 212).

Similarly, the internationalisation of modern sport began to spread to Iran from Europe from the late nineteenth and early twentieth centuries, along with the increase in travel opportunities and the influx of international workers. Early Iranian physical activities were heavily male-dominated and involved forms of wrestling, riding and training, among other things with clubs, in so-called *Zurkhaneh*, literally 'houses of strength' (Chehabi 2003: 276). Football became the most popular modern sport, boosted by the influx of, for example, oil industry workers (Chehabi 2003).

During the Pahlavi dynasty from 1926 onwards, physical education and sport were seen as part of the modernising agenda. The first Iranian physical-education specialist teachers were trained in 1935 and 1936 by military staff during a one-year course and in co-educational settings. In 1938, the first specialist teacher-training school of physical education was established in Tehran. A further school of physical education was established in Isfahan in 1951 for both men and women (Kashef 1999).

Under the Shah's regime, the sporting agenda was Westernisation and sport, and part of the nationalistic agenda focused on elite performers and international competitions in mixed-sex environments. In 1948, male athletes from Iran took part in the Olympic Games for the first time.

Compared with other predominantly Muslim countries, women's competitive sport in Iran has a long history. Iranian women appeared internationally in the Asian Games in 1958 (track-and-field athletics), 1962 (volleyball), 1974 and 1976 (fencing) (Pfister 2002). In 1964, the Iranian Olympic Committee sent four women athletes to Tokyo to compete in two disciplines, gymnastics and track-and-field. In 1976, four women participated in fencing in the Olympic Games in Montreal.

After the 1979 Islamic Revolution, Iranian women had to cover their heads and bodies in the presence of men in public places, in accordance with governmental and religious rules (Masteron 2007). All female physical-education classes at schools and universities had to be run by female coaches, teachers and professors: 'a mixed-sex environment is not acceptable to our Islamic ethics and order ...' (Chehabi 2003: 286). Women's competitions in the presence of men were stopped. Although physical activities of girls and women were accepted and even encouraged, resources were limited and unbalanced in favour of men. Shortage of female instructors (women had been coached by men before the Revolution) and facilities allocated to women were major problems for women's sport (Paidar 1995). This led to the initiation of a training cadre of women to facilitate sporting participation in roles of coaches, officials, organisers and administrators. The post-Revolution attitude of the Iranian government towards women's participation in physical activities was to steer women into Islamically appropriate sporting activity, and to broaden the agenda by supporting health-orientated participation for more of the population, as summarised in the following excerpt from Salam Iran, the official website:

> Sports play an important role in our social life because it helps women perform their maternal duty and nurture the new generation in the best manner within the sphere of the great Islamic system. The need for, and importance of, women's sports and physical education is quite obvious. Because women account for half of the population, specific programs should prepare physical capabilities and sport abilities ... in the years preceding the revolution no attention was paid to women's physical and mental health in governmental programs of the former regime. Rather, all facilities and opportunities were reserved for a handful of sportswomen, so-called, who were sent to international competition in total disregard of our society's traditional and ideological values.
>
> (www.salamiran.org, accessed 15 January 2008)

Elite Iranian sportswomen can only compete in sports where the governing bodies allow clothing that meets Islamic requirements, covering head, arms and legs. Success has been gained over many years, for example, at the Asian Games: in 1990 and 1994 in shooting, 1996 in fencing, 1998 in rowing and shooting, 2002 in horse riding, kayak, taekwondo, track-and-field and shooting (www.olympic.ir, accessed 10 October 2009) and 2006 in seven disciplines – taekwondo, chess, athletics, rowing, badminton, shooting and equestrian. Iranian women have also competed at Olympic level. In Atlanta in 1996, Iranian women competed in fencing, Sydney 2000 in shooting, Athens 2004 in shooting and, in Beijing 2008, three women competed in archery, rowing and taekwondo (Aali 2008). The fact that designers have started to take seriously the necessity and preference of some women to wear Islamically appropriate sports dress has opened international competition opportunities for many Muslim women. By modifying sports dress, Iranian women can participate in indoor and outdoor international soccer, basketball, volleyball and handball events, but participating in international events such as swimming, gymnastics and water polo (post-Revolution) remains impossible because of the lack of suitable dress (Elmi 2003).

Organisational development

As with participation, men's and women's sport and physical-education organisations developed collaboratively before the Islamic Revolution. The first organisation responsible for all physical education and sports affairs for men and women in Iran was established in 1934 as the National Association of Physical Education and Scouting in Iran, which had branches in regional centres. The Association provided instruction books and sports rules, employed consultants from the USA, notably Thomas R. Gibson, and its aim was the participation of men at the 1936 Olympic Games in Berlin. During this time, men and women shared sports facilities, and sporting practices did not meet Islamic requirements. While welcomed by some, the majority of Iranian women (being Muslim with strong Shia convictions) felt unable to participate in physical activities and sport in shared facilities and were therefore excluded from such developments (Women's Group 1981).

Since the 1979 Islamic Revolution, sport and physical-education organisations for girls and women have carried out the necessary changes to enable gender-segregated participation in large numbers. Systems have been changed and improved several times. A committee for the management of women's sport was first established in 1981 when all affairs concerning women's sport were transferred to the Sports Committee for Women. This became the Directorate of Women's Sports Affairs in 1985 and the Deputy of Physical Education and Sports Affairs for Women from 1989. At that time all women's sports affairs were governed by the Deputy. This body was attached to an umbrella physical-education organisation that was responsible for both physical education and sport for both sexes. In 1992 this Deputy was replaced by a Women's Sports Office (Figure 6.5) and most of its responsibility for governing women's affairs was given to federations (sports governing bodies).

In 1989, during the presidency of Ali Akbar Hashemi Rafsanjani, his daughter Faezeh Hashemi became head of the Women's Sport Organisation (WSO) (1991) and a vice-president of the National Iranian Olympic Committee (Chehabi 2003). She did much to improve women's sport in Iran. During that time, the war with Iraq was ended and more money was available for women's sport. Hashemi supported women's participation in many areas of physical activity, including cycling. She was 'supported by most women who believed the only way forward is to work with respect for the traditions and beliefs of Islam' (Hargreaves 2000: 59). The aspiration to support women's top-level sport, and the rules concerning sex-segregation, encouraged the idea of women-only sports competitions. Led by Hashemi, the Islamic Countries' Women's Sports Solidarity Council (ICWSSC)[1] was approved at the second session of the Iranian Executive Board in the National Olympic Committee (NOC) in 1991. A key facet of the work of the ICWSSC was the first international Islamic Countries' Sports Solidarity Congress for Women, which took place in 1991 in Tehran. Hashemi became president of this Council, and in 1993 she welcomed participants from 11 countries to the first international Islamic Countries' Women's

Sports Solidarity Games in Tehran. The competition was organised by the Islamic Federation of Women's Sport (IFWS) to meet Islamic requirements for sex segregation. This federation organises different sports competitions for Muslim and non-Muslim women in all-female environments, with an academic congress accompanying these events.

Between 1993 and 2005, these Games developed into an increasingly popular, four-yearly international event. The number of events, countries and participating athletes has increased steadily, and the inclusion of Muslim and then non-Muslim countries, as well as Muslim and non-Muslim female competitors, has increased its popularity (Benn and Ahmed 2006). Because men are excluded, women take over all the tasks and roles needed in such an event. This has meant the 'upskilling' of many Iranian women, for example in sports organisation, management and administration, and as referees and judges, as well as athletes. Figure 6.3 shows the increasing numbers of sporting facilities for women and Figure 6.4 the increasing numbers of female instructors, coaches and referees. Also, the number of women participating in all kinds of sport in sports clubs has increased. In 2008 there were 16 times more participants than two decades previously (CWS 2009).

Today, sport and physical education in Iran is still managed through an umbrella institution, the Iranian National Sport and Physical Education Organisation. This has formal links with the Iranian National Olympic Committee and federations, including IFWS. The Women's Sports Development Office oversees the provision of activities for girls and women. Separate associations manage resources, athlete development, elite and community sport for women and men in federations. Each region (state) has offices for managing physical education.

In summary, all girls have the right to physical education in schools, and women can participate in sporting activities, subject to Islamic requirements, from the recreational to the elite level. In 2008, the Iranian rower Homa Hossaini carried the flag for the mixed-gender Iranian team (49 men, three women) in the opening ceremony of the Beijing Olympics. In an interview with the BBC

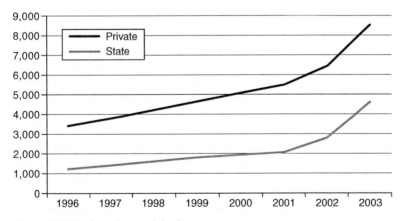

Figure 6.3 Number of sport clubs for women.

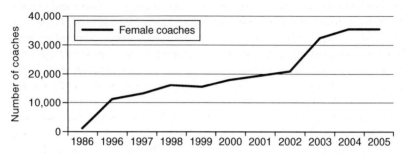

Figure 6.4 Number of female coaches.

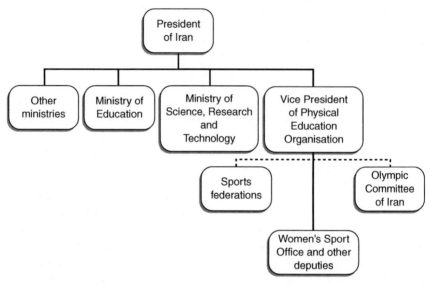

Figure 6.5 Brief organizational chart of sport in Iran.

(Leyne 2008), Hossaini said: 'We are not short of anything, and in fact some-times women get better support than men because of the sensitivity of the issue.' In response to a remark on Islamic dress, she answered: 'since we began to work with such clothing we got used to it.... Personally I do not have any problem with that and I don't think it is stopping me from making progress.' Clearly, the range of sporting possibilities is growing. The increase in opportunities for sport-ing participation is also reaching the community-orientated 'sport for all' move-ment. The mountainous nature of Iran has led to the growth of mountaineering sports. At present, skiing, mountaineering and rock climbing are popular and related to the geographical landscape of the country (Vishofer 1998). Amongst women, the most popular of these activities are mountaineering and skiing.

The right to be a spectator in sport in Iran is heavily influenced by state rules for modesty; for example, no men are allowed to watch women's sport unless women are covered, and women are not allowed to watch some men's sports. All these areas are contested, both in and beyond Iran, depending on the position of individuals towards issues of religion and state and personal interpretations of appropriate behaviour for men and women. Some Iranian women have challenged the existing rules regarding their exclusion from male sporting events by publicly protesting against their exclusion, for example at the 1997 football World Cup qualifying match at Tehran's Azadi Stadium and the World Wrestling Championships in 1998 (Hargreaves 2000). Today, women are allowed to attend some competitions as spectators, such as basketball, but they cannot attend other sporting events, such as football. This is justified by the authorities on the grounds that the football stadium is no proper place for women because of the safety risk. Furthermore, wrestling and swimming venues are considered improper because of competition dress-code requirements.

Barriers to women's participation in community sport activities in Iran

In Iran most of the research on sport is conducted in the recreational/community sector (Table 6.1). Results of this work illustrate many barriers to participation for Iranian girls and women. Opportunities and barriers differ according to the populations and locations across the country. According to the findings summarised in Table 6.1, barriers for women match those that many women face internationally and include the lack of free time, interest, money, motivation, professional trainers, transport and facilities, family and friends support, low levels of skills and physical fitness. According to a national study of urban women (age group: 20–65 years), for example, 43.5 per cent take part in physical activities for enjoyment but consider the shortage of facilities to be the most important barrier to women's participation in sport (Pourkiani 1999).

Future studies need to focus on the challenges, barriers and successes of elite athletes, as well as on the advancement of girls in the physical education programmes.

In terms of media interest, coverage of women's sport is increasing. Whilst television, radio and newspapers carry reports of women's events and individual successes, in comparison with men's sports coverage, especially men's football, women are marginalised in the mass media. Women, furthermore, can only appear on television or in photographs if they are wearing sports dress that meets Islamic requirements, as in climbing, horse riding, shooting and karate. Other sporting events for women cannot be attended by male journalists. On the one hand, this has led to the 'upskilling' of some Iranian women to embrace all these sport-related jobs; on the other hand, women remain marginalised from media attention that might be productive for augmenting resources and stimulating interest in the field for the benefit of all Iranian girls and women.

In conclusion, historical trends indicate long-established positive attitudes to physical education and sport for girls and women in Iran, amidst traditional and religious values that see separate, but equally valued, roles and responsibilities

Table 6.1 Synthesis of findings related to the barriers to participation in sport by Iranian women

First author	Year	Population (women)	Location	Type of physical activity	Outcomes
Atghia, N.	2008	Different ages (18–75)	Iran	Recreational activity	Barriers: shortage of facilities, high expenses and shortage of information through media
Keshkar, S.	2007	Different ages (over 18 years old)	Tehran	Recreational activity	Barriers: structural constraints (cost, time, facilities, skill and sport abilities), intrapersonal (attitudes, imaginations, psychological factors), interpersonal (lack of accompanying person and social relationships) constraints
Hamedinia, M.	2007	Different ages (18–58)	Sabzevar	Recreational activity	Barriers: free time (43.7 per cent), lack of exercise partner (31 per cent), boredom or laziness (29.4 per cent), high gymnasium registration fee (26.4 per cent), lack of suitable gymnasiums for females (25.9 per cent), lack of qualified coaches (24.8 per cent). 11.3 per cent of subjects exercised over 3 hours per week; 23.2 per cent exercised at home.
Sedarati, M.	2006	Different ages (25–55)	Tehran	Recreational activity	Barriers: shortage of sport facilities, improper time of gymnasiums devoted to women sport, high expense of sport classes, shortage of time, and lack of advocacy of family members. Women over 45 years old participate in sport programmes more than younger women, and married women more than singles
Vahida, F.	2006	Different ages (25–40)	Mazanaran state	Recreational activity	Positive related factors: family members sport activities, friend partnership, cost of activity, social support
Salami, F.	2003	Different ages (over 20 years old)	Tehran	Recreational activity	Barriers: physical problems such as disease, disabilities, obesity, psychological problems including impatience, stress, depression, lack of interest and lack of motivation, family attitude, economical status, facilities and cultural problems

Bagherzade	2002	School students	Torbate Heidarie	Recreational activity	Barriers: shortage of spaces and facilities, improper operating time of gymnasiums, lack of free time, cost. Involvement in school studies, lack of professional coaches, difficult transportation, little information in sport fields, parent disagreement
Dadashi, M.	2000	University students	Isfahan University	Recreational activity	Barriers: time, interest, money, facilities, information, skill, social relationship, vehicles and physical fitness
Iran TV	1998	Different ages (all ages)	Tehran	Recreational activities	Barriers: cultural-social (42 per cent), facilities and financial problems (80 per cent), information, media and management (19 per cent)

for men and women. Political and religious factors have influenced participation, regulations and environments at different times during the last century. As a predominantly Muslim country, the short period of modernisation in a Western direction, introduced by the former Shah, pleased some but excluded many women in the sporting arena who felt unable to renounce deeply felt beliefs about the body, modesty in interactions with men, and traditional and religious values of family obligation. Similarly, post-Revolution gender segregation had many supporters, but it also created dilemmas for a minority of others who are interested in mixed-sex sporting activities. Reconciling Iranian sports participation with stricter Islamic regulations has been accompanied by the development of an infrastructure that has empowered many women in the field at all levels of participation: coaching, teaching, management, organisation and administration. There are critics of the system in and beyond Iran, but the following personal statement by the author represents the voice of one who has grown up in post-Revolution Iran, and is a woman living and working successfully in the field of physical education and sport.

A personal note

Speaking as an Iranian woman born four years before the Revolution, when I compare my life experience in studying, recreational sport and social participation with that of my mother's generation, I can say that I have really enjoyed much progress and have had many opportunities in all aspects of my life. Spending 22 years in the field of education, in schools and at university, with the last six years as a lecturer and head of a university Physical Education department, I have been fortunate. There has been constant support for my participation in all aspects of physical activity, from my schooldays to my current career, from my mother, father, family and husband. My job has a high status and is well respected amongst fellow Iranians. It enables me to select research topics for study, to travel internationally and to exchange ideas on developments in the area of the sports participation and health of women in Iran. I have lived in a society where gendered roles are the norm but, in spite of this, much progress has been made in the provision of skilled women sports leaders, facilities and other resources for women's activities. Because of the need to comply with veiling within my religion, I accept it. Religious adherence has not limited my progress in sport or scientific fields, and many men support women's participation, especially with the aims of improving their health and enabling them to be role models for the next generation. In evaluating progress, further research is needed on barriers and facilitators for girls and women in physical education, community- and elite-level sports participation.

Note

1 The Women's Sports Organisation's name has been changed several times. At first it was recorded as the Islamic Countries' Women's Sport Solidarity Council (ICWSSC), but later it was changed to the Islamic Federation of Women's Sport (IFWS).

Bibliography

Aali, A. (2008) Zanane Irani dar Olampic [Iranian Women in the Olympics]. *Eetemad* [newspaper], February, 862, Tehran.

Amoli, A. (2004) Modiriate zanan dar sazenhaye gheire dolati [Women's management in non-governmental organisations]. *Reihane,* 7 July: 151–161.

Atghia, N. (2008) Arziabie zanane Irani az tabaghate mokhtalef da morede varzeshe hamagani [Needs assessment of Iranian women of different classes about sport for all]. *tahghigh da tarbiatbadi* [*Research on Sport Sciences*], Winter: 33–15.

Bagherzadeh, F., Hemayattalab, R. and Mottaghipour, M. (2002) Chera dokhtane dabire-stani dar varzeshhaye tafrihi sherkat namikonand? [Why do high school girls not parti-cipate in leisure-time sports?]. *Harakat,* 11, Spring: 23–32.

Beck, A.L. and Nashat, G. (2004) *Women in Iran from 1800 to the Islamic Republic.* Illi-nois: University of Illinois Press.

Benn, T. and Ahmad, A. (2006) Alternative visions: international sporting opportunities for Muslim women and implications for British youth sport. *Youth and Policy,* 92. Leicester: The National Youth Agency: 119–132.

Chehabi, H. (2003) The juggernaut of globalization: sport and modernization in Iran, in J. Mangan and F. Hong (eds) *Sport in Asian Society – Past and Present.* London: Frank Cass.

Council of Women's Statistics (CWS) (2009) Retrieved from the Women's Information & Statistics Center, www.Iranwomen.org (accessed 28 April 2009).

Dadashi, M. (2000). Mavanea faaliathaye varzeshie daneshjooyane daneshgahe Sanatie Esfahan [Barriers of recreational activities for students of University of Isfahan]. Unpublished MA Thesis, Isfahan University.

Elmi, H. (2003) Varzeshe zanan dar Iran [Women's sport in Iran]. *Rooznamaye Eetemad* [newspaper], 1614, 16 February 2006, Tehran. Online, available at: www. Magiran. com/nprview.asp?ID=1572441.

Hamedinia, R.M., Askari, R. and Moghadam, M. (2007) Mavanee mosharekate varzeshi dar zanane 20 ta 50 salaye shahrestane sabzavar [Barriers to doing physical activity among 20–50-year-old female citizens in Sabzavar City]. *Majalaye oloome varzeshi* [*Journal of Sports Sciences*], 1: 13–26.

Hargreaves, J. (2000) *Heroines of Sport: The Politics of Difference and Identity.* London: Routledge.

Iran TV and Radio (1998) *Didgahe zanane Tehrani dar morede moshrekate varzeshie zanan* [*Opinion of Women in Tehran about Women's Sports Participation*]. Tehran: Centre of Research, Study and Evaluation of Programmes on Radio and TV in the Islamic Republic of Iran.

Islamic Council of Women's Sports Federation (ICWSF) (n.d.) Online, available at: www.icwsf.org.

Jaafari, M. (1991) *Kashfe hejabe zanan* [*Taking Off Women's Covering*]. Markaze asnade farhangie Iran [Institute of Cultural Documents of Iran], Tehran.

Kashef, M. (1999) *Tarikhe Tarbiatbadi* [*Physical Education History*]. Tehran: Entesha-rate Payame Nour.

Keshkar, S. and Ehsani, M. (2007) Mavanee sherkate zanan dar varzeshhaye tafrihi dar Tehran ba taakid bar didgahhaye shakhsi [Constraints inhibiting women from partici-pating in recreational sports in Tehran, focusing on personal attributes]. *Motaleate Zanan* [*Women's Studies*], Autumn: 113–134.

Khalaji, A. (2002) Eslahate Amicaie va ghiame 15 Khordad [American refinement and 6th of June Revolution]. Islamic Revolution Research Center. 278, Tehran.

Koyagi, M. (2008) *Modern Education in Iran During the Ghajar and Pahlavi Periods.* Austin: University of Texas Press. Online, available at: www.Blackwell-compass.com/subject/history/article-view?article_id=hico_articles_bpl561. (accessed 14 November 2008).

Leyne, J. (2008) Interview of Homa Hosseini, Olympic rower, Beijing Olympics 2008, BBC News. Online, available at: http://newsvote.bbc.co.uk/mpapps/pagetools/print/news.bbc.co.uk/1/hi/world/middle_east/7537478.stm (accessed 16 August 2009).

Library of Congress (2008) Country profile: Iran, Federal Research Division. Online, available at: http://memory.loc.gov/frd/cs/profiles/Iran.pdf (accessed 17 August 2009).

Masteron, A.R. (2007) *Hijab in Iran.* Online, available at: www.islamonline.net (accessed 10 September 2009).

Mehdizadeh, S. (2006) Naghdi bar mehvarhaye davazdahganaye konferance Pekan ba kholasaie az vaziate zanan dar jomhoore eslamie Iran [Evaluating twelve aspects of the Beijing conference with a summary of women's status in the Islamic Republic of Iran]. *Women*, Spring: 4.

Motahhari, M. (1988) *Hoghooghe zanan dar Eslam [Women's rights in Islam].* Tehran: Entesharate Sadra.

Nashat, G. and Beck, L. (2003) *Women in Iran from the Rise of Islam to 1800.* Urbana: University of Illinois Press.

Olympic Committee (2009) Online, available at: www.olympic.ir/historymedals-asiangamesmedall.fa.html.

Paidar, P. (1995) *Women and Political Process in Twentieth-Century Iran.* New York: Cambridge University Press.

Pfister, G. (2002) Women and sport in Iran, in L. Hartman and G. Pfister (eds) *Sport and Women.* London: Routledge: 207–223.

Pourkiani, M. (1999) Arziabie emkanate varzeshe va estefade az an dar daneshgahhaye Iran [Evaluating Available Sports Facilities in Iranian Universities and their Usage]. Unpublished MA Thesis, Tehran University.

Rovshan nia, N. (2005) *Enghelabe farhangi dar Jomhoorie Eslamie Iran. [Cultural Revolution in the Islamic Republic of Iran].* Tehran: Markaze asnade jomhoorie Eslami.

Salami, F., Noroozian, M. and Mirfattah, F. (2003) *Tosife mavanee mosharekate varzeshie za. [Description of Barriers in Women's Sports Participation].* markaze tahghighate vezarate oloom tahghighat va fanavari [Centre of Sports Research in the Ministry of Science, Education and Technology], Tehran.

Sedarati, M. (2006) Barrasie emkanat va khadamate varzeshie zanan [Evaluating Availability of Products and Services for Women]. MA Thesis, Tehran Azzahra University.

Vahida, F., Arizi, F. and Parsamehr, M. (2006) Taasire hemayate ejtemaie bar mosharekate varzeshie zanan [Influence of social advocacy on women's sports participation]. *Journal of Movement Research and Sport*, Spring and Summer: 53–62.

Vishofer, Y. (1998) *Ancient Iran*, in T.B. Saghebfar: Ghoghnoos, Tehran.

Women's Group (1981) *The Status of Sports for Women in the Islamic Republic of Iran.* Tehran: Physical Education and Sports Organisation.

Women's Sports Organisation (WSO) (1998) *The Embassy of the Islamic Republic of Iran, Ottawa.* Online, available at: www. Salamiran.org/women/organizations/wso. html.

Zarrinkoob, A. (1998) *Tarikhe Iran [History of Iran].* Tehran: Sokhan.

7 وضع عمـــان ســـلطنة فــي والرياضـــة
الرياضـية التربيــة فــي والفتيــات والنســـاء

The Sultanate of Oman and the position of girls and women in physical education and sport

Yousra Al-Sinani and Tansin Benn

Editors' introduction

This chapter offers an original insight into the position of Omani girls and women in the field of physical activity in education, recreation and sport. Oman is one of the most recent countries to develop opportunities for women in physical education and sport. Understanding the location of women in the field cannot be decoupled from the geographical, historical, socio-cultural, political and religious context of the country. This knowledge is provided by the authors: Yousra Al-Sinani, the first Omani woman to gain a doctorate in the area of physical education, and Tansin Benn, who won a Leverhulme Research Fellowship which enabled her to live in the country of Oman in 2008 to investigate the lives of Omani women students and teachers of physical education and sport. The authors are indebted to Habiba Al-Hinai for her assistance in supplying information on Omani women and competitive sport.

Background

Oman is located on the Tropic of Cancer in the:

> far south east of the Arab peninsula and is bordered from the east by the Gulf of Oman and the Arabian Sea, from the west by the Kingdom of Saudi Arabia and United Arab Emirates, from the north by the Hormuz Strait and from the south by the Republic of Yemen.
>
> (Ministry of Information 1993: 40; Vine 1995)

The Sultanate occupies a total area of 309,500 km^2 and it is the second biggest country in the Arab peninsula. Its geography is diverse, including mountain ranges, desert landscapes and fertile plains. According to the General Census of Population and Houses for 2003, the country's population, which includes both Omani nationals and expatriates, is 2,331,391 (Ministry of National Economy 2003).

Oman is an Islamic country, predominantly Arab and tribal in organisation. There are also migrant workers from South Asia and Eastern Africa, but most residents are Omani nationals. Arabic is the main language, although English is now taught in schools as a second language and some education programmes in higher education are delivered in English. Some 86 per cent of the population is Muslim, and 13 per cent Hindu. Oman has a developing mixed economy, with the production and export of petroleum as its largest sector.

Until 1970, Oman was 'one of the least known countries in the world' (Riphenberg 1998: 144). Before 1970, Omani people faced severe political, economic and social conditions due to the country's isolation and 'closed door' politics. People depended on fishing, animal breeding, traditional agriculture and handicrafts. At the time, the Omani people lived in harsh, poor conditions in a repressive, isolated country on the brink of national collapse. There were three schools in the whole country, attended by boys, virtually non-existent healthcare with one hospital, and a shunning of anything modern like radios (Ministry of Information 2006: 6). This led to some internal instability and an exodus of large numbers of Omani nationals abroad to improve their living conditions and to avoid the difficulties in the unstable social, economic and political conditions at home (Al Nuaimi 1996). In 1964, oil was discovered in the Sultanate of Oman and was gradually to change the fortunes of the country. The accession of Sultan Qaboos in 1970 saw the first use of oil money for the benefit of the people.

With the accession to power of His Majesty Sultan Qaboos bin Said in 1970, the face of Oman changed and a rapid period of modernisation began, and it continues today under his reign. Regional, geographical and cultural challenges have led to great differences in the rate of modernisation across Oman. Some mountain communities, for example, remain relatively inaccessible, such as in rural parts of the enclave of Musandum on the northern tip of the Arabian peninsula. Some Bedouins continue to choose to live a nomadic way of life in tented communities in the desert regions, and some coastal communities still depend on the sea. Yet cities like Muscat have sophisticated facilities, the latest technology, first-class hotels, the Sultan's State University, modern sports and gymnasium complexes for women and men, and well-equipped hospitals. All of these factors ensure differences in aspirations, personal priorities, experiences of education, gender relations and life chances.

The Sultan's first drive was to unite the country through its people, engaging tribal leaders and regional communities in processes of change in political structures. He also made a deliberate move to open the borders to enable dialogue with other nations and improve international relations and opportunities for Oman, working for peace and harmony 'within a framework of mutual respect' (Ministry of Information 2006: 6–31). The country, for example, is now part of the six Gulf Co-operation Council (GCC) countries, the UN Arab League, the Arab League, the Organisation of Islamic Conferences (OIC), and enjoys good relations with countries in Asia, the West, Australasia and Africa.

Part of the modernisation of Oman was the Sultan's call for Omani citizens to return to their country to help build a better future: 'I would at the earliest do my best efforts for a better future for each individual and every citizen has to lend a helping hand in this context' (Ministry of Information 1996: 226). The process of

Omanisation encouraged investment in Omani citizens in the job market, supporting careers and socio-economic improvement for nationals. Sultan Qaboos has managed to establish a strong and positive identity for the people of Oman. A sense of pride in being Omani has been retained through values placed on the essence of Omani tradition and culture. The Sultan inspired a sense of purpose in contributing to development and a powerful loyalty in recognition of the massive social, political and economic achievements he has facilitated (Plekhanov 2004).

Through the modernisation process, the role of religion has stayed central to the way of life in Oman. Islamic beliefs, for example prayer regimes, organise and permeate daily life and the features of modesty in dress codes and gender relations are visible everywhere (see pp. 127–129). Tolerance and respect for non-Omanis and non-Muslims in the country provides a welcoming environment for Westerners. It is an Islamic country with Sharia (Islamic) law informing its legislative structure (Plekhanov 2004). In addition to religion, the Basic Law of the State was passed in 1996, clarifying:

> every aspect of the state apparatus and the fundamental rights and responsibilities of Omani citizens. The Basic Law guarantees the equality of all citizens before the law, freedom of religion and of speech, a free press, the right to a fair trial and the right to create and enjoy membership of national associations.
>
> (Ministry of Information 2005: 52)

Contradictions between Sharia and the Basic Law, especially in relation to equality for women in areas such as inheritance and polygamy, will become evident in the following section, but the Basic Law continued to move Omani society in a more equitable direction.

In summary, the succession of the current Sultan in 1970 became the catalyst for political, social and economic change in Oman, and although the pace of change is uneven, no corner of Oman has been left untouched by this process. Much of Oman has turned into a modern community with advanced scientific technology, comprehensive political, economic and social structures, and major investment in sectors such as health and education (Al Turki 1975). The post-1970 period is sometimes referred to as the renaissance in Oman.

Women in Oman

The post-1970 renaissance has had a great impact on the lives of women in Oman. Cultural practices which prohibited girls' and women's full participation in life and education were evident but have changed significantly: 'Oman has seen itself as something of a regional trailblazer in the way it has opened up all areas of opportunity to women, an approach that today can be seen to be paying dividends' (Ministry of Information (2005: 28).

In 1998, Riphenberg took a more critical view of the position of Omani women, comparing the policy framework for work and mobility, family, education, health and fertility and cultural realities. Riphenberg engaged with apparent contradictions between, for example, the political rhetoric of equality and minimal evidence of women in key positions of power, claiming that 'despite their important contributions, women in Oman continue to face formidable social, economic and political barriers' (Riphenberg 1998: 144). The research of Al-Sinani (2007) shows that barriers continue to exist for some Omanis, especially in rural communities. When a small number of qualified female physical-education teachers returned to their home communities to teach physical education and sport to girls, for example, they met with opposition to their dress codes and public visibility from some men in the community who thought it an inappropriate activity for women.

Despite such examples, there has been an improvement in the position of women in Oman, with large numbers entering the workforce. The current Sultan has done much to encourage Omani women to take their place as equal contributors in the modernising of Omani society. Al Hinai (2008), discussing developments in Oman, stated: 'women already account for a large proportion of employed Omanis in government, military and Royal Omani Police roles, and they represent the majority of those heading into higher education.' Feminisation is one policy process that encourages Omani women to enter the workforce. Primary teaching, for example (for children up to the age of ten years), is an all-female profession.

The rate of generational change in Omani women's aspirations is evident in Benn and Al-Sinani (forthcoming). Of 96 women student-teachers of physical education who answered questionnaires, not one had a mother in paid work. Yet all the students envisaged themselves as working women, managing the home, motherhood and careers in their future lives. The effects of rapid modernisation on the lives of women is obvious, at least for those fortunate enough to gain places at Sultan Qaboos University, the only state-sponsored university in Oman.

Gender relations cannot be fully understood through Western notions of equality. In Islamic teaching, women still have a high informal status in the family, enhanced by marriage and child-bearing. There are differences in financial status, with men retaining the responsibility to provide for their wives and children, but women being able to use their own earnings as they choose. Inequalities in legal rights are changing; for example, in December 2008 the Sultan changed property law to allow Omani women equal rights to free allocation of government land. Now each woman as well as man becomes entitled to a piece of land (Royal Decree number 125/2008, Sultanate of Oman, Ministry of Foreign Affairs, News, 17 November 2008). Inheritance law remains as prescribed by Sharia law, with men entitled to twice the legacy of women, justified by their responsibility for building family wealth. Polygamy is seen as permissible in certain circumstances, with men retaining more of the power of decision-making with regard to family matters.

Codes of dress and behaviour for men and women in public apply, and issues of sex segregation are more fluid and situation-dependent than before modernisation. In public gatherings, men are more visible than women. Most Omani men wear the traditional *dishdash* white robe and women the black *shalor* and *abaya*, with some still choosing to wear *niqab* or full-face veiling in public. There are many differences within and between Omanis of different age groups, communities and socio-economic background. It remains true that elite families are advantaged, for example, in terms of private and international education. Many also contribute to wider social support systems for less-advantaged women – for example, through the Omani Women's Association that has many branches across the country and has focused on projects such as literacy and nutritional education (Al Ghabshi 2002).

Religious and family responsibilities dominate everyday life for Omani men and women. For many who live in rural Oman, beyond the sophisticated cities of Muscat and Salallah, traditional systems of social structures remain, brightly coloured dress characterises regional communities and distinctive face masking for women is still visible. Living conditions, education and life chances for Omani women remain diverse but are much improved, largely driven by the views and support of the current Sultan. The recent development of tourism and restoration of ancient sites, mosques, forts and museums that celebrate Omani culture and the lives of its people, demonstrate how modernisation has been tempered with the desire to retain and celebrate the distinctiveness of Oman. Consequently, the country stands in stark contrast to evidence of modernisation in the neighbouring Dubai.

Education in Oman

From 1970 a state system of education for all boys and girls from the age of six years was initiated and rolled out over the ensuing years across Oman. This process has included the building of schools for every community, teacher training for Omani people and curriculum development. Such a rapid modernisation period required the massive adjustment of its people, and education became central to that process. It remains the Sultan's belief that education increases freedom, while ignorance reduces it. Mixed schools are now provided at cycle one (six–ten years), and separate schools are provided from cycle two onwards, ensuring that progress is respectful of Islamic requirements for separation of the sexes after puberty. Such development received the support of the Omani people, keen to retain customs, traditions and heritage that reaffirm values and beliefs. An illustration of the way in which Omani people value education is demonstrated in a study by Chatty in 1996 (cited in Mazawi 2006: 985–986). The Bedouin women of the Harasiis tribe in Oman challenged cultural sex-segregation assumptions which would have excluded their daughters from the right to formal education alongside the boys.

The education of females became one of the challenges facing Omani society in order for the basic rights of women to be met, and for women to exercise those rights by participating in different social fields (Ministry of Social Affairs 1998). Oman was the most deprived of the Gulf States in terms of the advancement of women in literacy and education in the 1970s. Azzam (1975, cited in Allaghi and Almana 1984: 22) found a 98 per cent illiteracy rate and the lowest percentage of girls enrolled in education throughout that decade (Azzam 1979, cited in Allaghi and Almana 1984: 23). Persistence in the advocacy of the positive values anchored in education for Omani girls was evident in the Sultan's messages. He encouraged women's education as a way for them to take on their responsibility for contributing to the development of Omani society. Cultural differences in the treatment of boys and girls needed to be challenged as schooling spread across Oman. Principles were developed, specifically aimed at girls, to safeguard equality of opportunity in the Sultanate. For example:

- girls have rights in education equal to males, and to their abilities and desires;
- girls have an entitlement to reach the highest level of qualification possible in their education. Their responsibilities for the home, the family and the raising of children ensure that the best-educated women will pass this on to their children and raise a high-quality generation to contribute to the future development of the country;
- families have the responsibility to take care of their female children in Omani society, to pass on the values and customs of Omani society, to ensure they know their rights and take up suitable jobs to play their natural role in the building of modern social life.

(Al Ghabshi 2002, translation by the author)

Physical education in the Sultanate of Oman

There is no well-sourced history of physical education in the early days of educational developments in the 1970s due to the momentous task of establishing general educational aims, objectives and strategies. The following, therefore, is based on limited documents and insider knowledge. Physical education existed on the periphery of learning, with the gradual expansion of a subject-based curriculum. In terms of priorities and subject status, education in Arabic, mathematics and science took precedence. As fields of studies opened in the 1980s, art, music and physical education received more attention. The building of schools was a priority, and these have been increasingly well resourced, most recently with IT equipment, as a more open Omani society has endeavoured to catch up with the outside world. Provision of suitable indoor facilities for physical education in state schools has been overlooked, which is highly problematic given the harsh, dry, hot climate, with temperatures often staying above 40°C for half of the year. However, the fact that a curriculum for boys and girls was devised and is currently part of the required national curriculum is to be celebrated.

All Omani girls and boys are entitled to physical education. Historically, outside influences, mainly from Jordan and Egypt, have been responsible for directing subject development, and many teachers have been brought in to deliver the subject because of the lack of qualified Omani teachers (see pp. 131–132). In 1976, the Ministry of Education used a Jordanian company to design the national physical-education curriculum, which replicated the curriculum model of Jordan, mainly based on games, gymnastics and athletics. In 1983 an Egyptian consultant was used and again aligned curriculum developments to those of his own country. When the Ministry of Education established the new Basic Education System in 1995, updated in 2005, the physical-education curriculum was re-shaped to meet the new goals for education in the Sultanate, again managed by the Egyptian consultant. Theoretically, the physical-education curriculum currently aims to develop movement competencies and sporting abilities, fitness, creativity, positive attitudes and an understanding of social values and responsibilities (author's translation).

Despite the need to applaud the recent policy-level development of the subject for girls and boys, it would be inaccurate to suggest the quality of provision is good. There is room for improvement in many Omani state schools, for example the provision of indoor facilities and equipment would make a difference. Current teaching methods are dominated by a didactic performance-orientated approach, which stifles learning processes, creativity and progress but which is maintained and reinforced through the inspection system (Al Sinani 2007; Al Rawahi 2008). Finally, traditional community opposition to girls' and women's involvement in physical activity is still experienced by some teachers when they return to rural areas of Oman to teach (Al Sinani 2007). The full potential for health and well-being, and the subject's contribution to physical, cognitive and affective development (Bailey and Dismore 2004), is still under-valued and under-developed.

Physical education, women and initial teacher training

It is not surprising, since there was no state education system before 1970, that developments in initial teacher training (ITT) are relatively recent. From 1975, generalist teacher training for Omani men and women was possible through one-year courses. Physical education was part of this training and consisted of sex-segregated football games for the men and volleyball for the women. The number of generalist teacher training institutes expanded to five in the major cities across Oman. The number of graduates at these institutes reached 2,521 teachers, of whom 45.5 per cent were women (Mohamed 1987; Al Raisi and Bilal 1989; Mawad 1992).

In the rapidly developing process of modernisation, dissatisfaction grew over the quality of teachers being prepared at the institutes. In 1984, the Ministry required two-year diploma-level studies for teachers, at the same time abolishing former institutes and establishing colleges (Mohamed 1987). It was recognised that deeper subject knowledge was required in teacher training, especially for cycle-two senior schools, but physical-education specialisation was not yet possible. Despite upgrading institutes with one-year training to colleges with two-year diploma-level training, concerns about the quality of teachers remained.

In 1986, Sultan Qaboos University became the first – and to date only – state-funded university in Oman. It started with five faculties, including the Faculty of Education, and 500 students. It now has eight faculties and 10,000 students with equal numbers of men and women. In 1991, three women and ten men (all those who reached the entrance grade and passed the fitness test) started the first four-year degree-level specialist physical-education teacher training programme. In January 1994, the first Ministry of Higher Education was created in Oman by Royal Decree with special responsibility for Sultan Qaboos University and for all higher-education provision, grants and scholarships. Confidence in the university degree-level training grew, and in 1998 the Ministry for Higher Education closed all diploma-level teacher training colleges, decreeing that all teacher training would be centralised in the four-year degree programmes at Sultan Qaboos University, Muscat (Benn and Al-Sinani 2007).

There are currently 35 men and 35 women specialising in physical education at Sultan Qaboos University each year. In line with Islamic requirements, separate practical spaces are provided for male and female students. Theoretical studies are undertaken in mixed-sex groups. With no Omani-trained specialists to lead the development of university-level physical-education specialist courses, programme design and leadership was led by Egyptian and other Arab experts. Recently Omani graduates have started returning from overseas with higher degrees, and the Omanisation process will ensure their influence in future developments at all levels of physical-education provision in Oman.

There are still challenges for initial teacher training in the degree-level programme at the university. There are rhetoric/reality gaps in terms of claims to deliver on differentiation, managing pupils with disabilities and widening teaching methodologies. There are much better facilities at the university than in state schools, for example air-conditioned sports halls, swimming pools and a wide range of equipment. Other challenges lie in the lack of 'joined-up thinking' between the university's physical-education department, the Ministry of Education, supervisors (inspectors) and practising teachers (Al Sinani 2007; Al Rawahi 2008). This is not to diminish the considerable achievement and developments in Oman of embedding the subject as a right for all children in the state-school system and as a degree-level teacher training programme in the higher-education system.

Omani women and sporting activity

Community sport

Beyond the educational context, which at least entitles all Omani boys and girls to physical education and sporting activity, the position of sport in the community in Oman is very different for men and women. In many parts of Oman, cultural and traditional attitudes still militate against women's participation in physical activity. Although the university provides for, and stimulates, interest and skills amongst young women leaders of sporting activities in Oman, a major problem for sport development is the lack of official women coaches in any sport. Almost the only physical activity that receives approbation is walking. Gradual change, however, is happening as Muslim women globally are taking more interest in this sphere of human endeavour (Pfister 2006). Certainly some of the wealthier Omani city women are attending the new women-only elite fitness gymnasia and pursuing exercise as part of healthier lifestyles. Many rural and Bedouin women still have demanding physical daily lives, often contributing to the family agricultural lifestyle and needs (Allaghi and Almana 1984; Benn and Al Sinani, forthcoming).

A series of community 'sports clubs' (with stadia-type facilities) was established across the regions of Oman. These grew essentially into men's football clubs although this is beginning to change in major cities. Recently, community women-only aerobic classes and other sporting sessions have been growing in popularity in these facilities, and more graduates of the university programme aspire to work in these contexts to encourage more community and sporting provision for women (Benn and Al Sinani, forthcoming). In 2008, the authors attended the award ceremony for the first Omani women's handball referee qualification course. There, 12 women received their certificates as a result of a collaborative training scheme initiated by the Ministry of Education and the Oman National Olympic Committee (ONOC). All were former students of physical education from the university course, illustrating the significance of the university programme and its graduates for community and sporting developments both in and beyond school. Handball remains a popular sport for women. It owes its development largely to foreign women resident in Oman and, unusually, the more talented and committed players are sometimes coached by men. This situation is starting to be mirrored in other popular sports such as volleyball and athletics. The rare opportunity for women to play and practise at a serious level ensures that many team members of Oman's national teams come from the training grounds of the university.

Elite-level competitive sport

Whilst physical education and sport have been part of the school curriculum for girls since the early 1970s, at least in principle, and specialist teacher training has been undertaken at the University of Sultan Qaboos from 1993, the development of competitive sport opportunities for women has been piecemeal, with no official records or database for research. Women only began to compete at a national level in the early 1990s. Organising bodies were not officially recognised and women were not allowed to represent Oman abroad. In the capital city, Muscat, enthusiasts began to form teams that competed in events organised by hotels and private clubs in such sports as netball, tennis, squash, volleyball and the martial arts. Some established sports clubs did open their doors to women sports enthusiasts, but the lack of suitable (sex-segregated) facilities and (female) coaches meant that there was little take-up and much of the initial promise was not fulfilled. In 1991, one local club did organise and run the first of four annual volleyball tournaments. Eight teams of women, made up of Omanis and expatriates, took part. Women's interest in volleyball can be traced back to schools, where the game is popular and a familiar feature of physical education.

A rare but significant opportunity for women to participate in sport at a high level – and also adhere to the required tenets of Islam – was established in 1993 with the Women's Islamic Games (see Chapter 6). Not surprisingly, the invitation to compete was extended by the Omani National Olympic Committee to past and current students of Sultan Qaboos University as there was no other mechanism in place to select and train a national team. Similar events have been organised following the success of this venture. Apart from tennis, and to a lesser extent athletics, there is still no systematic organisation of individual sports for women in Oman.

Al Hinai devoted many years to trying to stimulate, lead and support interest for Omani women's involvement in sporting events, becoming vice-chairperson of the Oman Volleyball Association (OVA) in April 2007. She is a former member of the Women's Sports Committee inaugurated on 30 April 2005 with six members, and they have organised some development work, including tournaments with local private schools. This committee started out as a sub-group of the Omani National Olympic Committee (ONOC). One representative from this sub-committee attends ONOC meetings. A Gulf Countries GCC Women and Sports Committee was formed in June 2007, and Al Hinai led a team of 62 women to the first GCC Women's Games in Kuwait in March 2008. The only GCC country not in attendance was Saudi Arabia. When interviewed on her return from Kuwait, Al Hinai (2008: 44) stated that Oman did not have enough practising women coaches or administrators to support a developing infrastructure for women in competitive sport. While making progress in participation, women were not fully involved in organising and decision-making positions, sometimes because they did not take up positions they had been offered, demonstrating the strength of traditional beliefs and values about the role of women in Oman.

Omani women's national teams that compete in the Women's Islamic Games, the GCC Women's Games and other international competitions are selected by the nominated coach in charge of events. As there are no national championships and few regional competitions, potential team members are invited to training sessions during which the coach makes the selection based on who turns up. It is significant that on the Oman Olympic Committee website the homepage introduction has a collage illustrating eight different sports, and while aspiring to a commitment to women, they are not yet visible.[1]

Sport for women in Oman is new and relatively fragile. Three sports – windsurfing, volleyball and athletics – had Omani women competitors for the first time at the Fifteenth Asian Games in Doha, Qatar, in 2006. Fatima al Nabhani, a promising tennis player, often features in newspapers for her successes, and recently figured in a school textbook as a positive role model. Interestingly, Fatima does not wear the *hijab* and plays in normally accepted tennis dress in the presence of male coaches. (A short film of Fatima playing tennis and being interviewed, called *Here I Am*, can be seen on YouTube.[2]) Safia bint Sakin Al-Habsi, the top windsurfer who competes for Oman, receives sponsorship.[3] Corporate houses are becoming interested in sportswomen as brand ambassadors, and the government publicly applauds the successes of these young sportspeople (Sacheti 2007). A 16-year-old athlete, Buthaina Yaqoub, became the first Omani woman athlete to compete in the Olympics in Beijing in 2008. In a recent meeting between the Omani and Chinese Olympic Committees about the 2010 Sixteenth Asian Games, Mr Al-Sinasi, General Secretary of the Oman Olympic Committee, spoke of Oman's readiness to host the next Asian Beach Games in 2010. He also said Oman would be sending 80 competitors to the 2010 Sixteenth Asian Games in Guangzhou, including seven women athletes (GAGOC 2009).

The sportswomen now receiving public acclaim through competing in international sport are in some ways a contradiction to the majority of Omani women. Their youth and pre-marital status might be influential in their current sporting success. To illustrate how unusual they are, when female final-year physical-education students at the university were interviewed for a study in 2008, the majority of the informants had mixed views about participating in the international arena, and many felt unable to participate wherever a male coach, official or spectator would be present (Benn and Al Sinani, forthcoming).

In conclusion, it can be said that there is diversity amongst Omani women in terms of urban/rural/mountain/desert location, socio-economic position and attitudes towards the body, Islam and cultural traditions. The participation of women in any kind of physical activity in terms of vocational training or sporting visibility is relatively recent and very much at an emergent stage. Physical-education teachers, for example, can still meet male opposition to their work on returning from training to their village schools. Some are forced to resort to teaching in full-length black *abayas* to retain a comfortable place in the community, despite the introduction of an Islamically appropriate 'uniform' allowing more freedom of movement for physical-education teachers that is supported by the government (Al-Sinani 2007). In contradistinction to this are the supportive sponsorship, media coverage and celebration of the successes of the small number of young international Omani sportswomen. Many challenges remain in working with communities to educate men and women about the values of physical activity. Also, resources are needed to provide more opportunities for gender-segregated facilities for women's participation in communities. Omani women in leadership positions are required as advocates for sport, including in coaching/training provision, and in national and international sporting bodies. The various ministries that govern Oman could work more collaboratively for the benefit of women's physical health and well-being through exercise and sporting participation – for example, the Ministries of Education, Sport and Social Affairs with other agencies such as the university and the Omani Women's Association. In the period of accelerated modernisation of the last 40 years, much has been achieved. The successes of Omani society, including that of its women in managing this process, are highly respected amongst Arab as well as other Islamic countries (Plekhanov 2004). As Al Hinai suggests, perhaps sport presents 'the last frontier for women' (Al Hinai 2008: 44). The greatest challenge is in managing the process of change in a manner respectful of the culture of Oman as well as of the new opportunities opening up for women.

Notes

1 www.omanolympic.org.om (accessed 20 October 2009).
2 Nike Women: *Here I Am – Fatma Al Nabhani*. Online, available at: www.youtube.com/watch?v=NB_HZZmI5KE (accessed 28 October 2009).
3 *Safia's Sailing Ambitions*. Online, available at: www.rahbc.pdorc.com/Sailing/Docs/Safia-sailing-ambitions.pdf. (accessed 28 October 2009).

Bibliography

Al Ghabshi, A. (2002) *The Use Of Media for Omani Women*. Cairo: Dr'Nasher.
Al Hinai, H. (2008) Women in Sport – The Final Frontier? Habiba al Hinai Talks About the Rise of Women in Sports Following the Inaugural GCC Women's Games Last Week. *theweek*, 19 March, 263, 44–45.
Al Nuaimi, T.S. (1996) *The Role of Education in the Assimilation Process of Modernity Attitudes Among Educated People in Oman*. Muscat: Case Study.
Al Raisi, I. and Bilal, N. (1989) *Assessment of Novice Teachers Professional Competencies*. Ministry of Education: Muscat.
Al Rawahi, N. (2008) The Beliefs and Practice of Omani Student Teachers and Teachers about Teaching and Learning in Physical Education: An Exploratory Study. Unpublished Thesis, Exeter University, UK.
Al-Sinani, Y. (2007) An Evaluation of the Effectiveness of the Physical Education Initial Teacher Training Programme for Women in Sultan Qaboos University in Oman. Unpublished PhD thesis, University of Birmingham, England.
Al Turki, A.M. (1975) *Basic Data About Oman and Development Direction*. Muscat: Unesco Projects, Research.
Allaghi, F. and Almana, A. (1984) Survey of Research on Women in the Arab Gulf Region. In F. Pinter (ed.) *Social Science Research and Women in the Arab World*. London: Unesco, Frances Pinter.
Bailey, R. and Dismore, H. (2004) Sport in Education (SpinEd) – the Role of Physical Education and Sport in Education. Project report to the 4th International Conference of Ministers and Senior Officials Responsible for Physical Education and Sport (MINEPS IV), December, Athens, Greece.
Benn, T. and Al-Sinani, Y. (2007) Physical Education in Oman: Women in Oman and Specialist Initial Teacher Training. *Physical Education Matters*, Summer: 57–59.
Benn, T. and Al-Sinani, Y. (Forthcoming) *Women in Oman: Education, Training and Teaching*.
China Olympic Committee (2009) 'Road of Asia' welcomed in Oman (GAGOC Chinese Official Website). Online, available at: http://en.olympic.cn/news/olympic_news/2009–04–02/1769216.html (accessed 20 April 2009).
GAGOC (2009) Olympic Council and the Guangzhou Asian Games Organizing Committee (GAGOC) 'Road to Asia' paves way to 2010 Guangzhou Games. Online, available at: www.china.org.cn/sports/news/2009.htm (accessed 1 November 2009).
Mawad, S.E. (1992) *The Importance of Education in Oman*. Egypt: Dr'nasier.
Mazawi, A. (2006) Educational Expansion and the Mediation of Discontent: The Cultural Politics of Schooling in the Arab States. In H. Lauder, P. Brown, J. Dillagbough and A. Halsey (eds) *Education, Globalization and Social Change*. Oxford: Oxford University Press.
Ministry of Information (1993) *Oman 1993*. Muscat: Ministry of Information.

Ministry of Information (1996) *Royal Speech (1970–1995)*. Muscat: Ministry of Information.

Ministry of Information (2005) *Oman 2005*. Muscat: Ministry of Information.

Ministry of Information (2006) *Tribute to His Majesty, Sultan Qaboos bin Said*. Muscat: Ministry of Information.

Ministry of National Economy (2003) *Census 2003*. Muscat: Ministry of National Economy.

Ministry of Social Affairs and Labour (1998) *Social Foundation Supporting Omani Women*. Muscat: Ministry of Social Affairs and Labour.

Mohamed, J. (1987) *Higher Education and Intermediate Colleges Diploma*. Ruwi: Al Alwan.

Pfister, G. (2006) Islam and Women's Sport: More and More Muslim Women are Taking up Sports, and Tehran is Setting an Example. *Sang Saeng* 16: 12–15.

Plekhanov, S. (2004) *A Reformer on the Throne: Sultan Qaboos bin Said Al Said*. London: Trident Press.

Riphenberg, C. (1998) Changing Gender Relations and the Development Process in Oman. In Y. Haddad and J. Esposito (eds) *Islam, Gender and Social Change*. Oxford: Oxford University Press: 144–168.

Sacheti, P. (2007) *Game for More*. Online, available at: www.boloji.com/wfs5/wfs882. htm (accessed 20 April 2009).

Vine, P. (1995) *The Heritage of Oman*. London: Immel Publishing.

8 الريـاضـة والمـرأة فـي سـوريا

Women and sport in Syria

Nour El-Houda Karfoul

Editors' introduction

This chapter makes history; it is the first detailed work on women and sport in Syria. The author is a prominent leader of sport in general, and of women in sport in particular, in Syria and the Arab world. The overview of Syria, the development, organisation and concerns for women and sport illustrate the prioritising of a secular Arab identity that has survived a long period of social and political unrest. In many ways, uncertainty and instability are ongoing in terms of geographical location and reputation as a homeland for refugees for displaced Arab people from neighbouring countries. The author's own life history exemplifies the message that opportunities do exist for girls and women in the field of physical education and sport in Syria. Gender, religion and ethnicity need not be barriers to participation. The post-1946 independence period has seen a growth in the provision of school-based, community and competition sports for girls and women. The evidence from the General Sports Federation's 2007 report, however, indicates that many women are not engaging with such provision, and that sport remains a male domain. Suggestions and recommendations are offered, and further research will develop an understanding of how to address the current imbalance in gender equity.

A brief overview of the country

Syria is an Asian country located on the eastern coast of the Mediterranean Sea, bordering Turkey to the north, Iraq to the east, Jordan and Palestine to the south, the Mediterranean Sea and Lebanon to the west. Syria is a country of the Arab Homeland, and the official language is Arabic. Mansfield (1985: 368) referred to the country as 'The Heart of Arabism'. Crucial to understanding Syria today is an awareness of its political history, especially the period before the First World War, when Syria was part of the Bilad-ash-Sham region under the Ottoman Empire. This included a vast territory whose national boundaries were later re-drawn. This large area came under French and English mandates following the Sykes–Picot agreement (signed in 1916, made public in 1917 and implemented after the war), with modern Syria and Lebanon under the French, and Jordan, Palestine and Iraq under the English.

The Bilad-ash-Sham region was, and continues to be, regarded as the heart of Arab Nationalism, where its people strove for the independence of an Arab homeland. Such aspirations became more visible again in Syria after independence on 17 April 1946, for example in the ideology of leftist political parties such as Al-Ba'ath and Nasserists with their socialist and secular Arab nationalist agendas. In this context, Syrian women have been encouraged to make fuller contributions to society in areas including education, literature, art and sport.

Today Syria is a republic with a president as head of state and a People's Council or Majlis al-Shaab (250 seats for members elected by popular vote to serve four-year terms). The legal system is based on a combination of French and Ottoman civil law, although Islamic law is used in family courts. Within this secular state, freedom of religion is tolerated. Whilst the vast majority (89 per cent) of the population is Muslim, 10 per cent is Christian and other religions make up around 1 per cent. The dominant political party is the Ba'ath Party which embraces secularisation and stresses pan-Arab unity. In 2007, the Syrian Central Statistics Bureau gave the population of Syria as 19.2 million, although this figure did not include expatriates or the Iraqi refugees, a figure estimated to be around 1.5 million. The urban/rural split is roughly equal. Syria has a rapidly expanding, young population with around 11 million under the age of 25 (www.champress.net).

Syrian law does not differentiate between men and women, or between religions. Women hold positions in the judicial system, government ministries, the diplomatic service, the police and the army. In the professions, women can be found practising law, medicine, engineering and business. Women have the right to stand for election to the People's Council, which currently has 28 women out of 252 members.

A historical perspective of sport

Syria has a long history of participation in sport, even producing Olympic champions at the original Olympic Games held in Greece. These champions came from different Syrian cites such as Antakya, Latakia (in ancient times known as Laodicia), Saida and Petra (Abu Nauwar 1983). The Syrian historian Dr Wadii Bashour (1999) mentions that Syrian women had taken part in the great sport festivals organised in the ancient town of Dafna in Syria in the era of the Emperor Antleokos.

Traditional sports during the 400 years of Ottoman rule, including wrestling, weight-lifting and swimming, were popular (for men). Post-1916, while under French and English mandates, sports clubs developed and recreational activities for men started, for example between the English and French soldiers, who played sport recreationally in many of the squares and other public areas of the main cities, introducing sports such as athletics, tennis, boxing and basketball. Political turmoil continued, however, with the Great Syrian Revolt from 1925 to 1927, which was a mass insurgency movement against French colonial rule.

It was during the occupation by France that sports clubs were formed. The first one was the Hamzasp Club in 1923, with its headquarters in the Anglican

Church, although in 1916 a football team had been formed at the Shibani School in Aleppo. Other clubs followed, and in 1928 the Barada Club and the Qasiyoun Club were established in the capital, Damascus, named after the city's river and mountain respectively. It was also during the French and English mandates that sport began to form part of the school curriculum. There were no specialist teachers, and providing the opportunity to play sport was left to the initiative of individual class teachers, although some young people organised matches between their schools and with local clubs.

Women and professional training

The strict Ottoman rule and subsequent unsettled state of Syria meant there was no schooling or sport for girls due to difficult social and political circumstances. Women and girls in urban areas were not encouraged to leave the home, either for learning or recreation, whilst those in rural areas were expected to work on the land or with livestock. It was not until 1947, after the end of the Second World War, when foreign forces finally left Syria to govern itself as an independent nation, that the situation improved.

In 1947, the establishment of the Ministry of Information was charged with ensuring the provision of sporting activities in all schools for boys and girls. This was the beginning of girls' engagement with sports clubs. Some of the more committed girls and women practised sport as a hobby, but later were able to enter a profession in teaching and coaching by graduating in sport education. In 1949, Siham Mahairi was the first woman from Syria to be sent from Damascus to the Higher Institute of Sport Education of Teachers in Cairo, Egypt to specialise in physical-education training, graduating in 1953. In the early 1950s, many women joined her at their own expense. Others were delegated by the state to institutes in Alexandria and Cairo, returning to take charge of sport in schools and sports teams at elementary, preparatory and secondary levels, as well as at local clubs. Syria started its own Sport Education Institutes later, the first being in Damascus for young men in 1968 and in Aleppo in 1969 for young women.

The first women graduates in the field of sport education were highly enthusiastic and strong believers in the value and importance of sport at both an individual and societal level. In the beginning they were exposed to direct and indirect social and religious prejudice against their pioneering role in encouraging and motivating girls to join sports clubs. There was also criticism concerning their organisation of competitions and sports festivals where participants wore sportswear. Among these pioneers was Nihal Amin, who graduated from the Higher Institute of Sport in Egypt in 1954. Back in Syria, she was subjected to critical articles against her and her activities, published in the newspapers of the stricter religious parties. The articles also criticised the men responsible for supporting women's sporting activities at clubs and schools. These pioneers and advocates of women's sporting participation persevered and made progress in the provision of sporting opportunities for girls and women in Syria.

The influence of Egyptian teacher training institutions on the professional training of Syrian women teachers meant that Egyptian curriculum and sporting models underpinned the early work in Syrian schools. The link between the two countries was further cemented during the union between Egypt and Syria (1958–1961), forming the United Arab Republic. In this period all policies were combined, including at Ministerial level. In education, the curricula were also unified, including in sport, with strong influence from Egyptian teachers working in Syrian schools. Even a combined Olympic Committee was formed. Under the United Arab Republic Olympic Committee, one team with athletes from Egypt and Syria participated in the Mediterranean Games in Beirut in 1959 and in the 1961 Olympic Games in Rome.

It is perhaps worth noting here that sport at a professional level in Syria is in its infancy, and currently the only professional sports are men's football and basketball. There are professional women and men coaches and a small number of elite athletes, both men and women champions, are given social and financial security, as will be seen later.

Physical education in schools

During the French mandate, the Syrian education system was developed and opened to all girls and boys. Physical education is known as sport education, as stated in the first Legislative Decree published on 22 May 1947, following independence in 1946. The Ministry of Information became responsible for sport education at all stages of state and private education. The first article of the decree obliged the Ministry of Information to pay particular attention to sport and the Scout movement in all its schools in order to ensure the good stature and sound growth of children, and to promote a spirit of order and obedience. To achieve these objectives, the Ministry officials were ordered to:

- examine the practice of sport and content of sports lessons in schools, both state and private;
- ensure that the necessary leaders and coaches for scouting and sporting activities in the schools were appointed, and that materials and equipment were purchased. Colleges and specialist students were also to be offered uniforms;
- construct playing areas in the schools;
- organise and stage scholastic sports festivals;
- hold training camps for coaches and leaders;
- encourage and support sporting and scouting trips outside school; and
- ensure that sufficient sports coaches and scouting leaders were trained to staff all schools.

This decree was signed by the then President of the Republic, H.E. Shukri Al-Quwatli. The requirement for well-equipped schools and trained professionals with competence both in and beyond the school is clear. With able women teachers taking the lead, girls started competing in their schools; the first Syrian Schools' Championships in netball, volleyball, athletics and badminton were organised for girls in 1955. Some girls joined sports clubs, especially in the larger conurbations such as Damascus, Aleppo, Latakia and Homs, where they were able to play basketball, table tennis, athletics, badminton and tennis.

In the 1960s and 1970s, some sport education teacher-trainees began to gain their qualifications even further afield at the Higher Sport Education Institutes of the former Soviet Union, as well as Eastern and Western Germany. The author of this chapter was the first of these trainees to graduate from the Central Higher Institute of Physical Education and Sport in Moscow in 1970, after five years of training. These new graduates, both male and female, were instrumental in the development of the sport-education curriculum in schools. Eventually they, too, began to occupy positions in National Sports Federations, the General Sports Federation and the National Olympic Committee of Syria. A number of others were employed to teach or manage the first sport-education institutes set up in Syria, one for men in Damascus in 1968 and later one for women in Aleppo in 1969. Young men and women who excelled in sport and gained a high-school certificate were admitted for training. They graduated after two years of study and became teachers and trainers of school sports teams. In Aleppo, Najat Kayali, who is one of the pioneering graduates from the Higher Institute in Egypt, had great influence on training in athletics.

A rapidly increasing young population and the consequential need for more schools, alongside a state policy of providing specialist teachers for all subjects at all levels of education, meant that the demand for qualified sport education teachers increased. This in turn required an expansion in the provision of training to four institutes, from which some 6,000 female sport-education teachers have graduated. These institutes were all-female establishments, which offered two-year training courses following high-school graduation. In addition to these institutes, today there are two university faculties that offer four-year training courses. These universities provide mixed-sex sports programmes.

Today, sport education is compulsory in state schools for boys and girls, and is included in the official examinations, along with the other subjects. From the first to the sixth grade of Basic Education (this is the name given to the first level of education), teaching is in mixed-sex groups, whereas from the seventh grade onwards the groups are separated. At all stages, however, teaching is carried out by specialist teachers of sport education. School matches and competitions are held for all stages of the basic and secondary grades in the eight sports taught in the national curriculum (athletics, gymnastics, swimming, football, basketball, handball, volleyball and table tennis). Badminton and chess are recent additions. Sport-education lessons include physical fitness exercises and playing principles and rules of the main sports. There are three principle objectives in the lessons:

- education – to promote sportsmanship, fair competition and self-confidence;
- health – to maintain good posture and the sound growth of children's bodies; and
- sport – to teach the principles of sports and identify talent.

School teams for girls are formed exactly as those of the boys at all educational stages. They have training opportunities in extracurricular time in the school facilities, where possible. If this is not possible, then facilities provided by the General Sports Federation or the local municipality are used. The school teams take part in the Pan-Arab School Games, which were first organised in 1949 and took place in Beirut, Lebanon. At this inaugural event, four countries took part – Egypt, Iraq, Syria and Lebanon – but there were only three sports: football, basketball and volleyball. At that time the games were for boys only; no girls' teams took part. The girls had to wait until 1975 before they were allowed to participate. The Games resumed after a break on a biennial basis and were held in Algeria in 2004, Beirut in 2006 and Jordan in 2008. Syria always enters both boys' and girls' teams.

The organisation of sport in Syria

The most significant milestone in the evolution of sport in Syria occurred in 1952 with the issue of Decree Number 199. This decree formalised the Sports Federation and the interrelationship between the Ministry of Information, National Sports Federations and Sports Clubs. Most importantly, the decree did not indicate any differentiation between males and females; rather, it was inclusive of all members of society. Further organisational changes were made following the political separation of Syria and Egypt, with the continuation of girls practising sports at schools and clubs, leading to the establishment of the Syrian General Sports Federation (GSF) in 1971. This government-funded organisation was charged with devising a strategic development plan for sport and became solely responsible for the guidance of the sports movement in Syria. It was required to certify National Federations and Sports Clubs as well as to organise internal sports competitions, festivals and training courses for coaches. This process of sports body formalisation is shown in Table 8.1. The GSF has branches in all 14 governorates of Syria and oversees the financing of the national federations.

A key element of the GSF's strategy was the establishment of training centres where top athletes in a variety of sports and talented youngsters could receive specialist training in good facilities. The ultimate objective of these centres was to support the national teams. Whilst funded by the GSF, the national federations retained a supervisory role with regard to the technical aspects of the training.

Women's status in sport and its organisation

In terms of legislation, access for women in sport in the General Sports Federation allows no distinction on gender or religious grounds. Coaches and referees are similarly remunerated although the fees they receive are insufficient to constitute a salary as these are not full-time occupations.

The same privileges and rights in practising sports are enjoyed by men and women. Affiliation to clubs is open to all individuals, as is participation in

Table 8.1 Process of sports body formalisation in 28 sports at national and international levels from 1938 to 2008

National federation	Foundation date	Affiliation date in IF	National federation	Foundation date	Affiliation date in IF
Football	1938	1939	Equestrian	1971	1972
Basketball	1946	1948	Shooting	1971	1980
Boxing	1948	1948	Chess	1972	1972
Swimming	1948	1948	Karate	1975	1979
Weightlifting	1951	1952	Badminton	1985	1988
Athletics	1952	1952	Sports medicine	1982	1983
Bodybuilding	1952	1983	Sports for handicapped	1986	1988
Tennis	1953	1953	Sport for all	1990	1991
Volleyball	1953	1953	Billiards and snooker	1998	2002
Gymnastics	1956	1957	Taekwondo	1999	2003
Cycling	1954	1957	Kickboxing	2000	2001
Wrestling	1958	1958	Rowing	2002	
Handball	1959	1962	Triathlon	2003	2003
Judo	1970	1975	Fencing	2008	2008

championships and matches scheduled by the national federations for all age groups. The special training centres, national teams and international competition opportunities are open to all who qualify.

Women have the right to stand as candidates for election in different sports institutions and are now represented on, for example, club executive committees, national federations and the National Olympic Committee. Women are present in influential decision-making positions related to sport. These opportunities and changes in the status of women in sport did not occur accidentally, but resulted from the persistence and leadership of pioneers. Female athletes in national teams, coaches and teachers worked together to raise the status of women in sport in Syrian society. The post-independence decrees relating to the organisation of sport nationally and the place of sport in schools, with their inclusive policies, were largely drafted by open-minded men who strongly believed in the value of sport and sport education in the building of a safe, cohesive society. This progress does not mean full equality yet, as demonstrated by the relatively low numbers of women in key decision-making bodies:

- clubs and the leadership of the General Sports Federation's branches – at least one in seven;
- individual national federations – from one to three out of seven to nine members;
- National Federation – 22 out of 196;
- General Sports Federation Executive (the highest sporting authority) – two out of 13;
- Central Council of the General Sports Federation – ten out of 65.

(GSF Annual Report 2007)

The National Olympic Committee (NOC) for Syria was founded in 1948 and affiliated to the IOC in the same year. A total of 24 national federations (NFs) are affiliated, and women are present in the leadership of 15, covering sports practised by girls in Syria. The number of women on the NOC Executive Board is three out of 23. History was made in 1983 when the author of this chapter became the first woman to be elected Secretary General of the Syrian National Olympic Committee. Until 2008 she remained the only woman in Asia to hold this office in an NOC.

On the participation, coaching and officials side of sport, there are also gender inequalities. The 2007 GSF Report indicated a dire situation: only 257 out of 9,865 coaches were female, and only 321 out of 10,445 referees. There were 380 certified sports clubs in Syria with 206,164 affiliated members, of which 19,740 were women (9.6 per cent). The number of female coaches and referees accredited by the national federations was 257 and 321 respectively. Sports practised by girls in the clubs were athletics, swimming, gymnastics, basketball, handball, volleyball, table tennis, tennis, karate, judo, cycling, shooting and equestrian; and, more recently, football, boxing, wrestling and fencing. Figure 8.1 summarises the proportion of women in sports leadership positions in Syria.

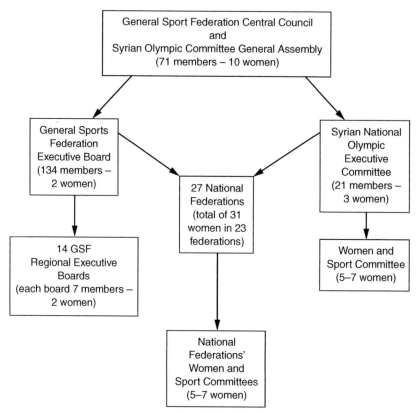

Figure 8.1 Decision-making bodies in Syrian sport and the number of women in leader-ship/decision-making roles.

Syrian women and elite sport

Teams and individuals can take part in the Pan-Arab, Asian, Mediterranean and international tournaments and championships as well as the Olympic Games. In addition, female Syrian teams (Muslim and non-Muslim participants) participate in the Islamic Women's Sport Federation's Championships. In the events in which both Syrian men's and women's teams take part, the proportion of women team members has never exceeded 15 per cent in the Pan-Arab Games, although this figure is slightly higher for the other events. In the modern Olympics, Syria has had a number of female representatives as indicated in Table 8.2.

By far the most successful female athlete from Syria was Ghada Shouaa, who competed in the heptathlon. She won gold medals at the 1994 Asian Games in Hiroshima, Japan, the World Athletics Championship in 1995 in Sweden and the 1996 Atlanta Olympic Games. She attained celebrity status in Syria and became the inspiration for many boys as well as girls to train as athletes. Postage stamps

Table 8.2 Syrian participants in the Olympic Games

Olympic Games	Year	Total in team	Number of men	Number of women	Female representative	Sport
Munich	1972				Malak Al Nassar	Athletics
Moscow	1980	67	65	2	Dia Totenji	Athletics
					Hala Al Moghrabi	
Los Angeles	1984	8	8	0		
Seoul	1988	13	13	0		
Barcelona	1992	9	8	1	Ghada Shouaa	Athletics
Atlanta	1996	7	6	1	Ghada Shouaa	Athletics
Sydney	2000	8	6	2	Ghada Shouaa	Athletics
					Marilla Mamoun	Swimming
Athens	2004	6	5	1	Zainab Bakkour	Athletics
Beijing	2008	8	6	2	Fadwa Bouza	Athletics
					Bayan Joumaa	Swimming

were issued bearing her picture and she became a figure of immense national pride in Syria. Injury limited the final years of her sporting career and eventually forced her into retirement. Sadly, whilst it would have been possible for her to have continued to contribute to the development of athletics, particularly among girls, in Syria, Ghada Shouaa chose to move to Germany.

Whilst never winning an Olympic gold medal, two Syrian men, Joseph Attiya and Nassar Al Shami, won silver in wrestling and a bronze for boxing in the 1984 and 2004 Games respectively. Syria has not enjoyed a large team presence at the Olympics, the representatives usually numbering between six and eight. The exceptions were at Moscow in 1980 with 64 competitors, of whom three were women, and at Seoul in 1988 with 13 competitors, although none were female.

As well as providing funding for special training centres for talented young people, the government continues to give strong support to top male and female athletes. Since 1981, a series of legislative decrees enacted by the then President of the Republic, Hafez Al Assad, has ensured social and financial security for Syrian sporting champions. Such rewards are given to those Syrian men and women who finish in any of the first three places at the Arab, Asian, Mediterranean and Olympic Games. Regardless of education or religion, they are provided with housing and permanent employment in a state institution of his or her choice. Remuneration is linked to further athletic success. At the end of their sporting careers, they may continue to work in the institution to which they were appointed and, subject to relevant certification, normal terms of promotion are applied until the retirement age of 60 years.

With regard to the *hijab*, there are no rules that refer to head covering in sporting participation in Syria. Girls and women may choose to wear it or not. Sex segregation in sport is not practised outside the secondary school system. Consequently, all school sports championships and national championships are held in open facilities and for anyone who chooses to participate, to enjoy as a spectator or to engage with via the media. Women are active members of the media, working as journalists on one of the five specialist daily sports papers, writing in the sports pages of the normal daily papers and as sports editors and reporters on television and radio. Although women's sporting activities do receive media attention, sports reporting is very much dominated by men's football, leaving relatively little room for other sports, and women's sports in particular.

Community-level provision, sport and physical fitness

Sports clubs and complexes first grew in the cities that had sports institutes, and then more widely after 1971. They cater for a wide provision of sporting activities, inclusive of men and women and people of all religions and ethnicities, from recreational to competition levels, as well as at regional, national and international levels. Outside their curriculum duties, trained teachers furthered sports development in Syria by providing opportunities for playing sports and by coaching in city clubs. Later, many of them occupied leading positions in the National Sports Federation and various sports institutions.

With the increase in general awareness of the importance of physical activity in all its forms for the health and well-being of everyone, the number of people taking up walking for health has increased, especially amongst women. Serious walkers can be seen in the streets, parks and sports complexes, where entry is free for both males and females. Exercising for fitness in the form of aerobics has also become popular in the state sports halls, where classes are provided at very low cost. The Syrian Arab 'Sport for All' Federation organises special courses for male and female coaches in aerobics, yoga and dance. In 2007, 613 female coaches were qualified. The number of private fitness centres and swimming pools that cater exclusively for women at specific times or in separate facilities has increased, but membership is relatively expensive. Commercially owned training centres, where boys and girls can play football, basketball and tennis and go swimming, have been built, but these too are relatively expensive to visit regularly.

The government recognised early that to develop sport effectively in the Syrian Arab Republic there needed to be a building programme of sports facilities both at city and club level. The GSF, the body responsible for sport in Syria, stressed the importance of the availability of sports facilities in every town and city. Large sports complexes were built, often to facilitate the hosting of major sporting events such as the Fifth Pan-Arab Games in 1976, from which Damascus and other neighbouring cities benefited. Similarly, in 1987 Syria held the Tenth Mediterranean Games, in Latakia, in which men and women athletes from Asia, Europe and Africa participated, and for which huge sports complexes were built in Latakia, Tartous and nearby towns.

Women and girls make up only 9.6 per cent of the membership of sports clubs, although the most talented and dedicated girls and women attend the GSF's training centres, where they receive specialist coaching, especially in artistic and rhythmic gymnastics, swimming, athletics, tennis, karate, judo, table tennis and badminton. In all, there are 55 such centres with ten to 15 sportswomen in each. National championships for these centres are held annually, developing a sound infrastructure for young women's participation and development of potential.

Difficulties and obstacles

The main obstacles for Syrian women in sport are social, technical and economic. Social obstacles relate predominantly to the culture of Syria and local traditions, still practised, especially in rural areas. These include early marriage and the reality that many women give up sport after marriage or at a certain age. Technical obstacles relate to the shortage of a female cadre of coaches and officials, and this is rooted in both economic and social obstacles.

Syria is an Islamic country in that 89 per cent of its inhabitants are Muslims, but what distinguishes it from a number of other Islamic countries, especially in the Arab region, is that no political or opposing religious group, internally or externally, affects the state's plans or strategies. There is abidance, by the religious men and different religious institutions in Syria, to the general policy of the state since the state permits, and assists them in realising, a number of religious freedoms. These include approving the construction of additional mosques and churches, the holding of sessions for preaching the Quran and Bible, and the opening of religious schools (Islamic and Christian). Consequently, any state-sponsored activities, including those related to sport, will meet with the support and encouragement of religious men and different religious institutions.

Whilst politics and religion are extraneous to sport, it is interesting to note the increase in girls wearing the *hijab* in sport as well. In my view, this return to religious appearance is attributable to several damaging global and regional political issues. Examples include the mistaken worldwide assumption that links terrorism to Islam, the accelerated spread of this belief through recent incidents and the lack of the establishment of justice in international politics. The latter is especially poignant with regard to the Palestinian situation and the continued dispute over the Israeli-occupied Arab lands, such as the Golan Heights in Syria. All these factors raise consciousness about faith and identity and the individual's desire to defend and protect such deeply held values, sometimes visibly.

Instability and lack of peace in the region bring social and economic pressures that affect progress, development and any scientific base for knowledge, such as accuracy in statistics and limitations to national census figures in monitoring accurately, for example, population and the health situation of Syrian citizens. In short, state regulations and laws in Syria currently afford women the right to live their lives as citizens in the same way as men, without any distinction, committing both sexes to the principles of sharing, collaboration and equal career opportunities, including their rights to practise physical education and sport. The greatest challenge for many Syrian women is to increase levels of awareness and the capability to overcome the constraints of some customs and traditions, and to gain knowledge and skills through education and qualifications that will enable them to contribute more fully to society.

Author's narrative

The author of this chapter, Nour El-Houda Karfoul, was a leading pioneer for women and sport in Syria. In the absence of detailed literature, and at the request of the editors, she has used her life experience and leadership in the area to write a first-hand account of women in sport in Syria, and her role and achievements in its development.

My own case has provided inspiration for many students in sports colleges and athletes in sports clubs who went on to occupy important positions in national federations or school sports. The decision to study sport education in the Soviet Union after obtaining the High-School Study Certificate in 1964 was undoubtedly revolutionary. For a young girl from a Muslim background to travel alone and live in a Communist, atheist country in 1965 was unheard of. I returned to Aleppo in 1970 to teach at the Sport Education Institute for Female Teachers, later becoming its Principal before taking up the principalship of a similar institute in Damascus in 1979. Later I was elected to the Executive Board of the General Sports Federation (GSF) and from 1982 served on the board of the Syrian National Olympic Committee (SNOC) and as the elected Secretary General of the Syrian Olympic Committee in 1983. Since this time I have served on the Women and Sport Committee of the Olympic Council of Asia (OCA) and have been awarded special recognition by the IOC on two occasions. In this part of my career as a sports administrator with the GSF and SNOC I was always the only woman amidst men. I never considered my position contentious, however; nor was there any sense of competition. I always felt confident in my qualifications, experience and abilities to perform my vocational tasks alongside all my colleagues.

In my career, certainly, there were great challenges to customs and traditions, but we have to bear in mind the important role and support of my family, my brothers, and later on from my husband, who believed in the woman's role in society and her ability to make a difference, as well as the state rules and regulations and the general political directives to support women. My husband, Mohammed Dayoub, is a retired engineer officer of the Syrian Arab army. He is a supporter of women's rights to work and to contribute to society in general. He understands and supports the careers in sport of myself and my daughter, Farah. Farah became the tennis champion of Syria in the cadet category, and later a member of the national tennis team in the junior and senior categories. She participated with the national team in the International Tennis Federation Cup for several years. Farah is currently a coach and coach educator, coaching the national tennis team for men in the 2009 Davis Cup. This is a rare phenomenon for a woman in any country of the world. Education has been significant for both our children; Farah is a graduate of Damascus University in architecture, and our son, Fadi, a basketball player in his youth, gained a PhD in engineering from the Ecole Central in Paris.

Family and state support helped me to overcome many obstacles. I have taken many leadership positions, which, in addition to those mentioned, include: Vice-President of the Commission for the History of the Sport Movement of Syria; Executive Committee member of the International Committee of the Mediterranean Games; President of the Sport Association of Arab Women and OCA Women and Sport Committee member. Through my education and life experience I had achieved academic qualifications and confidence in my capabilities. These gave me inner liberation from fear of customs and traditions, many imposed in the name of religion from my early years. I always endeavoured to maintain the real ethical values in dealing with others and to be moderate in conduct. I started from my understanding and respect of religions and their values of justice, tolerance and goodness, rather than outward performance of ritual and in some cases disingenuous action.

From my life experiences in Syria and internationally, I think the greatest challenges for the future are:

1   Establishing political and economic stability that can be reflected in the social position of all people, especially women, regardless of their religious belief. In-depth provision of sport for women requires such stability, especially economic, to become a reality and enable the state to offer the necessary resources and management.
2   Enabling women through education and training to become qualified in the scientific areas of sport that will assist them in fulfilling their role, for example as athlete, official, coach, referee, leader or administrator.
3   The greatest challenge is for the woman herself, her liberation from fear and the influence of some traditions, behaviours and ways of thinking, sometimes imposed in the name of religion.

Women in Syria have made good progress and development in all fields, including sports, and that progress has been rooted in societal structure over many years. To maintain this progress, in my view, women have to be armed with awareness, education and courage in facing the obstacles they meet which hinder both their development and contribution to society in every sense.

Conclusion

Syria is an Arab Muslim country that has been, and remains, a haven for Arabs in political crisis – for example Palestinian refugees since 1948; Lebanese refugees temporarily during the civil wars of 1958, 1975 and 2006 and the Israeli war in 2006; and Iraqi refugees expelled at the time of Saddam Hussein and later after the American occupation. Certainly, such numbers of refugees have had multiple economic and social effects on the Syrian people and consequently on all aspects of life, including the situation of women in sport. Sometimes other priorities have to take precedence. People in Syria, historically, possess a keen sense of belonging to the Arab Homeland and have the ability to overcome crises through patience and adaptation. The Syrian people, furthermore, do not lose hope of witnessing the victory of the values of justice and peace.

Bibliography

Abu Nauwar, M. (1983) Olympic Games: Ancient and Present, *Olympic Review*, Jordan: NOC.
Bashour, W. (1999) *A History of the Sport Movement in Syria*, vols 1 and 2, Damascus: General Sports Federation, Media and Education Department (in Arabic).
Central Statistics Bureau, www.champress.net (in Arabic) (accessed 1 May 2009).

General Sports Federation, Syria (2007*) Annual Report*, www.fgs-aleppo.org (in Arabic).
Mansfield, P. (1985) Syria: The Heart of Arabism, in *The Arabs* (4th edition), London: Penguin Books: 368–375.

Additional sources

The archive of the Syrian National Olympic Committee, which contains information on participation at the Olympic Games and the Arab Continental and Regional Games.
Presidential decrees relating to the organisation of the sports movement in Syria.

9 Güçlenmek için Mücadele

Türkiye'de Kadınların ve Genç Kızların Spora Katılımı

Struggling for empowerment
Sport participation of women and girls in Turkey

Canan Koca and İlknur Hacısoftaoğlu

Editors' introduction

The geographical location of Turkey, its secular government and majority Muslim population make it an interesting country for study when investigating the participation of Muslim women in sport. The authors explore historical and contemporary issues related to girls and women. Theoretically, modern Turkey encourages participation in school and community sport and exercise for all. In reality, some schools do not carry out the required national curriculum, and data suggests that, despite some provision, they provide very small levels of participation in physical activity. Turkish women can face social disapproval by taking part in sporting activities; the *hijab* has been banned in competitive sport since 1999; and opportunities are constrained by under-representation of women in all leadership positions in sport.

The history of modern Turkey

The history of modernisation in Turkey extends back to the institutionalised reforms of the Late Ottoman period. After the foundation of the Turkish Republic in 1923, reformers who aimed at modernisation through the Westernisation of the country made dramatic reforms to accomplish the process (Keyder 1997): the alphabet changed from Arabic to Latin, the calendar was adapted to the Gregorian calendar, the official day of rest changed to Sunday from Friday (the sacred day of Muslims), Evkaf (the umbrella organisation that oversees the running of all religious foundations in the Ottoman Empire) was taken over by the state, and religious education was regulated and patronised by the state (Lewis 1952).

The modernity project included a rational organisation of the state, bureaucratisation and organisational efficiency, as well as a social transformation including social, cultural and educational projects that aimed to bring forth modern citizens and modern gender identities based on secularisation (Keyder 1997).

Until the foundation of the Turkish Republic, Islam was a significant component of the Ottoman regime. However, after the foundation of the Turkish Republic, every religion was accepted if practised in private. In the public sphere religious signs and symbols became regulated by the state. In total, 69.58 million Turks are Muslims, representing 98 per cent of the total population.[1]

Although Turkey has preserved its secular regime, there has been an increasing emphasis on Islam in the political arena since the 1950s that can be interpreted within the framework of a critique of modernity (Kandiyoti 1997). Since the 1980s Islamic communities have gained power: influential Islamic-oriented TV channels have proliferated and many organisations and institutions have been founded, including newspapers, publishing houses, an Islamic-oriented labour union confederation and an Islamic-oriented businessmen's association (Gulalp 2001). In the 1990s, political Islam became more visible and powerful. In 1983 the Welfare Party was founded and in 1996 entered a government coalition as a partner. The rising electoral fortunes of the Welfare Party (Refah Partisi, RP), a party that differentiates itself sharply from the 'orthodox' parties of the right or left of the political spectrum by campaigning explicitly on an Islamist platform, constitutes the most obvious or visible sign of Islamic resurgence in the Turkish context (Onis 1997: 743).

The Welfare Party was forced out of power by the Turkish military in 1997 due to its alleged Islamist agenda. However, in 2002 the Justice and Development Party (AKP), whose founders were mostly from the Welfare Party or had an Islamic political background, won the elections and ruled as a single party. The party, which describes itself as Muslim and democratic, is still in power today. Thus, discussions on Islam and secularism have continued to be a controversial issue in Turkey.

As Turkey sought to establish itself as a modern republic in the early part of the twentieth century, it used Islam as one of its most potent symbols – for example the *hijab* (headscarf) for women – to distance itself from former regimes (O'Neill 2008). After the military coup in 1980, the military government introduced a Dress and Appearance Regulation Code. Head-covering was banned for women in public institutions. Furthermore, in 1982 with the Higher Education Law, universities were defined as public institutions and therefore head-covering was forbidden. Currently, the headscarf (the *hijab* in Turkey, strictly covering hair, neck and some parts of the cheeks) is one of the most controversial issues in Turkey. For religious women, the ban on *hijabs* is seen as an attempt to remove religious freedom since, for them, the *hijab* is a requirement of their belief. However, Kemalist (defending the policies rather than doctrines of Mustafa Kemal) authorities have claimed that the *hijab* is a most visible sign of radical Islam and that its wearers are in fact part of an anti-secularist movement aiming at the destruction of the modern Turkish state.

The situation of women in Turkey

During the Early Republican period, gender identities and enactments became products and signifiers of modernity in Turkey (Kandiyoti 1997). In 1924, a new education system, which was for both women and men, was introduced, and subsequently women gained equal rights with men in education. The new Civil Code in 1926, which replaced Sharia (the system of law based on Islam), gave women the right to divorce and to inherit, besides prohibiting polygamy and religious marriage. Civil marriage became a state requirement. Turkish women received the right to vote in 1930 and to be elected in municipal, state and federal elections in 1934. Through the modernisation processes, women gained access to citizens' rights; however, various groups, among them feminists, criticised the project of modernity because it ignored what women from different social and cultural backgrounds wanted (Arat 1997; Kandiyoti 1997; Toprak 1994).

With the increasing influence of women's movements in the 1980s (Özer 2006) and the ongoing attempt to gain entrance into the European Union (EU), Turkey signed the United Nations Convention on the Elimination of All Forms of Discrimination Against Women (1979) and the Declaration on the Elimination of Violence Against Women (1993). In 1990, the General Directorate on the Status of Women, attached to the Turkish Prime Ministry, was founded. Then, in 1995, Turkey joined the Fourth World Conference on Women and signed the Beijing Declaration.

In addition to the signing of international accords on women's rights and the founding of women's NGOs and the General Directorate on the Status of Women, several changes occurred in the legal field. First, the law on employment was changed in 1990, giving women the right to work without the permission of their husbands. A whole year of intensive lobbying and widespread campaigning by the women's movement throughout 2001 has resulted in reforms which have drastically changed the legal status of women in the family, and in the promulgation of the new Turkish Civil Code, which was passed by the Turkish Grand National Assembly on 22 November 2001 (WWHR 2002). The new Code sets the equal division of the property acquired during marriage as a default property regime, assigning an economic value to women's hitherto invisible labour for the well-being of the family household. After the promulgation of the new Turkish Civil Code in 2004, the new Turkish Penal Code was introduced which brings many changes on issues, ranging from rape to abortion, in favour of women.

Despite these positive reforms with regard to women's status in the Penal and Civil codes, according to figures from 2006 the proportion of women in the labour force is only 24.9 per cent, while that of men is 71.5 per cent (Turkish Statistical Institute 2007). Within the major occupational groups, the employment rate of women in high-prestige occupations is lower than that of men. The rate of women employed as legislators or senior officials and managers in the total women's labour force is 2 per cent, while for men it is 11.3 per cent.

However, the employment rate of women in agriculture is 33 per cent and in unskilled occupations 16 per cent, whereas the corresponding figures for men are 17 per cent and 3 per cent respectively (Turkish Statistical Institute 2007).

The most significant difference between men and women is to be found in political positions. There are only 50 women among the 550 members of the parliament (9.1 per cent). In 2005, women constituted 0.56 per cent of mayors and 2.32 per cent of general city councillors.[2] In addition, official education statistics show that, in 2000, 19 per cent of women were illiterate, while only 6 per cent of men were. According to figures from 2006, 77 per cent of women in the 25–64 age group had an education level that was primary school and below, and only 8 per cent of this age group had graduated from university (Turkish Statistical Institute 2007). Thus, although much has been done for women in Turkey, there is still a considerable difference between the social situation of men and women.

Sport and physical activities in Turkey

Following on from this brief account of the history of modern Turkey and the situation of women, the remainder of the chapter focuses on Turkish girls' and women's participation in sport and physical activities. This section addresses the school and community provision of sport, its organisation and the realities of girls' and women's participation. The barriers discussed include the ban on head-coverings, women's poor representation in leadership positions and the media's sports coverage.

The situation of physical education in Turkey and girls' participation

A new Turkish national physical-education curriculum was introduced for all primary schools in 2007, and the programme is standardised for all government and private schools. This new curriculum has changed the focus from traditional sport-based activities (e.g. gymnastics, track-and-field and wrestling) to physical activities that promote life-long participation (e.g. dance, games and outdoor activities). It has two main learning areas: (a) movement knowledge and motor skills, and (b) active participation and leading a healthy life (Ministry of National Education 2006). However, the former physical-education programme is still being used in many schools. Even though the national physical-education guidelines are standardised for all schools, there are substantial discrepancies in the implementation and contents of these guidelines.

Physical education is compulsory in all schools from ages 6–18; primary schools are expected to provide one hour of physical education per week for the first–fifth grades (ages 7–11) and two hours for sixth–eighth grades (ages 12–14). There are no differences for girls and boys in terms of physical education activities and environment. In accordance with Turkish secularism, coeducation in physical education is the norm for all grades. However, in many (especially private) schools, boys and girls are segregated in grades 6 to 8. The dominant sports in and out of school for the boys are football, basketball, wrestling and the martial arts; for the girls they are volleyball, gymnastics and badminton.

Schools are the key agencies in providing physical education for all young people, with additional opportunities for taking part in extracurricular activities. However, many studies revealed that numerous students did not participate in physical activities in and out of school and their activity levels were low (Hümeriç et al. 2005; Sönmez and Sunay 2001). For example, Hümeriç and her colleagues observed sixth, seventh and eighth grade students using SOFIT (System for Observing Fitness Instruction Time, McKenzie et al. 1991). They found that students spent little time in moderate to vigorous physical activity in physical-education classes and were generally standing or sitting in the observed physical-education lessons. Furthermore, girls' physical activity participation levels in and out of school were lower than boys' (girls had a mean of 50 METs[3] and boys had a mean of 66) (Koçak et al. 2002), and girls had less positive attitudes towards physical education and sport than boys (Koca and Demirhan 2004; Koca et al. 2005). This led to lack of interest in sport and physical activities among girls and women.

Physical-education teachers are trained at universities in undergraduate programmes in Turkey. There are more than 50 universities that offer physical-education teacher training programmes. These are four-year courses, aiming to train teachers for elementary school (1–8) and high school (9–12) physical-education classes. The programme consists of 144–156 credit hours of courses over eight semesters. The programme has applied courses and practicals such as Instructional Methods in Physical Education, Assessment and Evaluation, School Experience, Teaching Experience (Field Base Experience) and several sport branches that include team and individual sports.

Organisation of sports and physical activities in Turkey

GSGM, which is the government agency for sport, has the power to make all arrangements and take important decisions about sport-related events. According to the law (no. 3289), it has a responsibility of all 'sport for all' and 'elite sport' events (for example planning, programming, implementing and monitoring youth services out of school, the construction of youth centres, camps and sports fields, and organising courses for both professional and recreational athletes and coaches) in Turkey. There are a total of 59 sports federations (52 of them are autonomous) that are placed under the GSGM (www.gsgm.gov.tr).

There are a total of 8,593 sports clubs in Turkey: 5,636 youth sport clubs, 1,181 institutional sports clubs, 615 specialised sports clubs and 1,148 school sports clubs (www.tuik.gov.tr). However, one might assume that these clubs are not actively involved in organising and providing sports and physical activities. In recent years the municipalities of big cities such as Ankara and Istanbul have been providing outdoor physical activity opportunities and facilities such as sports centres, walking tracks and outdoor fitness apparatus for people. These facilities are established in most districts; for example, there are 23 walking tracks in Ankara which women and older people use not only because they are free of charge but also because they are accessible. Free public transportation is also provided for the members of some Ladies' Locals (LLs). However, this number is not sufficient for the number of inhabitants. Indeed, one might think that there should be more physical activity opportunities and facilities in a city like Ankara, which has a population of over 4.5 million (www.tuik.gov.tr).

Ladies' Locals, which were established in 2000, are community centres supported by the municipality of Ankara. There are 14 LLs, and the number of members was around 100,000 in 2007 (Ankara Government 2007). The primary objective of the LLs is to provide a space for women to spend their leisure time by participating in activities such as sports (for example, fitness, exercise classes and table tennis), as well as in educational and social activities (for example, music and drama courses). The socio-economic status of the LL participants is generally lower-class, with most rural migrants residing in neighbourhood squatter settlements. Besides these LLs, commercial sports centres are increasingly providing services in mixed-sex environments. Since they are expensive, these are only accessible for middle- and upper-class women. These sports centres are very popular among those women in pursuit of healthy bodies, and also because of the social pressure to be slim and meet modern notions of attractiveness.

Participation of girls and women in sports and physical activity

No state-wide/large-scale statistics on sport participation of the Turkish population have so far been collated. Turkey has a population of 70 million. However, the Turkish Sport for All Federation, which was established in 1990, has a very small membership of approximately 2,500 members. Research findings suggest that only 7.4 per cent of high-school students (88 out of 1,237 students) take part in organised sport or recreation programmes for eight or more hours per week, and 8.2 per cent (101 out of 1,237 students) for 6–7 hours per week, boys having more regular exercise than girls (Siyez 2008). In the case of university students, the research showed that 72 per cent of 1,097 students did not participate in any vigorous physical activity, and 68 per cent of them did not participate in any moderate physical activity (Savcı *et al.* 2006), male students being physically more active than female students (Aşçı *et al.* 2006).

In recent years there has been a significant increase in the number of women in competitive sports as well as in female athletes' participation and achievements in international sports competitions (for example, winning medals in World and European Championships and Olympics). According to information from the GSGM, while the number of active elite female athletes (56,651) is considerably fewer than elite male athletes (363,230), there has been a threefold increase in women's involvement in sport since 1997 (www.tuik.gov.tr). Most women are competing in volleyball (10,599), taekwondo (9,353), basketball (4,714), karate (4,101), swimming (1,952), kickboxing (1,924), handball (1,859) and judo (1,543). In addition, the highest participation of Turkish female athletes (21 athletes) in the Olympics was in the 2004 Games, where Nurcan Taylan became the first Turkish female athlete to win a gold medal in weight-lifting. A total of 20 Turkish female athletes competed in the 2008 Beijing Olympics, and they won four silver medals (weight-lifting, taekwondo and two medals in track-and-field). The most successful Turkish female athletes who won medals in the World, European and Olympics Championships achieved them in taekwondo, weight-lifting and track-and-field.

Little information is available regarding leisure-time physical activity participation rates of Turkish women. An increasing number of women from diverse backgrounds and circumstances are actively participating in sport and fitness centre programmes, particularly in big cities. The most popular leisure-time physical activities for Turkish women are aerobics (aerobic classes in sports centres) (60 per cent), walking (in outdoor locations) (48 per cent) and fitness activities using machines (exercise bikes, treadmills and strength training machines) (41.6 per cent) (Koca *et al.* 2007). Factors such as continuing modernisation and the growing attention paid by municipalities to physical activity for women have all motivated women in Turkey to participate in physical activities in different types of sports and exercise clubs (Koca *et al.* 2007). Many Turkish women, particularly lower-class women, still encounter constraints, such as traditional gender-stereotyped beliefs and pressure regarding their role in their families and social status, which compromise their participation in physical activities (Koca *et al.* 2009). Women emphasise family responsibilities and the ethos of care as significant constraints to their leisure-time physical activity, fitting their participation around family responsibilities such as housework and childcare. Moreover, the social disapproval for women venturing to take up a physical activity is strong in traditional Turkish families, and their participation is markedly affected by their husbands', relatives' and neighbours' approval or disapproval. Although the women in the above-mentioned study were trying to negotiate this lack of social approval, the authors argued that many other women are not allowed to participate in any leisure activities, let alone physical activity, in traditional segments of Turkish society.

The head-covering issue in sport

In Turkey there is a ban on wearing the *hijab* (headscarf) in competitive sport. Many Muslim athletes react to this constraint by not wearing a *hijab*, but others who are not willing to remove it cannot participate in competitive sports. For recreational sport, covered women go to women-only sessions or sports centres, such as the Ladies Locals in Ankara, to have a safe and private environment away from the 'male gaze'(Koca *et al.* 2009). However, the values of 'women-only' sessions or facilities are rarely recognised by sports governing bodies.

Women's representation in leadership positions

Women are significantly under-represented in decision-making positions in sporting bodies and institutions. There are two important sports organisations in

Turkey: the GSGM and the National Olympic Committee (TMOK). The so-called 'glass ceiling' for women seems to prevent them from assuming top positions in these two sports organisations. In 2007, there were 547 females and 4,943 males, i.e. a total of 5,490 employees, in the GSGM. Within this number, 853 (220 females and 633 males) were working at the headquarters in Ankara and 4,637 (327 females and 4,310 males) were working in provincial districts of the GSGM. In total, only 10 per cent of the employees in the GSGM were female. There were four females in the top-level management positions, two females in the middle and six in low-level management positions. Thus, females occupied 7.3 per cent of all management positions in the GSGM. Since the establishment of the GSGM in 1938, all the 25 General Managers of the organisation have been men. This means that sport policies are determined by men. In 2008, only 3.1 per cent of administrators and members of the executive committees of the 59 sports federations were women (www.gsgm.gov.tr). Only one federation (the Sailing Federation) is led by a women president, Nazlı İmre, who is also Assistant Secretary General of the National Olympic Committee (TMOK).

The TMOK for Turkey, which is an autonomous non-governmental sports organisation, has the control of Olympic sports in Turkey. As of 30 November 2008, there were two women (5.9 per cent) out of 34 members from all boards who had roles as Secretary General and Assistant Secretary General in the TMOK (www.olimpiyatkomitesi.org.tr). These women were members of the Executive Committee (11.8 per cent of a total of 17 members). Considering the established targets for women's membership of NOCs (10–20 per cent), it can be said that recruitment of women to the TMOK is not meeting these targets. In addition, the TMOK had no Women's Commission. Further, at present, there are no sports organisations exclusively for girls and women and no women's sections or committees in existing sports organisations in Turkey.

The same pattern is found in both coaching and refereeing. In one-third of sports federations (e.g. volleyball, sailing, wrestling, basketball and track-and-field) 22.6 per cent of all coaches and 15 per cent of all referees are women (taken from the Department of Sports Education in the GSGM). To conclude, girls and women are not represented in decision-making committees, which means that their participation in physical activities may often not be taken into consideration.

Turkish media coverage of women athletes

The most comprehensive research on the representation of women in the Turkish media has indicated that women are virtually ignored: 21 per cent of headline news includes women; 2 per cent of columnists are women; no political debate programmes broadcast on popular TV channels are led by women; and no main news presenters are women (MEDIZ 2008). Many researchers have also pointed to the under-representation of women in the Turkish media and the fact that, when women are represented, the coverage reinforces existing stereotypical norms presenting women as housewives, mothers or sex objects (Gencel-Bek 2001; Gencel-Bek and Binark 2000; Hortaçsu and Ertürk 2003).

The same trends are found in the media coverage of women athletes. Consistent with the results of studies in other countries, women athletes are markedly under-represented in newspaper and television coverage in Turkey. In one recent study, Arslan and Koca (2007) found that the number of articles about female athletes (6.05 per cent) was significantly lower than articles about male athletes (87.02 per cent). Another recent study indicated that women athletes who competed in the 2004 Olympics appeared to be of more interest to the media (28.74 per cent of coverage) than those who did not (only 2 per cent of non-Olympic coverage) (Koca and Arslan, forthcoming). These two studies indicate that male athletes received higher coverage than female athletes in both Olympic and non-Olympic articles. However, female athletes had a relatively higher coverage in Olympic articles than non-Olympic articles. An analysis of everyday coverage reveals the overwhelming dominance of male athletes' sports coverage in the Turkish media.

Conclusion

As can be inferred from the data in this chapter, women are under-represented at all levels, including coaching, refereeing, management and media, in Turkey. When the Republic was established in 1923, the equality of the sexes was introduced as part of the modernisation project. However, despite much progress, there are still significant gender inequalities in terms of access to and participation in the labour force, education and political representation, as well as in domestic and family responsibilities, which are still perceived as women's domains.

Turkey is a complex society where cultural, religious, social and economic forces constantly interact in women's lives. Therefore, the participation of Turkish women in sport seems to reflect the broader cultural context. Social and cultural constraints, contradictions between state secularism and religion, poverty, the low educational level of a large part of the population, inadequate sports and recreational facilities and the lack of opportunity, especially for females, frequently prevent women's and girls' participation in physical activity and sport. Likewise, the conflict between state secularism and the Muslim identity of religious women is a barrier that prevents their participation in sport. Moreover, the ban on head-coverings and mixed-sex environments in both competitive sport and many recreational sports restrict the access of women to these activities.

The small number of girls and women in both physical education and international sports, the lack of women in leadership positions and the lack of awareness about gender equality in the governing bodies of sport prevent the development of policies and strategies that might increase the participation of Turkish girls and women in sport. Therefore, it seems crucial to develop special plans of action to increase women's involvement in sport, especially religious girls and women.

For religious women athletes, the ban on head-coverings is the most limiting factor for their sports career. Because of this ban, many religious women who are unwilling to remove the *hijab* cannot integrate their religious and sports identities, and cannot participate in competitive sport. Currently it seems impossible to challenge this ban in the Turkish sports environment. Further research and a better understanding of the conflicts these women face will help to find ways to promote the inclusion of Turkish religious girls and women in sport.

Notes

1 There are no reliable statistics on the percentage of the Muslim population in Turkey. However, in most articles and reports it is written that Turkey is a predominantly Muslim country. Based upon the declared religion on the ID card of Turkish citizens, the Muslim population of Turkey is 98 per cent.
2 www.cities-localgovernments.org/uclg/index.asp?pag=stats_country. asp&L=EN&cnt_id=140&egn_id=3.
3 The energy cost of an activity can be measured in units called METS, which are multiples of an individual's basal metabolic rate.

Bibliography

Ankara Government (2007) www.ankara-bel.gov.tr (accessed 22 September 2008).

Arat, Y. (1997) The project of modernity and women in Turkey, in S. Bozdoğan and R. Kasaba (eds) *Rethinking Modernity and National Identity in Turkey*, Seattle: University of Washington Press: 95–112.

Arslan, B. and Koca, C. (2007) An examination of female athletes-related articles in Turkish daily newspapers regarding gender stereotypes, *Annals of Leisure Research*, 10: 310–327.

Aşçı, F.H., Tüzün, M. and Koca, C. (2006) An examination of eating attitudes and physical activity levels of Turkish university students with regard to self-presentational concern, *Eating Behaviours*, 7: 362–367.

CEDAW (Convention on the Elimination of Discrimination against Women) (1979) www.un.org/womenwatch/daw/cedaw (accessed 13 October 2008).

DEVAW (Declaration on the Elimination of Violence Against Women) (1993) Adopted by the General Assembly on 20 December 1993, UN Doc. A/RES/48/104.

Gencel-Bek, M. (2001) Medyada cinsiyetçilik ve iletişim politikası [Sexism in the media and communication policy], *İletişim 2001 Kadın Yaz Çalışmaları*, 213–235.

Gencel-Bek, M. and Binark, M. (2000) *Medyada Cinsiyetçilik [Sexism in the Media]*, Ankara: Ankara Üniversitesi, Kadın Sorunları Araştırma ve Uygulama Merkezi (KASAUM).

GSGM (n.d.) www.gsgm.gov.tr (accessed 11 November 2008).

Gulalp, H. (2001) Globalization and political Islam: the social bases of Turkey's Welfare Party, *International Journal of Middle East Studies*, 33: 433–448.

Hortaçsu, N. and Ertürk, E.M. (2003) Women and ideology: representations of women in religious and secular Turkish media, *Journal of Applied Social Psychology*, 33: 2017–2039.

Hümeriç, I., Kirazcı, S., Ince, M.L. and Çiçek, S. (2005) Assessment of health-related physical activity level, lesson context, and teacher behaviour in public and private elementary school physical education, *Journal of ICHPER-SD, XLI*, 4: 20–24.

Kandiyoti, D. (1987) Emancipated but unliberated? Reflections on the Turkish case, *Feminist Studies*, 13: 317–338.

Kandiyoti, D. (1997) Gendering the modern: on missing dimensions in the study of Turkish modernity, in S. Bozdoğan and R. Kasaba (eds) *Rethinking Modernity and National Identity in Turkey*, Seattle: University of Washington Press: 113–132.

Keyder, Ç. (1997) Whither the project of modernity? Turkey in the 1990s, in S. Bozdoğan and R. Kasaba (eds) *Rethinking Modernity and National Identity in Turkey*, Seattle: University of Washington Press: 37–51.

Koca, C. and Arslan, B. (forthcoming) Media coverage of Turkish female athletes in the 2004 Olympics, in T. Bruce, J. Hovden and P. Markula (eds) *Media Coverage of Women at the 2004 Olympic Games: Missing in Action*, New Zealand: Wilf Malcolm Institute of Educational Research-New Zealand and SENSE-Netherlands Publishers.

Koca, C. and Demirhan, G. (2004) An examination of high school students' attitudes toward physical education with regard to gender and sport participation, *Physical, Conceptual and Motor Skills*, 98: 754–758.

Koca, C., Aşçı, F.H. and Demirhan, G. (2005) Attitudes toward physical education and class preferences of Turkish adolescents in terms of school gender composition, *Adolescence*, 40: 365–375.

Koca, C., Bulgu, N. and Aşçı, F.H. (2007) Analysis of Turkish women's physical activity participation regarding gender and social class. Paper presented at the Fourth World Congress of ISSA in conjunction with the Tenth World Congress of ISHPES, Copenhagen, Denmark, July–August.

Koca, C., Hacısoftaoğlu, I. and Bulgu, N. (2007) Physical activity participation among Turkish women from different socioeconomic statuses. Paper presented at the Fourth World Congress of ISSA in conjunction with the Tenth World Congress of ISHPES, Copenhagen, Denmark, July–August.

Koca, C., Henderson, K., Aşçı, F.H. and Bulgu, N. (2009) Issues of participation in leisure-time physical activity for Turkish women, *Journal of Leisure Research*, 41: 225–251.

Koçak, S., Harris, M.B., Işler, K.A. and Çiçek, S. (2002) Physical activity level, sport participation and parental education level in Turkish junior high school students, *Pediatric Exercise Science*, 14: 147–154.

Lewis, B. (1952) Islamic revival in Turkey, *International Affairs*, 28: 38–48.

McKenzie, T.L., Sallis, J.F. and Nader, P.R. (1991) SOFIT: system for observing fitness instruction time, *Journal of Teaching in Physical Education*, 11: 195–205.

MEDIZ (2008) Women's Media Watch Group. www.mediz.org (accessed 23 November 2008).

Ministry of National Education (2006) *İlköğretim Okulları için Beden Eğitimi ve Spor Programı* [*Physical Education and Sport Programme for Elementary Schools*], Ankara: Milli Eğitim Bakanlığı Yayını.

O'Neil, M.L. (2008) Being seen: headscarves and the contestation of public space in Turkey, *European Journal of Women's Studies*, 15: 101–115.

Onis, Z. (1997) The political economy of Islamic resurgence in Turkey: the rise of the Welfare Party, *Third World Quarterly*, 18: 743–766.

Ozer, T.O. (2006) Women in Turkey and Turkish Civil Code. Paper presented at the annual meeting of the Law and Society Association.

Savcı, S., Öztürk, M., Arıkan, H., Inal Ince, D. and Tokgözoglu, L. (2006) Physical activity levels of university students, *Archives of the Turkish Society of Cardiology*, 34: 166–172.

Siyez, D.M. (2008) Health-enhancing behaviors among high school students in Turkey, *The High School Journal*, 46–55.

Sönmez, T. and Sunay, H. (2001) Study on effectiveness of physical education classes at secondary schools in Ankara province. Paper presented at the meeting of the Second National Physical Education and Sports Teacher Conference, Bursa, Turkey, December.

Toprak, Z. (1994) Türkiye'de siyaset ve kadın: Kadınlar halk fırkası'ndan 'Arşıulusal Kadınlar Birliği' kongresi'ne (1923–1935) [Politics and Women in Turkey: From the Women's Public Party to the congress of The Highest National Women's Association (1923–1935)], Kadın Araştırmaları Dergisi (İstanbul Üniversitesi Kadın Sorunları Araştırma ve Uygulama Merkezi): 5–12.

Turkish Statistical Institute (2007) *Turkey's Statistical Year Book 2007*, Ankara: TUİK, www.tuik.gov.tr (accessed 15 November 2008).

WWHR (2002) *The New Legal Status of Women in Turkey: Women for Women's Human Rights*, NEW WAYS Liaison Office. Publisher: Women for Women's Human Rights. Turkish National Olympic Committee, www.olimpiyatkomitesi.org.tr (accessed 10 December 2002).

Part III
Case studies

10 Die palästinensische Frauenfussballnationalmannschaft auf dem Weg in die Fußballwelt

Eine Fallstudie zum Zusammenhang von Religion, Kultur, Politik und Sport

Palestinian women's national football team aims high
A case study to explore the interaction of religion, culture, politics and sports

Petra Gieß-Stüber, Sarah Kremers, Steffen Luft and Jonathan Schaller

Editors' introduction

The study explores the lives of Palestinian women in the national football team. Interestingly, half of the team is Muslim and the other half Christian in a predominantly Arab, Muslim society. Participants' experiences of identity, sport, culture, religion and politics are recounted, demonstrating ways in which team membership has enabled the women to redefine themselves, gender relations and womanhood. Sport has become a social movement for self-determination, agency, peace and friendship in the lives of the women's national football team of Palestine.

Introduction

> It's a tough game. It's for boys and not for girls, and you should not play this rough-and-tumble game; you will be like boys. Don't just follow the ball; find a good man to marry! And look to the future!
>
> (Honey, captain of the team, describing Palestinians' conservative attitude towards women playing football)

Palestine is widely associated with pictures drawn by the media showing war, radical fighters wielding machine guns and a democracy that suffers from internal strife. Whoever travels to the Holy Land to get to know the country and its people will scarcely find these pictures. Instead, they will find a country, basically rural, with donkeys and horses among the old Mercedes cars, with progressively thinking people who discuss politics and have an above-average educational standard. A special effort is necessary, though, to master the challenges of a daily life which is seriously disrupted by the Israeli occupation and tensions between the Palestinian parties. In a life that is restricted by politics and military action, there are many surprising developments. One of these is the women's national football team. The authors would like to present a holistic picture of the challenges encountered by young women who play a male-dominated sport like football in a Muslim society – moreover, one which is beset by problems of conflict. It is impossible to trace and explore all the complex influences that affect the situation of the team, but this contribution is meant as an attempt to raise awareness for the opportunities and challenges of women's sport in Palestine.

Political background – Palestine

Palestine has a long and varied history that has been influenced by numerous cultures. Islamic heritage was, and continues to be, powerful from the time when Palestine became part of the Islamic world in the seventh century of the Christian era. For centuries Palestinian people from various faith communities lived in harmony under Islamic rule. But then, from the middle of the nineteenth century onwards, increasing numbers of legal and illegal Jewish immigrants from different parts of the world, but especially from Europe and America, followed the Zionist idea of settling in Palestine. The greater the numbers became, the louder the Jewish voices grew demanding their own state. Frequent conflicts took place between the local Arab inhabitants, who were worried about the loss of their own state, the Jewish immigrants and the British forces, who were in charge of protecting and administering Palestine from the First World War onwards. Severe problems, which still have an effect on the political situation today, were created when around 700,000 Arab citizens (about half the population at that time) lost their homes and were forced to move after Israel proclaimed itself a sovereign state on 14 May 1948. Refugee camps were built on the West Bank, as well as in Lebanon and Jordan. Even today Palestinians have kept the keys to their former homes in the hope of returning one day. The country has been shaken by wars and violent struggles ever since. The result is that high walls surround Palestinian cities in the Palestinian Authority areas, separating them from each other. In many districts, checkpoints have been built, and permits are required to travel from one place to another. To fly to another country Palestinians must first travel to Amman in Jordan due to the fact that they are not permitted to use Tel Aviv airport. Borders in conflict zones are heavily guarded, and crossings demand extraordinary patience since not everybody is allowed to leave and re-enter the country freely. Restricted freedom of movement, the loss of farmland and declining numbers of tourists in the Palestinian Authority areas, as well as heavy bombing in areas such as in the Gaza Strip, have led to high unemployment, poverty and despair. The Gaza Strip, a densely populated region inhabited by 1.2 million Palestinians and strictly closed off by the Israeli military, is totally separated from the West Bank. People there are still suffering from the effects of the Israeli bombings in December 2008 and the sporadic attacks in retaliation for rockets fired into Israel from Gaza.

At the heart of the conflict between Israel and Palestine lie unresolved questions concerning the return of Palestinian refugees to their homes in areas that are now Israeli territory; the construction of Jewish settlements on Palestinian territory; the sharing of Jerusalem as the capital of each country and as a common religious centre for Jews, Muslims and Christians; and, finally, the acknowledgement of each other as sovereign states. In addition to these problems with Israel, the Palestinians are faced with internal struggles between the two major parties, Fatah and Hamas.

Gender relations in the country are shaped by social, economic, political and religious factors, and are embedded in Palestinian culture, based on Islam. Internal strife and the Israeli occupation have led neither to decreasing gender segregation nor the participation of women in public affairs. On the contrary, the result has been an enhancement of traditional gender roles (Rizq-Qazzaz 2006). After a number of successes were achieved by women activists before the Second Intifada in 2000,[1] awareness building and struggling for gender equality 'was covered with the ripples of destroyed houses, high unemployment rates, alarming poverty, and the need to protect the family and children' (Rizq-Qazzaz 2006: 192).

The study

Jonathan Schaller's previous experience as a special coach for the goalkeepers of the Palestinian women's football team and assistant coach of the team for nine months in 2005/2006 allowed him to gain multifaceted insights into the practice and competition routines of female players in the Arab world. The team had been started by female coach Samar A. Moussa, Director of the Athletics Department at the University of Bethlehem, two years before. Since then, the team had been constantly developing. Support came through the Palestinian Football Association (PFA), and media interest increased when the team made its mark in Palestine and abroad. Moussa made quite an effort to introduce football for girls at clubs and schools. As a result, a growing number of clubs started to offer football training for women. In autumn 2008, a first league championship was held in Palestine. Girls from the different clubs are playing more and more national and international games, which has led to increasing popularity and awareness of football among girls in Palestine. Jonathan Schaller helped to organise a tour that took the female national team to Germany for three weeks in June 2007. The players met German football teams in Cologne and Freiburg, played games and participated in tournaments on the occasion of the thirty-first biennial Protestant *Kirchentag* (a nationwide inter-denominational Christian gathering) in Cologne. The authors accompanied, observed and interviewed the 16 Palestinian players and three officials during this trip. All participants gave permission for their names to be used and, consequently, no pseudonyms are needed.

The players' ages ranged from 12 to 23 years, and most of them were either high school or university students at the time. Half the players were Muslims, the other half Christians, an interesting split considering that Muslims constitute over 97 per cent of the Palestinian population. A probable explanation for this high percentage of Christians in the team is the fact that both the Muslim head coach and the Christian manager live in Bethlehem, a city with an above-average percentage of Christian inhabitants (cf. Ullrich 1998) and in which the first Palestinian women's football team was formed in 2003. Ten of the players come from Bethlehem district, one from Hebron district, four from Jericho district and one girl comes from Gaza. To gain an impression of their social background, a glance at their parents' professions shows that out of 15 fathers, one-third are businessmen and shop owners, one is in haulage, one an olive wood carver, two are teachers, one is a tiler, one a government official, one is jobless, one is in prison and two are dead. Out of 15 mothers, more than half are housewives, three are teachers, one is a tailor, one a secretary and two are employees, in a cultural centre and a bank. Due to the poor economic situation in Palestine, most of the families have to struggle with financial hardship.

All the team members who came to Germany voluntarily filled out a questionnaire in which they were asked their age, place of residence and the profession of their parents, as well as contributing information about their experiences as women in Palestine and as female football players. In addition, we asked them to give their own evaluation of the relation between sport and politics, as well as the political situation in general. The questionnaire was translated into Arabic to avoid misunderstandings. Afterwards we conducted interviews with seven players and the manager which focused on the following question: 'In which ways do religion, cultural traditions and social structures influence the lives of women football players in Palestine?'

The selection of interview participants was based on the idea of reflecting as wide a range as possible of the attributes of the team members, such as their function in the team, their religion, the area in which they live in Palestine and their political orientation. The manager of the team, the five players from Bethlehem and Beit Jala (Bethlehem District), the player from Hebron and the player from Gaza agreed both to be interviewed and to the future publication of the material. Five of the players, as well as the manager, were interviewed in English. Two of the interviews were conducted in German and simultaneously translated into Arabic by a bilingual university student.

The interviews were transcribed and analysed using the method of qualitative content analysis. Numerous problems were addressed in the interviews which could have been encountered by women in general, not just women footballers. Here we have decided to focus on the following problems: those caused by structural obstacles that arise in particular from the political situation; those caused by religious barriers; and, finally, those caused by the patriarchal structures of Palestinian society.

Two emergent overarching themes are used to shape the results. First, opportunities and challenges for women's football in Palestine will be discussed including the political situation for team management, sport and religion, and cultural traditions. Second, the significance of football in everyday life, which frames sub-sections concerning football as a means to personal development, football as a space of well-being and freedom, and football as a political messenger.

Opportunities and challenges for women's football in Palestine

Most of the players of the national team were between eight and ten years old when they first had opportunities to play football with their brothers in the back-yards of their homes and on the streets of their neighbourhoods: 'I often played with my brothers ... on the street, but it was strange for a girl to play in the street' (Fidaa). Much depended on where the girls grew up. In regions that were steeped in cultural tradition, girls experienced stricter restrictions on their sports activities than in cities like Bethlehem. Honey reported, for example:

> Hebron, you can't imagine, no girls without scarf, no girls, I was the only girl walking in the street.... Yeah, and they [schools and clubs] started working on that ... gathered from 30 to 50 girls who wanted to play basket-ball not soccer.... Basketball, yeah, it's a big step, very big step.

Some of the young women found their way into football at private schools: 'I found encouragement from my teachers ... because they saw that I am inter-ested, when they do games for boys, they involved me' (Honey).

The political situation and team management

'The political situation is an issue for team management.' This statement by the national team manager emphasises the problematic political situation of Palestine as a result of the Israeli occupation. The division of the country and internal Palestinian conflicts represent a massive hindrance to the practice of sports in Palestine. The first problem is the lack of sports fields, which has been aggravated by the destruction of the only playing field in the Gaza Strip by an Israeli rocket in 2006. A further serious problem is caused by restrictions on mobility:

> We don't have fields – grass fields – except one in Jericho. It's half an hour from Bethlehem by car, but because of the checkpoints we need three hours and we can't practise there every day because we don't go via typical routes. We have checkpoints everywhere so we have to take detours, and they are difficult roads, in order to reach Jericho.
>
> (Ghada)

Checkpoints ensure that Palestinians cannot enter Israeli-controlled areas without permission. Some roads (most often the shortest connection) are closed to Pales-tinians (Thomas 2006). In many cases it is necessary to take narrow roads through the mountains, even though here, too, cars are controlled at checkpoints. Thus, travelling takes a lot of time and energy.

As most international tournaments are played on grass fields, regular access to such facilities would be a necessary prerequisite for optimum practice conditions. In addition, since most girls acquire their technical and tactical skills by playing in small groups on the streets, it is even more important to train on regular fields to get used to playing with full-size teams. The political situation, however, does not only prohibit access to important infrastructure such as playing fields; it also makes it almost impossible to conduct training sessions with the whole national team. So far, the players have trained predominantly at their local clubs, for example in Ramallah, Jericho and Bethlehem as well as the surrounding villages, and occasionally they play tournaments against each other. Since the last escalation of the conflict between Israel and Palestine at the end of 2008, however, the players from Gaza have had to be excluded from the team because they are not allowed to leave the Gaza Strip. Consequently, it is extremely difficult for them to join the national team. Before international championships, the members of the squad try to meet and train together. Hala, who lives in the Gaza Strip, described the summer of 2008 situation as follows:

> We can't meet them and play games or train properly. Just telephone is available if I like to call anyone – or Internet. But, Jericho, one time we went to play in Jericho, but it was very difficult and hard. I think going to Germany is easier than going to Jericho.

Nevin notes that the circumstances of travelling, access to towns and obtaining permission to leave the country can change from one moment to the next due to the unstable situation. Crossing the Israeli border, which is necessary when travelling from Gaza to the West Bank, is extremely time-consuming and difficult. The players have to wait for hours in the sun, answer numerous questions and undergo many checks. Thus, the instability of the political situation has an enormously adverse influence on team activities. The erratic situation makes it impossible to make long-term plans for practice and competitions. It regularly ruins progress, as the team manager reports:

> Sometimes we get ready for a game, two months of practising, with careful scheduling, preparing ourselves to be at one level, and then something happens, political curfew or explosion in one place, they stop – we stop all the activities for one month or five weeks or two months and we will have to start once more from the beginning.
>
> (Samar Moussa, team manager)

Sports reflect the turmoil in all other spheres of everyday social life. Travelling abroad remains the only opportunity to practise and play with the whole team. One way of finding time for training together is to gather the players as early as possible at tournament locations abroad to give them the opportunity to train for at least two or three days.

Travelling abroad is not without its problems. It is expensive and, due to the dire economic situation in the Palestinian territories, the costs cannot be covered by the players alone. Invitations from other Arab countries often include financial support. If the team wants to fly, it has to use the airport in Amman, Jordan. Due to uncertainty about the duration of the procedures at the border, the players have to stay at least one night before the departure in Amman to make sure that they do not miss their flight. Obtaining all the necessary permits and visas is a time-consuming and exhausting process. The most important thing, however, is that the parents let their daughters travel. For these young women, involvement in sports is the only chance they have of leaving their country for a while.

Sport and religion

'Religion is of no importance when you are playing.' This is the way Fidaa, a Muslim defence player, describes her own attitude to religion and sport. It also reflects the team's tolerant ethos. Despite such comments, religion is a highly significant issue since the families, and their opinions about traditional religious values and practices, have a great influence on whether girls are able to participate in sports in the first place.

According to statements given by the Christian players, in their opinion objections to women's sports today are more common and uncompromising in Muslim communities than in Christian ones. Asked if she had any explanation for the ratio mismatch between Christians and Muslims in the team compared with the population as a whole, Honey remarks: 'Because it depends on the society we are living in, and actually Christians living in Palestine are more open-minded, I can say, in my opinion, they are freer than Muslims.' She referred to differences in the cultural traditions towards girls in sport as the only reason she could offer to explain her view.

Relations between Islam, gender and sport are complex. Islam does not forbid sports for women in principle, but there are reservations about modern sport, especially where religious and social obligations are concerned (Naciri 1973; Hassan and Schwendemann 2005). How families deal with and observe religious rules, for instance regarding the wearing of the *hijab*, or headscarf, varies considerably according to the country or region of birth, social class, level of education, the religious customs of the older generation and the location (for example, town or country) (Schirrmacher and Spuler-Stegemann 2006). The football players of the national team live in widely differing circumstances, which makes it impossible to describe them from a single religious perspective.

All the parents of the football players support their daughters' sports; hence, they seem to be a highly selective group in Palestine. They have one important principle in common: the activities of women and girls require the approval of their nearest male relatives. Changes in the family's situation can have abrupt and serious consequences for young women, as exemplified by the case of one of the Muslim players. When Nadine's religiously moderate father died, her freedom to play football without a headscarf ended. Besides having to cover her hair, she was not allowed by her uncle, who superseded her father as her guardian, to go out without being accompanied by an elder brother. In contrast, other Muslim girls in the team from religiously moderate families were allowed to wear shorts and shirts for sports.

Friends of the players did not often get permission to play sports. Nevin, a Muslim player reported: 'I am trying to enter this discussion about convincing my friends that women can [play football], because even the Islamic religion doesn't forbid me to do so!' Even one of the Christian players complains:

> My friends, Muslims with headscarves, my classmates, they always say, 'I wish that I could play like you!' I always tell them, go and just play … [and they say] 'We can't' … you know [that's just] the culture they live in.
>
> (Amira)

For Christian women footballers, other obstacles were mentioned which constrained participation in football, for example the lack of social acceptance for women who played football, parental restriction and financial difficulties, for example with transportation costs. It was also difficult to be freed from university for international travel.

In the Gaza Strip it is now even more difficult for Muslim women to play football, especially after the Islamic Hamas party came to power in 2007. Hala, the captain of the football players, reported that women's football was officially disbanded in the sports clubs. Football for women was kept alive unofficially, for example at universities in sports-related courses and free-time training groups. Since the Israeli military campaign in the autumn of 2008, however, playing football has become impossible due to the destruction of the university facilities and playing field.

In the women's football team, tensions between Muslim and Christian players were not observable. The general tenor of the interviews may be summed up in the following statement: 'The problem is not being a Muslim or a Christian, it's the game of soccer itself – [religion] is of no importance when you [are] playing!' (Fidaa). Within the team, religious tolerance was practised. Muslim players also practised during Ramadan, even though it was at the end of a hot day without food or drink; and their Christian team-mates drew crosses in the air when they passed a church or monastery. It was accepted by the Muslim players that the Christians took a break for a drink, even though it was not usual to drink in public or in front of those who were fasting. In the same way, it was taken for granted by the Christian players that bus trips were interrupted in order to give their Muslim coach the opportunity to pray. Sometimes the Ramadan dinner was taken together.

The glue that bound all the players together was their common Palestinian identity. Five of the seven players interviewed emphasised that being Palestinians was their most important common characteristic. Indeed, they affirmed that it was more important to them than being an Arab, a Muslim or a Christian, summarising the spirit of the team and the unifying potential of sport.

Cultural traditions

In traditional Palestinian society, a woman has to adopt the role of mother and housewife under her husband's authority (Velloso 1996): 'Women should stay home and marry a man.' Young women who have played football for several years in this cultural context must have gained an unusual measure of freedom and enjoyed the social support of their families. That this holds true for the members of the national team can be seen in the fact that the statement 'my family supports me playing football' was confirmed by 15 out of 16 players. The interviews showed that it is often initially one parent that encourages the daughter's sports, and is proud of the daughter's unusual experiences and skills. Of one family, the manager reported: 'Her father was open-minded, he is in politics ... [and because of that] now in prison but he encourages his daughter to play sports! He likes to give her freedom, to let her see the world.' In some families, the father's enthusiasm for sports overrules the mother's concerns about her daughter's health, since football brings with it the risk of severe injuries, a risk that is increased when playing on hard or uneven pitches. In other families it may be the mother's joy about the daughter's growing self-confidence that overrides the father's reluctance to let his daughter play. Success in sport, travelling abroad, positive reports of experiences at the dinner table, growing acceptance in the community, publicity and the daughters' increasing self-confidence all help to overcome scepticism in the families.

The extended family also plays a role in determining a girl's activities. Older people, especially those living in villages in rural areas, tend to have more traditional views than young people in university towns (Velloso 1996). Interviewees regularly mentioned comments made by either their grandparents or other close relatives expressing concern about the potential masculinisation of the girls and that this might impair their chances of future marriage: 'Do not play football! You will get muscles! You will look like a man! And nobody will want to marry you!' (a player's grandmother). But this kind of argument does not seem to have discouraged the girls. Amira, for example, a 19-year-old Christian who was also confronted with this stereotype, remarked: 'If I get married, if! Because I don't want to, OK!' Ghada likewise rebelled against this widespread objection to women's sport: 'I believe that it's ridiculous, saying "Find your future". I can't imagine that they believe that my future is only with the husband.' On account of the political situation in Palestine, the social pressure on women to marry could grow; for, when a country is at war, enlarging the population may be considered a weapon against the enemy. Having a large number of children is regarded as a woman's national duty. It was PLO Chairman Arafat who exhorted women to have no less than 12 children (Velloso 1996).

In both the survey and the interviews, the football players emphasised that there was a gender hierarchy in the structure of Palestinian society and that there were gendered norms and rules:

It seems that the man has the full right to do whatever he wants, even if he is wrong he says, 'who cares', he is a man, but when a woman fails or makes a mistake the whole society blames her and she'll be treated like an outcast.

(Nevin)

Within the family, the players were taught to fulfil typical gender roles. They learned what was expected of them in their future lives by helping in the household and serving the male members of the family: 'My sister always helps me but my brothers, they do nothing ... the men don't have to do anything!' (Fidaa). For women, to play football means not only breaking with restrictive traditions but also taking the role of a pioneer:

In Palestine playing soccer is a success in itself you know.... Because as I said ... the majority thinks that the girl ... she can't play soccer! So it's a challenge too, to prove that they are wrong and we can play!

(Ghada)

The young female sportswomen meet scepticism or even rejection from many sides, including members of the younger generation: 'No, at first my friends didn't accept the idea. But when they saw us on TV and now that everyone is talking about us they started to accept the idea. And now it's OK, all of them accept it' (Ghada).

The players of the young national football team were aware that they paved the way for other girls aiming at a career in sport. They were always careful not to behave in an 'inappropriate' way. One night after practice we witnessed a peculiar scene: the team captain, Honey, stopped her team-mates kicking the ball back and forth in the narrow streets of the Old Town in Bethlehem because she was afraid that this might cause some of the men to come out into the streets after their Ramadan dinner, possibly harming their families' reputations. In view of the numerous difficulties and obstacles these young women face, the question arises as to why they are still trying to play football and investing time and money in a controversial activity, especially since they have to pay their own expenses, such as travelling to practice.

The significance of football in dealing with everyday life

Football is more than a mere pastime for these Palestinian players; it is an essential part of their lives and their identity. How important football really is for these women is reflected in such statements as: 'I can't leave it!' (Tala) or 'There are a lot of things that are important in my life – but football I can't be without!' (Nevin). The interviews revealed the specific reasons for the intensity of their commitment to football. The sport provided them with self-esteem and an opportunity to find moments of relief from an everyday reality of deprivation and violence. It also allowed them to achieve a measure of liberation, both as women and as Palestinians.

Football as a means to personal development

Out of 16 players, 15 declared that playing football taught them rules of conduct such as self-discipline. All interviewees stressed that, in one way or another, playing football had changed their personalities for the better. They had learned such virtues as punctuality, respect for others, patience, endurance and accountability, as well as having improved their will power and interpersonal skills of communication and cooperation. 'It changed my personality – it made me stronger, more patient, more dependable, more responsible; all this changed my personality to be the best I can be and made me stronger and stronger!' (Honey).

These changes in attitudes and behaviour were confirmed by the team manager, who also emphasised that 'their personality is stronger than that of other people, which you find when you talk to them ... that they are not afraid of failing as they are used to a rough life!' (Samar Moussa, team manager). This development of character is of special importance in a patriarchal society, as Fidaa affirmed:

> it's a good change for my personality because I think when a girl plays soccer, it gives her [an idea] of free[dom], and this is good for the girl – to live free, to become strong in her society and maybe she will face everything and she can give the people outside of Palestine a good picture about the women in Palestine.
>
> (Fidaa)

Football as a space of well-being and freedom

The team captain mentioned that playing football enabled one to put aside everyday cares and problems: 'It's a way to feel comfort. Forget problems – just come and play soccer and forget negative things happening in life' (Honey). In Palestine's political environment this notion of freedom is especially important, and it was consequently emphasised by other players as well: 'I feel free, you know, and I feel everything that I need when I play soccer' (Fidaa). The team captain commented: 'It's a way of getting my frustrations out because [as we have] nothing [else] to do, we can get our frustration out with the ball – with playing ...' (Honey). As there are scarcely any alternatives for spending one's free time in the occupied territories, sport becomes a prominent leisure activity for the girls:

> It's the only thing we do in Palestine – playing sports because we don't have much else to do except studying and playing sport. We [can't go] out of Beit Jala, Bethlehem, because of the checkpoints and it's the only thing we do in our free time – playing sport.
>
> (Ghada)

Through trips abroad to training camps and international tournaments, the girls get a chance to see the world, experience new cultures and broaden their horizons. 'The national team improves the situation; it helps me to have contact with another world, and it also gives me the opportunity to have a tournament outside the country' (Hala). The national team captain, Honey, has similar views, but also stresses the function that sports have of releasing pressure from the social system:

> I can say that sport gives us the opportunity to feel the energy we have inside us and [to] divert it to other places. What is meant is, let the energy out from inside. It gives us the opportunity to apply it to sports instead of doing bad stuff … and so it gives us the chance to fill our time. It gives us a chance to express ourselves through sports, it gives us also the chance to visit the world … to be happy, to socialise as a team and talk about our daily lives.
>
> (Honey)

It became clear that the players we interviewed experienced sport as a means of acquiring self-confidence and as a source of pride that helped to shape an individual's identity. Football was a way of expressing a sportive lifestyle that channelled energy into ambitious performance. Social values such as responsibility and caring were included in this lifestyle and expressed during sporting activities within the team and towards other teams. The young female players, furthermore, saw their athletic talents as a chance to present an alternative image of womanhood, a new understanding of self-confident women who acted as emancipated individuals in sports. They were the first to have media attention in a traditionally male domain. They also observed the growing importance of their sport, with the establishment of a league for women and increasing amounts of money being given by the Palestinian Football Association (PFA) for developing women's football.

> It's a game – a challenge, first between the other teams and us, second for the society, because as you know [it's] a male-dominated society we live in; it's a challenge to prove that we are as good as boys and men and we can also play soccer as they do!
>
> (Ghada)

This Palestinian team wishes to encourage development towards a more equal society for men and women. As successful women, they hope to become role models in sport without negating traditional values. 'in our Islamic society, I can say that I am an example or a model for all the society! A good example for the society' (Nevin).

Football as a political messenger

One constant concern of the girls and women was to present their country in a favourable light and to demonstrate that there were positive developments despite political strife:

The role that our team is playing brings a message to the world that we are alive and well. We are not the 'terrorists' that some foreigners think we are as Palestinians. We have courage and motivation to show the world that we are still alive despite the situation we are in, despite the occupation, despite the walls. Despite everything we have a message for the world that Palestine is a good country and it is a country of peace, it is a country of good players – to show the best side of Palestine, and also to raise our flag all over the world and in the Arab world as well.

(Honey)

It remains to be seen whether it will be possible to use football as a medium for peaceful ends and whether it can entirely avoid being instrumentalised by politicians. In some of the interviewees' statements, a fear was expressed that any competitions with teams from Israel might be interpreted as a gesture of 'normalisation'[2] in the political situation. Palestinians want to avoid such a false impression of normality as long as occupation lasts.

Because of the explosiveness of the issue, the players were asked about their attitudes towards a fictitious game against an Israeli women's football team:

For me I have no problem [with playing against an Israeli team] because I always say that we are all humans. The problem is with governments and not with people. And I can be very friendly with Jewish people as I can feel that they want peace just like we do. I, as a Christian, believe in forgiveness and to love people even if they were our enemies and if they stole our land. For me I can forgive because God told us to forgive; so I have no problem. But the problem is when we play such a game they will think – the Arabs from the Arab side – that we are opting for normalisation and we accept the Israeli people in our land and we are happy that they are here and occupying us. That's the problem.

(Honey)

These concerns were shared by her team-mates, who were afraid of being branded as traitors for having friendly contacts with the occupying power. Therefore, she expressed reservations on the part of some players who were not wholly against having contact with Jewish women in sporting activities in principle, but against some misinterpretation which might arise from such encounters. The current leadership of the Palestinian Football Association favours the slogan of Palestinian passive resistance: 'No normalisation under occupation!'[3]

In contrast, Honey's Muslim team-mate Hala from the Gaza Strip stressed the potentially positive political effects of matches against Jewish players: 'If it's for peace and freedom … yeah … why not?' (Hala). Her team-mate Ghada argued similarly when asked whether she could imagine playing in a team with Jews. 'Yeah … I'd love to … to prove that I'm not against peace. On the contrary … I'm for peace. So I love the idea to play with them' (Ghada). Any game against a Jewish team would inevitably be emotionally as well as symbolically charged. It would be a very special and unique match, as team captain Honey underlined:

> I can see that, or I can imagine, it will be the strongest effort ever, because we would be able to show them that we can beat them, fair and square – we can compete with them for the best soccer ever – which is fair play. I can see that that would be the hottest game ever, because of the tensions between Israel and Palestine and I can imagine that we may ... we may beat them because of the inner feelings that we have, the courage and motivation that we have to prove ourselves ... that we are the opposite of what they think about us.
>
> (Honey)

Besides envisioning a possible game between two nations that have been fighting each other for decades, the players channel idealistic hopes into sport. The team manager described her hopes that sport would offer a chance for peaceful cooperation:

> I think sport is a language. [Laughs] It's the language of all people, because when we are on the field we can play within the rules of sports and everybody knows the rules of sports – we can communicate with each other even if we don't speak the language of all participants. It's a language – sports is a language of communicating peace and friendship and you know, when we go abroad all the girls meet with other players from other teams and they are friends to each other.... But the problem is with the political leaders – but sport is able to make peace in a wonderful way – I think it's the language of peace.
>
> (Samar Moussa)

Conclusion and prospect of things to come

To sum up the results of this study, it can be said that these women players are very aware of their society's traditions and norms, considering many of them to be unfair to women and a deprivation of women's personal freedom. Although they are subject to these norms, they occasionally question them. This experience together with the perceived misunderstanding of their country, Palestine, seems to mobilise a great amount of motivation and perseverance in the sense of struggle for recognition. For the young players, football is a means of realising a way of life that is not taken for granted in their society. Belonging to this extraordinary female football national team seems to be a valuable basis of identity formation. In their sport they find recognition and confirmation for identity constructions that help them to overcome societal restrictions. Furthermore, the women develop an alternative idea of society: to escape role expectations and to take part in a process that might slowly lead to change and the creation of a society with more freedom and equal rights. They can, to some extent, discard perceived helplessness and strengthen their self-esteem and locus of control. The development of personal identity and social movement are strongly connected.

Dedicated women such as Samar A. Moussa have successfully campaigned for the inclusion of women's football in the physical-education curricula of state schools.[4] Previously, women's football was played only occasionally, and only at private schools that are more liberal due to the influence of their Western benefactors. Last year, the city of Cologne sent experienced (male) football instructors to its twinned city, Bethlehem, to train local West Bank coaches (including women) in the pedagogy of football.

The majority of members on the council of the Palestinian Football Association (PFA) have also recognised that schools are key arenas in the development of women's football. They are now working on an adequate system of support, such as incorporating football for girls into the school sports curriculum, training women coaches and referees, giving financial support, building facilities and grounds and extending media coverage.[5] The most recent developments in creating a broader basis for nurturing women's interest in football are highly encouraging and promise to establish a more fundamental and lasting legacy of women's football in Palestine.

According to the team manager and a number of the players, sport provides opportunities to build bridges of friendship and peace, and for teams to display strength in difficult circumstances. By playing football, the players find that doors can open and new ways of thinking allow them to look towards the future with optimism and confidence. This study makes it quite clear that the Women's National Football Team of Palestine aims very high indeed!

Notes

1 Before the Second Intifada, much good work was done by women's movement activists, such as the integration of women in ministries, lobbying and advocacy for more schools for rural women, women's health projects and so on. But a fundamental depoliticisation of women's activism occurred as a result of the Al Aqsa Intifada and also a division within the women's movement itself. The complex background is unfolded in Johnson and Kuttab (2001).

2 A common slogan in Palestine that expresses the passive resistance against the occupation is: 'No normalisation under occupation!' This means that no steps, meetings or shared activities with Israel are to be undertaken by the Palestinians as long as the occupation lasts. The Palestinians want to avoid a situation in which in the course of time things become 'normal' to the rest of the world. Nobody should be able to say: 'Ok, there is occupation in Palestine, but look, it cannot be that bad, for they are playing football with Israel.'

3 Interview with the president of the PFA, September 2008.

4 Interview with Samar A. Moussa, September 2008.

5 Jonathan Schaller attended two meetings of the PFA in Ramallah on the development of women's football in the country in September 2008.

Bibliography

Amnesty International (ed.) (2005) *Israel and the Occupied Territories: Conflict, Occupation and Patriarchy. Women Carry the Burden.* Online, available at: http://web.amnesty.org/library/index/engmde150162005 (accessed 2 February 2007).

184   *P. Gieß-Stüber* et al.

Darvishpour, M. (2003) Islamic feminism: compromise or challenge to feminism? *Iran Bulletin – Middle East Forum*, Summer 2003, (55–58). Online, available at: http://www2.sociology.su.se/home/Darvishpour/Islamicfeminism.pdf (accessed 2 February 2008).

Flores, A. (2002) Islam, Islamismus und Nationalismus im Palästinakonflikt [Islam, Islamism and nationalism in the Palestinian conflict]. In U. Klein and D. Thränhardt (eds) *Gewaltspirale ohne Ende? Konfliktstrukturen und Friedenschancen im Nahen Osten* [*Spiral of Violence Without End? Middle East Conflict and Chances for Peace*], Schwalbach: Wochenschau Verlag: 50–66.

Hassan, S. and Schwendemann, W. (2005) Sport und Islam – ein paar Bemerkungen zu einer ungewöhnlichen Verhältnisbestimmung [Sport and Islam – comments on a special relationship]. In P. Gieß-Stüber (ed.) *Interkulturelle Erziehung im und durch Sport* [*Intercultural Education In and Through Sports*], Münster: LIT Verlag: 7–15.

Johnson, P. and Kuttab, E. (2001) Where have all the women (and men) gone? Reflections on gender and the Second Palestinian Intifada. *Feminist Review*, 69: 21–43.

Kroner, G. (2003) Von der Welt vergessen: Zur Situation palästinensischer Frauen im Gaza [Forgotten by the world: The situation of Palestinian women in Gaza]. *Frauensolidarität*, 43: 16–17.

Mernessi, F. (1975) *Beyond the Veil*, New York: John, Wiley and Sons.

Naciri, M. (1972) Die Einstellung des Islam zum Sport [The attitude towards sports in Islam]. In O. Grupe *et al.* (eds) *Sport in unserer Welt: Chancen und Probleme* [*Sport in Our World: Opportunities and Problems*], Berlin, Heidelberg, New York: Springer-Verlag: 652–654.

Pfister, G. (2000) Rekorde im Tschador [Records with chador]. *Zeitschrift für KulturAustausch, 1.* Online, available at: http://cms.ifa.de/index.php?id= pfister (accessed 2 February 2008).

Rizq-Qazzaz, H. (2006) Gender transformation in conflict? In U. Auga and C. von Braunmühl (eds) *Gender in Conflict: Palestine – Israel – Germany*, Berlin: Lit Verlag: 191–198.

Schirrmacher, C. and Spuler-Stegemann, U. (2006) *Frauen und die Scharia Die Menschenrechte im Islam*. München: Goldmann.

Thomas, A. (2006) *For Palestinian Women Soccer Players, a Field is a Dream*. Online, available at: www.csmonitor.com/2006/1204/p14s02-alsp.html (accessed 20 October 2007).

Ullrich, P. (1998) Zwischen Partizipation und Emigration: eine kultursoziologische Studie zur Lage der Christen in Palästina [Between participation and emigration: a study in cultural sociology of the situation of Christians in Palestine]. *Kultursoziologie, 2.* Online, available at: www.stud.uni-leipzig.de/~soz96jtv/pal/3demogra.htm (accessed: 2 February 2008).

Velloso, A. (1996) Women, society and education in Palestine. *International Review of Education*, 42 (5): 524–530.

Weiner, J.R. (2005) *Human Rights of Christians in Palestinian Society*. Online, available at: www.jcpa.org/text/Christian-Persecution-Weiner.pdf (accessed 2 February 2008).

11 Challenges facing South African Muslim secondary school girls' participation in physical activities, physical education and sport

Ilhaam Essa

Editors' introduction

The author/researcher of this study is a South African Muslim woman, a health professional, who became interested in the observed resistance of Muslim girls to active lifestyles. The study explores physical-education provision and the views of 14–18-year-old Muslim girls in two schools of the Western Cape Province. Issues pertinent to many adolescents arose, such as body consciousness and detrimental health habits, as well as those specific to religious needs that lead to participation resistance. These include inappropriate dress codes, gender organisation, male teachers/coaches and poverty of resources/provision. Instances of racism related to skin colour were also recounted. This is the first such study to be conducted in South Africa and is significant because of an increasing Muslim population and number of Muslim schools.

Author's narrative

As a Muslim woman growing up in pre- and post-apartheid South Africa, my main interest in, and contribution to, Muslim affairs, especially in relation to health, were as a member of school and community health committees and, eventually, through my professional life as a nurse and nurse educator. I come from a family where living Islamic values (for example, in trusting and compassionate relations with others and constant striving for excellence) was first in every context whether at home, school, on the sports field, at university or in the workplace. Only later in my professional life did I realise that I was classified as a South African coloured (although my great-grandparents came from India and the Netherlands). It was this combination of identity and professional interest that prompted me to ascertain more about the significance of identity groups by exploring why young girls in my chosen faith community do not seemingly embrace a healthy lifestyle (Phillips 2006; Walseth 2006: 85). In my own schooling experiences, I remember several Muslim girls in my class and other classes participating reluctantly in physical-education activities at school. Community provision in my area for young girls in sporting activities is poor, making the school arena particularly important. In Phillips' 2006 study into activity patterns of adolescent girls, including Muslim girls, in four high schools in the Strand area where I live, the results indicated inadequate activity levels to influence health in a positive way, but few reasons for this were explored. I became interested, consequently, in the factors that encourage or constrain South African Muslim girls' participation in physical activities.

The purpose of the study reported in this chapter was to identify and explore the opportunities and challenges of Muslim girls' experiences of physical education and school sport in relation to religious and cultural influences in their lives. The case study, conducted in two schools in the Western Cape Province, was based on the following three research questions:

- What are the opportunities and constraints that Muslim girls encounter in performing physical education?
- What is the impact of religion on girls' potential participation?
- How does culture influence their participation in physical activities?

Context – a brief introduction to South Africa and the Western Cape

After decades of apartheid rule, South African schooling is today no longer dominated by constitutional and institutionalised racial segregation. Schools, however, have remained important socialising agents for human activity, including academic, cultural, religious and sporting activities. South Africa's Constitution and Bill of Rights recognise freedom of association, expression and religious affiliation as long as the rights of other people are not unjustly violated.

One of the areas in which religious affiliation, movement and expression have been realised is in public and private schooling yet, paradoxically, some young people stay excluded from South Africa's post-1994 democratic shift, when the right of all learners to express themselves freely through physical activities, education and sport was recognised. What are the issues for Muslim girls in this area? Unless Muslim girls can enact their roles meaningfully in relation to South Africa's Constitution and Bill of Rights, schools cannot be said to have eradicated all prejudices, which characterised human actions during the days of apartheid.

South Africa is a multicultural and multi-religious society. Although a secular state, the Constitution recognises freedom of religion as an important human right. The Western Cape Province (one of nine in the country) is populated by approximately 40 per cent of the Muslims in the country. The Muslim community is not a homogenous group of people. By far the majority (about 90 per cent) belongs to the Sunni group of Muslims, whereas the minority comprises Shi'is. At a theological level, Muslims, whose ancestors were mainly from the Indonesian Archipelago, practise Islam mainly according to the Shafi'i school of thought whereas Indian Muslims, particularly those whose ancestors mainly arrived from the Indo-Pakistan sub-continent, adhere to the teaching of the

Hanafi jurisprudential school. At private Muslim schools Islamic discourses are taught according to these schools of theological/jurisprudential thought.

Although Muslims have widely enjoyed religious freedom and association, by far the most significant prejudices they encounter are amongst themselves, particularly between men and women. Contrary to normative Islam, some Muslim women in South Africa are discriminated against in areas which concern the apparent application of inheritance and marriage laws, as well as the freedom of movement in mosques and amongst the general public. The integration of women and men is not allowed in mosques, and Muslim private schools perpetuate this gender segregation. In public schools (Muslim[1] and non-Muslim) this separation is not practised.

The Muslim population of South Africa constituted 1.46 per cent (654,064) of the total population of 44.8 million in 2001 (Vahed and Jeppie 2005: 252). Post-1994, after the first democratic elections took place, South Africa was divided into nine provinces. Some 44.78 per cent (292,906) of the Muslim population is resident in the Western Cape Province, which is the southernmost part of the African continent. The Western Cape differs from the other provinces in that the coloured population represents the largest group, whereas in all the other provinces the black Africans form the largest group (Groenewald 2008). Afrikaans is the dominant language in the Western Cape followed by isiXhosa. The Western Cape scholastic results are rated as the best in the country. It also has the lowest unemployment figure (Groenewald 2008). After the Population Registration Act of 1950, South Africans were formally classified into four race groups: whites, Indians, Africans and coloureds (Vahed and Jeppie 2005). People belonging to the Muslim faith are found in all four race groups, with differentiation not only in race but also class, education, employment and income levels. In the Western Cape, most Muslims are found in the Indian communities and the coloured community (usually referred to as 'Malay', but this is a term that is contested as it includes descendants from South and South-East Asia, Mozambique, Arabs and Khoisan). Whilst the coloured and Indian groups make up the majority of the Muslim community (87.29 per cent), the African group is the fastest-growing, having increased by 52.3 per cent since 1991. The last census was conducted in 2001. Since 1994 there has been a tremendous growth in Muslim faith schools, which could be attributed to the democratic freedom attained, the secularisation of the schooling system and globalisation (Vahed and Jeppie 2005). Although these statistics might have changed in recent years, they were the only census data available at the time of writing. It is estimated, given the census data of 2001, that the Muslim population in 2009 has increased to almost 2 per cent of the entire South African citizenry.

Finally, physical education in South Africa has had a chequered history driven by changing political powers (Van Deventer 2007) and has been influenced largely by British and American systems. In 1972, the first multiracial committee for girls was formed, but academic subjects took precedence. In the 1980s, an attempt was made to develop greater educational equality for physical education, but this met with limited success due to serious under-resourcing. The

1990s saw many policy initiatives for schools (1996), higher education (1997), curriculum review (2000), and norms and standards (2000) (Waghid 2002: 1). This led to the introduction of the National Curriculum Statement (NCS) of 2005, in which physical education was subsumed into the Life Orientation curriculum. In this context, physical education lost much of its specialist subject status, and a limited time allocation diminished its place in many schools (Mohlala 2007). Current initiatives are reclaiming physical education as a specialist subject, but this is not yet widespread in the schools. This situation of racial and educational divide provides the context for the case study of the school-based experiences of South African Muslim girls. Before moving on to the research, it is important to explore the Islamic, gender, physical-education and health discourses in which the study was grounded.

Muslim girls and women, physical education, sport and health

According to Ansari (2006: 202), 'the Islamic philosophy of life is: No sound mind without a sound body.' In other words, Muslims should not only enhance their cognitive or intellectual progress but also their physical condition in order to lead a healthy, moral life. Ansari (2006: 203) states that this can only be achieved if 'every activity, be it intellectual, moral, social, aesthetical or spiritual is God-orientated'. Such views correlate with the viewpoint in the chapter concerned with an Islamic perspective on women in sport in this book. That is, that there are no religious laws that stop Muslims from participating in physical activities. Challenges that apparently minimise participation in school-based physical activities relate to requirements for religious adherence such as in body modesty. They include the Muslim girls' dress code, the changing/showering-room facilities, strenuous activities in the month of Ramadan and the scheduling of activities where they clash with obligations such as prayer times (Benn 2005). More positively, there are important desirable qualities promoted in the cultures of both Islam and physical education, which include perseverance, self-discipline and the pursuit of a healthy body (Benn 2005).

It is pertinent to note the importance of the current health agenda as a high priority in South African politics, and the role of physical activity and school-based physical-education provision as key to the pursuit of improved health. The National Department of Sports and Recreation's aim was to ensure that by the year 1999 every South African citizen should participate in at least one sport-related activity (Philips 2006). A survey conducted in 2007 by the South African National Food Consumption organisation shows that in urban areas one in every 13 children between the ages of one and nine is overweight (Mohlala 2007). These statistics, together with increasing rates of obesity amongst school children, led the National Department of Sports and Recreation, the National Department of Education and a private company to initiate sporting activities together with a bursary in order to motivate youth to become active again (Mohlala 2007). This initiative coincided with the Department of Education's five-year plan to reintroduce physical education into the school curriculum. In addition to the balanced and healthy lifestyle that sporting activity potentially inculcates in participants, it is also imbued with values such as physical and mental endurance according to the Minister of Sport and Recreation (Mohlala 2007). As a committed health professional, my rationale for examining Muslim girls' experiences in physical activities in South Africa is apposite.

Research method

An interpretive paradigm underpinned the qualitative approach to exploring experiences of 29 Muslim girls, aged 14 to 18 years, from two schools. A case study design offered potential for insights into lived realities that gave centrality to the perceptions of young people and the multiple realities they faced (Mouton 2005).

A public school (PUBL) and a Muslim independent school (PRIV) were selected for this case study. The reason for choosing these schools was to enable a comparison of factors influencing the participation rates of Muslim school girls in physical activities, physical education and sport, particularly in relation to provision for religious and cultural practices. For example, PRIV is a school only for girls, whereas PUBL is a mixed-gender school, and in Islam gender segregation post-puberty is a common practice. How does this system or other systems of organisation and practice affect Muslim girls' participation in physical education and school sport?

A purposive non-random sampling technique was used because the study is not concerned with statistical accuracy but detailed in-depth analysis or interpretation. The cases selected are pertinent examples of the phenomena to be studied (Terre Blanche *et al.* 2006). Permission was gained through the Western Cape Education Department (WESTERN CAPEED), the principals of both schools (head teachers) and respective educators (teachers) and learners (students), resulting in 29 volunteer Muslim girls participating in the study. Initially, 15 learners from each school group were identified, one educator from PRIV and three educators from PUBL. Two focus-group interviews were conducted at each school with the learners, and four individual face-to-face interviews with the educators. The interviews were arranged over two weeks but eventually took place over six weeks during 2007. At PRIV, both focus group interviews ($n = 10$–1, $n = 8$) and one educator interview (Muslim female) were conducted in one day. At PUBL, one focus group ($n = 6$) and one educator (Muslim female) were interviewed over one day and, on a separate day, the second focus group ($n = 6$) and two educators (both non-Muslim females) were interviewed. My dress code and name revealed that I came from a Muslim background.

My personal opinion is that the learners were comfortable with me also being Muslim. Initially, there was a reserved response, especially from the PUBL learners (who do not wear the *hijab*), but as they became more comfortable, their responses were as spontaneous as the PRIV learners (who wore the *hijab*). The learners who participated were all Muslim and during the interviews classified themselves as coming from Indian, Malay and coloured cultures. The interviews (educators and learners) lasted between 45 and 90 minutes each; only one learner (from PRIV) asked to leave during one of the focus group interviews and was allowed to do so as participation was on a voluntarily basis.

The data-analysis approach used consisted of five steps: familiarisation and immersion, identifying themes, coding, elaboration and, lastly, interpretation and checking (Terre Blanche *et al.* 2006: 322–326). Emergent themes of consensus or contradiction are used to present the findings. There are six themes and they are: dress codes, body consciousness, support from significant others, poverty, participants' cultural and religious perspectives, and racism and health issues.

The Muslim independent school situation

The Muslim independent school (PRIV) is situated in an urban area and opened its doors in 1995.[2] This case study school started, as did most of the Muslim independent schools in South Africa, through concerned Muslim leaders and community members identifying a need to have a school where an Islamic ethos together with secular teachings could take place. The school initially started with a staff complement of six, with 25 learners (all girls). Today the school has grown to 29 educators and around 600 learners (boys and girls) on two separate campuses (one for the girls and one for the boys), and boasts an average matriculation pass rate for the last five years of 93 per cent. The curriculum of PRIV consists of all the learning areas prescribed by the Western Cape Education Department (WCED) for grades 8–12 and also includes Arabic, Quran Studies, Islamic Studies and Computer Literacy/Science. Although most of the learners attending PRIV are Muslim, there is also a small percentage of non-Muslims. The majority of the learners come from a middle-class Malay background (Peck 2009). The available sporting facilities include a netball court, which is also the parking area, an athletics field a few kilometres away, and a hall where table tennis and badminton can be played.

The public school situation

The public school (PUBL) has been in existence for 57 years. It was built in the apartheid era for coloured children. Currently, coloured and black African learners attend the school (the coloured learners are in the majority) and it is also a mixed-gender school with learners of different faiths (Christians, Muslims, Jews) attending. The catchment area of the school includes urban and semi-urban areas, and most of the learners attending the school come from a middle to low socio-economic class background. According to an annual survey (WCEDEMIS 2007), the PUBL had 732 female learners and 586 male learners. My focus was on the grade-8 to grade-11 female Muslim learners. There are 39 educators (thirty-37 employed by WCED and two are school governing body posts). PUBL is classified as an open school; in other words, any school-age learner may attend the school and the annual school fee for 2007 was R750.[3] It follows the National Curriculum of the WCED and has one rugby field and two netball courts that are also utilised for volleyball.

Discussion of results

As stated above, the results are organised under the six themes of dress codes, body consciousness, support from significant others, poverty, participants' cultural and religious perspectives, and racism and health issues.

Dress codes

It is well-documented (Benn 2005; Flintoff and Scraton 2005; Nakamura 2002) that one of the barriers Muslim girls and women experience in participating in physical activities is accommodation to a flexible and modest dress code. The same concerns were raised in PUBL when learners had to participate in sport: 'If you participate in sports [athletics or netball], you must wear specific clothes, which are a tight-fitting vest or top, tight-fitting shorts and a leotard.' The learners prefer the physical activities during the LO (Life Orientation) period because they do not have to undress: 'Enjoy, do not need to undress.' Some feel that the immodest dress code in sport inhibits their progress: 'We would definitely go further in sport if it were not for the clothes.' As previously stated, none of the learners at PUBL wore the *hijab* (literally referring to headscarf), but the majority showed an unwillingness to wear tight-fitting attire. The diverse response is similar to that found by Nakamura (2002), i.e. that Muslims differ in the practice of dress codes. With regard to swimming, some learners (three) felt that it is fine to swim in a bathing costume, but the majority (nine) wore shorts or a T-shirt over their bathing costume.

Concerns that learners from PRIV raised regarding the dress code during the LO period were that they practise in their school uniform (pants and long shirt), which creates discomfort afterwards because their school does not have any shower facilities. A theme that came across very strongly at PRIV is that learners associated Islam with having internalised faith and this was not necessarily dependent on the outward modes of dress: 'The teachers stress about how you look and dress and whether you speak to boys, but then there are things ... like learners that talk and laugh when they salaah (pray), that swear but whose attire is correct'; 'yes it [the headscarf] is part of the religion, but it does not make a person, it is the person herself. The wearing of a scarf or having the correct attire is not as important as having a good heart, it is pointless being fully covered if you are not clean from inside'; 'I know of learners that dress appropriately but spread bad gossip all the time, will swear and go clubbing'; 'I also feel learners wear proper uniform, but have no respect for their educators'.

Body consciousness

A second theme that connects with the first is that of shyness and self-consciousness of their bodies. In PUBL, learners prefer not to do physical education because of shyness in exposing their bodies. As some learners commented: 'sometimes it is about the figure, for example myself I am shy because I have a big bust and if I jump I feel I draw attention to it and I don't like it' and 'if you participate in sports you must wear specific clothing and then everything shows and other learners look at you, you feel uncomfortable, then I just say I am not going to participate any more'.

The PUBL learners also experience adjustment problems, for example some mention: 'I am not actually used to these people, I was used to Muslim children … when I came here there were Christian children and different religions and I felt uncomfortable' and 'when I came to high school I stopped doing anything because the workload was too much'. They also felt at a disadvantage and inadequate because it seems their coaches did not teach them regularly and inform them of the correct rules; they then become 'the laughing stock when they play other schools, especially one of the previously white schools'.

A lack of interest in participating in physical activity, physical education and school sport seems to be present at both PUBL and PRIV schools: 'generally girls are not interested in physical activity, the interest they have is in MIXT [chat room], men, cigarettes and oka [sheesha] pipe' and 'learners themselves also do not want to go outside with the following excuses: we do not know how to catch a ball, it is too hot or too cold'.

Support/lack of support and stereotyping from significant others

Lack of interest, adjustment problems and self-consciousness may be prevalent in the learners of both schools, but the question arises: how are they supported by educators and principals? Learners at both schools felt that educator enthusiasm, support and encouragement for physical activity were not always forthcoming. There is a high turnover of staff in PRIV, which breaks down continuity of support for building skills and confidence in the area. Additionally, learners are concerned about the lack of time offered for physical activity:

> We participate at the beginning of the year in athletics with other Muslim schools and at the end get Life Orientation [LO] twice during the week. In the one period class work is done [attention probably being given to the other learning outcomes of LO], in the other period they sometimes or seldom go outside to play with a ball…. Sometimes they just stand around and don't do anything, there is no structure.

PRIV only has one LO educator for grades 8 to 12 who is responsible for both the boys and girls (moving across campuses). In PUBL, learners' perceptions are that educators do not seem to encourage them to pursue physical activity, or as two learners expressed it: 'Educators tolerate learners who do not want to do physical activities in the LO period but prefer to do other work' and 'Some of the educators do not feel like exercising or working, and the learners just stand or sit around doing nothing specifically, unless they are told the activity will be counting towards their marks for LO'. PUBL has four educators that teach LO from grades 8–12.

The lack of female coaches and presence of male coaches also presented a barrier. PUBL has female LO educators, but when they play against other PUBL schools, male coaches may be present. For some of the PUBLs' fathers, this is not acceptable.

A further barrier learners encountered was with regard to their choice of sport, for example: 'the educators also felt it was a boys' sport [soccer] and said no for a couple of times ...' and 'the educators classify the sports into boys' and girls' sport and netball and table tennis are girls' sport'. The principal of PRIV was also seen as 'the biggest barrier' as 'he classifies what sports girls can participate in and what sports boys can'. This is consistent with what Scraton (1992) found in her study of teachers' attitudes and expectations relating to girls, where teachers had very specific ideas on girls' physical capabilities and which physical activities were appropriate for girls.

Parental influences seem to be positive in encouraging learners to participate in physical activities. Some parents are trainers at sports clubs. These findings are applicable to both PUBL and PRIV schools, where families play an active role in promoting physical activities. What was interesting to note was the influence of gender in the different schools. Fathers are more prominent in PRIV, and mothers in PUBL.

Poverty

Comparatively, the learning situation is impoverished in PRIV due to poorer resources, only one educator and a constant turnover of staff. This is not only in terms of time split between boys and girls but also the range of specialisms that can bring enrichment through diversity. The girls complained that when their activity space was occupied, for instance by a car, they did not have a lesson. The athletics field was a distance from the school and had neither showering facilities nor an adequate supply of water; at times 'the water gets put off' and 'we don't have either the facilities or the money, or coaches; we must coach ourselves'. In PUBL, resources are also limited as they only have a netball court and a shared space for volleyball. Financial sponsorship for travel is not easily available to these girls, especially when they have to participate in provincial tournaments. Lastly, the girls can only travel the long distances often required to compete against other schools if their parents or a trusted, responsible person can take them.

Participants' cultural and religious perspectives

The learners of both schools felt culture has less of an influence than religion in their decision to participate or not participate in physical activity, physical education and sports. The few aspects of culture that do have an influence are parents allocating specific roles to PRIV girls such as home chores and also determining what type of sport they may participate in: 'a girl is supposed to be at home, help with the cleaning, cooking, and the man is supposed to work, support and do sport' and 'it is unacceptable for a girl to play soccer or rugby'. Boys were perceived to be afforded more freedom than girls to partake in physical activities. Excelling in their academic work is still considered more important than any other school activities by parents of both schools. This, together with high-school workloads and having to attend madrassahs after school, limits the free time available for PRIV and PUBL learners. In turn, this affects girls' participation in physical activity, as was found in the Nakamura (2002) study. The most positive cultural aspect seems to be for those learners, across both schools, whose families were active and who therefore gave the greatest support to the girls' participation.

Like PRIV, PUBL parents seemed to be opposed to learners being trained by men. In PUBL, Muslim girls were reluctant to participate in sport as a result of not being encouraged to intermingle with males, there is gender integration at the school and during athletic gatherings. In PRIV, sports were gender-segregated, and inter-school competition was only with other Muslim girls' schools. Although gender integration has been perceived as enabling girls to have equal access to a physical-education curriculum (Flintoff and Scraton 2005), this would not be an acceptable practice in the majority of South Africa's independent Muslim schools, where in most cases there is segregation of the sexes. In PRIV, the girls associate participation in physical activity with the life experiences of the Prophet Muhammad who, according to them, encouraged horse riding, wrestling and swimming, and especially encouraged his wife to run with him. PRIV learners had clear views on Islam and sport: 'Yes, religion affects the kind of activities because you know that you cannot just do what you want, everything must be within certain boundaries, but within those boundaries there are ways and means in dealing with things ...' Many also felt that if certain needs were addressed or accommodated, then participation would increase:

> there is also the time factor where we may be busy with a match and it is prayer times, they cannot just stop in the middle of the match. They don't take that into consideration, but if they did, it wouldn't be a problem ...

In PUBL, the same sentiments were shared, alongside concerns of Islamophobia at a national level:

> some people are very anti-Muslim, for example Hashim Amla [a cricketer] when he said that he does not want the emblem of the SAB [South African Breweries] on his shirt, people had a problem with it, also because he has a beard and he did not want to shave it. Islam does set boundaries, but you can participate in sport.

Even at this age, they recognise social and structural barriers to sporting participation for Muslim men and women.

Racism and health issues

Additional barriers mentioned at PUBL were racism and health issues. A so-called 'coloured' learner took part in swimming at a local club and seemed to experience various forms of racism. According to her, there were only two coloured youths who belonged to the previously all-white club, indicating very small change post-apartheid. When she was chosen to compete at a provincial level, no administrative or monetary assistance was given because she was the only member of the club that was chosen. This did not match the full assistance given to a white person who, in the same situation, had been selected previously, indicating remnants of racism persisting.

Heavy smoking was an issue for some learners. They preferred not to do physical education because they could not keep up with the physical activities due to smoking-related fitness issues. They deemed themselves to be unfit. Another learner had asthma and her father did not want her to participate because he was afraid of complications. The girls raised many issues that would be shared by all young girls, for example these fitness concerns, as well as some that would only be shared by Muslim girls.

Conclusion

In conclusion, evidence indicates that girls are afforded some opportunities to participate in physical activities at school during Life Orientation, as statutorily required in South Africa, albeit with inequities in resourcing at every level. Some girls also have the opportunity to take part in wider sporting activities and join sports clubs or communal dance groups with other family members. Parental influences are strong, positively and negatively, dependent on parental attitudes and behaviours towards participation in physical activity. These findings were evident across participants from private and public secondary schools. There were also examples of so-called 'coloured' girls suffering subtle forms of prejudice and discrimination in funding and travel opportunities regardless of sporting talent. The participants raised a range of issues: some they would share with many adolescent girls, for example related to body consciousness and fitness levels; and others they would share with many Muslim girls, for example meeting their needs for gender segregation, participation in appropriate (preferred) activities and dress codes in sport. There was evidence of valuing private, internalised Islam in preference to hypocritical religious displays, for example in the form of strict Islamic dress codes that were not matched by Islamically valued, moral behaviour. The study also raised issues about the quality of physical-education provision under Life Orientation, for example insufficient educators and poor attitudes of some with inadequate specialist knowledge of the subject. A range of other issues were raised, such as the significance of same-sex staffing to increase participation of Muslim girls, the importance of continuity in staffing, timetable and space protection for physical education/school-based sporting activities, and improvement of facilities and resourcing. Knowledge levels of the health and other benefits of participation in physical activity were poor, with academic subjects being regarded as much more important and taking priority in curriculum time.

Such inequities in provision are not commensurate with the country's Constitution and Bill of Rights, which states children be afforded opportunities by others (teachers) to express and live their freedoms. Policy rhetoric needs to be matched with positive action. Responding to the challenges raised in this study would ensure more equitable experiences among all young people in school-based physical education and sporting opportunities in South Africa. As Benn (2005) states:

> Schools do provide the only guaranteed access to all facets of physical education, sport and dance.... Schools become an important arena for respecting difference, encouraging potential, for providing positive role models and opportunities, to experience breadth of activities, within an equity framework, concerned with justice and fairness.

Unfortunately such provision has not yet been achieved in all schools of the Western Cape as indicated by the case study. Improved school-based opportunities are essential for South Africa's youth, and the future health of the nation.

Notes

1 Often, Muslim private schools are funded by the local community. These schools follow a curriculum designed to meet the educational requirements of their local educational authority. Muslim public schools are state-funded, and the curriculum taught is a state curriculum with Islamic studies being integrated as an additional subject at school. Muslim schools produce good academic results, with many of the students pursuing tertiary education after schooling.

2 In 2006, only 8 per cent of Western Cape schools were independent (receiving no or a small subsidy), 92 per cent were public, subsidised by the national Department of Education with additional funding found through the school governing body (Baxen 2008). Most Muslim independent schools started because of a perceived deterioration in the quality of education at most public schools, a perceived moral decay of Western Cape society in townships and to inculcate an Islamic ethos in Muslim learners (Fataar 2003). Since 1994, 12 Muslim schools have been established in the Western Cape: four primary schools, three high schools and five schools from grade 1 to grade 12. Fataar (2003) identified four types of governance at the high schools: mosque-based, expatriate-belonging (Turkish), ideological closure and ethnicised identity production (Indian); funded by mosque-based community structures, Turkish expatriates (business and professionals), businessmen and Indian professionals, and business people respectively. Learners attending these schools come from Malay, Indian and Turkish communities with backgrounds ranging from working class to upper middle class. School fees range from R1,200–R8,000.

3 According to the South African Schools Act of 1996, public and independent schools could be established (Chisholm 2005). The subsidies for schools are categorised according to quintiles, with quintile one being the poorest schools and quintile five the wealthiest, which means that most schools have to generate extra income. One mechanism of achieving this is through the paying of school fees. The South African

Schools Act of 1996 declared that schooling is compulsory and free from grade 1 to grade 9, but because school governing bodies have the authority to determine school fees, most, if not all, of the schools impose a monetary value on education.

Bibliography

Ansari, F.R. (2006) *Islam to the Modern Mind: Lectures in South Africa 1970 and 1972.* Paarl: Paarl Printers.

Baxen, J. (2008) Population and education in the Western Cape. In R. Marindo, C. Groenewald and S. Gaisie (eds) *The State of the Population in the Western Cape Province.* Cape Town: HSRC Press.

Benn, T. (2005) Race and physical education, sport and dance. In K. Green and K. Hardman (eds) *Physical Education: Essential Issues.* London: Sage Publications: 197–219.

Chisholm, L. (2005) The state of South Africa's schools. In J. Daniel, R. Southall and J. Lutchman (eds) *State of the Nation: South Africa 2004–2005.* Cape Town: HSRC Press.

Fataar, A. (2003) Muslim Community Schools in Cape Town: exemplifying adaptation to the democratic landscape. *Annual Review of Islam in South Africa*, Volume 6.

Flintoff, A. and Scraton, S. (2005) Gender and physical education. In K. Green, and K. Hardman (eds) *Physical Education Essential Issues.* London: Sage Publications: 161–177.

Groenewald, C. (2008) Western Cape: an overview. In R. Marindo, C. Groenewald and S. Gaisie (eds) *The State of the Population in the Western Cape Province.* Cape Town: HSRC Press.

Mohlala, T. (2007) Games plan to get children active. *The Teacher* 12(3): 15.

Mouton, J. (2005) *How to Succeed in Your Master's and Doctoral Studies.* Pretoria: Van Schaik.

Nakamura, Y. (2002) Beyond the *hijab*: female Muslims and physical activity. *WSPAJ*, 11(2): 21–48.

Peck, N. (2009) Personal interview. 7 May, Strand.

Phillips, J.S. (2006) Concerns about physical inactivity among adolescents in the Strand. *South Africa Journal of Community and Health Sciences* 1: 39–45.

Scraton, S. (1992) *Shaping Up To Womanhood: Gender and Girls' Physical Education.* Milton Keynes: Open University Press.

Terre Blanche, M., Durrheim, K. and Painter, D. (2006) *Research in Practice: Applied Methods for the Social Science.* Cape Town: UCT Press.

Vahed, G. and Jeppie, S. (2005) Multiple communities: Muslims in post-apartheid South Africa. In J. Daniel, R. Southall and L. Lutchman (eds) *State of the Nation: South Africa 2004–2005.* Cape Town: HSRC Press.

Van Deventer, K.J. (2007) A paradigm shift in life orientation: a review. *South African Journal for Research in Sport, Physical Education and Recreation* 29(2): 131–146.

Waghid, Y. (2002) *Democratic Education: Policy and Practice.* Matieland: Stellenbosch University Printers.

Walseth, K. (2006) Young Muslim women and sport: the impact of identity work. *Leisure Studies* 25(1): 75–94.

12 Din ve devlet

Bir elit Türk sporcusunun hikayesi

Religion and the state
The story of a Turkish elite athlete

Canan Koca and İlknur Hacısoftaoğlu

Editors' introduction

The case study recounted in this chapter is focused on the experiences of one Turkish woman. 'Zeynep' (pseudonym) was a Muslim woman who rose to the top of international competition in her sporting field. Her case provides an example of how tensions between religion and the state can be reflected in the life experiences of women athletes in Turkey.

Background to the study

The role of women and their respective liberties within any society have been vulnerable to broader political and social conflicts and processes of change. The question of appropriate dress for Muslim women has been a particularly controversial issue as women struggle to maintain harmony between personal identity and societal norms. In Turkey, where most of the population is Muslim, women's feelings about themselves and their identity as Muslims are often reflected in their participation in sport and exercise (Hargreaves 2007). Dress code can be an important dimension of that reflection because of the Islamic requirement for modesty in followers and the religious symbolism this represents to others. Consequently, the dress code for women to engage in official sports activities, as well as in other spheres of public life, has been a focal point for disputes regarding religion in the political sphere of modern Turkey.

In order to understand the dress code discourse and the role of Muslim women's involvement in sport in Turkey, it is important to analyse the historical reforms that have fuelled much of the controversy today. In the transition from the Ottoman Empire to the Turkish Republic, the discourse regarding the role of women in Turkey greatly transformed. During this period, enhanced freedom for women was seen as a symbol of modernisation.

Wide-ranging reforms were instituted in a top-down process as reformers eradicated old institutions of the Ottoman Empire. These changes were especially prevalent in the religious and political spheres. For example, 'reforms initiated by the founders of the Turkish Republic were part of a spate of legislation which amounted to a radical break with Ottoman Islam and its institutions' (Kandiyoti 1991: 22). Furthermore, the Ankara government abolished the Sultanate in 1922, and the Turkish Republic was proclaimed in 1923. In 1924, the Caliphate was abolished, the state had a monopoly of control on the educational system, and the madrassas (religious schools) were terminated. Religious affairs were put under the authority of the office of the Prime Minister. The new secular government, in 1928, also eliminated the constitutional provision which recognised Islam as the official religion of the state (Kandiyoti 1991). Hence, as Özdalga (1998) stated, Turkey became the only country in the Middle East where secularism became the official ideology of the state. The significant political and social changes during this period, as well as the framework of the modernisation process, had many effects on the legal status of women.

As a part of the modernisation/Westernisation process, the Turkish Civil Code, inspired by and almost identical to the Swiss Civil Code, was adopted in 1926. In 1930, women were granted suffrage in local elections in 1930, and at the national level in 1934 (Kandiyoti 1991). Women in Turkey have always been at the centre of changes in the relationship between religion and the state, as in other Muslim countries (Hargreaves 2007). In the Republic of Turkey, after the new government adopted secular legal and political reforms, the wearing of more modern dress and the abandoning of the veil were considered symbolic of progress. Indeed, Atatürk, founder of the Republic, urged women to adopt modern styles of dress (Kandiyoti 1991).

In the 1920s and 1930s, after the establishment of the Republic, although women's head cover was not forcefully removed by the state forces, unveiling marked the commitment of women to the republican reforms, particularly to its new secular regime, principles of gender equality, and development; hence it became the sign of western modernisation while veiling was the sign of the rejected Ottoman past.

(Saktanber and Çorbacıoğlu 2008: 519)

Wearing the headscarf (*hijab*, referred to as 'turban' in Turkey) in public institutions was banned, as this was interpreted as being a contradiction to the secular characteristic of the state (Sündal 2005). Currently, there still exists a ban on the wearing of the headscarf in public institutions, for example schools, courts, universities, Parliament and official sports competitions. Göle explains: 'the public sphere [in Turkey] is institutionalised and imagined as a site for the implementation of a secular and progressive way of life' (2002: 176).

The last three decades have been marked by the rise to power of political Islam in Turkey (Özdalga 1998), and with it the increase in the use of the *hijab* by Turkish women. The wearing of the headscarf epitomises the secular–Islamic struggle (Howe 2000). The question of veiling often accompanied public confrontations with state authorities as well as the secular sections of civil society (Saktanber and Çorbacıoğlu 2008). While women who wear the *hijab*, together with many other women and men of different political persuasions, oppose the ban as a violation of human freedom as well as religious freedom, Kemalists (people who defend the policies rather than doctrines of Mustafa Kemal) oppose any kind of religious dress as a betrayal of Atatürk's reforms (Howe 2000). Because of the ban on the *hijab*, women who choose to wear it are not allowed to work in state institutions or compete in official sporting events.

Although since the year 2000 there has been a significant increase in the number of Turkish women in sports, and Turkish female athletes have been successful at the international level (for example, winning medals in World and European Championships and the Olympics), there are significant gaps and challenges with regard to the access and participation of women in sport generally. According to information from the General Directorate of Youth and Sport, while the number of elite female athletes (330,258) is less than that of elite male athletes (856,572), there has been a five-fold increase in women's involvement in sport since 2002 (www.gsgm.gov.tr). According to the statistics, the number of female competitors was roughly 66,000 in 2002, this number increasing to around 350,000 in 2007. In addition, the highest number of Turkish female athletes at the Olympics Games was in 2004 in Athens, where Nurcan Taylan became the first Turkish female athlete to win an Olympic gold medal. This was for weight-lifting. In the 2008 Olympics, 20 Turkish female and 48 Turkish male athletes competed. The Turkish Olympic team won eight medals, of which female team members won four silver medals. In the 2009 IAFF World Championships in Athletics, Melis Karin won the bronze medal in the long jump event. This was the only medal won by the Turkish team in the competition.

The ban on the headscarf in official sporting competitions restricts the access of women to competitive sports. Although some Muslim women acquiesce and remove their *hijab*, those who do not wish to do this are, effectively, banned from representative, competitive sports.

The following case study draws on the life experiences of a Turkish woman who was both Muslim and a top-level athlete. The aim of the study was to increase our understanding of how complex identities are managed in the context of sport and religion in modern Turkey. Zeynep was selected because her career in sport epitomises the struggles that top-level Muslim women athletes face. She has always spoken freely about the conflict of sport and faith in her life and when approached to be interviewed for this case study, she willingly agreed.

Method

An interpretive case study was conducted on the life of Zeynep, one of Turkey's most successful sportswomen. The purpose was to understand more about her personal life as a Turkish Muslim woman and elite athlete in the sport of judo. This martial art is the second most popular sport, after football, in Turkey. Of the 193,000 registered participants, 50,000 are women. A total of 50,000 Turkish men and women are competitive athletes in this sport (Maden 2009). The researchers conducted a 90-minute semi-structured interview which probed successes, issues and challenges encountered in the history of her participation. In particular, we were interested in her career experiences as a woman athlete, from first encounters with judo to international sporting success and beyond. We asked about her religious beliefs and how religious influences may have impacted on her career. Furthermore, we asked how the religious beliefs of significant others influenced her development. Finally, we probed Zeynep's views on how public opinion had influenced her sport engagement. Analysis of the transcript sought to identify key emergent themes in order to increase understanding of ways in which Zeynep managed the complexities of her life history and identity. Three interrelated themes are discussed: (a) judo, early years and family influences; (b) judo after marriage; and (c) managing multiple identities – Turkish woman, Muslim woman and sporting champion.

The story of Zeynep[1]

Zeynep was born in Ankara, Turkey. At the time of the interview she was 30 years old, married with an 11-year-old daughter and still competing and coaching in her sport. She started to practise judo as a young child. Zeynep began to compete locally, nationally then internationally, reaching the highest level of success with many national and international titles, including World Champion in her weight category at the age of 16 years in 1995, bronze medallist in the Sydney Olympics and bronze in the 2008 European Championships in Italy. Although she also trained as a physical-education teacher, Zeynep has dedicated her life to judo. However, she took a break from judo in 1995 and returned in 1998. She grew up in a religious Islamic family and considers herself to be a religious person. She did not wear the *hijab* in her youth, but began to wear it in 1996. After returning to her judo career, she participated in competitions wearing the *hijab*. In 2000, she decided to wear a bandanna (a cloth head band that partially covers the hair and does not visibly symbolise Islam) to cover her head. This was in response to a ban on head covering in national and international competitions.

Judo, early years and family influences

Zeynep started to practise judo at the age of seven with her sister. She explained that she and her sister were interested in martial arts movies. When a martial arts club opened in their neighbourhood, they were thrilled to have the opportunity to practise. Judo was the most popular activity in the club, and this was the martial arts form that they decided to take up. Throughout her primary, secondary and high-school years, she was involved in training and competition at national and international levels. She subsequently became a member of the national judo team, becoming World Champion in 1995 at 16 years of age.

Family influences shaped opportunities and constraints for Zeynep. With her elder sister she had found her interest, but being the younger sister proved to be an unexpected advantage. The elder sister met more insistence on following cultural traditions for adopting the *hijab*, expectations of womanhood, marriage and child-bearing. Sport was not considered appropriate as her sister moved through adolescence, and she was eventually stopped from participating by her parents. This did not happen to Zeynep. In addition to her position in the family, her outstanding early successes also made a difference to the way her parents treated her:

> Actually they [my family] always supported me but they did not support my sister. We were exercising together but I was more successful [than her].... She was three years older than me. My family said that she was growing up, she was a young woman, she should not do sport.... They did not allow her to do judo. They allowed me since I was the youngest and a tomboy in their mind.... Later, they also forced her [my sister] to cover her head.

This experience links with cultural interpretations of Islam that allow girls, before puberty, more freedom to participate in any physical activity, including in a mixed-sex environment out of the home. Girls and boys practise judo together in most sport clubs in Turkey. What is interesting is how success brought a shift in parental views of cultural adherence.

Zeynep spoke excitedly about going to practice when she was in primary school. However, her teacher tried to stop her since partaking in judo, for girls met with disapproval in her local community/town, as indicated in this narrative:

> I never forget what my primary school teacher did. She thought that girls should not do male sports. I remember well, the teacher asked a friend of mine to follow me and check whether I was going to judo or not. I asked my coach if I could exercise behind a column where it was impossible for her to see me. I think the teacher was uncomfortable with what I was doing. She said you are a girl, why do you play with boys? I was playing football with boys rather than jumping rope with girls. She [the teacher] wanted me to be feminine.

Here we see traditional views of masculinity being associated with sports that have aggressive and fighting elements, alongside expectations of appropriate/ inappropriate sports for girls. It also demonstrates the significance of both teacher and coach in shaping experiences of young Turkish girls and how Zeynep, as an athlete, had a certain amount of power to manipulate situations to gain advantage for her personal ambitions.

Her main goal was to compete in judo and to win a gold medal:

> I always wanted to have a gold medal. I mean being good at judo was extremely important for me. I remember when I won my first gold medal [European Championship, 1994]. At the end of the match there was a trophy ... and a medal. Having a gold medal meant much more to me than being second or third.

Zeynep gained many successes in the European Championships in 1994 and 2000, becoming World Champion in 1995, 1999 and 2001, and winning the bronze medal in the 2000 Sydney Olympics.

Zeynep decided to quit judo after becoming World Champion in 1996. Although judo had become a priority in her life, she thought that she had reached her highest level in winning the most prestigious championship:

> I just thought that winning the World Championship was the most important goal in a sport career. I had no idea about the Olympics. I had never heard of it before. You know I was 16 years old and this was the biggest achievement for me. I had to protect my title. If I competed in another championship and I won the silver or bronze medal, everybody would say, 'Hey look, she was a World Champion but now she became a second'. It would be a scandal. I mean ... I did not want to be in this situation.

Although she was very young when she ended her sporting career, she quit judo to protect her status as World Champion. This indicates dilemmas that many 'achievement-oriented' top sports people face with regard to their sense of identity and achievement. Whereas striving is extrinsically driven and connected with ambitions of reaching the top, once achieved there is a feeling of having nowhere else to go.

In this case, the way that Zeynep perceived her success in judo can be better understood in the context of Nicholls' achievement goal theory (1984). This theory states that individuals can be categorised as low or high in two separate dimensions: task orientation and ego orientation. Athletes who are high in task orientation define success relative to their ability to perform certain tasks or activities competently. However, athletes who are high in ego orientation define success relative to external factors such as the right equipment and rewards. Research has revealed that athletes high in task orientation believe success in sport is achieved by receiving external rewards (Duda and Nicholls 1992; Duda and White 1992; King and Williams 1997). Consequently, ego-oriented athletes usually foster external motivation. In the light of these findings and the comments made by Zeynep, it could be argued that Zeynep is ego-oriented and the reason for her decision to quit sport might be explained by her extrinsic motivation. Further, as can be seen by the rest of her story, she started to compete in judo again since she enjoyed being a successful sportswoman.

Judo after her marriage

After she had dropped out of sport in 1995, Zeynep married in 1997 and began to live with her husband's family. This was the point when she began to cover her head as a personal choice and as a sign of her religious belief: 'I wanted to be covered, not because of my family ...' However, she was living in a religious family (both her own family and her husband's family), and most of the women around her did wear the *hijab*. Further, she added that there were many other women athletes in judo who wore a head covering.

Two years after getting married, Zeynep had a daughter. In the interview for this case study she mentioned several difficulties in adapting to family life. She thought that it was difficult for her to deal with family responsibilities, childcare and living with relatives. Besides, while she had competed in judo, she had earned her own money. After dropping out and getting married, she became dependent on her husband financially. She was a housewife, but this did not satisfy her:

> I had a baby and I was a housewife, but I used to have an active life. Besides, I had no economic independence ... and I said to myself that this was not my life. The best thing I could do was judo.

Again, we see dilemmas in identity and a growing multiplicity of views on who she was, her life priorities and aspirations.

In 1998, Zeynep decided to return to her sports career, saying: 'I wanted to do lots of things in judo.' She took up her training three months after having a baby and she forced herself to train regularly: 'Just jogging along I had bleeding and I could run for only ten minutes. I was observing other athletes' training.... I mean, I made every effort to retain the discipline of training for each day.'

Her family's reaction was negative to her return to a sporting life: 'My husband did not want me to do judo. My mother-in-law told me that I was a bride' (a term used in Turkey for married women). She would always be a bride to them, first and foremost a family member, wife and mother:

> I had to stay at home to look after my baby and my husband's family. But, I said that I was determined to do judo. I said I wanted to. My own family did not support me either. They thought that I was married and a mother [so not a sportswoman], but I decided to practise judo ... in spite of their rejections.... The head of the federation at that time was very supportive to me.

This comment indicates that she was driven by inner motivation to continue despite family opposition and new responsibilities.

In many ways, Zeynep's story reflects her efforts to resist and to undermine dominant norms and the expectations that society had of women, especially mothers. Being a woman athlete and a mother was looked upon as an irreconcilable contradiction against the normative role of a woman in Turkey. For instance, she emphasised that, though there were societal expectations and pressure to adopt these 'ways of being', she also came to the conclusion that social norms caused many constraints on continuing her career as a competitive athlete. Her life was constructed by the socio-cultural structure of Turkish society, which included patriarchal views of a woman's subservience to fathers and husbands. She mentioned specific constraints, such as family responsibilities and social disapproval for her sports career. However, she was determined to defend her right to continue judo by ignoring negative comments from her environment. Zeynep was mainly constrained by lack of family support. She tried to persuade her family that her training had no negative effects on her family responsibilities and the care of her child. The evidence suggests generational differences in attitude within families, although Zeynep's sister became her main childcare support, bringing the baby to the gym when she was training and enabling the breastfeeding of her young baby to continue.

Zeynep's case is not typical of a Turkish mother in terms of deciding to do something for herself. As Kulacac *et al.* (2006) found, many Turkish women had to sacrifice their leisure time and freedom in order to satisfy the needs of their children. In a more recent study (Koca *et al.* 2009), family responsibilities and the ethos of care/childcare are found to be significant constraints on Turkish married women's participation in physical activities. Further, the authors point out that the approval of husbands and relatives are very important for Turkish women's being able to take up a physical activity. Zeynep's story shows, on the one hand, the constraints that Turkish women experience when they wish to embark on a (sports) career, but it also demonstrates that there are ways of resisting obligations and negotiating concessions.

Despite these difficulties, Zeynep was selected for the Turkish national judo team again. In 2001, she was selected for the Turkish World Championship team, and in the same year she also started to study at university. Zeynep regarded this time as a very difficult period of her life due to her struggle to continue judo at the highest level, to integrate family life and to resume her education:

> I had to organise my life around family, education and judo. I was looking after my daughter, going to training and going to the university. There was a pressure on me. I mean, you know, I had a kid and I was married and I was old to compete. The other coaches and the athletes thought that the World Championships was a big challenge and I would not be able to motivate myself. They thought that I could not cope with the problems in my life. When we were in the camp for the 2001 World Championships, they were always watching me whether my performance was good or bad. I had to exercise regularly and I had to take care of myself. I had an injury, but I could not tell anybody.

She felt the disapproval of the coaches because of her age and family responsibilities, yet she was determined to prove them all wrong.

Multiple identities: Turkish woman, Muslim woman, sporting champion

Zeynep is a 'covered woman' (in her own words), and in 1999 covered women were banned from entering sports competitions in Turkey. The GSGM (Gençlik ve Spor Genel Müdürlüğü) (Youth and Sport General Directory) has the power to formulate and apply sports policies at both national and international competitions. In

1999, according to the Dress Code of National and International Sport Competitions, formulated by the GSGM, athletes were required to wear sports dress conforming to the basic national principles (secularism in this case) of the Turkish Republic:

> Item 4: Athletes must wear uniform (sports dress), which is determined by the GSGM in national and international sport competitions. Item 6: Athletes and other staff in sports competitions must wear clothing which does not belong to any religion and political views. Item 8: ... Athletes who do not obey this code will be banned from participating in sports competitions for one to three years.
>
> (www.gsgm.gov.tr)

This code is based on the law of dress code (no. 2596, item 2) which is decreed by the Council of Ministers.

Zeynep did not quit judo because of this ban, but nor did she give up covering her head. This was a tradition of her family and community, and something she had always associated with being the kind of Muslim she wanted to be. She decided to wear a bandanna instead of the full headscarf in sports competitions. According to Zeynep, her decision was accepted in the Turkish sporting community because a bandanna is not regarded as a religious symbol. Furthermore, it is not visible under the headgear required for judo. In many respects, Zeynep had negotiated a compromise for herself that enabled her identity as Turkish Muslim sportswoman to remain protected in a politically pressured position. However, she was never entirely comfortable with this as it did not cover hair and neck fully, as the headscarf did. Zeynep had often faced the problem of wanting to adhere to her religious beliefs and modest dress code in the face of opposition from sports bodies during her career. In the interview, she cited one particularly memorable example at the training camp for the judo World Cup in 2001, which had upset her:

> Before going to the World Championship [in 2001], short-sleeved T-shirts were distributed to the team. I sewed red fabric to the T-shirt to make the sleeves longer. He [the General Secretary of the national team] said, 'Remove those things from your arm and your head. I can't allow you to wear a long-sleeved T-shirt and a headscarf, get out.' This time they wanted me to discard headscarf and long sleeves in training as well as competition and I did not want to. First I cried and decided to go back home. Then my coach persuaded me to wear the short-sleeved T-shirt and not to wear a turban. I competed and became the World Champion.

According to Zeynep, there is a basic right of the freedom of conscience and belief (vicdan ve inanç özgürlügü):

> I should not be banned from competing just for wearing a headscarf and long sleeves or just because of my religious belief. I am not putting pressure

on other female athletes to cover their heads. I mean, it seems they are afraid of my influence on other female athletes ...

Zeynep was not happy with the dress code ruling and she questioned it. Although the bandanna was a compromise for a head-covering, there was no such solution when given the choice of wearing short-sleeved tee-shirts or leaving the national team. As a young woman competing for the first time in a World Championship on behalf of Turkey, her sporting identity took precedence and she competed according to the rules. The personal cost, evident in the quote, related to issues of conscience about having to discard her religious preferences for a less modest dress code.

The power of Zeynep's sporting drive is clear from the following quote:

> The most important thing in my life is my daughter. To be honest, only when the Turkish National Anthem is played, I swear, that is the only moment that I don't think about her. I just want to cry. There is such a spirit in that moment. That's why I can't leave judo. That's why I am taking the headscarf off.

Zeynep described herself as 'a competitive top-level athlete' but she felt judged by significant people in sport on her overt religious affiliation. She knew about the headscarf ban in Turkish sports policies, but she expected a kind of tolerance for her religious needs regarding the dress code because she was successful for Turkey in international competitions. Zeynep assumed that her sporting environment would respect her wishes because of her international achievements for Turkey:

> I know that I don't feel comfortable with myself if I uncover my head and my arms. I just want them to accept me just the way I am. Yes I am a Muslim, wishing to cover my head, but I am a top-level athlete too and I am very enthusiastic to win medals on behalf of Turkey. This should be the main point.... I have been competing in judo for 14 years. I am the most elite athlete in the team.

In addition, Zeynep expressed her great frustration with the lack of Turkish media interest in her athletic achievements and their focus on her religion:

> My athletic successes are not important for the Turkish media. I'm a good asset for them because I've both success and many things causing sensations in terms of being married, having a child and wearing a headscarf. They are mostly interested in my religious beliefs. For example, there was a World Championship in Europe. I was sitting in the stands with my female team-mate and waiting for a final competition. A journalist wanted to take my photo. The articles were published in the newspapers with the title of 'backwardness [to the Islamic order] in judo'. In the photo we were

presented as head covered ... both of us were sitting in the stands but there was only my name. At that time, I had an injury on my head. I said I had had an injury on my head that is why I wore a bandanna. But if I said 'I'm covered', things would be getting worse for me. I mean it would be difficult to join training camps and competitions. Maybe I would hurt many women athletes who want to be covered by wearing a bandanna or women who join competitions with a bandanna.

The serious dilemmas faced by Zeynep as a Muslim woman, who in pursuit of her sporting goals is forbidden from being visibly Muslim, are evident in the ambiguity of her words. It seems she has to hide her religious identity, avoid displaying any symbol of her faith in public in order to ensure favourable press coverage as a top woman athlete in Turkey. Her apparent fear in 'coming out' as a believer might, contrary to her views, make it easier for many others to fulfil both their religious and sporting identities who have not enjoyed her success and the national attention this brings. According to Zeynep, it is not possible to simultaneously follow religious laws and compete and gain sporting glory for Turkey. Although Turkey is a predominantly Muslim country, Turkish policies and the Turkish media regard the religious laws and the principles of a secular state as incompatible. Further, the mainstream media also voiced its belief that supporting this kind of religious behaviour whilst representing Turkey, particularly at such a high level, threatened the secular ideals of the Turkish Republic.

Conclusion

In this case study, we wanted to provide an insight into the life of a top-level woman athlete and an understanding of the range of opportunities, struggles, resistance and constraints of women's lives in Turkey. Despite being a dedicated athlete, Zeynep had to struggle with many constraints, which made it difficult for her to continue judo during her sporting career. Some of them are related to gendered social expectations. Zeynep shares these expectations with all other women living in a patriarchal society. Other constraints are caused by the cultural and political conditions prevailing in Turkey with regard to religion and secularism. These competing ideologies are explained in the introduction to this chapter.

Zeynep had to fight, resist and negotiate hierarchical gender relations and hegemonic notions of femininity that led to oppression from her family and environment, particularly during early marriage and motherhood. In a patriarchal society that discourages women from being physically active, women's participation in sport challenges traditional values (Whitson 2004). From this point of view Zeynep, as an athlete in a male-dominated sport, represents a challenge to patriarchal society. Despite her pioneering position as a World Champion, her story shows that she experienced many problems due to her preference to adhere to dress codes in accordance with her Muslim identity. Because of the ban on the headscarf in official sports competitions, she felt permanently constrained in her sporting career. She constantly had to choose between her sporting career and her religious values and preferences. Zeynep, as a Muslim woman and top-level athlete, emphasised the concept of freedom, which is guaranteed in many countries. She argued that she should have the freedom to simultaneously fulfil her religious duties and compete in sport. However, as has been mentioned, the decision to cover the head is understood in Turkey not as a matter of freedom but as a powerful religio-political message. This situation is not unique to Turkey.

During the interview, Zeynep focused on explaining the effects of this situation on her life experience as a sportswoman. The emphasis on her religious beliefs in the media obscured the celebration of her athletic achievements as a Turkish champion sportswoman. The story of Zeynep shows a path of not only restriction, struggle and negotiation, but also success, acknowledgement and pride in outstanding achievements as a Turkish Muslim sportswoman able to reflect on the influences that have both shaped and constrained her life story.

Note

1 Parts of this story have been fictionalised to help maintain the anonymity of the athlete.

References

Duda, J.L. and Nicholls, J.G. (1992) 'Dimensions of achievement motivation in school-work and sport', *Journal of Educational Psychology*, 84: 290–299.

Duda, J.L. and White, S.A. (1992) 'Goal orientations and beliefs about the causes of success among elite skiers', *The Sport Psychologist*, 6: 334–343.

Göle, N. (2002) 'Islam in public: New visibilities and new imaginaries', *Public Culture*, 14: 173–190.

GSGM (Gençlik ve Spor Genel Müdürlüğü) [Youth and Sport General Directory]. Online, available at: www.gsgm.gov.tr (accessed 16 February 2009).

Hargreaves, J. (2007) 'Sport, exercise and the female Muslim body: negotiating Islam, politics and male power', in J. Hargreaves and P. Vertinsky (eds) *Physical Culture, Power, and the Body*, New York: Routledge: 74–100.

Howe, M. (2000) *Turkey Today: A Nation Divided Over Islam Revival*, Colorado: Westview Press.

Kandiyoti, D. (1991) 'End of empire: Islam, nationalism and women in Turkey', in D. Kandiyoti (ed.) *Women, Islam and the State*, London: Macmillan: 22–47.

King, L.A. and Williams, T.A. (1997) 'Goal orientation and performance in martial arts', *Journal of Sport Behavior*, 20: 397–411.

Koca, C., Henderson, K., Aşçı, F.H. and Bulgu, N. (2009) 'Issues of participation in leisure-time physical activity for Turkish women', *Journal of Leisure Research*, 41, 2: 225–251.

Kulakac, O., Buldukoglu, K., Yilmaz, M. and Alkan, S. (2006) 'An analysis of the motherhood concept in employed women in south Turkey.' *Social Behaviour and Personality*, 34: 837–852.

Madan, E. (2009) 'Turkish Taekwondo demands more media attention', *Sunday Zaman* e-gazette. Online, available at: www.sundayszaman.com/sunday/detaylar.do?load=detay&link=172837 (accessed 27 May 2009).

Nicholls, J.G. (1984) 'Achievement motivation: Conceptions of ability, subjective experience, task choice, and performance', *Psychological Review*, 91: 328–346.

Özdalga, E. (1998) *The Veiling Issue, Official Secularism and Popular Islam in Modern Turkey*, Richmond: Routledge.

Saktanber, A. and Çorbacıoğlu, G. (2008) 'Veiling and headscarf-skepticism in Turkey', *Social Politics: International Studies in Gender, State and Society*, Special Issue.

Sündal, F. (2005) 'Invisible women visible Islam: Engendering everyday lives of educated Islamist women in Turkey', *Sosyal Bilimler Dergisi*, 1: 109–130.

Whitson, D. (2004) 'The embodiment of gender: Discipline, domination, and empowerment', in D. Scraton and A. Flintoff (eds) *Gender and Sport: A Reader*, London: Routledge: 227–240.

13 المتحدة:المرأة، الإعاقة، و الرياضة
دراسة حالة من الإمارات العربية

A case study on the United Arab Emirates
Women, disability and sport

Eman Gaad

Editors' introduction

The author of this chapter is currently seconded from the British University in Dubai to be the Director of Disability Services in the Dubai Government's Community Development Authority. She is a researcher/practitioner/advocate who is committed to improving the social inclusion of people with disabilities in the United Arab Emirates (UAE), where she lives and works. In 2004 she started the UAE Down's Syndrome Support Group, which uses sport as one domain through which young people can engage with wider opportunities and greater equity of life chances. The chapter is significant because it addresses the importance of recognising intersecting axes of oppression – culture, gender and disability – as well as the challenges and opportunities faced by young Muslim women with an intellectual disability.

Introduction to the case study

Despite good efforts in many countries to promote the social and educational inclusion of young people with physical and intellectual disabilities (learning difficulties), there remains much to be achieved regarding the quality of life and education of such individuals in the Arab, Muslim world. The status of social inclusion, particularly for females with learning difficulties, reflects an alarming reality in most Arab countries. A very small number of these girls attend regular schools and few participate in sporting events, which can be effective tools to promote inclusion in society. Barriers to social inclusion have had their origin in cultural beliefs and practices, but financial and human resources also have an effect.

This chapter focuses on the challenges and recent successes in the UAE and describes the contribution that sport can make towards improving quality of life. It is necessary, however, to consider the country context, as well as socio-cultural issues related to gender and disability, before an understanding of education and community sporting provision can be gained. The use of sport by one support group, the UAE's Down's Syndrome Association, which grew into one of the largest registered non-governmental organisations (NGOs) in the country, is examined. It was the first group formed to protect the rights of these people and is proactive in the pursuit of its aim to improve the lives and life experiences of children with Down's syndrome. The chapter concludes with recommendations to improve inclusive practices using sport as the main vehicle of delivery.

The context of the UAE

The United Arab Emirates (UAE) is a federal state located in the Arabian Gulf and was founded in December 1971. The country has seven emirates: Abu Dhabi, Dubai, Sharjah, Ajman, Umm al-Quwain, Ras al-Khaimah and Fujairah. Abu Dhabi is the capital city and the neighbouring countries are Saudi Arabia, Qatar and the Sultanate of Oman. The individual emirates are sheikdoms or monarchies which are federated (Burden-Leahy 2005: 130) to form a central government. In 2007 the first National Council was formed and some of the members, both men and women, were for the first time publicly elected.

The total area of the UAE is 83,600 km^2, much of which is desert. High temperatures and very little annual rainfall are characteristic of the climate (Camerapix 1998; Heard-Bey 2004).

The economy of the UAE evolved rapidly following the discovery of crude oil in the 1960s. Great wealth created investment and development possibilities which were seized upon by nationals as well as businessmen and entrepreneurs from all over the world (Khan 2005). The rapid modernisation process, driven initially by the oil and gas industries and later by tourism, was characterised by displays of conspicuous wealth in the form of hotels, futuristically designed office buildings and extravagant residential developments. Hundreds of thousands of foreign workers from neighbouring Arab countries, Iran, the Asian sub-continent, the Philippines, Europe and America entered the UAE to service the needs of the construction industry, tourism and the lifestyle of the sizeable wealthy communities (Whetter 2000; Heard-Bey 2004). So numerous has been the influx of foreigners that, of the total population of the UAE, some six million, only 16.5 per cent are Emirati nationals. Indians make up the largest group of workers, numbering in excess of one-and-a-half-million (arabianbusiness.com 2009). Such large groups of people bringing their own customs, religions and cultures will inevitably have an effect on those of the native Emirati population.

Socio-cultural issues related to gender and disability in the UAE

An insight into the historical changes that have shaped UAE culture and attitudes to religion, gender and disability is necessary in order to understand the experiences of young women with disabilities today. The small Emirati section of the UAE's population has a strong local culture, where the fundamentals of the Islamic faith 'dominate the cultural, moral, social, economic, legal and political' aspects of life (Heard-Bey 2004: 135). Although UAE legislation is based on an Islamic constitution,

> gender inequality in the Middle East in general and in the Arabian Gulf region in particular, has socio-economic and political roots as opposed to religious roots ... there is a wide gulf between Islam and cultural practices misconstrued as Islamic.
>
> (Randeree and Gaad 2008: 70)

The UAE and Arab-Gulf culture has had a negative influence on gender relations and the lives of people with disabilities. Only recently has the attitude towards the education of women and girls been challenged, and international human rights campaigners have turned their attention to the rights of children with disabilities to be educated in mainstream schools or in special schools.

Girls and women in UAE society

The status and the role of women in the UAE have changed rapidly during the modernisation process. Up to the 1940s, the Bedouin and tribal lifestyle were the norm, centred on herding, wider agricultural activities, fishing and pearling. Bedouin values influencing women's lives were rooted in patriarchal notions of the male-dominated family, which included 'honour, chastity and the seclusion of women' (Randeree and Gaad 2008: 70). With oil and modernity came affluence, education, the lack of economic necessity to work and the resources to employ domestic (expatriate) labour. Modern life in the UAE centres on a knowledge-based economy in which education is highly valued and women, at least in the major cities such as Dubai, have taken new opportunities to address the equity imbalance between the sexes, although there is still a long way to go:

> Over two thirds of university graduates in the UAE are women. They account, however, for less than 12 per cent of the entire workforce ... very few of those who make it to the labour markets make it to the boardrooms or upper echelons of leadership and management.
>
> (Randeree and Gaad 2008: 69)

Traditional family attitudes towards the role of women have to change to enable women to contribute more fully to life in the UAE. Calls for change have support at the highest level: 'women's participation in public life is required and we must be ready for it' (Sheik Zayed bin Sultan Al-Nahyan, former UAE President, *UAE Yearbook 2003*, quoted in Randeree and Gaad 2008: 72). Such encouragement forms part of an 'Emiratisation' process that aims at reducing dependence on expatriate labour and building a better future for Emirati citizens in their own country. In researching the barriers to progress for women, the study with Emirati women reported by Randeree and Gaad (2008) found that, for many men and women, the overriding concern was freedom of choice rather than cultural or religious restrictions. This was not to deny that many women still felt societal and parental pressures to conform to the traditional roles expected in Emirati society. Although there is great diversity of women's experiences within and between each Emirate, the trend over the last 15 years has indicated a movement towards an improvement of opportunities for women.

Challenging culturally negative attitudes towards people with disabilities

The recognition of people with disabilities is a relatively recent phenomenon. Prior to the 1990s there was a general societal denial of their existence. Disabled children, particularly those with learning difficulties such as Down's syndrome, were frequently kept hidden away. As a result of this, there was little understanding of such conditions amongst the general public in the UAE. Attitudes towards people with disabilities, particularly intellectual disabilities, can be based on misinformed beliefs and superstitions and can impact on the lives of such individuals. For example, as Gaad (2006: 134), writing of the UAE region, states:

> The condition of Down's Syndrome is nearly a taboo topic in this part of the world. . . . With only a handful of pupils with Down's Syndrome included in regular schools, and with many myths and misconceptions surrounding the syndrome and individuals . . .

There is a lack of awareness about the wide variety of ability levels and attributes associated with this condition, which inevitably leads to stereotyping and low expectations. Additionally, in such a climate of ignorance, damaging myths evolve, for example: 'Young women's marital relationships and possible marriage plans were directly affected by the presence of a child with Down's Syndrome in the family, especially in small communities where everyone knows everyone else' (Gaad 2001).

Despite improvements in international legislation on the rights to inclusion in education and wider society, realities for individuals with this syndrome are often disappointing. Negative attitudes amongst UAE generalist teachers towards the inclusion of children with intellectual disabilities are evident in earlier research by Gaad (2004). Many parents who have children with disabilities want to hide them, and they have mixed emotions of shame and inadequacy when asked to talk about their children. This is due to a cultural stigma that still exists to a certain extent, despite efforts from government and NGOs to eradicate it. An example of how difficult any conversation related to Down's syndrome has been until recently can be seen in a personal experience encountered when I (the author) tried to start the UAE Down's Syndrome Support Group (UAEDSSG) in 2004. Working closely with local hospitals, I was able to identify families with a Down's syndrome member (of all ages). On telephoning the families to introduce the idea of a support group, I discovered that the majority denied at first that they had a family member with Down's syndrome.

International studies have revealed the increased marginalisation of people with learning difficulties with the transition to adulthood; for example, a narrow range of leisure opportunities or workplace chances and continuing dependency on parents are factors often ignored by wider society (Thomson *et al.* 1995: 325). The situation in the UAE is not any better than Thomson describes because, until recently, there was no discourse concerning intellectual disability. The segregation of those affected, either by keeping them closely confined to the home or, in a few cases, educating them in separate schools, meant that there was little acknowledgement of the existence of such people by the general public. Few attempts were made to move towards a more inclusive society, despite the passing of a federal law to protect the rights of persons with special needs and disabilities (federal law number 29: 2006, Ministry of Social Affairs).

The position of girls and women with intellectual disabilities in all countries in the Federation, is influenced by cultural attitudes to both gender and disability. They form a group of particular concern in terms of accessing education and gaining equitable life chances, including through physical activity, in order to achieve quality of life. Much of this evidence underpinned the motivation of the author to start the UAE Down's Syndrome Support Group.

Education, inclusion, physical education and sport in the UAE

With little systematic education earlier than 1971, the new federal state established an educational entitlement for all children in the UAE. Girls and boys became entitled to free public education at all levels (Bahgat 1999: 130). A federal Ministry of Education and Youth was made responsible for education in the public sector. A fast-growing private sector emerged to meet the needs of so-called 'expat' communities (Bradshaw *et al.* 2004: 50).

The private/public school duality in education provision is reflected in educational provision for people with special educational needs (SEN). Where it is offered, it is in the form of government centres, all outside mainstream schooling, and under the umbrella of the Ministry of Education. These institutions are currently referred to as 'Centres for People with Special Needs', and only nine such centres currently exist across the UAE. These particular rehabilitation/therapy centres are exclusively for UAE nationals, although there are some specialist private therapy centres that are open to all nationalities.

Until recently, there was no federal legislation stipulating access to education for people with special needs (Bradshaw *et al.* 2004: 51). In government and private schools, children with highly visible or profound special educational needs are not enrolled but are referred to the special centres. Without such a referral, they are kept at home (Bradshaw *et al.* 2004: 52).

In the rapidly developing UAE, social justice issues concerned with inclusion and the rights of all children, including those with learning disabilities, are high-profile media topics (Gaad 2004: 322). Recent change towards wider inclusion followed the federal law, No. 29/2006, which was enacted to organise and protect the rights of learners with disabilities. Article 13 of this law states: 'The Ministry of Education … shall be committed … to securing the complete participation of students having special needs.' The then Minister of Education, His Excellency Dr Hanif Hassan, stated that 'something wonderful is happening to children throughout the United Arab Emirates. They are learning that all people are entitled to equal opportunities. They are learning to understand, respect, and appreciate people with physical or intellectual differences' (Gaad and Thabet 2009).

Theoretically, physical education is an entitlement for all children in schools but in boys' as well as in girls' schools, the subject is currently taught by expatriate teachers because there have never been opportunities for Emirati women to train to teach physical education in their own country. Specialist training for men did exist for a while at the large federal university (UAEU), but this ended in the 1990s when an accreditation process conducted by the American National Council for Accreditation of Teacher Education (NCATE) led to the closure of the programme (Al-Ameri 2003). The provision of physical education in schools, consequently, is dependent on mainly Arab expatriates, with experience, working in the UAE on temporary contracts, although some do stay for long periods of time. In the centres for special needs, the story is much the same, and one will rarely find an Emirati physical-education teacher working with learners with special needs and disabilities.

Physical education is a low-status subject in schools and universities, and there are various cultural and traditional reasons for this. UAE is an Islamic country despite its tolerance of other religions. The stigma and sensitive nature of the suitability of 'Western' and 'liberal' dress, associated with sport, could be the prime reason. There is also a 'tacit rule' regarding traditional disapproval of what might be deemed 'inappropriate' activities for women, for example those involving the display of their bodies in public spaces and in the presence of men. In stark contrast to this is the popularity of sport in general among male Emirati society, where male-dominated sports and major international sporting events are extensively pursued and televised. Until recently, Emirati women's engaging in sporting activity as participants, administrators or leaders has been virtually non-existent across the seven states. This is despite the diversity of the modern Emirates and the popularity of sporting activity amongst 'expat' communities. The exception to this low level of activity is amongst a small number of members of royalty, including the daughter of Dubai's ruler, Vice-President and Prime Minister of UAE, Princess Sheika Maitha Bin Muhammed Al Maktoum. She became the first Gulf woman to take part in an Olympic Games, representing her country in the 2008 Beijing Games in taekwondo, and has won many titles. Now a prominent international sports figure, she attracts a great deal of attention amongst women in the Arabian Gulf. Following the 2008 Beijing Olympics, Ebrahim Abdul Malek, General Secretary of the National Olympic Committee, told a UAE daily newspaper, *The National*, that Sheikha Maitha had been deeply moved when she was asked to carry the flag during the opening ceremony, describing it as her 'historic moment'. He continued:

We are making history here. This is something that every UAE citizen and anyone connected with the country can feel really proud of. We are sending a clear and powerful message to all women in the UAE that now the government strongly supports sport across all sectors of society and that there is no difference between male and female. If they work they will get their chance.

(www.arabianbusiness.com/527161-sheikha-maitha-makes-history-at-olympics (accessed 16 November 2009))

Such role models are essential for Emirati women who live in a culture where women's participation in public exercise and sporting activity is a relatively new phenomenon, and one which can challenge traditional notions of appropriateness for women and their bodies. Some parts of the UAE are much more conservative than others. The rate of change in the modernisation process is uneven across the individual states, and this is reflected in the progress on inclusion for people, particularly women and those with disabilities, in education, sport and beyond.

Down's syndrome and the activities of the UAE Down's Syndrome Association

The final part of the chapter focuses on the UAE Down's Syndrome Association. This community-based venture was started by the author in 2004. Its aim was to fill a void and change attitudes through positive action, using sport, alongside arts and other activities, as a means to achieve better social acceptance and quality of life for this group of marginalised people.

Down's syndrome is a leading cause of intellectual disabilities, occurring in one in 800 live births worldwide. Its prevalence in the UAE is almost double the global rate due to high maternal age, whilst the number of other genetic causes for disabilities in general, and intellectual disabilities in particular, are also higher than the global rate:

The UAE has a high incidence of single gene defects which accounts for the high rate of autosomal recessive disorders. This is related to the high rate of consanguineous marriages, which is around 51 per cent of marriages between UAE nationals.

(www.cags.org.ae/news 2003)

In 2004 the first UAE Down's Syndrome Support Group was formed in response to the need for positive action to improve the life chances of those with Down's syndrome. People with an interest in Down's syndrome came together to support individuals, their parents and care-givers. The group grew to become the first ever registered charity with more than 200 members of all ages, and became an NGO known as the Down's Syndrome Association in the UAE (UAEDSA). In addition to the quality of life of people affected with this syndrome, the Association's mission statement aims to offer comprehensive support to them and their carers. The four main objectives of the Association are to:

- increase awareness of Down's syndrome in society;
- promote inclusion into society of those individuals with Down's syndrome;
- provide an emergency professional support unit for parents and carers;
- establish a UAE database for Down's syndrome.

Initially the Dubai Ladies Club offered a location and financial support for events and activities, for example day trips and regular nursery meetings for people with Down's syndrome, their friends, parents and care-givers (mostly mothers and children). The Association managed to secure a residence and has long-term employees. Recently it has attracted funding to spread awareness about Down's syndrome among school children.

The sports committee of the Association works closely with a network of local sports clubs such as the Dubai 'Special Sports' Club to plan and implement sporting activities for people with Down's syndrome. The Association's view is that sport is an effective vehicle as a means of including this group in society, strengthening participants' health and improving their quality of life. Another important objective was to use sport to include and empower girls and women with Down's syndrome in a society where there is little awareness of the needs of people, particularly girls and young women, with intellectual disabilities.

Research undertaken by Gaad (2006) has shown that sport can be useful to aid the inclusion of children with Down's syndrome. The UAEDSA encourages siblings and family members to participate in all outings and activities. One respondent to the interviews conducted in the research was a young woman aged 16 with Down's syndrome. She was not enrolled in any school and had received only a few years of education in a centre for Preparation and Rehabilitation for the Handicapped (as it is referred to in the UAE). When she was asked about the activities taking place through the group, she said:

> I do games ... I like games.... I go out with my sister ... she go[es] ... to school but I am different I don't ... I stay home ... and ... erm ... I am happy I go out with my sister ...

> (Gaad 2006: 137)

For her, it was not only the activity on this occasion but also the sibling contact and the wider social space and network accessed through the opportunity that was significant.

The UAEDSA networks and supports activities of members through established sports providers along with arts and other activities. The Association, for example, has links with the Dubai Club for 'Special Sports', which helps to prepare men and women with special needs and disabilities to compete in disability sports events. The club is partially funded by the government, although there are NGOs that help to promote women's sport in the field of disability and special needs. Riding for the Disabled Association in Dubai (RDAD, www.rdad. ae), a charity organisation founded in 1998, offers free riding lessons to children with special needs. It works in conjunction with schools for special needs children in Dubai. The Riding for the Disabled Association's patron is yet another female Royal figure, Her Highness Sheikha Hassa bint Mohammed bin Rashid Al Maktoum, who launched the programme by donating three of her horses to be used for therapeutic riding in 1998. October 2008 marked the beginning of the RDAD's tenth season of therapeutic riding lessons. Currently they have approximately 60 children enrolled in the riding programme. Examples of the riders' various disabilities include autism, cerebral palsy, spina bifida, Down's syndrome and other intellectual disabilities.

At the Special Olympics level, the UAE has seen small numbers of competitors but great achievements. In 2006, in the swimming events, Nada Abdullah of the UAE won gold in group two for the 15–34 years category. Fatima Mosimany clinched a third gold medal for the UAE in Bocce, and Kawtahar Eisaily and Hala Abdoony from the UAE won silver and bronze medals respectively, creating a new wave of female athletes bringing home honour and glory (www. archive.gulf news.com). In an interview following the event, flanked by male and female members of the UAE's Special Olympics National Team, Majid Alusaimi, National Director of Special Olympic UAE, commented that the country is learning increasingly about people with disabilities thanks to sports, arts and other cultural and social initiatives that challenge stereotyping. He valued the role of sports in changing the lives of male and female citizens with special needs and disabilities, stating: 'There's still a lot of work to do but things have changed a lot. . . . Public awareness has increased and the parents of these athletes are very proud of their sons and daughters' (www.archive.gulfnews.com).

The UAEDSA offers a multi-faceted, multi-activity programme to improve quality of life for people of all ages with Down's syndrome, as well as their families and carers. The aim of making a difference, giving opportunities and improving quality of life is achieved through networking and proactive activities wherever there is mutual interest across private, public and governmental organisations. Sporting activities are valuable means of improving lives in enjoyable, healthy ways, and the high levels of success some achieve are celebrated by all. There is no room for complacency; only the tip of the iceberg has been touched in the area of gender and disability inclusion in the UAE.

Conclusions and recommendations

This chapter has raised a number of issues and challenges that affect UAE girls and women in general, and in particular those with an intellectual disability, with regard to social inclusion. The UAE can celebrate some recent achievements in terms of women's success in education, visibility in the workplace and success in sports arenas. The accomplishments of these women pave the way for others, and challenge stereotypes and negative attitudes. Moving from stigma to acceptance is a slow process; and the role of engaging communities with the reality of disability using a range of physical activities has been one successful strategy followed by the UAEDSA. Approaches used in sport through informal activities, inclusive of people with disabilities, as well as more formal special sports events, have facilitated acceptance and appreciation of what people with Down's syndrome are able to do for themselves, for others and their country. Maximising opportunities has meant sustained effort for visibility through the media, the raising of public awareness and networking. Attitudes are changing. There is much work left to do; for example, equality in education does not yet exist for children with disabilities. The training of teachers to cope with special needs is poor, and training for women (and men) in the field of physical education and sport does not exist anywhere in the country. Consequently, there is no cadre of specialist knowledge in mainstream or special needs provision at school or community level. The dearth of post-school opportunities for young people with a disability and life-long dependence on family care-givers needs greater recognition and action. Finally, some recommendations to continue along the path to positive change for girls and women and people with disabilities would be:

• raising awareness of gender and disability and their intersection through research and dissemination of knowledge;
• sharing good practice across the states of the UAE, the Gulf Council Countries and the wider Arabian Gulf region, where similar problems are faced;
• developing awareness programmes for schools and communities;
• establishing systems for sustained co-operation through networking that allow multi-agency support to address needs arising from inequality in terms of gender and/or disability;
• celebrating success at every level through quality media reporting.

Bibliography

Al-Ameri, N. (2003) Evaluation of the Opinions of Teachers and Parents in United Arab Emirates Concerning Physical Education Cultures. Unpublished EdD thesis, University of Arkansas, USA.

Al Taboor, A. (2008) *History of Education*, UAE Ministry of Education official website, www.moe.gov.ae/English/Pages/HistoryofEducation.aspx (accessed 10 September 2009).

Bahgat, G. (1999) Education in the Gulf Monarchies: Retrospect and Prospect. *International Review of Education*, 46 (2): 127–136.

Bradshaw, K., Tennant, L. and Lydiatt, S. (2004) Special Education in the United Arab Emirates: Anxieties, Attitudes and Aspirations. *International Journal of Special Education*, 19 (1): 49–55.

Burden-Leahy, S. (2005) Addressing the Tensions in a Process-based Quality Assurance Model Through the Introduction of Graduate Outcomes: A Case Study of the Change Process in a Vocational Higher Education Institution in the United Arab Emirates. *Quality in Higher Education*, 11 (2): 129–136.

Camerapix (1998) *Spectrum Guide to United Arab Emirates*. Kenya: Camerapix Publishing International, 5.

Cassell, C. (1997) The Business Case for Equal Opportunities: Implications for Women in Management. *Women in Management Review*, 12 (1): 11–16.

Gaad, E. (2001) Educating Children with Down's Syndrome in the United Arab Emirates. *British Journal of Special Education*, 28 (4): 195–203.

Gaad, E. (2004) Cross-Cultural Perspectives on the Effect of Cultural Attitudes Towards Inclusion for Children with Intellectual Disabilities. *International Journal of Inclusive Education*, 8 (3): 311–329.

Gaad, E. (2006) The Social and Educational Impacts of the First National Down's Syndrome Support Group in the UAE. *Journal for Research in Special Educational Needs*, 3 September: 134–142.

Gaad, E. and Thabet, R. (2009) Needs Assessment for Effective Inclusion in United Arab Emirates Government Schools. *International Journal of Interdisciplinary Social Science*, 4 (6): 159–174.

Heard-Bey, F. (2004) *From Trucial States to United Arab Emirates*. UAE: Motivate Publishing.

Khan, L. (2005) A Study of Primary Mainstream Teachers' Attitudes Towards Inclusion of Students with Special Educational Needs: A Perspective from Dubai. Unpublished Master's dissertation, The British University in Dubai, UAE.

Randeree, K. (2006) The Impact of Historical and Cultural Effects on the Advancement of Women in the K-Economy in the Arabian Gulf Region: Participation of Women in the Arabian Gulf. *International Journal of Knowledge, Culture and Change Management*, 6 (1): 65–68.

Randeree, K. and Gaad, E. (2008) Views on the 'Knowledge Economy Project' of the Arabian Gulf: A Gender Perspective from the UAE in Education and Management. *The International Journal of Diversity in Organisations, Communities and Nations*, 8 (2): 69–77.

Shaw, K., Badri, A. and Hukul, A. (1995) Management Concerns in the United Arab Emirates State Schools. *International Journal of Educational Management*, 9 (4): 8–13.

Thomson, G., Ward, K. and Wishart, J. (1995) The Transition to Adulthood for Children with Down's Syndrome. *Disability and Society*, 10(3): 325–340.

Whetter, L. (2000) *Live and Work in Saudi & The Gulf*. Oxford: Vacation Work.

Websites

www.7days.ae/lifestyle/why-every-child-deserves-a-chance.html (accessed 14 September 2009).

http://archive.gulfnews.com/indepth/olympics08/specialreport/10234626.html (accessed 10 August 2009).

http://archive.gulfnews.com/indepth/specialolympics/sub_story/10082486.html (accessed 10 August 2009).

www.arabianbusiness.com/527161-sheikha-maitha-makes-history-at-olympics (accessed 16 November 2009).

www.cags.org.ae/news2003.html (Dr Yousef M. Abdel Razak, Vice-Dean of the Faculty of Medicine and Health Sciences at UAE University and Chairman of the Scientific Committee of the Shaikh Hamdan Foundation) (accessed 10 September 2008).

www.rdad.ae (accessed 5 October 2008).

www.thenational.ae/article/20080806/SPORT/462368441/1119 (accessed 18 August 2006).

www.xpress4me.com/news/uae/dubai/20011398.html (accessed 22 May 2009).

Part IV
Narratives

14 Iskustva rata u Bosni i Hercegovini njegove refleksije na tjelesne aktivnosti djevojaka i žena

Experiences of war in Bosnia and Herzegovina and the effects on physical activities of girls and women

Fadila Ibrahimbegovic-Gafic

Editors' introduction

This chapter offers rare insight into the author's experiences as a Professor of Physical Education and Sport at Sarajevo University who experienced life in Bosnia and Herzegovina before, during and after the 1990s' war. As a moderate Muslim country with strong European influences, women have historically enjoyed participation in many forms of physical activity. The country hosted the 1984 Winter Olympics in Sarajevo. Much of the country's infrastructure was destroyed in the war, and the atrocities of 'ethnic cleansing' to remove the Bosnian Muslims from their homeland can never be forgotten. Girls and women found ways to keep important aspects of their identity and social networks together through sport. Today there are successful women athletes in many sports from boxing to speed skating, but there are many more successful men. There is a need to develop women's coaching and leadership skills to counter the dominance of men in the field.

Introduction

To understand sport and physical education in Bosnia and Herzegovina (B&H) today, it is necessary to examine historical events that have laid the social, political, economic and religious foundations of the country. B&H is located in south-eastern Europe in the West Balkans, surrounded by the republics of Croatia, Serbia and Montenegro. It has been at the crossroads of East and West, a place of struggle where different forms of culture, religion, trade, wealth and poverty have met. The country has a long history of turmoil, but for the latter part of the twentieth century, from 1945 until 1992, the people enjoyed a period of stability with the coexistence of Bosniaks (Muslims), Serbs (Orthodox Christians), Croats (Catholic Christians), Jews and people of other religions.

B&H was formerly one of the six federal republics of Yugoslavia. During the break up of that country in the early 1990s, B&H declared independence on 1 March 1991 after a referendum, which was boycotted by Bosnian Serbs. In 1992, Bosnian Serbs joined with Serbs from neighbouring Serbia and Montenegro to begin hostilities against B&H, using the weaponry and army of the former state of Yugoslavia. The intention was to destroy all non-Serbs, with the main focus on Bosnian Muslims, in order to create their own ethnically cleansed state called the Republika Srpska. They started with the systematic shelling of civilian buildings all over the territory of B&H, expelling people from the homes they had lived in for centuries, starting fires and killing men and women. Many women were raped, as well as teenage and even younger girls. The war lasted from 1992 to 1995, including the 1,479-day siege of the capital, Sarajevo. Atrocities were committed all over the country, including genocide in a number of places. In Srebrenica alone, located in the north of the country, Serbs killed between 8,000 and 10,000 Bosnian Muslim males, from young boys to old men, in the presence of the UN Dutch troops who were stationed in the town to protect the UN-proclaimed 'safe haven'. Women and children were separated from men and expelled from the town. The bodies of thousands of husbands, sons, fathers, brothers and relatives, who were killed there, have not been found to this day.

From the census figures of 1991, it is known that there were 4.5 million citizens of B&H: 44 per cent Bosniaks, 37 per cent Serbs, 17 per cent Croats and 2 per cent of others. Some 200,000 citizens, with the highest percentage of Bosniaks among them, were killed during the 1992–1995 war, and about one million were forced into exile all over the world. The war and its atrocities impacted on the lives of all the people in the country, on many women and girls who survived, often with no male family members, and also on the whole infrastructure of the society, including education and sport.

The cessation of hostilities was achieved by the signing of a peace accord in Dayton, USA. As a result of this accord, NATO forces led an international peacekeeping force in the country, which was gradually reduced to a stabilising force and eventually reduced further to a European Union force. The pre-war borders remained, and a joint, multi-ethnic and democratic government was established at the state level, entrusted with conducting foreign, diplomatic and fiscal policies. Administratively, B&H was set up as a state of two entities with their respective governments: the Federation of B&H (FBiH) and the Republika Srpska (RS). Today, Bosniaks and Croats make up the majority in the Federation of B&H, while Serbs make up the majority in the Republika Srpska.

After the war, politicians have been unable to agree on the terms of another census, so that we do not have precise percentages of the current population; however, there still remain three main constituent groups: Bosniaks (Muslims), Croats (Catholics) and Serbs (Orthodox Christians), as well as several other religious groups such as Jews, Protestants, etc. Today the country's policies are based on the acceptance of multi-ethnicity and multi-religion. Children and young people go to the same schools and mix in public places, except that there are some ethnically homogeneous areas and specific faith schools for Catholic or Muslim children.

Today women, including Muslim women, participate freely – and success-fully – in sports in B&H. It is interesting to note, however, that the majority of successful women in individual sports are Muslim, whilst in team sports like basketball, volleyball, handball and winter sports there is a mix of the ethnicities living in the country. Today sportswomen such as boxer Irma Balijagic, basket-ball player Razija Mujanovic, tennis player Mervana Jugic-Salkic, the best per-former in rhythmic gymnastics Amila Terzimehic, and most of the best women in karate (Arijana Jaha, Arnela Odzakovic – gold medallist at the 2009 World Games in Taiwan) and judo (Larisa Ceric, 2009 junior World champion) are all Muslims.

Islam, as practised in B&H, is moderate, with women wearing predominantly European-style clothes, although many Muslim women also choose to wear a head covering to comply with Islamic requirements. Girls studying at madrasahs and Faculties of Islamic Studies dress exclusively according to Islamic princi-ples. During physical-education classes in school, however, they dress conven-tionally, although in public competitions they wear tracksuits and scarves.

As for prayers and fasting, they are matters of personal choice except for the students of the above-mentioned institutions, who meet all Islamic demands in this respect. There are no women who adhere to strict Islamic dress and behavi-our codes, however, among top sportswomen.

Sport for girls and women in Bosnia and Herzegovina before the war

The rights of women were laid down in the legal system in the period between the Second World War and the 1992 war, although, socially, women have always been in an inferior position compared with men – and this was reflected in the sporting world. School-based physical education and training opportun-ities for young people during that period varied, and depended on the qualifica-tions of staff, infrastructure and facilities available such as indoor sports halls, outdoor sports grounds and swimming pools. This generated differences in the quality of provision, the experiences of young people and their future lifestyle choices as adults. Some enjoyed and pursued physical activities, while others disliked them or did not take part in them at all.

In public (state-run) schools, girls and boys were usually taught together in elementary and secondary school physical-education lessons. Classes at univer-sities were also mixed-sex. Sometimes, if there were enough male and female teachers and facilities in schools, physical-education lessons were given sepa-rately for boys and girls. Today only Muslim faith schools have retained the practice of separate-sex classes in physical education and sports. Most of these schools are the oldest educational institutions in the Balkans, possibly in Europe. Students attending them come from families with a variety of socio-economic backgrounds but share an adherence to traditional Islamic socio-cultural values and practices. There are also those, however, who want to develop a greater, personal, Islamic awareness.

In general, women were rarely involved in systematic sporting activities because of the poor provision of suitable facilities for recreation. The sports clubs tended to cater for the more 'serious' sportspeople. There were, however, annual workplace community sporting events for women. Various communities of workers, for example textile workers, food-processors or metal industry workers, organised competitions in activities such as volleyball, some athletic disciplines, rifle shooting, table tennis and bowling. Teams had minimal training and practice for these events. Walking in the hills and mountains to enjoy the scenery, taking some exercise and sharing time with friends and family was also a form of activity accessible to women. The geography of the country made winter sports very popular in the snow-covered mountains for men and women of all ages. Skiing and skating were in focus during the Fourteenth Winter Olympic Games, held in Sarajevo in 1984, and remained popular afterwards. Owing to the closeness of the Adriatic Sea, many families used to spend their summer vacations at the seaside or by rivers and lakes, where swimming was a favourite activity despite there being few public swimming pools available. Around 1970, the all-female sport of rhythmic gymnastics started to gain popularity in B&H. Many young girls wanted to participate, and the number of clubs increased to cater for this growing demand.

Sport during the war

The 1,479-day siege of Sarajevo changed the lives of its people forever. The Serbian aggressors were joined by Serbs who used to live in the same streets as those they now wanted to kill. They attended the same schools, universities and workplaces. Citizens of Sarajevo resisted the attacks successfully and defended their city with inadequate weapons as they endured the longest siege and isolation in the history of humankind. Citizens suffered from the effects of four million shells and sniper fire that came from the hills surrounding the besieged city. Thousands of civilians, women and men, children and old people, were injured or killed. The people lived in constant fear for their lives. Electricity, water, gas and fuel were in very short supply. The city was turned into a ghetto where people died as they did in concentration camps during the Second World War. In such chaos people were killed at funerals, in hospitals, in ambulances, in classrooms, in the streets, and in queues for water, bread and fuel.

Many sportsmen and women, despite the deprivations and difficulties, tried to maintain a sense of identity by exercising wherever possible, mostly at night, in the ruins and in cellars. Some even managed to escape the siege to attend competitions in other countries. Amazingly, sportsmen and sportswomen from B&H managed to attend the Olympic Games that took place while the war was raging in their homeland in 1992. Helped by the international sporting world, many went to friendly countries to exercise and train and, with the support of sports governing bodies, to compete. The activities of the 'Bosnia' rhythmic gymnastics club in Sarajevo were outstanding, as it produced one of the three most successful teams in the former state. Competitors from this team continued to train regularly throughout the war period and, again, the international sporting community reached out. With the help of the United Nations Protection Force (UNPROFOR), women competitors from B&H left for France and stayed in the city of Evry from 1994 to 1995 at the invitation of the SCA 2000 Rhythmic Gymnastics Club, where they trained with French gymnasts. In 1994, together with a club team of Bulgarian Rhythmic Gymnasts, they participated in the World Clubs Cup in Japan. The Japanese federation also invited them for a month to train and compete. After returning to France, the team travelled to Slovenia, Norway and Belgium, and took part in several other competitions in Europe. Supported by the Embassy of Norway in B&H, the team competed in the European Championship in Oslo in 1996, where they were placed eighth in the group section.

Recreational physical activity also retained the interest of women of all ages in war-torn Sarajevo. They organised small groups to meet and exercise in their apartments and basements, where it was safer than exercising in the open. They did aerobics and therapeutic gymnastic exercises because it was necessary for them to be fit, able to move fast and with agility, and to be strong to deal with the extra physical demands of their new life and environment. These examples of sporting participation during the war period exemplify the enormous resolve, courage and determination of the besieged population, and the value placed on physical activity.

The post-war period and current situation of women in sport

Cessation of war meant the end of the killing and the beginning of normal everyday life. The scale of destruction was enormous; for example, in Sarajevo many of the public buildings and factories were gone, as were the maternity hospital and paediatric clinic. The National and University Library and the Institute for Oriental Studies were also completely destroyed in a deliberate attempt to obliterate the centuries-long heritage of Bosnian Muslims. In such a situation it was necessary for the authorities to determine priorities in the regeneration of Bosnian society. There was a need to repair or rebuild everything, including houses, hospitals, roads, schools, sports facilities and cultural institutions. Now, over a decade later, normality is gradually returning but it will take many more years before the human, psychological scars are healed. Lost lives cannot be restored nor destroyed families repaired, but life continues and progress is being made.

In schools today, physical education fills between two and four hours a week for all children. The majority of schools have sport halls and highly qualified staff educated in four-year degree programmes at well-equipped specialist Physical Training and Sport Schools at universities, where a two-year course for sports coaches is also offered. There are five such university sport schools in B&H. Of the total number of female students studying in these institutions, 30 per cent actively compete in sports.

Gender inequity is evident at the universities. The majority of professors at the Physical Training and Sport Schools of Universities are men. Women teach only rhythmic gymnastics and a small amount of theory or technical skills. This is probably the result of both prejudice and traditional male discrimination against women on the one hand, and the general situation in which there are fewer women in this field on the other. The under-representation of women begins with their choice of study. Far fewer female than male students attend the two-year Higher Coach study programme, which is staffed largely by male coaches. These two factors combine to perpetuate the circumstance that there are currently very few female coaches in B&H. Even in clubs where the majority of members are female, coaches and managers are predominantly male. There are no women at all holding the position of president of a club or sports federation, and very few doctors attached to sports federations are women. Rhythmic gymnastics is an exclusively female sport, although, even in rhythmic gymnastics clubs where coaches and some managers are women, the club presidents are all men.

Women in sport at the elite level

Due to the increasing successes of female athletes, women's sport in B&H is gaining momentum, but the ratio of men to women competitors is still heavily weighted in favour of men. It is in the area of contact sports, perhaps surprisingly, that the women in the country are gaining international honours that surpass those of the men. Elite-level female athletes train and compete in sports up to international standard. Most of these, however, are not currently Olympic sports. At the 2008 Olympic Games, the only female in B&H's Olympic team of eight competitors was Lucia Kimani. She was born in Kenya but is married to a B&H citizen living in Prijedor, part of the Republika Srpska. Her husband, Sinisa Mocetic, is both her coach and manager.

There is much interest from women in sports such as boxing, karate and judo, with success at international level. The greatest success to date came from women's boxing in 2008, when Irma Balijagic-Adler won the world-championship title in the featherweight division of the Women's International Boxing Association. For the 26-year-old woman boxer from Sarajevo, that was the ninth match in her professional career as a boxer, which came after reaching high levels in other sports including basketball and kick-boxing (European champion in 2006). In September 2009, Irma defended her title of World Women's Champion, defeating the Bulgarian champion Galina Gumiliiska in ten rounds. She is proud of her abilities in sport and of the fact that it is women, particularly in contact sports, who are bringing B&H the most medals in international competitions.

Judo is the second most popular contact sport among girls. Junior and senior teams from B&H have won second or third place at the Balkan Championship since 2001.

In 2006 and 2008 the junior teams were outright winners. Arijana Jaha was the individual gold medal winner at the 2005 Balkan Championship and is now the coach and secretary of a judo club. Larisa Ceric became World Junior Champion (78 kg category) in October 2009. In this championship, 450 players from 70 different countries competed for the title.

Successes in karate are similarly impressive, with B&H women winning many international honours since 2000 across weight categories and age groups at team and individual levels. The honours were gained at World Championships, World Games, European Championships and Mediterranean Games events. One of the most successful athletes is Arnela Odzakovic, who won the gold medal at the World Games in July 2009. She was declared 'Sportswoman of the Year' in 2008 by the Sports Federation of B&H.

Although not matching the successes in contact sports, an increasing number of women are now playing team sports such as basketball, volleyball and handball. Basketball is less popular among women than men, but there are some good women's clubs and players. Strong basketball clubs, whose players make up the bulk of international teams, include: 'Mladi Krajisnik' Basketball Club of Banja Luka, champions of the Adriatic League, Zeljeznicar UNICA Basketball Club, Celik of Zenica and Jedinstvo of Tuzla. These clubs have women's teams in three national-level leagues. A large number of successful women basketball players from B&H play in clubs throughout Europe and the world. An outstanding player, and Europe's most famous woman basketball player, is Razija Mujanovic. She started training at the age of 14 and played for 23 years at the 'Jedinstvo' Club in Tuzla, which in 1989 won the European Club Championship. The first foreign club she later played for, accompanied by her elder brother, was the Italian club, Bari. She also played in Spain, Hungary, Brazil and the USA. She gained four European Championship medals. In her career, she won Olympic and European silver medals, and a gold medal at the Mediterranean Games. Razija ended her playing career in 2008 at the age of 41, having helped B&H to qualify for the European Championships. Currently she lives in Sarajevo; she is planning to become a basketball manager and aims to help the country's women's basketball to greater success.

Volleyball is played by many young girls in B&H. It is popular in schools, and there are many clubs offering women's volleyball. Team handball is played in some parts of the country. There are clubs competing in the Premier League with many good players who travel abroad and play for European clubs, including the German *Bundesliga*. Teams representing B&H have done well at European B Championship levels since 2004.

The interest in women's football in B&H reflects the worldwide upsurge in the numbers of girls and women players. A Premier League has been formed, in which the 12 best women's football clubs play. Some of these teams regularly qualify for European and World Championships, although so far they have not managed to qualify for the second competition phase. The most successful women's football team is Jedinstvo from Brcko, where the 2009 B&H Cup competition was held, and it emerged victorious. Dijana Vasic from the same club was proclaimed 'best player' of the tournament.

Individual sports, other than martial arts, are also gaining popularity in the country. The most accomplished tennis player, for example, is Mervana Jugic-Salkic, ranked among the top 100 women tennis players on the World List. There are many private tennis clubs, but tennis remains an expensive sport to play and, consequently, is enjoyed predominantly by the rich and more privileged. Interestingly, there are around 200 girls who have taken up nine-pin bowling. They have had some success in international competitions playing in mixed-doubles teams. In 2004, the national team was placed third at the World Championships. One notable player is the current secretary of the B&H Bowling Federation, Bubija Kerla, who previously competed at the 1984 Sarajevo and 1988 Calgary Winter Olympic Games in speed skating.

Weight-lifting was not a particularly popular sport with women, mainly due to the dispute over its 'appropriateness' as a sport for females. In recent years, however, it has become more available to women, and in 2006 competitors from B&H were placed first in the Balkan Promotion Competition. At the Alpe-Adria Tournament in 2008 the national team was placed third out of eight national teams taking part.

Athletics is not a mass sport in the country, with only a small spectator following and little media interest, although there are clubs with many talented men and women athletes, some of whom gain national and international representation. Women athletes, mostly juniors, have participated in several international competitions including the European Cup, the Balkan Junior Cup, the Junior World Championships, the Balkan Cross-Country Race and the Junior European Championships. The only female athlete from B&H who participated in the 2008 Beijing Olympic Games was marathon runner Lucia Kimani. She was placed forty-second (of 82 athlete women participants), breaking the national record. She has taken part in several half-marathons in Europe and neighbouring countries, and won first place in the 5,000 m and second place in the 3,000 m races in the European Cup Second League in 2008.

Young girls and adolescents are most active in rhythmic gymnastics clubs, where they train in groups for both recreational and competitive purposes. Every year an international memorial tournament is held in Sarajevo, dedicated to the first victim of the war in the city, a young medical student who was killed whilst protesting against war and violence. Despite the popularity of the sport, international successes have been few to date. The best results at senior level were gained by Amila Terzimehic, who came third in both 2006 and 2007 at the annual Bulgarian International Tournament. Amila is currently studying at the Academy of Performing Arts.

There are many people with disabilities in B&H as a result of the war and war-related violence. Sport for people with physical disabilities is very popular. Girls and women are active in various sports such as athletics, basketball and rifle shooting. There has been some success at the international level, for example in the Paralympic Games. The most successful teams have been those playing volleyball, with B&H recognised as having the best teams in the world for more than a decade. At the 2008 Paralympic Games in Beijing, Klico Djenita competed in three athletic disciplines, finishing sixth in her category for the discus throw. As is usual in sport in B&H, the coaches of the disabled athletes are men.

Recreational physical activities

The numbers of girls and women participating in recreational physical activities are much greater than those training in sport at the elite level. Popular activities include aerobic gymnastics and fitness training in gymnasia. Outside the club structures, it is not unusual to see girls, alone or in groups, running for pleasure and exercise. Dance, in many different styles, is another popular activity. Since B&H abounds with folk dances, there are many folk clubs that cultivate the authentic and traditional folk dances along with music and customs from the regions of the country. Many people in B&H feel bound together by these dances and music, and such gatherings bring great happiness.

A personal narrative

At the editors' request, the chapter finishes with a personal narrative of the author, Fadila Ibrahimbegovic-Gafic, and her life in the field of physical education and sport. She is the only female scholar in the field writing about women in sport in her country for an international audience.

> I am a Muslim from Bosnia and Herzegovina (B&H), where I was born and where I grew up, a country that used to be part of ex-Yugoslavia. In my youth, people lived together harmoniously despite their different ethnicities and religions. In school, physical education and sporting experiences became important to me. I loved all physical activities and sports, participating in folk dancing, gymnastics, handball and volleyball, mountain climbing and skiing in my home town of Travnik, which lies at the foot of Mt Vlasic. This love of sports led to my family's support when they took me to Sarajevo to attend the Secondary School of Physical Education. The school was attended by students from all over ex-Yugoslavia, with 20–25 per cent of them girls. I continued to take part in all activities, including folk dancing and athletics, and was B&H's record holder for the 400 m race.
>
> On graduation, I worked as a physical education teacher at primary and secondary schools in Travnik. Later I enrolled in the Faculty of Sports at the University of Sarajevo; at that time there were very few women with a university degree in sport. When I attended, only 10 per cent of the students at the faculty were women. Since I was the first in my year to graduate, I was employed by the Faculty as a teaching assistant at its Centre for Physical Education and Sports for Students. Later I became a lecturer and professor at the Faculty of Medicine of Sarajevo University (sub-department of Physical Education and Sports), contributing at the university to physical education classes for students of the Faculty of Dentistry, the Faculty of Pharmacy

and College of Nursing. I also trained male and female student teams for the Sarajevo University intercollegiate as well as regional inter-university competitions. This lasted for 32 years and included gaining a Master's degree at Belgrade University and doctorate at Sarajevo University. Currently I am teaching physical education and sport at the Faculty of Pharmacy of Sarajevo University and Rhythmic Gymnastics and Dance at the Faculty of Education of Bihac University (some 300 km from Sarajevo).

For two decades I was an associate with the B&H Gymnastics Federation and B&H representative in Yugoslavia's Gymnastics Federation. Having established a rhythmic gymnastics club, I became the first B&H citizen to become an International Rhythmic Gymnastics Judge (Brevet 1). My research focused on problems of the movement abilities of students, women in particular, in order to counter the dominance of research on men in sport.

Throughout this time, my family has supported my professional career and commitment to sports. My parents and siblings followed my sports and academic achievements, especially my elder brother, who is a journalist. Later on, in my immediate family, my husband, a sportsman himself and working in education management, and my daughter, who is excellent at several sports, although she is a professor of music, continued their support.

I am the only woman in the country trying to reach an international audience by writing about women in B&H sports. The gender issue is not simple. I research with female researchers on male subjects and with male researchers on female subjects. Many male coaches train female athletes, and physical activities take place in mixed-sex environments except in an all-female sport such as rhythmic gymnastics. However, the number of female coaches is almost negligible. In leadership positions the situation is the same, with very few women in positions of club management despite some of them having higher qualifications.

As far as faith is concerned, I believe that my faith is a personal matter and it does not interfere with my profession. I think that it is deep inside me and is not to be publicly manifested because, when I am before God, I address Him directly. What matters is to work, make progress, be honest and fair, and study, study and only study ... (which is what Islam prescribes as well). With regard to clothes, I have always dressed according to the standard European fashion, compatible with the milieu, as we in B&H are European Muslims having our own tradition. However, when at prayer, addressing God Almighty, which is especially intensive during the month of Ramadan, the time for fasting, then I adapt my clothing to Islamic principles.

Conclusion

A large number of women in B&H are university-educated, holding MAs and PhDs in all fields – professors, lawyers/barristers, medical doctors, physicists, engineers, experts, writers, poets and many more. Yet their number is insignificant when it comes to positions of leadership. Men still dominate, even if they are less competent than many women. B&H remains a patriarchal society in many ways.

As a woman who has lived through the experiences of war and its effects, the author has shared the traumas and successes of women and girls in sporting participation before, during and after the 1990s' war in B&H. It is a small country that has suffered great turmoil. Restoring a war zone to a state of stability, improving the living and working conditions of its people and healing the deep wounds has taken time and resources. With fewer means than most countries endeavouring to develop sporting opportunities for girls and women, the country is doing well at every level of participation. Representation is multi-ethnic in all national teams, which is an aim in all spheres of the new country. Sporting activities are one beacon, helping to unite young people of different ethnicities and showing them ways to work together for a better future. The advancement of women in leadership positions is an area for future development.

Bibliography

Atletski savez Bosne i Hercegovine (2008) *Godišnji izvještaji za period 2004–2008 (Athletics Federation B&H – Annual reports for the period 2004–2008).*

Avaz (2008–2009) Various editions.

Cekic, S. (1995) *Agresija na Bosnu i genocid nad Bošnjacima 1992–1993 (The acts of aggression against Bosnia and genocide against Bosniacs 1992–1993).* Sarajevo: Ljiljan: 442.

Cigar, N. (2000) *Uloga srpskih orijentalista u opravdavanju genocida nad muslimanima Balkana (The role of Serbian journalists in the justification of genocide against Muslims in the Balkans).* Sarajevo: Institut za istrazivanje zlocina: 139.

Drinjakovic, M. (2008) Gracija *Prvi BH magazin za suvremenu zenu* (Gracija *First B&H magazine for the modern woman*) 45: 36–38.

Karate savez Bosne i Hercegovine (2008) *Godišnji izvještaji za period 1992–2008 (Karate Federation of Bosnia and Herzegovina. Annual Reports for the Period 1992–2008).* Online, available at: www.karatebih.ba.

Košarkaški savez BiH (Basketball Association of B&H) (n.d.) Online, available at: www.basket.ba (accessed 2009)

Odbojkaški savez Bosne i Hercegovine (2009) *Izvještaj za period 2006–2009 (Volleyball Federation of Bosnia and Herzegovina. Report for the period 2006–2009).* Online, available at: www.osbih.org.

Oslobođenje (2008–2009) Various editions.

Rukometni savez BiH (Handball Association of B&H) (n.d.) Online, available at: www.rsbih.com.

Sport (2008–2009) Various editions.

Teniski savez BiH (Tennis Association B&H) (2009) Online, available at: www.tsbih.ba.

Zeco, E. (2008) Gracija *Prvi BH magazin za suvremenu zenu* (Gracija *First B&H magazine for the modern woman*) 95: 14–19.

15 Les femmes et le sport en Afrique du Nord

Voix d'athlètes marocaines

Women and sport in North Africa
Voices of Moroccan athletes

Fatima El Faquir

Editors' introduction

It is from the position of a dedicated and distinguished life as a Moroccan athlete, leader and advocate of women in sport that Fatima El Faquir offers this chapter on North-African women, with particular focus on Morocco and track-and-field athletics. From her background in the development of sport in North Africa, the focus shifts to Morocco, the setting for the ensuing life stories. Through her own biography and life-history interviews with two Moroccan athletic champions, the reader is given insights into the personal qualities of such women, factors important to their perception of a culture of acceptance, the management of complex identities as Arab, African, Muslim women athletes, and the ways in which devotion to sport and religion were not seen as compromising in any way.

Introduction

Contained by the shores of the Mediterranean to the north and the arid sands of the Sahara to the south, the countries of North Africa were heavily influenced by ancient European civilisations such as Rome, as well as the more recent expansion of Islam. They were also subject to European colonialism, which has markedly influenced their ways of life.

During the eighteenth and nineteenth centuries, North Africa was colonised by France, the United Kingdom, Spain and Italy. Prior to the 1920s, many women did not venture far from their homes, fulfilling many household and family duties, but between the 1920s and 1950s they were encouraged to participate in the struggle for independence. This was a great opportunity for emancipation from patriarchal and cultural constraints. During the 1950s and 1960s, and into the 1970s, all of the North-African states gained independence from their colonial European rulers, except for a few small Spanish colonies on the far northern tip of Morocco, and the Western Sahara, which went from Spanish to Moroccan rule. It is a point of consideration that, had it not been for colonialism, the North-African countries would not have witnessed the signs of modernity that are found in many areas of North-African societies today.

The Kingdom of Morocco achieved independence, after being a French Protectorate (part of France's Trans-Saharan Empire), on 2 March 1956, and additional territories held by Spain achieved independence shortly afterwards: Northern Marruecos on 7 April 1956, Tangier on 29 October 1956 and, finally, Tarfaya (Southern Marruecos) on 27 April 1958. Algeria achieved independence on 3 July 1962 after 130 years of French rule. The country has had a history of conflict through the National Liberation Front's fight against the French colonial administration, which continues in the current struggle between the country's military and Islamic militants.

Since the independence of Morocco in 1956, the situation for the majority of women has improved very slowly. More people live in the cities rather than in rural communities (37.8 per cent in 1975, rising to 57.5 per cent by 2000). Women constitute 51 per cent of the population and 34 per cent of the working population, which looks promising when compared with 30 per cent in Spain or 39 per cent in Germany. However, the positions and status of workers in the urban areas are low, with women making up only 25 per cent of the workforce. Of these, 44 per cent work in the craft industries and 47 per cent in commerce, domestic roles and general administration. The illiteracy rate amongst women is 61 per cent, and only half of the working women hold any formal qualification (Cincera 2004).

In 1963, women won the right to vote and be elected to governmental and parliamentary positions. Between 1997 and 2007, the number of women engaged in parliamentary work quadrupled, and women's involvement in political decision-making at all levels is now increasing at a rapid rate.

Heavily influenced by their Muslim heritage, North-African countries have a keen sense of tradition as well as a strong sense of unity. The inhabitants are, in view of their proximity to southern Europe, also attuned to Western lifestyles, as can be seen in the people's dress styles and other customs. Although they have differing histories, current policies and practices, the people of North Africa share a mixture of Arab and African identities and a predominantly Sunni Muslim faith (97 per cent in Libya, 98 per cent in Algeria and 99 per cent in Tunisia and Morocco). Libya has a population of 6.3 million, Tunisia 10.5 million, Algeria 34.1 million and Morocco 34.8 million. They also currently share a fascination for sport, as well as great admiration for successful sportsmen and women. Enthusiasm for sport originates from the early days of colonisation. It can be claimed, justifiably, that modern forms of sport such as tennis, swimming, basketball, gymnastics, fencing, football and athletics were largely 'imported' during the period of colonisation in Algeria, Tunisia and Morocco. Military training systems were also established alongside sports clubs and associations. These were, however, predominantly for men, with discrimination from the church and schools continuing women's marginalisation in sporting participation on the grounds of gender inappropriateness (Zeleza and Eyoh 2003).

The presence of females in the sporting arena increased gradually between the 1950s and 1970s, with the opportunities for girls in school to take part in sports competitions rising rapidly from the 1960s (Zeleza and Eyoh 2003). With the introduction of statutory physical education for boys and girls and a growing number of sports clubs in the cities, more girls were able to take part in sporting activities.

In 1972, the first two Moroccan women competed at the Olympic level in Munich, one of whom was the author of this chapter. Track-and-field athletics and the achievement of African female athletes has been significant in the recognition and improvement of opportunities for all women in the region, although there is still a long way to go:

> During the post-Colonial era African female athletes have utilised their fame to challenge gender inequalities at home. Female Olympians from North Africa brought international attention to struggles between Muslim women and the misogynist practices of Islamic fundamentalists during the late 1980s and early 1990s.
>
> (Zeleza and Eyoh 2003: 518)

Track-and-field athletics has been the most influential sport in raising the profile of women in sport in North-African countries, most notably in Algeria and Morocco. Both countries have produced a small number of outstanding sportswomen who have led their field in international competitions on the world stage, at the Olympic Games and World Championships. Some of these champions have gone on to hold high positions in sports leadership and administration in their countries and beyond. Perhaps the most famous is Nawal El Moutawakel, the first Moroccan, African and Muslim woman to win an Olympic gold medal, in the 1984 Los Angeles Olympic Games. She continues her life's work for the benefit of sport, having achieved many national and international honours and positions, including IAAF membership in 1995, Secretary of State for Sport in 1997, membership of the IOC in 1998, President of the Evaluation Committee for the 2012 Olympic Games and Minister for Sports and Youth in Morocco from 2007 until July 2009.

The lives of these North-African champions have not always been easy in countries where traditional cultures have clashed with modernity, and experiences still vary in and between countries across a diverse region. Most elite-level female athletes from these North-African Islamic countries compete in athletic shorts and vest tops. In the past this has created religious tensions regarding different notions of appropriateness in dress for Muslim women, as in the case of the Algerian athlete Hassiba Boulmerka. She won a gold medal at the Tokyo World Athletics Championships in August 1991, but not everyone joined in the celebrations:

> Both representatives of state (official) Islam and certain personalities within the so-called 'Islamist' (political) movements criticised the non-Islamic

dress ... which was described by one of the imams of Algeria as 'scandalous' (Fates 1994: 10).... This view was not shared by all Algerians, however. For the so-called 'secularist' women's associations in Algeria, Hassiba Boulmerka's victory was considered as a victory against men's domination.... As for Hassiba: 'When I won in Tokyo, I wasn't comfortable with being the centre of attention.... I like to keep things simple, not to be a star. But I've become a representative of all Algeria, and of young women in particular. I've gotten so many letters wishing me courage ...'

(Moore 1992: 58 and 61, cited in Amara 2007: 546)

For many women in North Africa, these champions came to dispel some deep-seated taboos regarding women and physicality, helping them to discard an epoch characterised by deeply held beliefs about womanhood that precluded many from aspiring to the highest levels of athletic achievement. The efforts and courage of these early pioneers paved the way to sporting participation as well as to sport-related careers as teachers, officials, administrators and journalists.

North-African women remain under-represented in key posts of responsibility and decision making at every level of the sporting structure:

Africa has a long way to go before gender parity is achieved in sport. Nevertheless, the success of female athletes from all parts of the continent has provided inspiration to a new generation of young girls, while simultaneously forcing national and international sponsors to take notice of women's athletic potential.

(Zeleza and Eyoh 2003: 528)

One has to take into consideration, however, that this situation is similar in many countries of the world, as is the marginalisation of women in leadership positions despite the declarations and recommendations made in Brighton in 1994, Lausanne, 1996, Paris, 2000, Montréal, 2002, Marrakech, 2004, Kumamoto, 2006, Jordan, 2008 (International Olympic Committee, www.ioc.org; International Women's Group, www.iwg.org).

Since the first Olympic appearance of Moroccan women in 1972, other North-African women have been successful at Olympic and/or World Championships, including: Nezha Bidouane (Morocco), Nouria Mérah-Benida (Algeria) and Hasnaa Benhassi (Morocco). In addition, there has been regular representation of female athletes from North Africa in events such as the Mediterranean Games, Pan-African and Pan-Arab Games. With sport remaining a male-dominated arena in the region, it is not surprising that international success came to the men before the women in North Africa, notably from the 1960s in the Olympic Games and World Championships. Outstanding medallists at Olympics or World Athletics Championships include: Abdeslam Radi (Morocco); Mohamed Gammoudi (Tunisia); Said Aouita (Morocco); Brahim Boutayeb (Morocco); Khalid Skah (Morocco); Nourredine Morceli (Algeria); Salah Hissou (Morocco); Hicham El Guerrouji (Morocco); and Jaouad Gharib (Morocco). Despite the merits of these men, it has been the successful women athletes who have acquired considerable fame within their own societies.

The second part of the chapter focuses on the successes and challenges for track-and-field athletes in Morocco, including narratives of the lives of three successful Muslim women athletes.

Morocco – challenges and successes

The information about women and sport in Morocco is based on the expertise of the author, who is one of the first successful female athletes in the country and whose life story comes later. At the beginning of Moroccan independence, in 1956, King Mohammed V insisted on promoting physical activity and sport for all at schools and in the army. This developmental momentum increased under the rule of King Hassan II (1961 to 1999). The period from 1961 to 1970 saw the setting up of sports federations, the development of military sport, the growth of sports clubs and associations, as well as the creation of ministries with responsibility for sport. Regional events were established across the Maghreb area (Morocco, Algeria, Tunisia and Libya) in schools, universities and local communities. Competitive sport grew in the 1960s with men participating in events such as the Olympic Games, the Mediterranean Games and the Maghreb Games. Television started to bring public attention and celebrity to the sport of athletics following the great successes of the male athletes, such as Gamoudi Mohammed from Tunisia, in the Olympic Games of 1964, 1968 and 1972. The fame of these sports stars motivated teenagers, male and female, to try to emulate such role models.

Opportunities to compete at the elite level began for women in the 1970s, and the participation of female athletes in high-ranked competition increased from the mid-1980s. The first steps to a professionalisation of sport and the emergence of new systems and ideas for training found the approval and support of royalty, for example the late King Hassan II. His particular love of track-and-field athletics ensured interest and support in this area, which helped to attract sponsorship from sources such as the Office Chérifien des Phosphates, Moroccan Telecommunication and the sportswear manufacturer Nike.

Since 1978, elite-level competition in track-and-field athletics has been based on the centralised control of talent selection and systematic training for the development of men and women athletes. This strategy included a concentration of facilities and coaches in an environment where new training methods and ideas could be developed.

A National Institution was founded in 1978 where sports space, resources and personnel could come together to develop athletic talent. This institution started as the Collège des Athlètes and became the Ecole d' Athlétisme in 1988, Ecole Nationale d' Athlétisme in 1990 and the Institut National d'Athlétisme in 1995. Athletes training in the Institute, under the auspices of the Royal Moroccan Federation of Athletics, are professionals with regular salaries. This allows them to train full-time and at the same time support their families.

Despite the success of some Moroccan women in track-and-field athletics, opportunities for female athletes remain limited to a small number of talented girls. School programmes could do much more for young girls. Provision of physical activity opportunities for women, aimed at health and well-being, could also be improved.

The remainder of the chapter is devoted to the narratives of three women athletes who reflect on their lives, the successes and the challenges they have faced.

Life stories of Moroccan women track-and-field athletic Olympians

This section starts with a biography of the author, followed by the narratives of two outstanding Moroccan women track-and-field athletes derived from interviews she conducted with them. All athletes are African, Arab, Muslim women who grew up in Morocco and volunteered to share aspects of their lives and thus contribute to an understanding of women's sport in their country.

Fatima El Faquir: author and pioneer

Fatima El Faquir has sustained a long and distinguished career in the field of sport, and more widely in terms of improving women's engagement in their social and political world in Morocco and North Africa. She describes herself as Moroccan, Muslim, African and Arab, and has made a significant contribution to the region as an athlete, teacher, coach, manager, organiser and activist. As an athlete, in 1972 Fatima became the first of two Moroccan women to participate in the Olympic Games in Munich, the first to win the African championship in the 400m hurdles in Dakar in 1979, and she has held many National, African and Arab records.

Fatima's interest in physical activity started at the age of nine years at primary school, where she developed a lasting passion for sporting activities. Her first love was classical dance, but the physical-education teacher steered her towards athletics and there began a life path of commitment. Fatima represented her school teams in athletics, handball and basketball, and her teacher introduced her to an athletics club: the OM: Moroccan Olympic.

At that point she experienced 'real' training in mixed-sex groups with male coaches. Her mother was concerned about the intensity of the training, but gave her support to Fatima provided that her school studies were not allowed to deteriorate, a condition that Fatima was happy to accept. Being Muslim in this environment was an issue for her conservative family, but she was very quickly established as a 'colleague' amongst the boys and appreciated her opportunity to train with the best coaches available, even though they were male. Later, Fatima attended a mixed-sex high school to study Economic Science, where she was one of only five girls, but found no difficulties integrating. Having been born and brought up in a Moroccan society that favoured tolerance, encouraged participation in physical education and sport by boys and girls, and imposed no restrictions on sports clothing, helped her develop a career in competitive sport. Consequently, in Fatima's experience, growing up in Morocco and being Muslim never necessitated sex-segregation or covering of the body. Success on the track brought selection for a university place, and Fatima studied Physical Exercise and Sport in Romania from 1973 to 1978, then at Canada's Montreal University from 1980 to 1982. She married and raised a family with her coach, Azid Daouda, who studied with her at the same university and shared her passion for athletics and raising standards in Morocco.

Many years of dedication to the development of other athletes followed, particularly in the area of talent identification. One of the most distinguished athletes that she discovered, later coached by her husband, was Nezha Bidouane, who became World Champion and an Olympic bronze medallist. Fatima became a professional national coach in athletics, being the first to coach Nawal El Moutawakel in hurdles and relay events, bringing successes such as in the Mediterranean Games of 1983.

In Morocco, success in sport often brings further life opportunities. Fatima became a Professor of Higher Education and Training in Sport at the Institute of Sports Moulay Rachid, where she worked for nine years on research and research supervision in the field of motor learning, performance and coaching. Her responsibilities have included work on training systems for the Moroccan and International Association of Athletics Federation (IAAF) and management of major athletics events such as the Pan-Arab Games (1985), Francophone Games (1989), Cross Country World Championship (1998) and the Youth World Championships, which was organised in Marrakech (2006). Fatima has also worked for six years to promote sport for women in Islamic countries, and was the first Vice-President of the Sports Federation for Muslim Women.

Fatima became an advocate for the improved education of women to enable them to realise their potential in the socio-economic and human development of the country. As part of this work, she started the National Association for Women's Physical Activity and Sport (ANFAPS) in 1993 with the aim of disseminating physical exercise as an integral part of women's development, promotion and emancipation. She also chairs the Northern Region (Maghreb) of the African Federation of Athletics (CAARN) which includes Morocco, Tunisia, Algeria and Libya.

This life history of success and contribution has earned Fatima many royal honours from the late King Hassan II, the present King of Morocco, Mohammed VI, the president of the International Association of Athletics Federations (IAAF), the Arab Union of Sports and the Moroccan Royal Association of Athletics (FRMA). Apart from these honours, her life in athletics has allowed her to travel and make friends with people all over the world, and enjoy the life-enhancing experiences of being involved in competition at the highest level, both as performer and coach. Despite her success, Fatima is keenly aware of the help and support that she received from her family, fellow coaches, teachers and professors. It is with this in mind that she now strives to increase the opportunities for girls and women to access sport and exercise.

Nezha Bidouane: Morocco's first woman world champion

In 2008, the Confederation of African Athletics named Nezha Bidouane as 'one of the greatest athletes in history'. This was in honour of her many international achievements and long service to athletics. She continues to work for the benefit of Moroccan society.

I am a practising Muslim. I am always in the habit of reading the Quran before I begin any race. I see it as an additional source of psychological strength. Islam has given me a sense of justice and acceptance of others. It has helped me, also, to accept competition results as they happen, both in winning and losing. With regard to the dress code, to cover my body is not a necessary part of my faith, but I can point to the Bahraini athlete Ruqaya Al-Ghasara and her dress in leggings, arm and head-covering. She was able to reach the semi-finals at the Olympic Games, a great achievement, but her tight-fitting sporting uniform by no means hid the outline of her body as some Muslim athletes feel they need to do. Non-Muslim athletes may wear a similar uniform but adhering to her dress code did enable Ruqaya to compete and meet Islamic requirements to her satisfaction. Concerning other sporting uniforms that are proposed for Muslim athletes, I think they cannot make for easy movement for high-level sport. However, they are valid for practice and general physical activity for the sake of fitness and well-being.

Turning to the separation of the sexes for sporting activities, I can say that, personally, I have always participated in training with male athletes, I have had most success with male coaches and I see no harm in that. Those who wish to see such restrictions respected ought not to impose their view on the majority of athletes within the framework of universal sport.

I was born in Rabat on 18 September 1969, and embarked on a professional career as an athlete in 1991. I worked hard to become the African/Arab/Muslim woman to receive the widest range of titles in her career, including a bronze medal at the Sydney Olympic Games in 2000, and World Championship titles in the 400 m hurdles in 1997 in Athens and 2002 in Edmonton. Between 1990 and 2004, I travelled the world, gaining, and retaining, many titles in multiple events including 100 m, 200 m, 400 m, 100 m hurdles, 400 m hurdles, 4 × 100 m and 4 × 400 m relays. I competed in a wide range of competitions, such as the African championships, Pan-Arab Games, Arab Championships, Francophone Games, Mediterranean Games and Maghreb Games. There have been challenges in my life to achieve such a career. From an early age I did face a battle to persuade my traditional family to allow me to participate in gymnastics, which I loved, because it happened in a mixed-sex milieu. Not only did I manage to persuade them, but my mother, Hajja Fatima, became my first and constant ally. She took me to events, bought sporting clothing and gave all sorts of encouragement despite the reservations of my father and brothers. This stage was very important for me in terms of determination to participate and succeed and, at 15 years of age, I was identified as a talented athlete and passed the selection tests to attend the training school for athletics in the Prince Moulay Abdallah Sporting

Compound of Rabat. I showed my early ability quickly, making the Junior National team and gaining increased competition opportunities.

Early in my professional career I was able to contribute to decisions related to training, even persuading the Federation's managers to agree to my choice of coach, Mr Aziz Daouda, who had trained Saïd Aouita, one of the greatest legends in Moroccan athletics. I thought I could improve and perform to the best of my ability because of the quality of his coaching.

A great family tragedy changed my responsibilities during my sporting career. Soon after the passing away of my father, two of my brothers were killed in an accident. This placed a heavy responsibility on my shoulders to attend to the family both morally and financially. It became a turning point in my life and instigated my determination, motivation and inspiration to further my sporting ambitions, build on achievements to date and do this for the sake of my family. In 1992, at the age of 21, I became champion at the Mediterranean Games and won seven gold medals in the Pan-Arab Games, carving a place for myself in the sporting world.

Another challenge has been injury, a constant part of my life. One example was in 1996, as athletes were preparing for the Atlanta Olympics, when I was faced with the disappointment of not attending because of the need for delicate surgery on an Achilles tendon. Many feared that this operation would put an end to my career, but that was not the case. I resumed training and went on to win the World Championship title in 1997 in Athens, the first for Morocco. Driven by a desire for challenge and achievement, I continued to contribute to refining athletic technique, helping to advance technical and tactical knowledge, especially in the 400m hurdles event. In recognition of my accomplishments, the International Amateur Athletics Federation appointed me as an ambassador to Africa on the occasion of the Year for the Female Athlete (1998). This was a great honour for me as it reflected my reputation both in Africa and across the world.

In 2001, after more injuries and further Achilles tendon surgery, many thought that I was too old to compete. Seeing this as another challenge, I regained the 400m hurdles title at the World Championships in Edmonton, Canada, being the only athlete to have won the 400m hurdles twice. In recognition of this achievement, King Mohammed VI honoured me with the Throne Decoration (the highest-ranking decoration of the Kingdom of Morocco), the order of an officer.

I decided to devote 2002 to having my first baby after ten years of marriage. Mohammed Yassin was the name chosen for him by King Mohamed VI. I also announced that I was not retiring from athletics and would endeavour to make a comeback for the Olympic Games in Athens 2004. Athens was the city where I had obtained my first regional title in 1991 (the Mediterranean Games) and first world title in 1997. Unfortunately, recurring injuries meant an early withdrawal from the Games that time, but they did not dampen my spirit and, in that year, I gained three gold medals at the Pan-Arab Games in Algeria.

A growing interest in my life has been the opportunity to contribute in other ways to Moroccan society through social work and television appearances for the benefit of those less fortunate than myself. Projects have included working with children who have cancer, people with intellectual disabilities and sporting competitions for young girls from poor neighbourhoods. In addition, I have been appointed by Her Royal Highness, Princess Lalla Amina, as a member of the Board of Administrators of the 'Special Olympics Morocco'.

In January 2005, I announced my retirement, after 15 years as an athlete at a ceremony organised by the Moroccan Royal Federation of Athletics at the Mohammed V National Theatre in Rabat. The event was to celebrate the best athletes for the year 2004 and pay tribute to former icons. The social work continues, and in September 2007 there came a second son, whom His Majesty King Mohammed VI named Yassir. Much time is now devoted to my family, but also to important causes, currently as president of the Women, Achievements and Values Association. Athletics demanded much in my life but also gave me much in return, a chance to overcome personal challenges, aspire to achieve something worthwhile and an appetite to work hard on a day-to-day basis.

Finally, my message to other Muslim women in sport is to have faith, first and foremost, then to have self-confidence and passion for sport and your country. Everyone should encourage women to practise sports. Women are indispensable pillars of society.

Hasnaa Benhassi: Olympian

Hasnaa Benhassi has sustained a record of medals in elite-level international athletic events since 1997. In 2005 she was voted Morocco's top sportsperson in a radio poll and this is her first opportunity to tell of the challenges and successes of her life.

I was born on 1 June 1978 in Marrakesh. My story with athletics began when I was attending lower-secondary school. Before then, I did not have the slightest idea about athletics, nor did I watch any races on TV or know anything about Moroccan champions.

One day my school staged a race to choose girls who would subsequently participate in the regional cross-country running championship. I won the girls' race. At that time I was 15 years old. The following week I participated in the regional championship and managed to come second, though I had never received, or understood, what was meant by training.

Immediately after the race the professor of the Physical Education Department suggested that I join a club, arguing that I could become a great champion. When I returned home, I told my mother excitedly that I was going to join a club and become an athlete. My mother was worried about my studies, but I assured her that I would pursue my studies and train only on Saturdays.

I was lucky to receive every encouragement from my family and friends. I practised sports freely, and nobody objected to that. Then I joined the Kawkab Al-Marrakeshi Club, where I met the coach who taught me the basics of athletics, how to run with a good technique and how to train. He taught me many things. We would go for training three times a week. We were a group of young athletes, training and playing together without any idea that we could be champions in the making. One day my coach told me that I would take part in the qualifications for the Throne Cup in the 800 metres. We made preparatory training at this distance and I managed to achieve a good time. I enjoyed this distance very much. Thus began my story with the 800 m, in which I won the Moroccan girls' championship.

In 1996 I was invited to join the national team. I went to Rabat to the Al-mandar Al-Jamil training centre. There I met Idriss Ouahou, who became my coach. I was introduced to all the athletes and we became like one family. We used to spend almost nine months of the year training in a friendly atmosphere. I started to make good progress in the 800 m and 1500 m. In 1997 I participated in the Mediterranean Games and won the gold medal in the 800 m. It was a strange feeling, and I started to entertain the dream of becoming a world champion. I was watching closely the outstanding achievements of great champions like Hicham Guerrouj, Nezha Bidouane, Salah Hissou, Zahra Ouaziz and others. Then I took part in the Athens World Championship and reached the semi-finals.

In 1999 I participated in the World Indoor Championship and reached the finals. I did not finish the season, however, due to sustaining a fracture of a shin-bone in June, which prevented me from participating in the Seville World Championship. By the end of the year, I was married to Mohsin Shehibi, an athlete who was with us in the national team and who was pursuing his studies at the Royal Institute for the Training of Executive Staff.

The early years of the new millennium were exciting. In 2000 I took part in the Sydney Olympic Games and qualified for the finals. The following year saw victory with a gold medal in the World Indoor Championship in the 1500 m. After that I gave birth to my daughter and gave up running for 18 months. Frankly, I was very thrilled to be a mother and gave up thinking about becoming the world champion for a while. It was a different feeling to being an athlete. It is beautiful to be a world champion, but it is more beautiful to be a mother and to feel familial warmth. Six years after the birth of my daughter, I resumed training, as I was still only 23 years old.

In the beginning it was difficult for me to come back with the same vigour as before but I persisted for two years. In 2004 my husband told me that he was convinced I could reach the podium in the Olympic Games. I was encouraged by always finishing in the top three during several big races before the Athens Olympics. In the 2004 Athens Olympic Games, whilst I did not win a medal, I did break the national record. Since then I have won a bronze medal in the 2005 World Championship, silver in the World Indoor Championship in 2006, bronze in the 2007 World Championship and silver in the Beijing Olympics in 2008. I still aim to compete in my fourth World Championship and take my place on the podium again.

Important as it is to me to be a successful athlete, it is more important that I am a Muslim, and this gives me strength and confidence. I have had no difficulty practising my sport, from when I was young until the present moment. On the contrary, I received great support from everyone I knew, above all from my own family. The closest person to me, who is my husband as well as my coach, has never ceased to support me wholeheartedly. I have learned much through sport which has also allowed me to improve my living standard (as a professional athlete). Athletics has given me the chance to travel to many places in the world, meet people very different from myself and build friendships.

This is why I encourage Muslim women to emancipate themselves and practise sports freely, because this is a way in which they can change our society's view about women and help to shape an open society where the spirit of sport is valued. Sport is vital to our lives in these times. It can help prevent youths indulging in drug abuse and make them more health-conscious, thus producing a healthier society. When I retire from athletics, I would like to pass my experience on to young girls and encourage them to practise sport.

The challenges that sportswomen face in Morocco have declined, as most African countries have appreciated the importance of sports, both with regard to health and the promotion of their countries. The majority of the problems that athletes face are concerned with the management and provision of financial resources.

Editors' conclusion

The chapter has given insights into the sporting history of North Africa, Morocco and the lives of three women athletes in this significant region. The athletes are from three generations. The first was a pioneer in elite-level athletics from 1964 to 1982, the second from 1986 to 2002, and the third is still performing and expects to take part in the London Olympic Games in 2012. What emerges is evidence of the early influence of successful male athletes as role models for younger boys and girls, and the significance of early Moroccan women champions in opening possibilities for others by challenging restrictive regimes. In Morocco it is acknowledged that the number of successful female athletes is small. Many challenges remain at school and community levels that restrict the participation of girls and women in physical activity, including poor education about the value of exercise to health, resources such as coaches, adequate spaces and training; and continuing cultural constraints in rural areas. Through the life stories of the three athletes profiled, an understanding of the possibilities of self-determination, influence of family and environment, as well as the significance of royal patronage in enabling life-long careers and status for top athletes, is made visible. Ways in which these women internalise their religious belief, yet hold it to be pre-eminently significant in their lives, illustrate how they have resolved the integration of their Muslim/athlete identities without personal compromise.

Bibliography

Amara, M. (2007) An introduction to the study of sport in the Muslim world, in B. Houlihan (ed.) *Sport and Society: A Student Introduction* (2nd edition), London: Sage, pp. 532–553.

Cincera, M. (2004) Marché du travail et genre Maghreb-Europe, Proceedings of the International Conference in Rabat April 2003 – *Labour Markets and Gender: Magreb-Europe*, Brussels Economic Series: 3, Université Libre de Bruxelles, Dept. of Applied Economics (DULBEA).

Confederation of African Athletics: www.webcaa.org.

Daouda, A. (2008) L'Athlétisme au Maroc: Conférence présentée lors du symposium international sur l'athlétisme en Afrique.

Rahmouni, H (1988) Ouvrage realisé sous la direction de Mr Hassan Rahmouni, in *Sports Education, La Grande Encyclopédie de Maroc*. Vol. 11 Novembre. '*Les femmes fonctionnaires au maroc et la réforme administrative.*' Par: leila DINIA Mouddan, p. 229.

Royal Moroccan Federation of Athletics: www.frma.ma.

Zeleza, P.T. and Eyoh, D. (2003) *Encyclopedia of Twentieth Century African History*, London: Routledge.

16 العراقيـــات فـــي الحـــرب والرياضـــة قصـــص للنســـاء

Women's narratives of sport and war in Iraq

Nadhim Shakir Yousif Al-Wattar, Fatima Hussein and Alla Abdullah Hussein

Editors' introduction

This contribution offers experiential accounts of the lives of five practitioners in women's sport in Iraq. The insights gained indicate the serious issues of the rise of conservative forces, dogmatic religious forces and ethnic tensions that have impacted negatively on the opportunities for women in the field of sport generally. The position for Iraqi women currently living and working inside the country is difficult (for a fuller examination of this, see suggested reading in the bibliography). The recent war and occupation has left much turmoil, differently experienced in the various regions of the country. Iraqis face huge political, religious, social and economic challenges in the rebuilding of their country. In this situation we are privileged, through the efforts of the authors and the willingness of participants, to share the voices of Iraqi women working in the field of sport who have volunteered to contribute to the book. Three contributors requested that their real names and affiliations be used (Aamirah, Ghadah and Nawal), while two have been given pseudonyms (Almina and Raqiya). An initial section containing background information on women in sport in Iraq is followed by extracts from the personal reflections of the women – as they felt able to express them at the time – recounted in the interviews.

Authors' brief overview of women in sport in Iraq

The decision to contribute this chapter formed part of a long-standing mission agreed between us (the three chapter authors) to exchange information amongst academics in order to seek solutions for problems related to the deterioration of women's sport in Iraq. Current problems include not only the lack of resources and the under-representation of women, but also restrictions on and negative attitudes to participation. Our work in the Colleges of Physical Education has drawn attention to this important trend in the Iraqi sporting community, exacerbated by the American occupation since 2003.

The American invasion of Iraq on 9 April 2003 has led to a new cultural era. So-called 'democracy' has become a cover for many phenomena which were not hitherto common in Iraqi society such as religious and social radicalism on the one hand, and ethnic and national conflicts on the other. Unfortunately, the building of a new cultural framework includes changes in all things, regardless of their previous success, based on the claim that if it was a part of the past political regime, it needed changing. The radical political, cultural and religious trends now present in the country have had negative consequences and have even led to conflicts. One example has been calls for people to adopt radical attitudes against woman who practice sport. Realities have included actions ranging from exclusion and marginalisation to forbiddance and absolute prevention. As a consequence, many families have decided to forbid their daughters from participating in sporting activities since they are afraid of the security situation, the armed gangs, denominational militias, kidnapping and raping incidents. These are some of the reasons for the declining participation of girls and women in sport at school, club and university levels in Iraq since 2003. All such reasons are embedded in the nature of current religious and political struggles. The rights of women are one aspect at the heart of the struggle.

There have been more successful times for women in sport. When we were students at college, we read and enjoyed the history of Olympic sports in modern Iraq, which started with the establishment of the first Iraqi National Olympic committee in 1948. The writer Dhiya'a AlMunshi (1987) told us about an important period in the sporting history of our country during the British occupation after the First World War and how British soldiers brought a number of sports to the country, including football. Iraqi men learned this game in many cities like Basrah, Baghdad, Mosul and Habaniyah, and football became very popular. Although modern Iraqi sport (for men) was popularised by foreigners, there was also a long tradition of other sports, such as wrestling, which were rooted in the Iraqi, Assyrian and Babylonian civilisations.

Sport in schools and the provision of specialist teacher education was initially for boys and men. Training for professional qualifications in physical education (for men) started in 1938 in Baghdad with a cohort of seven. However, poor economic and political conditions led to its discontinuation, and a system operated in some places in which high-school teachers trained elementary school teachers in schools. In 1954 the Higher Institute of Physical Education in Baghdad started to recruit men for teacher training; the length of study was three years. In 1956, moves were made to establish a branch of physical education for girls, linked to the Faculty of Education for Girls at Baghdad University. The first women graduated in 1960.

During the regime of the Al-Baath Party (1968–2003), the same principles that underlay women's equality with men in all aspects of life were also applied to physical activity and competitive sport. To promote the participation of women, the Iraqi Women's Sport Federation was founded in 1992, initiated by the Iraqi Sports Council with the approval of the Iraqi National Olympic Committee. Its role was to develop women's sport in the provinces with the formation of four clubs for girls (Al Anbar, Najaf, Karbala and Mosul), the provision of clubs later extending to ten provinces in places such as Kerkuk, Baghdad,

Wasit, Maysan, Muthanna and Basra. By 2001 the experiment had succeeded in increasing the number of female participants in individual and team sports, and of qualified trainers, referees and organisers (Abd Maleh and Hassan Mohammed 2002). Increased interest and activity was motivated by women's domestic competitions, hosted by the Women's Federation through its annual programme, and the move by the Arab and Asian International Federation to broaden its programme of seminars, conferences and activities. This great period of advancement for women in sport disintegrated after 2003.

Sport in the period before 2003 was imbued with political ideologies of the former regime. The son of the former president, Uday Saddam Hussein, was President of the National Iraqi Olympic Committee for many years. Although there were many criticisms about the style and nature of the leadership of sport in Iraq at that time, we cannot ignore the social and cultural development of that secular political regime in relation to women. Many women practised sports alongside men without any religious or cultural restrictions. In addition, there was a popularisation of the role of women in training and leading Iraq's youth, and in joining the national teams. A time was reached when there were no constraints on sportswear, travelling or practising sports that remain problematic in some Arab countries.

Looking ahead to the future, the election of the new Iraqi Olympic Committee in 2009 has brought cautious optimism. Mr Ra'ad Hamoudy, who is a very popular figure in Iraq, it is now its head. The expectation is that sport, especially women's sport, will receive great support in a way that differs from the past few years. The situation in Iraq continues to change daily, of course, and remains unstable in many ways, but there is a hope that the rebuilding will begin again in a positive way for the men and women of the country, including in the field of sport.

The massive changes that war and occupation have brought in recent years have led to a significant decline in women's sport in Iraq. We think, consequently, that it is important and necessary to share vignettes, through excerpts of interviews with five professional sporting women. The authors conducted four interviews. The last is an interview reported in the *Al-Sabah* newspaper on 16 February 2008. The interviews capture the participants' views and experiences of women's sport in Iraq, and are shared here in the hope that this contribution will help Iraqi women in the future and bring our current challenges to the attention of a wider international audience.

Aamirah's story

Aamirah Ashamma has worked actively for women in sport in Iraq for many years, and is the current Head of Alfatat Sports Club in Mosul. Alfatat clubs were established first in Mosul, Basrah, Kirkuk and Najef in 1992, then later across the country. Their purpose was to enable young women to participate in athletic, social, cultural and artistic activities, to raise the status of Iraqi women and strengthen their self-esteem. They offered a new era in sport for women.

Although conditions in Iraq are bad, Aamirah remains committed to helping young women in sport and considers that, whenever she succeeds with an event or festival, she is helping society to move forward.

Q: I heard you once talking about your childhood and sport. Would you tell us about this?

A: When I was a child, sport attracted me and I became interested in it. I became very fond of games, of their movement and vitality. When I started school, I loved lessons of physical education and started to participate with my friends in games and competitions. I felt very happy when first nominated to represent my school team in basketball. When I got back home, my mother used to assign easy jobs to me in accordance with my age; so I did them running.... When my relatives visited us they used to say: 'This child does not walk like us; whenever we see her we notice that she is running continuously.'

Q: Were you ever inspired by men's sport?

A: Yes, as a matter of fact – and, as you know – sport for women in our country has been prohibited in the past, especially during the 1960s. I was a child at that time and used to go to a sports club which was located in a very popular neighbourhood near to our house. I used to watch male athletes practising sport, and I remember becoming very happy when a ball flew out of the stadium and I could rush to return it. It was all very interesting for me.

Q: Did you find it difficult to practise sport in such a society?

A: I tried to find a sports club in my city that paid attention to women and helped them to achieve their athletic ambitions, but unfortunately I could not, so my activity remained only within school and university teams.

Q: What about Alfatat Club?

A: Alfatat Club was established in 1992; at that time I had reached an age where I was not allowed to practise athletic activities as a competitive athlete, as I had hoped. Thus, I preferred to develop administrative work, but with the same spirit, desire and motivation in order to achieve for others what I could not achieve for myself.

Q: Can you tell me more about Alfatat Club?

A: Alfatat was the first club in Iraq dedicated to women. It was a hope we fought for and finally achieved after much effort. The club was not devoted exclusively to athletic activities; it offered many other activities. It was a real school for Iraqi women and was characterised by its breadth of opportunity.

Q: What else can you tell me about it?

A: There is a lot to talk about in this respect. The club was supported by the Olympic Committee at that time, and several championships were held between all Alfatat Clubs in the country. We arranged training courses for women in swimming and sports activities, particularly during summer vacations. The club attracted the special attention of the local government and was supported financially by the local university. A piece of land was donated as a site for building a larger club, but the war on Iraq started in 2003 and curtailed progress.

Q: So what has happened since 2003?

A: We face many problems such as a deficit in the budget, lack of financial support, families forbidding their daughters from practising sport, women's fear of practising sport because of the security situation, religious radicalism and changes in athletic and university administrations, which were accompanied by changes in the aims and the philosophy of the club.

Q: Now you are the head of the club. Can you talk about the impact of the current state of affairs on active women athletes?

A: Sport is forgotten here completely, placed 'on the shelf' because of the current situation and the security fears, as I told you. However, there is insistence from some women – I am one of them – who pull together and keep on working for women in sport in Iraq.

Q: Are you depressed?

A: Of course not, because there is always hope, and Iraq will recover. But there are problems such as shortages of donations from the Ministry of Youth, weak attendance of girls at the club because of religious radicalism. And I think that the problem in the south of Iraq is more serious than in other places because the religious philosophy elsewhere is less complicated and rigorous.

Q: So what about the northern part of Iraq?

A: The situation there is completely different. Athletic activity is better, and there are athletic school and university teams. Normally we would compete with athletic teams from the north of Iraq.

Q: Do you think that the current situation in Iraq will help in developing more positive trends towards women taking up sporting activities?

A: Of course not, because the new cognitive structure and the coercive nature of its composition will not serve society. Iraqi society had become used to more openness and equal participation by women in society over several decades. Omitting or eliminating all this within a short period of time will bring psychological crises and pressures, affecting women's lives. When we close the door of sport to them, it means that we have closed the door on their opportunity to shelter themselves from the complicated social situation.

Q: Do you think that women in Iraq are oppressed?

A: No, I don't think so, but they are excluded for the time being, and their roles are restricted to some national and social occasions.

Q: Is there any particular situation or event that has attracted your attention after the year 2003?

A: Once on TV I saw Iraqi folklore dancing in Basrah; it was very beautiful, but all the girls who performed the dances were veiled.

Q: What is wrong about that?

A: The veil is not the problem; what I mean here is the apparent contradiction in the use of the body between dancing and wearing a veil. Sometimes women will wear a veil to avoid problems with radical politicians.

Q: Do you have a special wish?

A: I wish that sport could take its place in our society and that those in power reconsider the matter of the participation of women in sport.

Raqiya's story

Raqiya is a teacher of physical education at a school in Iraq. She trained to teach at her local university and was a basketball player in the women's university team. This interview was conducted by one of the authors, who shared university years with her in the same group of friends.

Q: Do you remember the old days when we were students at the college?

R: Yes, I always remember them and I feel sadly emotional for those days when we practised sport freely. I also remember our participation in university championships, the great games and the scores we achieved. It is now like constantly replaying a video-recording in my mind, I cannot forget that.

Q: I suppose that you are sad when you talk about this subject?

R: Not sad exactly, but it is a sort of depression. We had been working for the sake of great things, but now we are back to square one again.

Q: Let us move on to other things – how did your interest in sport begin?

R: My starting point with sport was not that encouraging because I grew up in a devout [Muslim] family that did not easily accept a woman practising sport; therefore, I was not involved very much with sport. When I grew up, with the spread of the mass media, press and television channels in Iraq, accompanied by cultural developments in values and trends of Iraqi families, my family started to look at sport more positively. At the beginning of the 1970s, I found my family gathering in front of the television to watch a famous sports programme [*The Week's Review of Sport*]. At that time I felt that something had changed in the culture of society, saying to myself: 'If my devout family had started to change, what must be happening in more moderate families?' When I completed the secondary school stage [high school] I was encouraged to ask my family if I could attend the College of Physical Education, and I was really lucky to get their approval, which reflected a massive social change.

Q: What happened at the College of Physical Education?

R: I was particularly interested in the practical classes [applied lectures], practising sport and different athletic games. One day I was introduced to one of my athlete colleagues – he is my husband now – and he was a very distinguished person at the college. He encouraged me to train and participate in the teams of the college and the university. He changed many things in my life; he used to listen to me, understood my athletic ambitions, and helped me in my training. He is an open-minded human being and respects women. When he asked me to marry him, I was still a student, and my family insisted that I must continue my studies. That was a great joy for me because I realised that my family was completely in support of my sport-related training. Having my husband's interest and support made my parents even more confident. I became skilled in games, memorised rules and attended every training session and match.

Q: What happened then?

R: I graduated and was appointed to the Sports Unit of the university.

Q: What is your job now?

R: Unfortunately I left my job at the university, which was the dream job of my life, after the American occupation of Iraq in 2003. I moved to work as a physical education teacher at one of the secondary schools [high schools] in the city.

Q: What happened? Can you tell me?

R: You are living in Iraq now, and of course you know what is happening. The university's Sports Unit is very far from my house, I had to cross the bridge daily from the house to get to work, and there are six checkpoints on the way. These checkpoints are really very annoying, with the guards treating people very badly most of the time. When there was any incident, they used their guns and shot at people randomly. This exposed me to danger daily. In addition, these situations made me late getting to work and getting back home after finishing my day's work. It was too risky and difficult to continue.

Q: Now that you have the chance of working in schools, what do you think of school sport?

R: Sport is the victim of changing attitudes. Now there are social and religious restrictions, accusations that women who practise sport are immoral, and there is a deterioration in the security situation. Women have become victims of the current circumstances, losing much support from society. There is no safe place to hold a schools' championship, besides the problems of financial support for sport. Other common problems include the neglect of sports lessons by some schools' administrators, the replacement of some sport supervisors in schools by people who are socially and culturally conservative and do not value or acknowledge sports lessons. Others do not accept the new knowledge, theories and methods in teaching and coaching.

Q: So the situation is really very difficult?

R: Yes, that is right, but I expect that things are going to change in the next few years because society will not let this situation continue.

Q: What is the difference between the past and the present?

R: The difference is huge. Before, there was much more space and freedom to work, and people valued your activities and respected them. The security situation was stable and there were women's unions, Alfatat clubs and women's universities. The biggest problem, though, was the impact of the economic embargo against Iraq, which lasted for more than 12 years and exhausted the country. Iraqi sport was boycotted by international sports federations during that period of time, so international competitions could not be held in Iraq. These sanctions contributed towards destroying the infrastructure of sport in Iraq generally and women's sport in particular. Then came the American occupation, which destroyed the rest.

Q: Is there anything else you would like to raise?

R: As a matter of fact, I am very grateful to you because you have made me recall my beautiful memories. I hope that I will see a new Iraq without wars and interference, a time of peace and a better life for all.

Almina's story

Q: What were the highlights for you in the history of women in sport in Iraq?

A: When talking about the highlights for women in sport in Iraq, we must remember everything and be realistic when conveying information because the next generations will read what we say and write. Sport was an aspect of the social freedom experienced before 2003. School sport was the best evidence of this, especially in the 1970s. There were big sports events for all levels of capabilities. After the nationalisation of oil, when Iraq started to control the exports, the financial capacity of the state grew. There was great investment in sports activities for men and women.

Q: Were there any low moments for you?

A: During the 1980s I was moved to military training, similar to the regular training of the military units. One task was training on how to use the gun in primary schools, and this happened on Thursdays during the ceremony of saluting the flag. That caused sport to take a different direction and started to cause fear among pupils who were terrified of the sound of the gun shots at the beginning of the school day. When the sanctions were imposed on Iraq after the Gulf War, it was a rare thing to find a football or basketball in the school sports class. It became very hard to provide a sports team with equipment to play a game with another team. The situation remained like that until the invasion of Iraq in 2003.

Q: What happened later?

A: After 2003, the situation became more complicated. The schools were looted and some of them were burned; the thieves sold the sports equipment. The same thing happened at the universities; unknown parties looted the apparatus on a regular basis. Radical religious militia emerged and started to lead the sports boards and started to impose restrictions on the form and the nature of the women's sports. The security problems added even more complications.

Q: Anything else?

A: The political strife and problems between the various political and sectarian factions led to the exclusion of qualified members from sports establishments and organisations for sectarian or political reasons, for example those who had former political associations, especially in the field of sport and education. They were replaced with unqualified, untrained members who had no previous expertise. This led to a further deterioration of the educational process in general, but sport in particular.

Ghadah's story

Ghadah Addabagh is the former head of Alfatat Sport Club in Mosul. She worked for many years in sport for women and is currently a member of the teaching staff at the College of Administration and Economy in the University of Mosul.

Q: When did you work at Alfatat Club?

G: I have worked at Alfatat Club since its establishment in 1992 and was a member throughout the early period of its establishment. From 1993 to 1996 I was responsible for financial affairs, and then I was elected Head from 1996 to 2004. I did many things including attending all meetings of the Women's Sports Federation in the Iraqi Olympic Committee in Baghdad, and all the meetings of the Olympic Committee's local branch. I also headed the women's chess team in the Third Women's Championship, which was held in Tehran in 2002.

Q: What were the most important sporting activities at the club?

G: The club had many activities; from 1996, teams were formed in volleyball, basketball, table tennis, handball, women's football, shooting, tennis, swimming, badminton, fencing, track-and-field, chess and bowling; in addition to courses in tailoring, painting, music, fine arts, artistic galleries and festivals. The club won the first and second places for many terms in various sporting activities.

Q: How were these activities funded?

G: The Iraqi Olympic Committee and the local government strongly supported our activities, as well as using self-funding methods – for example, loans against training course earnings. This situation continued until the war started in 2003.

Q: What did you do after the start of the war in 2003?

G: The results of the war were catastrophic; all the club's property was stolen because the club was located inside the university, which also was robbed – laboratories and athletic equipment, many things were completely destroyed. The situation was very dangerous. Then we started to rebuild the club and we bought furniture and new athletic equipment.

Q: Did you face any sort of obstacles in trying to rebuild the club?

G: Yes, I faced many obstacles; one was the poor financial support from the authorities, another was the broken promise concerning the rebuilding of the club on a piece of land dedicated to that purpose by the Iraqi Ministry of Youth and Sports.

Q: What are your ambitions concerning the club?

G: I was hoping during my work for the club that we could make a separate centre for the club, building an enclosed pool for women and new sports halls.

Q: You worked for the club for a long time. How do you feel about it now you have left?

G: I'm OK, but I still feel that I belong to that club, and I have a great desire to give more in the future.

Q: Why did you stop working at the club?

G: I was given a position at the university because I had the opportunity to study for a PhD degree. This did not leave me enough time to run the club – and, of course, the current conditions.

Q: How do you evaluate the current situation in Iraq, particularly for women?

G: Women in Iraq are confined religiously and socially. We need to help them to start again and not let them go backwards because the progress made in the past should continue. We do believe in the freedom of women and their right to a happy and healthy life.

Nawal Al-Abeidi's story

Dr Nawal Al-Abeidi is Dean of the College of Physical Education for Girls in Baghdad. Her interest in sport started in 1962 when she was at school. She represented her school in basketball, gymnastics and other games. Her family, especially her brother, who was a recognised athlete for Iraq in 1948, encouraged her to join a sports club from an early age. Nawal went on to participate in competitions in various Arab countries. Between 1972 and 1976 she studied for a degree at the department of Physical Education at Baghdad University. Later she returned as a tutor in the same department. Nawal represented Iraq in table tennis internationally and became a high-level coach of women's teams. Throughout this time she continued her studies, gaining her doctorate in Poland in 1989. She continued to gain recognition for high-quality work in the field of women's physical education and sport, and was appointed Dean of the College of Physical Education for Women, Baghdad, in 2005. Nawal continues to be proactive in her struggle to improve conditions in Iraq for girls and women in the field. She travels to international seminars and conferences, when possible, to ensure that Iraq is given the best opportunity to move forward from current setbacks.

On 16 February 2008, *Al-Sabah* newspaper reported an interview with Dr Nawal Al-Abeidi on the nature of sport for women in Iraq in general and on the School of Physical Education in particular. The purpose was to hear about the obstacles they face and need to overcome in order to improve the situation at the college and in the women's sport-related movement in Iraqi society. The interview is reported here with the kind permission of Dr Al-Abeidi.

Q: The interview focuses on the poor-quality resources and facilities at the College of Physical Education for women Baghdad. Can you tell me a little about this?

N: The College lacks a swimming pool, sports halls, an athletics stadium and necessary equipment. Historically, it was very good with excellent students; we had sports teams representing Iraq, competing in various parts of the world, with some winning gold medals in international competitions. It was a time when women's sports were as good as men's in terms of achievements, ambitions and competitions, but now it is not up to standard. Women's sport is no longer as good as men's sports in terms of achievements, ambitions and competitions.

Today women's sport has witnessed a dangerous recession, and women have been absent repeatedly from international competitions, even local ones. Athlete representation is confined to a few clubs and groups here and there. The reason for this recession is the absence of planning, no support, no finance and an attempt to marginalise the sports movement.

There have been many factors that have led to a slowing down, if not a complete stagnation, of this important movement in Iraq despite all the scientific and academic progress that was made. In 1996 the women's movement established the College of Physical Education for Women in Baghdad as a scientific sports institute to prepare a generation of sports teachers, coaches and sports officials. We have been able to maintain a minimum of such academic activities against all attempts at marginalisation and rejection.

Q: When and how was the Physical Education College established?

N: The College was set up in 1996 in response to the demands of students' parents that there should be a College specifically for women in this subject, rather than the previously combined men and women's courses. The sports curriculum is divided into two parts, practical and theoretical, although the practical side takes more time than the theoretical one. The students study for a degree over four years. In the first year there are special subjects taught such as anatomy, rehabilitation, sports medicine.... In doing this, we really prepare them scientifically and practically.... There are some exceptions: we do not teach some of the sports which are predominantly men's sports such as boxing and wrestling, but apart from that we do sports like tennis, swimming, basketball, badminton ...

... we are very aware of the importance of changes regarding new ideas and technology, at least theoretically, and, as a result, we have incorporated new ideas about women in sport in our curriculum. We have done as much as we could in order to be able to open up to the outside world and catch up with the latest knowledge and international rules and developments through the Internet and international events.

We know that physical-activity knowledge always changes, and we should catch up with that particularly from the health side, like physiology and sports medicine, body preparation, the healthy body and how to manage injuries. Cardio-vascular exercise and balance – all these are important – we are aware of these things and want to incorporate them in the programme to ensure graduate students are well prepared to do the job. We also need the degree to be recognised internationally ... to allow women to work in the field regionally and internationally; hence we are trying to ensure our curriculum would be on a level with the university sports curriculum internationally.

Q: Do you use the latest technology and equipment to teach the physical-education students?

N: Yes, but that depends on the money we receive, and the budget currently does not allow us to buy all this equipment according to international standards. But within the current constraints we are able to offer the basic necessities ... we do our best in the circumstances to provide the best possible resources. A new laboratory will be available in the future.... We desperately lack computers – so important to catch up with the latest research and reports.... At the moment we have one computer to every five students, although we have been promised more by the university.

Q: Do you have enough staff and do you have an able staff?

N: We have enough staff and we have planned each year to take 15 students for Master's degrees and 15 for PhDs. We use the best of these to help with the teaching of the undergraduates.... Most of the women who teach at the College were themselves sportswomen and they have experience in the Olympic Games and high-level competitions. We have some scholarships for PhD students and we have sent four to Syria, Jordan and Bahrain ...

So we have professional and experienced staff when it comes to sport, knowledge and experience.

Q: What kind of relationship is there between the College and the Ministry of Youth and Sport and their Olympic Committee and sports clubs?

N: We aim to produce graduate women who later should be welcomed and supported by the Olympic Committee for the knowledge and experience they offer. The teaching staffs of schools have to be supported and jobs allocated by the Ministry of Education. It is obvious that the right person has to be in the right place. The Olympic Committee should offer opportunities to our graduates. The Ministry of Education should also support the teachers of physical education. In reality this is not happening. In all honesty the Olympic Committee refuses to accept any female graduate, and the evidence for this is that the Executive Board of the Olympic Committee now has no female representation among its members and this is the same with all sports clubs. This is a dangerous indication of lack of interest, collaboration, exchange of sport expertise and able sportswomen.

Two years ago the Olympic Committee took a decision to form a sports union for women in Iraq, and I was chosen as President of that Union. This was a positive gesture to restore the integrity of sport for women in Iraq. But this never materialised because the Olympic Committee did not invite me to form the Union and did not respond to my correspondence or demands to take up my position. I say, with regret, that there is no cooperation between us and the Olympic Committee. The fact that we were not asked to be represented in the recent Arab Games, which took place in Cairo, is an indication of the attempt to marginalise women's sport in Iraq. Women's sport is a main component of sport in Iraq. We need to be proactive and encourage the provision of facilities to restore our Olympic sport position for women in all domains, and this will not happen without sincere cooperation and collaboration between the Colleges and the official sports institutions. We are ready to encourage this and reactivate links to make sure that women can participate in sport activities inside and outside the country. We should distance ourselves from empty arguments and avoid replacing qualified personnel with untrained people. There has been a favouring of certain unqualified people at the expense of people who are qualified and have gained international achievements.

Q: What are the obstacles that you face in your life?

N: There are too many obstacles. Apart from the ones I have mentioned, like the lack of cooperation between sports institutions and my College and constraints in financial resources, we are chasing problems in the infrastructure of the College. The building is very old, built in the 1960s as the first College for Physical Education for women in Iraq, and as a result we suffer from a lack of, for example, a swimming pool; the training halls are very old.... And the same is true of other parts of the College: they need refurbishing or rebuilding in order to have enough suitable facilities for modern sport.

Q: What is your strategic plan to improve the College of Physical Education for Women?

N: The first aim is to build a new College in the complex of Jadrayyah (the main complex of the University of Baghdad), and it should be equipped with the latest equipment and the standards should be at least equal to the standards in other Arab countries. If we achieve this, it will push ahead the Sports Science Studies for women in Iraq. We aim to establish international sport and scientific relationships and have exchange programmes with the universities and sports institutions in the neighbouring, regional and other countries. Then we wish to participate in the Olympic Games and encourage women, especially those with potential, through training to achieve success. We also need to improve, update and expand the curriculum in relation to what is going on in the field. We have a plan to initiate a private consultancy unit that could advise and provide services with regard to sports activities in particular and Iraqi society in general.

Editors' conclusion

It is an extraordinary privilege to be able to include these voices of Iraqi women telling their experiences in the field of sport in this book. Women are often the silent victims of war and here they tell of the impact of past and present situations on culture, personal lives, hopes and aspirations. The vignettes shared by these women reveal a life-long passion for sporting activities, as well as for giving opportunities to girls and women in physical education and sport in Iraq. The women's continued endeavours in the field, despite dangers and obstacles that challenge the principles of their life's work, is an example of dedication to the rest of the world. As indicated in the author's preamble, the position of women in sport in Iraq has deteriorated into a serious state of marginalisation.

From the interviews it can be seen that there have been both successes and difficulties for Iraqi girls and women participating in physical activities. The interviews, for example, tell of girls being unable to continue taking part in sports 'beyond a certain age', of parental restrictions, coercive forces and religious radicalism. There are recurring themes of the religious and social confinement of women in recollections of the 1960s as well as in present-day Iraq. The women talk of the need to 'fight for facilities to allow women's participation' and the need to change attitudes in some families in order to gain support. Regional differences add to the complexity of the current picture, and the unstable political and economic situation in the regions has affected the provision of opportunities for girls and women. The Iran–Iraq war of the 1980s, the invasion of Iraq in 2003 and the present, ongoing, internal political conflicts are all detrimental factors. Many Iraqi people are also fearful of openly discussing subjects, such as women's freedoms, that are considered sensitive in the current climate. The contributions of the interviewees and Professor Nadhim Al-Wattar give an international readership an insight into the first-hand experiences of Iraqi women in sport and the current problems they face.

Bibliography

Abd Maleh, F. and Hassan Mohammed, L. (2002) *The Obstacles Facing Girls' Clubs in Iraq.* Unpublished paper delivered at the College of Physical Education for Girls, Baghdad University.

Al Sabaath newspaper (2008) Published interview with Dr Nawal Al-Abeidi on the College of Physical Education for Women in Baghdad (number 1822), 16 February. Online, available at: www.alsabaah.com/paper.php?source=akbar&mlf=interpage&sid=57163 (accessed 22 November 2009).

Dhiya'a Al-Munshi (1987) *The Olympic History of Iraq*, Baghdad: Dar Al-Thoura.

For further information on the overall situation of women in Iraq, especially after the invasion of 2003, see the following books:

Al-Ali, N. and Pratt, N. (2009) *What Kind of Liberation? Women and the Occupation of Iraq*, California: University of California Press.

Al-Ali, N. and Pratt, N. (eds) (2009) *Women and War in the Middle East*, London and New York: Zed Books.

Holt, M. and Jawad, H. (2010) *Women and Islamic Resistance in the Arab World*, Boulder: Lynne Rienner.

Conclusion

Tansin Benn, Gertrud Pfister and Haifaa Jawad

> People with global mindsets have the ability to continually expand their knowledge; have a highly developed conceptual capacity to deal with the complexity of global organizations; are extremely flexible; strive to be sensitive to cultural diversity; are able to intuit decisions with inadequate information; and have a strong capacity for reflection.
>
> A global mindset thinks and sees the world globally, is open to exchanging ideas and concepts across borders, is able to break down one's provisional ways of thinking. The emphasis is placed on balancing global and local needs, and being able to operate cross-functionally, cross-divisionally, and cross-culturally around the world.
>
> (Marquardt 2000: 4)

All women have been the subject of prejudice and discrimination in the sporting world. Indeed the modern Olympics started in 1896 as a male preserve where women were deemed fit only to crown the heads of the victors (Pfister 2000). Today there is hardly a sport, or even an event within a sport, for example athletics, that is not open to women. Whilst women rarely compete against men, for valid physiological reasons, they are now accepted as officials in men's competitions at the highest level. Research across a range of disciplines has slowly brought about change, from an excluding to an including discourse (Pfister 2000), but this has been a journey led predominantly by Western activists and academics and it has largely ignored cultural differences and knowledge of people's lives beyond Western societies. This book brings important contributions together from across the Middle East, Africa and Europe in the consideration of life experiences of Muslim women in sport, connected by religion and their commitment to sport-related physical activity. While many of the barriers Muslim women face are similar to those of all women, such as social and economic forces, there are, as illustrated here, important faith-based and cultural differences situated in distinctive contexts which are significant in shaping people's priorities and preferences for their lives in the twenty-first century.

The experiences of Muslim women in sport recounted in this book are built on the premise that physical activity is beneficial to human development, health and fulfilment; and that within the religion of Islam, women's participation in physical activity is encouraged (see Chapters 1 and 2). It is also acknowledged that some girls and women live in challenging cultural, economic and political situations that deny them life chances in terms of education, freedom to move and equality of opportunity to contribute to their society (Sfeir 1985). The many accounts in this volume position some Muslim women as agents of change, role models for others and pioneers in the area of physical activity in their respective countries and regions, which is in contrast to the dominant discourses of the West.

A global issue

Approximately one-fifth of the world's population, 1.3 billion individuals, are followers of Islam, the second-largest global religion. Muslim people live on every continent, in around 57 countries, in different social, political and economic situations (Esposito and Mogahed 2007: 3). Some claim that Islam is the fastest-growing religion in the history of the world (F.A.I.R. 2006), but culture and life experiences within Islam are diverse. Countries such as Iran are Islamic countries which are governed by Sharia law; others, such as Syria and Turkey, have Muslim majority populations but separate religion from state; and other Islamic groups are part of the Diaspora that positions Muslim people as a minority in a predominantly non-Muslim country. In spite of the size and the global occurrence of Muslims, very little is known about their diverse cultures and their conditions of life, and even less is understood about the body cultures and physical activities of Muslim girls and women. Public attention to date has focused on top-level athletes at the Olympic Games, or fatwas, by religious conservatives, on Muslim women who choose to wear sports clothing considered to be un-Islamic (lacking in modesty). One example was the case of tennis player Sania Mirza who, despite her popularity with the Indian population, has been the centre of controversy and opposition from fundamentalist religious groups. Threats led her to travel with bodyguards (Gentleman 2006), and it was reported in 2008 that she had considered withdrawing from playing in India, despite her love of her country, because of religious controversy (www.all-about-tennis.com/sania-mirza.html, accessed 9 December 2009). Such examples highlight the need to focus on authentic experiences of Muslim women from within different cultures and listen to their personal histories of living in the sporting world.

As realised through the chapters of this volume, the experiences of Muslim women go largely ignored. The life experiences described in this book provide a basis for further dialogue and help to increase understanding of factors influencing women's participation in sport and physical activities, including religious, cultural, political and economic issues, and the effects of modernisation processes. Despite the efforts of the authors and the wide range of original contributions, this book is only a first step.

Diversity, religion and sporting cultures

The chapters focus on diverse groups of girls and women. Ways in which faith and sporting identities are managed by sport participants mentioned in the book indicate a wide spectrum of positive and negative encounters of Muslim women in sport-related activities. There are athletes for whom religion is a private aspect of their lives, who see no need for adoption of the *hijab* and non-conventional sports clothing, as exemplified by the women Olympians in North Africa. There are other participants whose 'embodied faith' necessitates the adoption of the *hijab* and whose religious identity is compromised by sports governing bodies and political regulations that ban the wearing of the *hijab*, for example in Turkey. In Palestine, when engaged in playing a football match in a Muslim–Christian national team some young women prioritised their national over religious identities, perhaps not surprising in the current political situation of the region. In Oman most women physical-education teacher-training students regarded modest Islamic dress and gender-segregated sports spaces as both a religious requirement and Omani cultural expectation. There are some exceptions to this as a small number of Omani women step into the international women's sporting arena.

Diverse attitudes towards physical activity prevail amongst Muslim women in European countries. For example, in Denmark and Germany, current discourses of immigration, assimilation, integration and inclusion ensure political good-will towards immigrant populations. Sporting opportunities are many and the climate for participation is positive, but the structures and practices are culturally designed by and for a Westernised/European understanding of social relations and body culture. This can create inevitable conflicts for some participants and providers of sporting environments in Diaspora situations.

Diverse situations are also evident in Iran, where gender-segregated sporting structures have led to a separate but active women's sport movement. In contrast, authors who have lived through recent and rapid modernisation processes, for example in Syria and Morocco, told of struggles endured for the acceptance of women's rights and sporting opportunities alongside those of men. Women's sport in the Gulf countries is in its infancy with differences in and between the countries that relate to urban/rural lives, socioeconomic conditions and cultural traditions. While Bahrain led the region in the provision of sporting opportunities for women at university level, other countries in the region still do not have such arrangements. In the UAE, physical-activity opportunities are making a difference in the lives of young people with intellectual disabilities, but public acceptance of this disadvantaged group is recent.

On a positive note, all countries mentioned in the book have a commitment to the provision of physical education for girls and boys within their education systems, at least in theory, although this is not yet a global phenomenon (Hardman and Marshall 1999, 2005). As illustrated in the chapters, in some countries there can still be barriers to participation for those girls who wish to adhere to Islamic requirements for modesty in their schools. In addition to this desire, other barriers may also be present, such as a hostile climate, poor or inappropriate facilities, inflexible policies, lack of teacher understanding, cultural/parental resistance, lack of student motivation and an increasing consciousness of body and religion among the girls.

A major factor in determining opportunities for women in physical activities and playing sports is a country's 'sporting culture'. Where there is a long history of modern sport,[1] albeit a male-dominated model, sport is integrated into the infrastructures of school and communities, as in Germany and Denmark. It is the relatively recent numbers and patterns of immigration that have raised new challenges in Europe for inclusion of people with different beliefs, values, expectations and needs in their sport discourses and practices. In many of the Muslim countries, modern sport is not rooted in traditions but arrived with colonialism and alongside Westernisation projects with migrant workers. Globalisation processes such as commercialisation, internationalism and politicisation have led to Western models of sport becoming part of the global sports business, televised and available worldwide on a daily basis.

The culture of commercially popular elite sport today has an aura of spectacle, glamour and wealth, but is also criticised (Bale and Christensen 2004) for exploitation (including of women), cheating, gambling and drug abuse. While there is criticism, rarely do critics touch upon issues related to complex overlaps between religious and secular values, resulting in a potential for difference in value-positions. High-achievers in modern sport are frequently considered as role models for aspiring, or even participating, sportspeople. The spectacle, consumerism, fanaticism and inappropriate behaviour, however, that surround many sports and sporting 'heroes' could be seen as an antithesis of an Islamic lifestyle.

Diversity, faith identities and women's agency

Sporting opportunities have given many of the women discussed in this book the self-determination, confidence and perseverance to resolve multiple complexities in and between religious beliefs, gender relations, body and sporting cultures. Such personal attributes can be lost where shifting balances of political power leave women relatively powerless. The atrocities suffered by girls and women in periods of instability, such as the wars of Bosnia and Herzegovina and Iraq described in the book, are a reminder of the structural fragility of some societies and the effects of war on the lives of women – but also of the positive role sport can play at such times.

A common thread across the chapters of the book was the support most women found from their families, parents, siblings, husbands and children. Some women allude to changes in the attitudes of parents once they understand how determined their daughters are to pursue sport-related activities and/or careers. Most countries have sports organisations or educational institutions where girls and women find: support in terms of understanding; expertise to further their abilities; other women with a shared interest; and a safe space in which to develop their interest. Examples include the athletic clubs of Morocco and Iraq, the Down's Syndrome Association in UAE and the physical education department of the University in Oman. In other Muslim countries, such as Morocco, the support of the state and/or royal family is essential to legitimising participation, the status, acceptance, and, in some cases, life-long careers of sports women.

Muslim women were able to adapt to situations required by their sporting situation; for example, when sports halls became unsafe, the women of Bosnia and Herzegovina moved exercise classes to their homes. Some women also changed and transformed sporting practice; for example, the Turkish judo athlete, Zeynep, who fought to be allowed to wear Islamic dress in competitions, negotiated with parents, coaches and sports bodies, eventually adopting the bandanna (head band) as a compromise between her religious and sporting identities. Other Muslim sportswomen adopted Western dress and demanded acceptance of the decision by their families and peers. Young women of Turkish heritage in Germany developed bicultural identities that differed from those of their parents, the social networks in the sports clubs providing a means of learning about the host culture and gaining social acceptance.

The chapters of the book focus on both elite sport and recreational physical activity. Thus, we gain an insight into the broad variety of sport and exercises of the majority of women. In Turkey, the Local Ladies initiative is popular, devised by and for women, as is the Alfatat Club network in Iraq. In other countries, cultural and economic barriers contribute to the lack of participation of women in regular exercise, for example inappropriate sporting environments (public and mixed-sex spaces in Diaspora contexts), lack of understanding of the importance of exercise for health and well-being and low socio-economic status of the immigrant population. The lack of a sporting tradition in many Islamic societies or other forms of resistance, connected to body cultures, also contribute to a disinterest in physical activity amongst girls and women. Muslim girls in South Africa are, for example, unmotivated in their school-based sporting opportunities and unable to see positive connections between physical exercise and their lives. Other factors, such as curriculum change and inadequate teacher training, influence such attitudes, as does the lack of understanding or accommodation of their Islamic religious needs by their teachers.

A small number of female athletes in Muslim countries have made a considerable difference to the recognition of women's potential and capability in sport. They have used their fame and influence to support the development of opportunities in sport for others, although few women have had opportunities to engage with decision-making processes within sports governing bodies, which were, and still are, predominantly male preserves. Despite some success for female sports leaders in Syria, statistics suggest that there is still a long way to go for women in sports leadership positions to gain equality with men; this includes access to international bodies. Women's occupation of decision-making positions in sports governing bodies and administrative agencies is worse in those countries just emerging in the field of sport and physical activity provision for women, such as Oman, and those in political and economic recession such as

Iraq, where increased religious dogmatism has had a deleterious effect on a formerly well-established women's sport movement.

Recommendations

Before any consideration of what support may be offered to increase the opportunities for Muslim girls and women to participate in physical activities, it must be repeated that they live in different situations, come from a wide variety of backgrounds, and have different priorities, aspirations and needs. For example, while some may aim at top-level competitions, others participate in physical activities to become or stay healthy or slim, and yet others are disinterested. It should be regarded, as a principle, that sport and physical activities – their conditions, contents and aims – must be oriented to the needs of these different groups.

Schools, sports organisations/clubs, youth centres or women's groups should develop concepts and programmes that follow the principles of equal rights, equal opportunities and inclusion, as well as acceptance and tolerance. The following guidelines make sense in sports programmes for (Muslim) girls and women in Western as well as in Islamic countries:

Girls and women who choose to wear the *hijab* and adhere to strict gender-sensitive religious requirements may be encouraged to participate in sport if:

- only females take part in these activities;
- the course leaders are female;
- boys and men have no access to the facilities when used by females;
- clothes are accepted which cover the body;
- separate changing and showering facilities are available;
- the sports facilities are within easy reach of the girls' and women's homes;
- the sports courses take place in the afternoon or early evening;
- participants may bring their friends or acquaintances;
- male family members can be won over to support the sporting activities of their daughters, sisters or mothers;
- the activities are significant and meaningful for the groups which may differ in their expectations;
- activities offered are oriented, in particular, towards health and fitness;
- culturally valued movement forms, such as traditional dance, can be integrated.

Furthermore, girls and women should be made familiar with a variety of physical activities in order to give them a chance of choosing the activity that best fits into their lives.

In addition, in Western countries it may be helpful, in some cases, if the courses are run by a woman of the same cultural background. The question remains, however, whether it is better to organise physical activity/sports courses exclusively for ethnic minority groups or whether immigrant women should be integrated into multi-ethnic groups. On the one hand, it is important not to isolate immigrants, while on the other hand, it makes sense to encourage the preservation of ethnic groups in order to strengthen cultural identity and offer a 'safe haven'. Therefore, both opportunities for doing sport should be available.

Girls and women can be empowered in and through sport, but there is still much to be done in order to provide sports for females and to motivate females to take part in sports. At least some initiatives do exist that work not only for, but above all with, minority girls and women for their empowerment.

Finding pathways – the negotiation of change

The chapters of the book will contribute to increased understanding of the significance of 'situation' with regard to the participation of Muslim girls and women in physical activity in its widest sense – schools, communities and clubs. At local levels, Muslim women are negotiating change and opportunities for themselves in arenas of physical activity, in line with Henry's (2007) concept of 'situated ethics'. Local initiatives are commendable, but these can only become universal with the widespread dissemination of knowledge and understanding as well as the willingness to facilitate the provision of opportunities for girls and women to participate in physical activities and sport.

Reaching consensus in the 'Accept and Respect' Declaration in the Oman 2008 international study week (see Introduction, p. 00) was a learning process through which differences between the delegates were better understood. The group consisted of Muslim and non-Muslim people with different religious and ideological views of the world and attitudes towards women's involvement in sport. They came from countries with widely diverse cultures; for example:

- Oman is an Islamic country that might be described as 'emerging' in terms of the acceptability of women in sport;
- Iran is a country where political Islam demands compulsory public covering and sex-segregated sporting participation;
- Denmark is a country with a Diaspora population;
- Bosnia and Herzegovina and Iraq are countries devastated by war;
- Turkey is a secular state with a 98 per cent Muslim population where the *hijab* is banned in sports competitions; and
- Syria is known as 'the heart of the Arab Nationalism'.

Notwithstanding those differences, through a process of exchanging experiences, listening and negotiating, the architects of the 'Accept and Respect' Declaration reached a consensus. The Declaration stands between universal human rights that ignore cultural difference and cultural relativity that may accept discriminatory behaviour justified in cultural and religious terms. 'Accept and Respect' was a product of post-modern 'situated ethics' (Henry 2007: 317, 319) where 'absolute standards are rejected in favour of the requirements of a particular situation', in full recognition of the fact that 'consensus has limits and ... some groups will almost invariably stand outside the consensus achieved, but that consensus is an on-going constructer upon mutual respect and dialogue'. Through the Declaration, and now the research and practice evidenced in this book, negative stereotypes of Muslim women are challenged, awareness of difference is increased and solidarity of support for the rights of *all women in sport* is entrusted to 'accepting and respecting' the choices and voices of others.

Note

1 Modern sport started towards the end of the nineteenth century in Europe with the formalisation of national then international rules and regulations that enabled competition to take place. Many sports governing bodies were formed between the 1870s and 1890s. This development was part of major societal changes, particularly industrialisation and the spread of ideas and lifestyles internationally with ideologies such as Athleticism, Olympism and Imperialism.

Bibliography

Bale, J. and Christensen, M. (eds) 2004) *Post-Olympism? Questioning Sport in the Twenty-First Century*. Oxford: Berg.

Ehsani, Kouzechiyan, Honarvar and Sharifryan (2005) Role of Professional Sport in Muslim Women's Sport Development, in *Toward The Future*, The Fifth International Sports-Science Congress of the Islamic Federation of Women's Sport, 24–25 September, Tehran (IFWS): 67–69.

Esposito, J.L. and Mogahed, D. (2007) Who Speaks for Islam? What a Billion Muslims Really Think. New York: Gallup Press.

F.A.I.R. (2006) Forum Against Islamophobia and Racism. Online, available at: www.fairuk.org/introduction.htm (accessed 26 July 2006).

Gentleman, A. (2006) India's most wanted. The *Guardian*, 5 February. Online, available at: www.guardian.co.uk/sport/2006/feb/05/features.india (accessed 30 September 2009).

Hardman, K. and Marshall, J. (1999) *World-Wide Survey on the State and Status of Physical Education in Schools*, Conference Proceedings – World Summit on Physical Education, Berlin, 3–5 November, ICSSPE/CIEPSS, Berlin.

Hardman, K. and Marshall, J. (2005) *Update on the Status of Physical Education World-Wide*, Second World Summit on Physical Education, December, Magglingen, ICCSPE/CEIPSS.

Henry, I. (2007) *Transnational and Comparative Research in Sport: Globalisation, Governance and Sport Policy*. London: Routledge.

Marquardt, M. (2000) *Successful Global Training: Business Skills*. Alexandria, VA: ASTD.

Pfister, G. (2000) *Contested Her-Story: The Historical Discourse on Women in the Olympic Movement*, Pre-Olympic Congress Sports Medicine and Physical Education, International Congress on Sport Science, Brisbane, Australia.

Sfeir, L. (1985) The status of Muslim women in sport: conflict between cultural tradition and modernization, *International Review for the Sociology of Sport*, 30: 283–306.

Index